The Random House
Guide to Basic Writing

The Random House Guide to Basic Writing

Sandra Schor
Judith Fishman

both of Queens College
The City University of New York

Random House   New York

First Edition
9876543
Copyright © 1978 by Sandra Schor and Judith Fishman

Library of Congress Cataloging in Publication Data

Schor, Sandra.
  The Random House guide to basic writing.
  Includes index.
  1. English language—Rhetoric. 2. English language—
Grammar—1950–   I. Fishman, Judith, joint author. II.
Title. III. Title: Guide to basic writing.
PE1408.S316   1978   808'.042   77-27469
ISBN 0-394-31201-5

Manufactured in the United States of America

Designed by A Good Thing Inc.

Acknowledgments

"On Keeping a Diary" by William Safire. © 1974 by The New York Times Company. Reprinted by permission.

Excerpt from "Writing American Fiction" by Philip Roth. Reprinted with the permission of Farrar, Straus & Giroux, Inc., from *Reading Myself and Others* by Philip Roth, Copyright © 1961, 1975, by Philip Roth.

"Discovery of a Father" by Sherwood Anderson, from *Sherwood Anderson's Memoirs*. Reprinted by permission of Harold Ober Associates Incorporated. Copyright 1939 by Eleanor Copenhaver Anderson. Renewed.

Excerpt from *Manchild in the Promised Land* by Claude Brown. Reprinted with permission of Macmillan Publishing Co., Inc. Copyright © Claude Brown 1965.

"Oh, Those Grippes of Yesteryear! That Certain Soup . . . And Mom's T.L.C." by Mimi Sheraton. © 1977 by The New York Times Company. Reprinted by permission.

"Skid Road Stroganoff," from *The I Hate to Cook Book* © 1960 by Peg Bracken. Reprinted by permission of Harcourt Brace Jovanovich, Inc.

"Why I Want a Wife" by Judy Syfers. From *Ms.*, December 1971. Copyright © 1971 by Judy Syfers. Reprinted by permission of the author.

Portion of advertisement on page 106 reprinted by permission of Easton Press, a division of MBI.

Advertisement on page 110 reprinted by permission of The Advertising Council, Inc.

Excerpt from "Big Two-Hearted River" is reprinted from *In Our Time* by Ernest Hemingway by permission of Charles Scribner's Sons. Copyright 1925 Charles Scribner's Sons.

Portion of advertisement on page 116 reprinted by permission of the North Carolina Department of Commerce.

Advertisement on page 118 reprinted by permission of Killington Ski Resort.

Advertisement on page 121 reprinted by permission of Liggett Group Inc. All rights reserved.

Portion of table of contents reprinted from the January 19, 1976 issue of *People Weekly* magazine by special permission: © 1976, Time Inc. All rights reserved.

Advertisement on page 126 reprinted by permission of the copywriter, Ron Finkelstein, CBS Records.

Portion of advertisement on page 127 reprinted by permission of R. T. French Company.

Portion of advertisement on page 128 © 1977 by E. C. Publications, Inc. Reprinted by permission.

Advertisement on page 128 reprinted by permission of Import Record Service.

"Dear Abby" © 1975 by *The Chicago Tribune*. Reprinted by permission of Abigail Van Buren.

Portion of advertisement on page 133 reprinted by permission of California Almond Growers Exchange.

Portion of advertisement on page 135 reprinted by permission of Weider Health and Fitness.

Portion of advertisement on page 146 © by The New York Times Company. Reprinted by permission.

Excerpts from "Heather Lamb, telephone operator," from *Working: People Talk About What They Do All Day and How They Feel About What They Do* by Studs Terkel. Copyright © 1972, 1974, by Studs Terkel. Reprinted by permission of Pantheon Books, a division of Random House, Inc.

Portion of advertisement on page 150 reprinted by permission of Howmet Aluminum Corporation.

Portion of advertisement on page 151 reprinted by permission of General Mills, Inc. ® Wheaties is a registered trademark of General Mills, Inc.

"The Bear Who Let It Alone" by James Thurber. Copyright © 1940, James Thurber. Copyright © 1968, Helen Thurber. From *Fables for Our Time,* published by Harper & Row. Originally printed in *The New Yorker*. Reprinted by permission of Helen Thurber.

Portion of advertisement on page 153 reprinted by permission of Dale Carnegie & Associates, Inc.

Excerpt from *Nigger: An Autobiography* by Dick Gregory with Robert Lipsyte. Copyright © 1964 by Dick Gregory Enterprises, Inc. Reprinted by permission of the publishers, E. P. Dutton.

Portion of advertisement on page 159 reprinted with permission of The IBM Office Products Division.

Excerpt from "I Remember" by Joyce Maynard. Reprinted by permission of Curtis Brown, Ltd. Copyright © 1975 by Triangle Publications, Inc.

Portion of advertisement on page 160 reprinted by permission of American Motors Corporation.

Portion of advertisement on page 161 reprinted by permission of *Cosmopolitan*.

Portion of advertisement on page 161 reprinted by permission of The Mennen Company. Photo used with permission of The Mennen Company.

Portion of advertisement on page 163 reprinted by permission of N. W. Ayer International.

Portion of advertisement on page 163 reprinted by permission of Saturday Review Magazine Corporation.

Portion of advertisement on page 164 reprinted by permission of Triangle Publications, Inc.

Excerpt from *Slouching Towards Bethlehem* by Joan Didion reprinted with the permission of Farrar, Straus & Giroux, Inc. Copyright © 1967, 1968, by Joan Didion.

Excerpt from *The Greatest—My Own Story* by Muhammad Ali with Richard Durham. Copyright © 1975 by Muhammad Ali, Herbert Muhammad, Richard Durham. Adapted by permission of Random House, Inc.

Portion of advertisement on page 179 adapted by permission of The National Center for Voluntary Action.

Portion of advertisement on page 179 adapted by permission of The Coca-Cola Company.

Portion of advertisement on page 180 adapted by permission of Harley-Davidson Motor Co., Inc.

Excerpt from *Guinness Book of World Records* © 1976 by Sterling Publishing Co., Inc., New York. Reprinted by permission.

Portion of advertisement on page 204 reprinted by permission of Trifari, Krussman & Fishel, Inc.

Excerpt from review of Olivier's "Hamlet" adapted from *Agee on Film* by James Agee. Copyright © 1958 by The James Agee Trust. Used by permission of Grosset & Dunlap, Inc.

Excerpt from review of "The Graduate" from *The Figures of Light* by Stanley Kauffmann. Copyright © 1967, 1968 by Stanley Kauffman. By permission of Harper & Row, Publishers, Inc.

"The Best and Worst, the Most and Least in 20 Star-Filled Months of Dining Out" by John Canaday © 1975 by The New York Times Company. Reprinted by permission.

"The Fact of the Darkness" by Sandra Schor. Reprinted by permission of the Editors of the *Journal of Popular Film* from IV, No. 4 (1975), p. 296.

Headline on page 218 © 1976 by The New York Times Company. Reprinted by permission.

Obituary of Otto Soglow © by The New York Times Company. Reprinted by permission.

Adapted sentences from "Sharks" by Elizabeth Keiffer © 1975 by The New York Times Company. Used by permission.

Excerpt from "An Irrevocable Diameter" from *The Little Disturbances of Man* by Grace Paley. Copyright © 1956, 1957, 1958, 1959 by Grace Paley. Reprinted by permission of The Viking Press.

Excerpt from *The Autobiography of Bertrand Russell 1872–1914* by Bertrand Russell. Copyright © 1969 by George Allen and Unwin. Reprinted by permission of Simon & Schuster, a Division of Gulf & Western Corporation.

Excerpt from *Blackberry Winter* by Margaret Mead. Copyright © 1972 by Margaret Mead. Reprinted by permission of William Morrow & Co., Inc.

Excerpt from "The Case Against Regular Physicals" by Richard Spark © 1976 by The New York Times Company. Reprinted by permission.

Excerpt from "Life after Death" Copyright 1976 by Newsweek, Inc. All rights reserved. Reprinted by permission.

Excerpt from "The Road Less Traveled" by Michael Parfit © 1976 by The New York Times Company. Reprinted by permission.

Excerpt from "Soliloquy on James Dean's Forty-Fifth Birthday" by Derek Marlowe. Reprinted by permission of John Cushman Associates, Inc. Copyright © 1976 by Derek Marlowe.

Excerpt from "Neither Witch Nor Good Fairy" by Brenda Maddox © 1976 by The New York Times Company. Reprinted by permission.

Excerpt from "A Black Conservative Dissents" by Thomas Sowell © 1976 by The New York Times Company. Reprinted by permission.

Excerpt from "The Rhetorical Stance" by Wayne C. Booth reprinted by permission of National Council of Teachers of English.

Excerpt from pages 83–84 of *Lyndon Johnson and the American Dream* by Doris Kearns. Reprinted from "Who Was Lyndon Baines Johnson?", Part 1: "The Man Who Would Be Loved," by Doris Kearns, which originally appeared in *The Atlantic*. Copyright © 1976 by Doris Kearns. Reprinted by permission of Harper & Row, Publishers, Inc.

Excerpt from "Welcome Freshmen" © 1976 *Yale Daily News*. Reprinted by permission.

Excerpt from "I Dreamed I Stopped the Show" by Nora Ephron reprinted and adapted by permission of International Creative Management as agents for Nora Ephron. First published in *Esquire* magazine, December 1974.

"Eating Out" reprinted with the permission of Farrar, Straus & Giroux, Inc., from *I Would Have Saved Them If I Could* by Leonard Michaels, Copyright © 1972, 1975 by Leonard Michaels.

Excerpt from "The Bankrupt Man" by John Updike reprinted by permission of the author. First published in *Esquire* magazine.

Excerpt from "Behold the Crazy Hours of the Hard-Loving Wife" by Hilma Wolitzer, reprinted by permission of William Morrow & Co., Inc. from *In the Flesh*. First published in *Esquire* magazine.

Portion of advertisement on page 273 reprinted by permission of Longines-Wittnauer Watch Co., Inc.

Portion of advertisement on page 273 reprinted by permission of College Entrance Examination Board.

Excerpt from review of "Sunset Boulevard" from *Agee on Film* by James Agee. Copyright © 1958 by The James Agee Trust. Used by permission of Grosset & Dunlap, Inc.

Excerpt from "A Right to Replay" reprinted by permission from *Time*, The Weekly Newsmagazine; Copyright Time Inc. 1977.

Photograph and caption on page 297 © 1977 by The New York Times Company. Reprinted by permission.

"Short Trip" by Robert Lipsyte © 1967 by The New York Times Company. Reprinted by permission.

Excerpt from "Interference by C. B. Radios Causing a National Earache" by Wayne King © 1977 by The New York Times Company. Reprinted by permission.

Portion of advertisement on page 306 reprinted by permission of Nissan Motor Corporation in U.S.A.

Excerpt from "The Eagle Has Landed: Two Men Walk on the Moon," by Thomas O'Toole. © 1969 by *The Washington Post*. Adapted by permission.

Portion of advertisement on page 329 reprinted by permission of Christian Children's Fund, Inc.

Portion of advertisement on page 338 reprinted by permission of Primauté Advertising, Inc.

Portion of advertisement on page 338 reprinted by permission of BMW of North America, Inc.

"Cool Caper on a Hot Rock" reprinted by permission of Liz Smith. First published in *Cosmopolitan* magazine.

Portion of advertisement on page 359 reprinted by permission of RCA, Inc.

Portion of advertisement on page 359 reprinted by permission of Sony Corporation of America.

Portion of advertisement on page 361 reprinted by permission of Ralston Purina Co.

Portion of advertisement on page 364 reprinted by permission of the California Almond Growers Exchange.

Portion of advertisement on page 367 reprinted by permission of Hunt-Wesson Foods, Inc.

Portion of advertisement on page 368 reprinted by permission of Fedders Corporation.

Portion of advertisement on page 373 reprinted by permission of Western Electric Co., Inc.

Excerpt from *The Peter Principle* by Laurence J. Peter and Raymond Hull © 1969 by William Morrow & Co., Inc. Reprinted by permission.

Excerpt from "I Dreamed I Stopped the Show," by Nora Ephron. Reprinted by permission of International Creative Management. First published in *Esquire* magazine December 1974.

Portion of advertisement on page 377 reprinted by permission of Eastern Airlines.

Portion of advertisement on page 377 reprinted courtesy of Keye, Donna, Pearlstern, Inc., for Realty Hotels, Inc.

Portion of advertisement on page 378 reprinted by permission of the Swiss National Tourist Office.

Portion of advertisement on page 378 reprinted by permission of The Stride Rite Corporation.

Portion of advertisement on page 403 reprinted by permission of Colgate-Palmolive Co.

Portion of advertisement on page 403 reprinted by permission of Sears, Roebuck & Co.

Portion of advertisement on page 411 reprinted by permission of Shulton, Inc.

Headline on page 413 reprinted by permission of The Reader's Digest.

Excerpt from "Splashy" reprinted by permission of The New Yorker.

Portion of advertisement for Top Choice dog food on page 416 reprinted by permission of General Foods Corporation.

Portion of advertisement on page 417 reprinted by permission of BMW of North America, Inc.

Portion of advertisement for Novara brand Oil of Youth Moisturizer on page 423 reprinted by permission of Schmid Laboratories, Inc.

Excerpt of text on Eleanor Roosevelt reprinted from the Life Special Report "Remarkable American Women" by special permission; © 1976, Time Inc. All rights reserved.

Excerpt from "The Little Pub" by Patricia Zelver adapted and reprinted by permission of Wallace & Sheil, Inc. Copyright © 1976 by Patricia Zelver.

Excerpt from "Drowning in Drink," by Ben Patrusky reproduced courtesy of *Signature* magazine. © 1975, Diners Club, Inc. From Reader's Digest, July 1975.

Portion of subscription card on page 431 reprinted with permission of *The Wall Street Journal.*

List of homonyms on pages 447 to 450 adapted from "Homonyms," *The Lincoln Library of Essential Information,* by permission of The Frontier Press Co.

Excerpt from *Readers' Guide to Periodical Literature* reproduced by permission of The H. W. Wilson Company, publisher. *Readers' Guide to Periodical Literature* © 1976.

Excerpt from "The Scary World of TV's Heavy Viewer" by George Gerbner and Larry Gross reprinted by permission from *Psychology Today* magazine. Copyright © 1976 Ziff-Davis Publishing Company.

Excerpts from *Brief Lives,* edited by Louis Kronenberger, reprinted by permission of Little, Brown & Co. in association with The Atlantic Monthly Press. Copyright © 1971 by Little, Brown & Co.

For Joe and Ross

To the Student

A student in one of our basic writing classes wrote about himself as a writer in this way:

> When I start to write, it presents a lot of problems. For example, I am self conscious of what I am writing and I am always fearful of using incorrect grammar. Another problem I have is staying on the main topic. When I write, it's like having mini-explosions going off in my mind. Thousands of words, sentences, and ideas keep flashing in and out of my head. It is a nuclear war between my hand and my brain. The actual results usually amaze me. In my mind it is clear and concise on paper it becomes a jumble.

To many of you, this battle is nothing new. Most college students would like to write well but arrive at college shaken by previous skirmishes or with little or no real writing experience. A few believe they are already good writers only to find that the first paper they hand over to their college English instructor carries back disappointing news. Have they been misled? Or does the news from up front mean that here is yet another English teacher to be "psyched out" with another personal set of requirements they must learn to satisfy?

You may be one of these people, in one group or another, victimized by the mysterious demands of a mysterious skill. It is our belief that at least some elements of the writing process can be demystified, and this book has grown out of that conviction. Certainly we don't promise you a set of formulas that guarantee you will write effortlessly. Nor do we say that writing well will automatically land you a good job one day. But writing well has never *hurt* anyone's chances for a job and has *helped* a lot of people get their thinking in order. We know that in any art the magic of excellence eludes recipes. But we also know from our own writing and from our years teaching in the classroom and working individually with students in the writing lab that there are methods writers use and habits they cultivate to make writing less of an ordeal and, perhaps, an occasion for quiet pleasure. We hope the *Random House Guide to Basic Writing* will serve you in and out of class as a reliable guide to writing and as a flexible reference handbook to grammar and usage. It puts together writing and grammar, laying out the basic principles of writing essays and strong English sentences before it offers advice about problems in usage that cause most of the errors writers make.

Our purpose from the start is to get you writing and keep you writing, so that any improvements in organization and in grammar relate closely to your own writing. Because English grammar is at work everywhere, we exhibit grammatical forms from the writing all around you. For example, turn to p. 118 to see how an ad for a ski resort demonstrates parallel structures and the use of *-ing* words. Plenty of exercises are included in all the chapters, but the crucial exercise is the final one back on your own paper, because continuous drill work without reference to your own purposes can be as unproductive an exercise as sleepwalking.

We have tried in this book to create the atmosphere of purposefulness and trust that exists in a good classroom, where students feel supported and not judged, where practicing writing will build your confidence and not seal your doom. You will fall in and out of love with your own sentences, and that is to be expected. Since writing includes re-writing we encourage you to do many things that may have been drummed out of you: risk mistakes, start with what you may think are trivial ideas, seek reactions from friends and teachers before you hand a paper in, revise and recast the ending, the beginning, or any sentence in the process.

Chapters 1 through 5 begin with methods for getting started, getting something down on the page. We start with freewriting as a ten-minute exploration to uncover ideas and then move swiftly to a whole piece of writing—essays, letters, journal entries. From the whole, we coax lessons in the smaller units. We use the method of the "writing cycle" (discussed in Chapter 1) to give you a base of support you may never have had. You will find that every writing task requires you to perform roughly the same acts—among them getting started, writing a rough draft, getting reactions, revising—which you can repeat and reverse wherever and whenever the stream of your writing requires it. You will discover that each fresh demand to write need not be a detached and threatening ordeal. These repeatable acts offer you a degree of assurance and confidence that may well make the difference between writing and a hard time.

Throughout the book we direct your attention to the whole essay *and* to sentences, because a writer's struggle is with sentences, and the sentences of a piece of writing pass through many stages before they are "ready." Chapters 6 through 9 guide you through the processes of seeing and writing sentences. Chapter 8 will help you eliminate fragments and run-ons while your sentences steadily gain power. Consult Chapter 16 on punctuation when you think your problems with sentences are not grammatical but concern your skill in separating into sentences the stream of writing on your page.

Chapters 10, 11, and 12 strengthen your control of the small parts—paragraphs, sentences, and words—by introducing options to make your writing not only correct, but effective.

The usage section, Chapters 13 through 17, continues to provide reference support and exercises for your uncertainties on verbs, subject-verb agreement, pronouns, punctuation, and spelling. Clearly, not all writers are stalled by all these problems, and you will begin by attending first to the issues you (and your teacher) consider urgent in your writing.

Finally, the book recognizes that, ready or not, you will soon be putting your skills on the line, and a lot may hang in the balance. Taking exams, writing research essays, and writing job résumés often require knowledge of a few added conventions so that your writing can go public. Chapters 18, 19, and 20 provide a closer look at these practical concerns.

We hope you will take advantage of the scope of the *Random House Guide*. Both publisher and authors feel that students in basic courses deserve, in a single book, a comprehensive guide to writing. But the book, remember, will never be a substitute for your own writing. When you are learning to write, your own writing is the primary text. Many whole essays are nonetheless included, some written by professional writers, others by students like yourself. Though you may feel you write better or worse than these students, we can assure you that your serious observations about the essays of your classmates are an indispensable turn in the "writing cycle." Since your writing deserves the reactions of a range of readers, not only those of your instructor, all of what you write need not be read by your instructor at all. Writing is a lifelong skill that should be tested in more places than on the English teacher's desk. Not until other people report to us how our words move them do we know exactly what the words on our page have managed to say. Now we invite all of you—students and teachers alike—to respond to this book in that same spirit, offering observations on what we have written and suggestions for change.

ACKNOWLEDGMENTS

The ideas in this book have had many allies along the way, and a few adversaries, all of whom deserve gratitude. They forced us to stop teaching long enough to talk about writing and answer some hard questions. Thanks go to our colleagues at Queens College in the Composition program and in the Writing Skills Workshop, in particular to Donald McQuade for his advice and indispensable encouragement and to Robert Lyons, who created a spirited atmosphere where good teaching and ideas about writing were equally marketable. Betsy Kaufman, Rosemary Deen, Edmund Epstein, and Michael Timko have our thanks. Special indebtedness to two colleagues: to Marie Ponsot, who tested portions of the manuscript with wisdom and authority, and to Aileen Grumbach (Nassau Community College, SUNY) for her excellent ideas about rhetoric.

We are indebted to many students over the years, and in particular to those whose writing-in-progress appears in this book: Dexter D. Jeffries, Alex Gonzalez, Howard Guralnick, Douglas Manley, Paul Nims Horton, Paul Goldberg, Donna Simms, Hanna Hechinger, Sheryl Reiss, Valerie Babb, Joseph Bertolino, Suzan Abouel-Ela, Karen Rieger, Tom Coppola, Kathleen Hyatt, Rebecca Burgoon, Athena Artemiou, Rich Barakat, Mark Tricarico, Adam Epstein, Fernando Bustelos, Walter Bruckner, Frank Renna, Keith Edwards, Michael Beller, and Frank Crane.

Assistance often came to us in print rather than in person. We acknowledge the influence of Paul Roberts, Leo Rockas, Francis Christensen, James Moffett, Ken Macrorie, Peter Elbow, Kenneth Bruffee, Mina Shaughnessy, and Richard Young, Alton Becker and Kenneth Pike as well as the teachings of the late Edwin L. Peterson of the University of Pittsburgh.

To Sondra Perl (Hostos Community College, CUNY) and particularly to Richard Larson (Lehman College, CUNY) who saw the project through from beginning to end, we owe a runner's debt for holding us to continuing exercise and training in the prudent revision of our thought. A separate sentence of appreciation to Alan Ehmann (University of Texas at El Paso) and Joseph Trimmer (Ball State University) for participating in our ideas with so much optimism and care.

Talking and working with the team at Random House has taught us a great deal about putting together a book. Appreciation to Richard Garretson, our Editor, and to David Follmer, June Smith, and Murray Curtin for their attention to this project. To Betty Gatewood, our Project Editor, special thanks for holding the innumerable details of our universe in her head for so many months.

A final statement of thanks to our parents, for their love and understanding.

But to the seven people in two houses who let this project move in on them, this book is gratefully dedicated: Joe and Ross; Starry, Josh, Gideon, Sharon and Lauren.

Sandra Schor
Judith Fishman

Contents

9 Modifying   182

PART 3 Choosing Effectively

10 Writing Convincing Paragraphs   226

12   Choosing Exact Words   289

PART 4 **Choosing Correctly**

13 Verbs   316

17 Spelling   429

PART 5 Being Practical

18 Writing the Research Essay   464

Part One

The Writing Cycle

Chapter 1 / Writing Immediately

THE WRITING CYCLE In your mind, the notion of writing may be uncomfortably linked to writing an "assignment," a chore you desperately undertake to satisfy a deadline for a teacher or a boss. If you have this dread of writing, it may be because you never write anything unless you have to. A lot of people share your dismay, but certainly not all. On the contrary, there are many people who write often and willingly, people who would confess to you that writing has a private value of its own. Independent of assignments and deadlines, teachers and jobs, writing is a system of acts you can come to depend on to help you find out what you think. And knowing what you think can be a secret weapon in your life, a continuing source of personal confidence and pleasure.

This book invites you to think of writing not as a single act but as a *cycle* of acts that you repeat with increasing confidence every time you write. As you work on a piece of writing, intermittently writing and thinking and writing again, you are gathering strength as a writer. Here at the outset, we want to emphasize that you improve as a writer not because you're learning to show someone else what you know, but more importantly because you're *exercising and widening your ability to think*. Since every time you write you'll be required, among other things, to get started, to discover what interests you, to put down a first draft, and to express your thoughts in sentences, you'll be practicing and improving the same skills every time you write. The idea of the cycle may be a particularly reassuring one, therefore, because you can count on going over the same acts every time you move through another piece of writing.

Like many beginning writers, you may wonder how you can get at all

2

the ideas you have. Whether you're writing a letter to a friend or composing a business memo, the first thing to do is to write, for you can discover ideas *as you write.* When you write, just as when you think, you're moving forward and backward, bumping into unexpected thoughts, adjusting your thinking as you try to capture some of them in words. Often, by looking into your own sentences, you can see the ideas still locked in the words you've already written. Regular writing practice makes it easier for you to bring out your ideas, and, once your ideas are in writing—even in the crudest form—it's easier to see connections among them. Nor should it be a surprise that connections between thoughts are almost inevitable: one thing you do relates to another and another and another, and the thoughts jammed into your mind begin to assume a shape, an arrangement that makes writing and rewriting more orderly. But writing is not entirely a private matter. The reactions of other people to what you write may later send you back for more ideas, plainer connections, a better way to arrange your sentences on the page, before you're satisfied that you have landed on what you want to say—and said it.

Unfortunately, thinking of writing as a cycle may not save you time at first. The only immediate shortcut lies in the flexibility of your behavior. Instead of feeling trapped in a rigid start-to-finish sweepstakes or becoming stalled midway in your writing by not knowing what else you can say, you are able to reenter your thinking process at any point and recognize precisely which actions you need to perform to get your piece of writing moving again. "I need to do some freewriting." "I need to produce more details." "I need to discover what the details in the third paragraph mean." "I need to rewrite my opening because at last I know what I'm saying." The amount of time saved has a way of showing up later, since the experience you gain from working on one piece of writing increases your confidence and control as you begin to take charge of your next piece of writing.

FREEWRITING Your very first action is to write, not a finished assignment, but an exercise. This exercise is called *freewriting.* Take out a pen and a pad of paper, sit quietly for a moment, and relax. Think about whatever you want: nothing, or where you are, where you've been, or what you want. Set a clock for ten minutes. Put your pen to your paper and begin.

Remember only *not to stop.* Keep writing for ten minutes. You may babble, you may yammer, you may feel silly and embarrassed, but don't stop. And don't go back to correct spelling, to change a word, or to cross out. Keep writing. There is no such thing as a writer's block when you do freewriting.

If you can't think of what to write next, just repeat your last word or phrase until a new word rises, rises, rises, rises, rises. . . . Or write, "I'm stuck, I'm stuck, I'm stuck. . . ." When you get tired of "I'm stuck," another word will happen. At the end of ten minutes, *stop.*

For now, let's not ask why. Begin.

Samples of freewriting Here are some freewriting exercises done by students in college writing classes. The first ones are by people just starting out. The last two are by people who've been at it for a while.

What to write what to write next, will I have a lot of stuff to do at work today. I'm never going to be able to do this for ten min. What did I put down so far will the bookstore be crowded, will they have the book I have to get how did he write a whole page so far. I hope we don't have to do this often. I don't want to have to read this in front of everyone. I better write down something because this isn't enough.

This class ain't bad. I think I like it. They're smoking. I want to but I don't want to. I wonder where she is now. If she's on campus yet. I feel bad I didn't call. Everybody's writing. Now I feel like the kids on the paper. I gotta get a job. I need money. This room is half a classroom. I don't think I can write for ten minutes straight. I shouldn't be doodling. I should be writing. I haven't wrote anything in so long—my hand writing is very sloppy and spelling even worse. 10 minutes is almost up. I'm hungry. I could go for some nice pizza. Old cars on his shirt. This course doesn't seem to be a study-study course. It's just you. Gonna need a lot of paper in this class.

Right now I got a tooth ache and a head ache. I want to go home. I want to go home, and lay down. Go to McDonald's and get something to eat, but my tooth is hurting too much. "hum" "hum" What am I going to write about? I don't know what to write about. This is one of the problems I always had. I want to go swimming or play ball. Should of stayed in bed. Wish that I had money. My tooth is killing me but I am going to fight the pain. Everyone else is writing a lot of things and I don't know what to write. I want to go home. One more class to go, I do not think I can stand very much more of this tooth ache. I can't write any more because I have nothing to say. OK yesterday I went to the park.

I think that I have adjusted a little better to college now that this is my third day here. I have found that there is a lot of different things in college than in high school. Perhaps more difficult, but the idea that one has to adjust to these new ways of learning. Right now I am uncertain about what to write thinking, thinking, thinking, something has just come up in my mind. It's about my art teacher. He looks mean and, and, and, and, and, old fashion. He speaks much too fast for me to take notes. The course is not what I expected. To me it's kind of boring to stay for 2 hours in this class and listen to this stranger. I am undecided if I should drop this course, I think I won't because this girl I know goes to this class, maybe it's foolish just to go to a class you don't like because there's a nice girl you know in the class. But I think that with a little bearing down I can adjust to this teacher's way of teaching. I want to go home and eat, and talk to all my friends, and go and play basketball.

At this moment I am sitting here very nervous thinking about how I would stand in this English class. Would I like it or not. Will I be able to do well. I am also watching the other people in this classroom, what they're doing to hide their nervous habits, some of the students are smoking, some are playing with their hair or clothing, or what ever he or she feels like doing. While I am thinking about what to write I see Alex smoking a cigarette, but then I realize it's his way of covering up for being nervous. I don't like cigarettes, I feel they are terrible in so many ways, for example they're expensive, it doesn't smell good, it's pollution,etc.

I'm smoking. Why? My chest feels so heavy it's as if someone had been sitting on it all night. Yet I love to smoke, especially when I'm nervous like now. The fly in the room is bothering the hell out of me. It keeps buzzing around in my head and near my writing hand which holds my pen. My pen. My pen which is grey in color. I remember the pen I took with me cross-country and how I screwed it up when I dropped it in this guy Ron's fire and how I couldn't write letters home because I needed to buy a pen but in Alaska if you don't have a car it's hard to get around to the store to buy a pen. My pen, my pen my pen my pen my pen my pen my pen my pen I wonder how long the days are in Alaska now? Is it a period of only 2 hrs. of darkness or 4 or 6? Someone told me that in the winter the sun only comes up at noon and then it goes down at 12:15. That sounds like lunch time. I'm hungry. I didn't bring my lunch today, so I'll have to spend some money. I can't afford to buy a greasy lunch here in the caf. The caf. Loud music, pinball machines, rattling of plates, smells of food, vending machines, garbage on the floor, people smoking pot, girls in halter tops, tops, tops, tops and short shorts and I want to get off this track so tell Judy there's 6 minutes left right and how I didn't really want to move to Canada and how lucky I am.

What is it like to write? I remember when I would look at the paper and it would stare blankly back at me. It hardly happens now, maybe because too much is happening. The more that happens the more I have to write to clear and sort. Writing is clearing, writing is sorting. I can't get over the flow when I remember my first freewriting experience. I want to say a lot but a piece is always held back so what usually ends up on paper is only a surface reflection of the deeper depth. What is it like to write. What is it like to live? I can't separate the two, I need one to do the other & wouldn't think of doing one without the other. My head always wins the race & my pen & cramped hand slowly come in a poor second. If I could write what I think, put the thoughts down. Not so much the thoughts that I can verbalize, but the ones that just hang, waiting to be formed into thoughts by a mind too weak to gather them all together.

Writing is wondering if you can write & writing what you wonder.

You may be asking what practice like this can do to help you. A careful look at the samples may justify "writing immediately" as a way of plunging into writing ice cold.

YOU CAN WRITE IMMEDIATELY—YOU HAVE THE GRAMMAR

For one thing, you can write immediately in English because you know the language. Our method in this book is to demonstrate that you already know the grammar of English. You can see in the freewriting exercises that although not everything written there is a sentence, every writer knows how to compose acceptable sentences:

> I hope we don't have to do this often.
> I woke up at six this morning for nothing.
> My tooth is killing me but I am going to fight the pain.

> What am I going to write about?
> Will I be able to do well?
> What is it like to live?

In ten minutes of nonstop writing, these writers, and you too, rely on a grasp of English grammar to write sentences without thinking about grammar at all. Although you may not realize it, you have been seeing grammar wherever you turn—in books, in advertisements, in newspaper headlines, even in the yellow pages of your phone book. When you speak or read, you don't have to think about grammar because you use it and respond to it automatically. For example, you can understand the following advertisement because you understand English grammar:

Why do you smoke?

Without a second thought, you know you are being asked a question, and you know it long before you reach the give-away question mark at the end. You don't need to study this book to understand that *yes* is not an acceptable answer to the question *Why do you smoke?* On the other hand, *it's a habit, because I'm nervous, to keep my hands out of the Hydrox cookies* are acceptable answers because they meet the demands of the question word *why*.

Throughout this book, sentences are illustrated through headlines, advertisements, and the prose of good writers. Your own writing and the writing of other students will also provide many more illustrations of grammatical structures. The book assumes that you know grammar, but it does not require that you be familiar with grammatical terms and labels, even though you were probably exposed to these terms and labels during many years of grammar lessons. In fact, we ask that you start again, stripping away whatever assumptions about grammar may be closing your mind, and opening it to the fresh evidence in this book.

The grammar of any language describes the systematic way words are used to make sentences in that language. French, Swahili, Japanese, and Hebrew each has its own system. This book is concerned with English grammar, particularly with English sentences. Sentences, after all, are what you will be writing. In love letters and in your personal diaries, just as in encyclopedias and magazines, ideas generally travel in sentences. In English —and this is true of other languages as well—written sentences are variations of basic patterns. Americans from different parts of the country who *write*—regardless of the way they *speak* in their part of the country—all follow the common requirements of what we call standard American English in their sentences. This is the public English you will find on your evening newscast, in the *New York Times,* in *Sports Illustrated,* in this book, and in most books in your library.

Ever since you were a baby, you have been hearing English and training yourself to produce the language approximately as you heard it. *Don't cry any more. Here I come with a bottle. You're such an angel. What are you hiding under your jacket?* These represent some of the basic patterns of English sentences. You use them confidently as you speak because, if you are a native speaker of the language, English is the system you know best.

Still, there may be a few variations based on the sentences you heard at home or among friends. If as a child you heard *Don't cry no more* for *Don't cry any more* or *Here he come* for *Here he comes,* you will have to focus on practicing the standard forms so that your writing can go public.

In Part Two of this book, the parts of the sentence are unraveled and then knit back together again. This is one of the most important processes a writer needs to grasp. Some lucky people write sentences and punctuate them just as intuitively as they say sentences. Others aren't so lucky. But the process can be studied, and writers can learn a precise way to test what they have written to see if they have produced sentences. The Food and Drug Administration requires that antibiotics be tested by a quality control department to see that all bottles of a drug have minimum potency. Similarly, your sentence power depends on a kind of grammatical potency. You can begin to insure the quality of your writing by testing it for the minimum requirements of a sentence.

You will also see in Part Two the process of moving beyond minimum sentence requirements. Soon you will be able to make connections within and between sentences so that you aren't limited to writing only short, safe sentences. You'll be able to pry open your sentences and see the possibilities that they hold.

Elsewhere in this book, you will concentrate on usage problems that cause the greatest uncertainty among beginning writers—problems with verbs, pronouns, agreement, and spelling. About these points, the public language offers you no choice: they are right or wrong. However you describe it—educated American, edited American, standard English—the single most important dialect for college students is the dialect that has been standardized. You may think of this as another form of quality control.

Although you may feel that there are trouble spots in your grammar, these shouldn't prevent you from writing immediately. We hope to take some of the guesswork out of your decisions by giving you a step-by-step understanding of how sentences work. You don't need to understand sentences perfectly *before* you write because you will learn *as* your writing gets under way. This book does not postpone writing until after you master fifteen weeks of grammar drills. The truth is that you can write *immediately*. Writing and writing in sentences are two simultaneous processes that begin the writing cycle. We assume you'll leave behind your dread of grammar once your freewriting shows that you know more about grammar than you think. Although we couldn't print the first two parts of this book, "The Writing Cycle" and "Seeing Sentences," on the same pages, you can profit from using the two together. You can consult the grammar and usage sections of this book as you need them to understand the processes of writing sentences, and you can use them as a handy reference guide when you need answers to specific questions.

You will be working on sentences all the while you are writing whole essays, learning that you can proofread for "correctness" after you have tried out your ideas in writing. Every day that you write, you progress as a writer, building confidence, making use of the skills you already have and extending them through regular, nonpressured writing practice, a kind of writing practice you may never have had.

YOU CAN WRITE IMMEDIATELY—YOU HAVE THE IDEAS

Another glance at the freewriting samples may persuade you that you already have in your head not only enough grammatical structures but also enough memories, experiences, doubts, ideas, and dreams about your own unfolding life to allow you to begin writing right now. Asked to write about anything, is it any wonder that freewriters begin by writing about writing? That is their immediate concern—ten minutes of writing. But see how they move from writing into all kinds of ideas and feelings:

> *Fear:*   I don't want to have to read this in front of everyone.
> *Desire:*   I wish I had a car.
> *Observation:*   My handwritting is very sloppy and spelling even worse.
> *Memory:*   Yesterday I went to the park.
> *Speculation:*   I think I can adjust to this teacher's way of teaching.
> *Observation:*   I am also watching what other people are doing to hide their
>   nervous habits.

All of these are "living" ideas, glimmers of thought released at a given instant from people's heads. Your own freewriting is no different. It is an exercise that puts you in touch with your own thinking.

Invention, or discovering something to write about, is the writer's first concern, and freewriting, as we have seen, is the first broad swing in that direction. *Writing itself produces ideas and brings them forward so that you can see them.* Your page of freewriting may be messy and disconnected; it may defy everything you have ever learned about editing your work and being careful; it may simply turn inside out the disordered thoughts in your head; but *after ten minutes you will have a page of thoughts written down* that you can get at for further consideration if you wish or that you can simply get out of your way. This kind of writing is free and exploratory. It is like freethinking or daydreaming on paper. Your pen follows wherever your head takes it. Your thoughts drift from the present moment to a word or a phrase or a memory that pops into your head by means of some private association. You may eventually come upon a subject that preoccupies you (getting a job, going to Mexico) or that holds out some special appeal or fear (moving into your own apartment). Freewriting loosens you up, limbers your muscles, strengthens your hand and mind. Writing is no longer an exercise that tires you quickly or an act that you distrust because it has embarrassed you. Rather, it gets you into shape for the athletics to come.

Freewriting is your best method of invention because it makes immediately available to you some of the ideas that are in your mind. That is why we begin with it here. Your daily freewriting exercises bring your thoughts out to a place where you can reach them. Just how ideas come to us as we write, we don't know. But, for whatever reasons, putting words on paper leads us to think of more words and the patterns to hold them. Although there is another stage of freewriting (discussed in Chapter 2) that focuses on a subject and has as its special intent rounding up loose ideas for an essay, for now we will concentrate on the freest writing. First, however, we need to add a few words about personal experience as the raw material for that writing.

A professor we know tells a story about the most fluent, the most articulate person he ever met, a person never stuck for the next word. Another professor? Not at all. He is a truck driver whose truck has been rammed by a convertible speeding into a left turn from a right lane. The truck driver is full of clear ideas and you can bet lively language. He is fluent because he is telling about an event that matters to him, an event that he both knows the truth about and feels powerfully about. Having his trailer smashed by a maniac on the wrong side of the road makes him eloquent. He never swerves off the subject. He is convinced, and he convinces everybody listening, that he is the only one on earth who can tell this story.

Each day some of us are truck drivers rammed by convertibles. We want to yell our heads off about something we have experienced. We want to make somebody understand the truth of what happened to us and how we feel. Sometimes the convertible is a teacher, a landlord, or a strange idea about marriage. But it rams us in the side when we least expect it.

As a writer, you are now entering a new relationship with such experiences because the one agreement you must keep with yourself is to write about things that matter to you. Which of the day's experiences keep your mind's motor running long after your car's motor is shut off? What ideas won't be put to bed when your body is ready for sleep? To enjoy writing is to explore ideas that steal your attention, to write about them and allow them to explain the unprecedented demands they place on your thinking.

But perhaps you consider yourself to be a person who doesn't feel such a passion about events. You are a take-it-or-leave-it person. Things don't faze you much, you say.

We doubt that. Take-it-or-leave-it symptoms are often the result of unsureness, and there *are* events that we all experience that leave us unsure. We don't know exactly how we feel. We can't yell our heads off even when we think we should because we haven't made sense out of what we've been through. Writing can be a way of working through these experiences because the demands of writing teach us to observe our experiences more intelligently.

Suppose that you were riding home from work on a crowded bus. There you were, sitting in the first row, behind the driver. The bus crept through rush-hour traffic. At the Maple Avenue stop, a dozen people filed into the bus, tossing coins into the hopper. The last one on was an elderly woman. She came up close to the driver and whispered that she had left her purse at home, that she had no money. The driver answered, "Sorry, Ma'am. This bus doesn't give free rides." The woman pleaded. The driver refused. The passengers began to murmur, but the woman stood fixed. The bus driver said, "I'm not moving until you leave this bus." The woman didn't budge. A man in the back row offered the woman the fare. She refused, saying, "I don't take handouts." The bus driver stared out the window. The woman finally left the bus.

These observations leave you with dozens of judgments: the bus driver was stubborn. The bus driver was following orders. The woman was a spy from the bus company, testing the driver. The driver had given free rides in the past and had been reported. He was guarding his job. The woman had a lot of pride. She tried to get a free ride, but she wouldn't accept the fare. That's a strange kind of pride. Was it pride or was it something else? If the bus hadn't been so crowded, maybe the bus driver would have agreed. The bus driver had had a bad day. The woman had done this before. The bus driver had her number. The woman was a wealthy eccentric who got her kicks out of doing strange things. She had a roll of $100 bills in her pocket.

We all have experiences, and we all wonder about what we observe during those experiences. Writers turn their experiences and their wonderings into writing.

As you sit on the bus every day, you *see*. As you work at your job in the supermarket or in the library or in the liquor store, you *see*. You have experiences with customers. You overhear conversations. You think about your boss. You wonder where she goes after work and what her love life is like. You wonder about dreams—about your own and others'. You wonder about "where you are" in life and "where you're going." You think about college and why you're here. You wonder whether the woman next to you in your English class will look at you. You wonder whether the man across the room in your French class will smile back if you smile first. Should you take the chance? You wonder. You sit in your class and your mind wanders. You remember your first date. You remember your first funeral. You remember the first time you won something after a struggle with your parents. And now here you are tempted to say, "I have nothing to write about."

That's the most common complaint of beginning writers, "I have nothing to write about." But when beginning writers tap their experiences and call upon their memories, make observations, and think about their lives, they often find that they have too much to write about and not enough time. The following exercises are designed to tap your own resources. As you work through the ones that interest you, keep in mind that you are opening yourself to what may be new experiences and new ways of thinking about your experiences. Concentrate on what you see rather than on how you feel.

1. Write down everything you see as you leave your English class.
2. Stand for at least fifteen minutes in a corner of the college union or the college "hangout" and record what you see and hear. Take in all you can. Notice the man in a rush. Notice the woman wearing sandals in the snow.
3. As you go home from work or school, observe. If you're walking, look at the houses, stores, empty lots, trees, whatever you're accustomed to racing right by. If you drive, slow down—take in what you can. If you take public transportation, watch people, eavesdrop on what they're saying.
4. Record a vivid dream exactly as you remember it.
5. Sit in a corner of a room. Write down what you see. Now close your eyes for two minutes. When you open your eyes, write down what you see. Are there differences?
6. Write down what you hear. Now cup your hands over your ears for two minutes. After you remove your hands, record what you hear. Do you notice differences?
7. Watch a young child. What do you see? Write down exactly what the child does.
8. Record a "first" experience—a first day of school, a first date, a first job, the first time you were refused something important. Concentrate on what happened, who did what, who said what.

The observations you just made were recorded without comments. For example, "Record a 'first' experience. Concentrate on what happened, who did what, who said what." You tried to eliminate your feelings and restrict yourself to an accurate record of observable events. You left out how you were affected, whether you thought an event was terrible or terriffic. The result is like a photograph.

But listing a series of events, no matter how accurately, can grow boring:

> I got up out of bed at 5:00. I studied my chem notes until 8:00. Then I grabbed a piece of toast and a cup of coffee. I picked up Jeannette on the way to class and talked about the atomic number of a few elements. Later I told her about my date with Karen the night before. We got to the lecture hall at 9:28. My hands were pretty sweaty. Jeannette appeared calm.

As a writer, you need to recognize that all of the events you experience are raw material. Even at the very beginning of the writing cycle, your freewriting encourages you to explore the events of your daily life for vivid personal details. Eventually, your writing takes more shape. You become more aware of a reader who wants to find out what the details mean to you, the writer. To find out, ask yourself questions about the events you observe:

> Why did I get out of bed at 5:00 in the morning?

> Why did I have to study my chem notes? Do I usually cram for tests? Didn't I study before? If not, why not?

> Who are the characters in this little drama? Does each one matter?

> Does Karen have anything to do with my chemistry test?

> And what about Jeannette, what do I really think of her? How does she affect me? Does she make me feel nervous? jealous? stupid? How do these events relate to the way I usually take tests? to what I *must* do in school? to what I want to do for the rest of my life?

Now the writing cycle is turning. You have gone back to ask questions that lead to more ideas for your writing. Here is another stage of the same piece of writing incorporating some of the answers to the questions:

> I got out of bed at 5:00 because the test wouldn't let me sleep. With only the test on my mind, I studied my chem notes because I hadn't gotten to them last night. Oh, that was a great night with Jeannette's friend Karen, though badly timed, badly timed. Timing, in fact, is a big problem for me. I do reckless things at the last minute, perhaps to give myself an excuse for not doing well on my tests. Then I try to cram and my guilt feelings increase as time slips by. I managed to eat some toast and coffee and stopped for Jeannette on my way, hoping to pick her brain about the

atomic number of uranium, but she wanted to talk about Karen and what I thought of her, since Jeannette, after all, had spent the evening at home, studying like crazy. Sometimes she makes me feel stupid, or at least regretful that I am such a coward and can't face up to trying my best without excuses. I wished my feet would take off in a direction away from Lecture Hall 301 but there they were, keeping step with Jeannette's, all the way into the room. I sat down like a robot. I am a very poor test taker while Jeannette is all cool. She sat there chatting amiably with some guy she wanted to make time with later. When the tests arrived, I wondered why I subject myself to these horrifying ordeals, and I wondered if I would ever get to engineering school. I was in a panic. Jeannette, however, was calmly placing an extra Bic pen and her pocket calculator next to her paper as she began.

Usually you can count on the details you select to attract readers. Answering questions that matter to you uncovers why *your* subject is different from all other subjects—what single feature of it is unforgettable to you. People are interested in what is important to other people, interested in how they perceive differences among similar habits, similar people, similar tests. You secretly want to compare the way you study with the way Jeannette does, your methods of surviving in the world with hers.

And since you are the world's expert on you, you are ready right now to begin your research—to freewrite into your mind and memory—as your first writing acts.

Later discussions in this book will attempt to give you insight into *form*—into ways of arranging your ideas and emphasizing the one idea that matters most. You will begin perhaps by telling a story out of your own experiences. Telling a story is a form. You will then be urged to look for a "point" in the story. Arranging your story as an illustration of that "point" is another form.

But arrangement of raw material comes later. Let us practice now the earliest moments of your writing cycle. Perhaps today you do a ten-minute freewriting exercise. Suppose that here and there in it you mention the beach. Your research has already begun. The beach is on your mind, and you are the only living expert on your own beach-going activities. You reread your freewriting to locate a special idea about the beach; you look for sentences that reveal your attitude about why you go to the beach. You think about the beach and remember your feelings the last time you went. You may identify a conflict, a tension that pulls you in two directions at once—for example, "I remember going to the beach every Saturday in July and August even though I despised it." That is an idea that arouses your curiosity. What didn't you like? What drove you there? Had you merely stated your activity—"I spent every Saturday and Sunday in July and August at Oak Neck Beach on Long Island Sound"—the sentence might have led to nothing more than a shrug and a *so what?*

Later you will see how to underline the sentences in your freewriting that arouse the most questions in you and how to jot down the questions. An idea with sparkle may be well hidden. It's up to you to search for the one that *matters* to you.

Take your time. Read your freewriting carefully, but don't be too hard on yourself. And don't expect consistency. You may have produced a fantastic page of freewriting on Tuesday only to find that on Thursday your page is dull and embarrassing. Remember how you felt on Tuesday, how much you unearthed in your writing, and keep writing.

Your writing cycle begins with an emphasis on freewriting because it is one form of research into your mind and into your memory that produces the raw material quickly. Chapter 2 discusses other ways to get started, methods other than freewriting that help you notice your experiences and find ideas in them. Freewriting will not mislead you. You may add other methods later. For now, in ten-minute turns, you will be relying on all the living you have done until now, the raw material of your life. You have been through a childhood; twelve years of schools and teachers; assorted relatives—siblings, parents, aunts and cousins; friends. You have lived in one or more places; visited around the corner or across the world. You have worked for money, had a boss and a job to do. You have been exposed to religion or ethical teachings. You have been aware of your own sexuality and the sexuality of others. You dress a certain way. You eat certain foods. You go to the movies and look at a newspaper. You may have had to master a skill, driving a car, or turning a dowel on a lathe. You dream. In short, you may not be an expert on most things, but you are a specialist about yourself. And beginning writers learn fastest when they include themselves in their subject. You are your own most specific subject, and you can interest your reader. As one freewriter on page 4 says, "This course doesn't seem to be a study-study course. It's just you. Gonna need a lot of paper in this class."

Yes, you are. Keep your pen and paper ready because you can untangle what is happening to you in your life through your writing. As you coax your surface ideas onto paper, you may soon find the roots of what bothers and burdens you. Writing and thinking and rewriting will help you think more clearly and with more complexity. Another freewriter on page 4 said, "Maybe it's foolish to go to a class you don't like just because there's a nice girl in the class." Is that a problem worth poking at? Maybe, though it will take his personal time and effort to find out. Writing is probably one of the few great solo acts left.

As you begin to think of writing as a cycle, and of all the separate acts you have to perform, your optimism may dip suddenly. That is to be expected. Writing is not, after all, an instantaneous act. No immediate high lies in store for you as you unload your first word. But with regular practice, you will improve, and a few months from now it will be interesting to reread what you have written today. Writing, like any process you are trying to perfect, requires your time, your patience, and your effort. We think you'll find you're worth all the time and effort that it takes.

Getting Started

Chapter 2

When Brooklyn College opened its writing center to all students who wanted to improve their writing, the staff surveyed the reasons students gave for walking in and asking for help. "Getting started" was the reason most frequently given:

> I have to write a paper on some aspect of the movies, and I can't seem to get going with it. I've known about it for two weeks, and now it's due tomorrow but I still can't get started. It's such a big subject that I don't know where to begin.

Or:

> My teacher assigned us a topic to write about. We have to select an event that changed our lives in some way. So I have to come up with an important event in my life and say how it changed me. I told him nothing important has ever happened to me. I sit down to get started, and, as usual in my life, nothing whatever happens. It's due Friday. Maybe if I don't turn it in, something important will happen? *Help!*

Chapter 1 has already suggested freewriting as a way to get started. But after you freewrite, there are other workshop methods you can use to move any further blocks out of your way. College students who come to writing workshops learn how to rely on these methods for self-help. Although getting started may sometimes seem to be a matter of luck, you can, in fact, turn to specific techniques for inventing ideas before your essay itself begins to take shape. These techniques, called *prewriting strategies,* occur early in your cycle of skills but may be repeated whenever you need another rush of ideas.

FOCUSED
FREEWRITING

We hope you are convinced by now that freewriting, or "nonstop" writing, is an actual—not a trial—step in the writing process because it brings something onto paper when you need it most, when you are working hardest to get ideas down on a page.

One way to get closer to a piece of writing is to reread your free-writing, since hidden in the spill of your freewriting may be a subject that attracts your attention. Sometimes you may have a need to write in a general subject area (to satisfy some personal interest or for a class assignment)—a subject that is still very large and vague to you. You can begin by focusing your thoughts on that subject at the moment of writing. This *focused* freewriting may take any form whatever. If your subject is the movies, you may tell how envious you were of the actor who starred in the movie you saw last weekend; you may write about late night reruns on TV and how your family always hollers when you stay up to watch; you may run a page or two on the comedy and confusion that results when you and your friends fill your Chevy for an evening at the drive-in; you may ramble on about Barbra Streisand or the Marx Brothers; you may jot down vague expectations you feel each time you take a seat in the dark. More likely your focused freewriting may contain all, some, or none of these thoughts, in a free-flowing stream of ideas spilling freely and form-lessly into one another. Here's what to do.

> Freewrite for ten minutes.
> As you begin, focus your thoughts on your general subject (going to see a movie).
> Don't stop. Keep writing for ten minutes.
> If your thoughts wander, let them.
> This is the focused freewriting of a student in a freshman writing class.

It begins at the movies. Where does it end?

"Where the Lilies Bloom"—I often sit back and think about the movie.
I remember it vividly. The trees, the mountains, the girl singing that song
as they buried her father. It wasn't so much the theme or the plot of the
movie that interested me. It was more the feeling that I had while watching
it. I liked the sister the best, the eldest. I watched her carefully throughout
the movie, letting my mind drift, imagining myself as she not in her
situation but in the way she moved, in the way her mind went on carelessly, even more in the way she dressed, the things she liked, her playing
the guitar or on top of the hill picking wild flowers. I sat and watched
as if all the things I am, all the things I would really like to do were being
viewed in front of me. I loved it. It made me happy, it also made me
quite sad, for after the movie was over I realized that all I had lived was
only within me—all the freedom I imagined was nothing more than
imagination. It reminded me of all the limitations being put on me by
society, my surroundings, even myself. I love simplicity, simple dress,
living, everything down to earth. If you'll excuse the cliché, the girl dressed

just the way I would like to dress. But I can't always be barefooted with a skirt made out of a pair of old jeans—I can't because my situation won't allow it. I can't imagine myself walking into an office or a class dressed like that. I don't think there is anything wrong with it. It's that it just is not so easily accepted, or is it? I don't know. My father looks at that kind of dress as being hippie. He looks at a person who dresses as such as not normal because she goes against the so-called (*normal*) way of doing things.

The second stage in your focused freewriting is to read what you have written. Read it through quickly, underlining any sentence or phrase that seems outstanding, either for its truth, its importance to you, the striking way you said it, or any other reason.

This is the time to ask yourself what matters most about all these raw thoughts. How did you feel while watching that movie? Were you frightened? envious? happy? hopeful? disappointed? depresssed? Why do you remember this movie above so many others? Did one of the characters remind you of yourself? Which one? Why? Did you like him or her? Did he or she bring you glamour? insight into your own problems? a plan of action? Is there any place in the freewriting where you reveal what you felt about this experience at the movie?

Underlining important sentences As you read your focused freewriting, keep asking questions such as these. Treat your writing with respect. Expect to find answers there. Underline those sentences and phrases that mean something important to you.

Here is the same freewriting with key passages underlined:

Where the Lilies Bloom—I often sit back and think about the movie. I remember it vividly. The trees, the mountains, the girl singing that song as they buried her father. It wasn't so much the theme or the plot of the movie that interested me. It was more the feeling that I had while watching it. I liked the sister the best, the eldest. I watched her carefully throughout the movie, letting my mind drift, imagining myself as she not in her situation but in the way she moved, in the way her mind went on carelessly, even more in the way she dressed, the things she liked, her playing the guitar or on top of the hill picking wild flowers. I sat and watched as if all the things I am, all the things I would really like to do were being viewed in front of me. I loved it. It made me happy, it also made me quite sad, for after the movie was over I realized that all I had lived was only within me—all the freedom I imagined was nothing more than imagination. It reminded me of all the limitations being put on me by society, my surroundings, even myself. I love simplicity, simple dress, living, everything down to earth. If you'll excuse the cliché, the girl dressed just the way I would like to dress. But I can't always be barefooted with a skirt made out of a pair of old jeans—I can't because my situation won't allow it. I can't imagine myself walking into an office or a class dressed like that. I don't think there is anything wrong with it. It's that it just is not so easily accepted, <u>or is it?</u> I don't know. <u>My father looks at that kind of dress as being hippie.</u> He looks at a person who dresses as such as <u>not normal</u> because she goes against the so-called (<u>normal</u>) way of doing things.

The underlined passages contain honest, personal ideas, some of which may be interesting enough to give you a start on a paper about the movies. Isolating them gives the writer the drift of what is on her mind. She has added comments in parentheses:

> The trees, the mountains, the girl singing that song as they buried her father. (I love the country.)
> It was more the feeling that I had while watching it. I liked the sister the best, the eldest.
> I sat and watched as if all the things I am, all the things I would really like to do were being viewed in front of me. (That was *me*).
> All the freedom I imagined was nothing more than imagination.
> All the limitations being put on me by society.
> I love simplicity, simple dress, living, everything down to earth.
> The girl dressed just the way I would like to dress.
> But I can't always be barefooted.
> Or is it? (I mean: Or can I???????)
> My father looks at that kind of dress as being hippie . . . not normal.

What is the drift of these thoughts? A natural setting, a simple young woman, and the writer's father combine to awaken powerful feelings in the writer. Identifying with the eldest sister, the writer gets caught up in the simple, natural lifestyle projected on the screen and imagines herself as that young woman. The movie shows dramatically and in life-size detail the simple life she secretly yearns for. But is that simple life possible for her? Why does she feel so many constraints? Why can't she dress in jeans and go barefooted? The writer begins her underlinings with a sentence about the eldest sister's father and concludes with a sentence about her own father. Her focused freewriting has moved her toward the realization that it is her father who prevents her from living the simple life she admires. Finally she acknowledges that her father condemns such living as "hippie" and "not normal." This movie and the freewriting about it have led the writer to question the interference of her father in her own choice of lifestyle.

Narrowing the subject Now she approaches the paper she wants to write with questions that have become more complex. What might her paper be about? It might be about her father's rigid code of conduct. But she plans to write about the movies. Is there a connection? Has she discovered a link between the movies and her own life during this freewriting? Will she write her paper about this movie or about movies in general? What is her attitude toward this movie? toward movies in general?

The writer tests her ideas by writing several general statements, any of which might become a controlling idea for an essay. In each case, as you see below, she thinks first about the particular film she has seen, and then about films in general; finally, she attempts to write a sentence that summarizes the content of her proposed essay.

THIS FILM:
* I believe this movie showed me a lifestyle I admire.
FILMS IN GENERAL:
* I believe that movies allow me to compare my lifestyle with other lifestyles.
CONTENT OF MY PAPER:
I could compare my constrained lifestyle with the lifestyle of the barefoot girl in the film *Where the Lilies Bloom*.

THIS FILM:
* I believe that experiencing the freedom of the eldest sister in the film helped me see how bound up I am.
FILMS IN GENERAL:
* I believe that experiencing the problems of characters in a film helps me with my own problems.
CONTENT OF MY PAPER:
I could tell the story of the film *Where the Lilies Bloom* and then explain how it relates to my life.

THIS FILM:
* This film made me profoundly unhappy the next day.
FILMS IN GENERAL:
* Films that give me dreams I can never achieve make me dangerously unhappy.
CONTENT OF MY PAPER:
I could discuss three or four movies (*The Way We Were, Where the Lilies Bloom,* and so on) that hold out dreamworlds "ordinary" people cannot hope to achieve, thereby frustrating them.

Whichever topic the writer decides on, her paper will be more than a movie review. The opening sentence for her paper might be any of the sentences marked with an asterisk, depending on which idea means most to her and how narrow she wants to keep her topic. Every one of the ideas uncovered in her freewriting assures that the writer will interweave her own personal feelings and observations with the large subject area of her paper, the movies. Since her problem was to confront a subject too large to write about, her focused freewriting has been a way to narrow down the subject. Focused freewriting allows you to search freely through your mind, funneling a large and often vague subject into a narrower topic for writing that touches one of the centers of your own life.

CONSULT YOUR JOURNAL

Another instrument of research and another source of ideas for writing is a journal you might keep to help you remember, collect, and explore your thoughts and experiences.

Buy a hardbound notebook, and keep it exclusively as a journal. Write something in it almost every day. Enter the date. Chiefly, a journal is not a diary of everything you do in a day, but an account of "what got to you that day." It is a record of special feelings, observations, confusions, and unexpected attitudes that you don't want to forget. Oddly enough, what makes a writer's journal special is that it is about ordinary events—events involving friends and jobs and passers-by—that bring out reactions worth noting. A journal trains you to notice how you feel because you must take ten or fifteen minutes to put your feelings into sentences. A journal helps you preserve ordinary events for private, extraordinary reasons. It can be a free-wheeling playground of your mind as you select the most impressive confrontations of your day-by-day life, and it keeps these events for your later use. Selection is the key to a good journal.

Do not record everything you do. Record only what grabs you: intimate ideas about the events of the day that you consider personally outstanding. Since many writers keep journals, you may want to look at some of the entries they make, usually in longhand, at the end of the day.

Here are two student journal entries:

My fingers are so fat! I couldn't believe what happened at the bowling alley today. My fingers got caught in the ball. I felt like a fool. I had to wash the ball off. I was so embarrassed. I felt like everyone knew what was going on.

Well, bravo for women's lib! seems that in McDonald's there is an unwritten law that the grill person must be a guy, but today I challenged this so-called rule. One of the reasons it was thought that girls should not work this station was because they weren't fast enough. But contrary to this opinionated fact, girls can be just as fast as the guys, as we proved to the manager today. I think he left me *alone* at the grill on purpose to see if I would break under the pressure. But I didn't, and surprisingly enough the manager admitted that I was just as capable as any of the guys.

This entry is by a student who drives a cab on the weekends:

What a day! I'm beat. I'm tired, physically and mentally fatigued. Drove from 5:30 A.M. to 4:40 P.M.—11 hours—191 miles—booked $65. It was Mother's Day. A lot of people were on the move. Never drove so much in my life.

I noticed a couple of things. Rich people were a little more angrier than usual. They can treat me bad but why were they turning the screws so hard today? It took me a while but I figured it out on Park Ave. No doormen! All those dudes are on strike. Nobody to open the rich folks' doors. Nobody to salute, tip their hats, say, "Good morning, good this, good that." Nobody to hold their umbrellas while they get in and out of a cab. Nobody to see and feel better than. Those doormen are in the rich folks' private army. They wear uniforms. They follow orders and give none.

Yeah, those doormen are way down on the economic scale, like me, but I've never had any sympathy for them. If anything, I have a lot of antagonism. When I drive up to a big hotel or apartment house on 5th Avenue, they look at me like I'm nothing. They've got their rich costume uniforms on, hats, braids over their shoulders, and shiny shoes. I'm wearing my old army field jacket, dungarees, and imitation earth shoes. But damn! I don't know what these guys got against me.

Well, I guess I know. They're just like any other person. They want to feel better than someone else. And I guess I'm the same, because every now and then I prove to that doorman that he's no match for a young taxi driver when it comes to hustling these rich folks. Sometimes I drive up to a hotel, and before you know it I'm out my door, around to the other side, and I'm opening the door for the rich dude. Do you know what that means? That means that I get my regular tip, plus the doorman's quarter. You should see that sucker's face when I drive away. But I think to myself, this capitalist system's got me and this poor doorman fighting for the scraps, just the crumbs of their big old pie.

Well, got to keep on driving and think better thoughts.

These entries come from the diary of the writer Franz Kafka:

Sunday. I must go see my sister and her little boy. When my mother came home from my sister's at one o'clock at night the day before yesterday with the news of the boy's birth, my father marched through the house in his nightshirt, opened all the doors, woke me . . . and proclaimed the birth as though the child had not only been born, but as though it had already lived an honorable life and been buried too.

When I begin to write after a rather long interval, I draw the words as if out of the empty air. If I capture one, then I have just this one alone and all the toil must begin anew.

Every few days, reread your journal entries and underline passages that strike you as interesting, thoughts that you want to give more time to. On a separate sheet of paper or in the back of your journal, list your underlined sentences. As an exercise, you may want to underline key passages in the sample journal entries on these pages.

The following essay by William Safire talks about the importance of taking charge of your own diary, of knowing that you are writing "a private letter to your future self."

ON KEEPING A DIARY

Diaries are no longer dear; as the invention of the telephone began the decline of letter-writing, the invention of the tape recorder has led to the atrophy of the personal diary. Many of us record our words but few of us record our thoughts.

Why is a diary stereotyped today as the gushing of a schoolgirl or the muttering of a discontented politician, unworthy of the efforts of a busy person? Perhaps because we are out of the habit of writing, or have fallen into the habit of considering our lives humdrum, or have become fearful of committing our thoughts to paper. . . .

Diaries remind us of details that would otherwise fade from memory and make less vivid our recollection. Navy Secretary Gideon Welles, whose private journal is an invaluable source for Civil War historians, watched Abraham Lincoln die in a room across the street from Ford's Theater and later jotted down a detail that puts the reader in the room: "The giant sufferer lay extended diagonally across the bed, which was not long enough for him . . ."

Diaries can be written in psychic desperation, intended to be burned, as a hold on sanity: "I won't give up the diary again," wrote novelist Franz Kafka; "I must hold on here, it is the only place I can." Or written in physical desperation, intended to be read, as in the last entry in Arctic explorer Robert Scott's diary: "For God's sake look after our people."

But what of people who are neither on trial nor freezing to death, neither witnesses to great events nor participants in momentous undertakings? To most of us, a diary presents a terrible challenge: "Write down in me something worth remembering," the neatly dated page says; "prove that this day was not a waste of time."

For people intimidated by their own diaries, here are a handful of rules:

1. *You own the diary, the diary doesn't own you.* There are many days in all our lives about which the less written the better. If you are the sort of person who can only keep a diary on a regular schedule, filling up two pages just before you go to bed, become another sort of person.

2. *Write for yourself.* The central idea of a diary is that you are not writing for critics or for posterity but are writing a private letter to your future self. If you are petty, or wrongheaded, or hopelessly emotional, relax—if there is anybody who will understand and forgive, it is your future self.

3. *Put down what cannot be reconstructed.* You are not a newspaper of record, obligated to record every first time that man walks on the moon. Instead, remind yourself of the poignant personal moment, the remark you wish you had made, your predictions about the outcome of your own tribulations.

4. *Write legibly.* This sounds obvious, but I have pages of scribblings by

a younger me who was infuriatingly illiterate. Worse, to protect the innocent, I had encoded certain names and then misplaced my Rosetta Stone; now I will never know who "JW" was in my freshman year at college, and she is a memory it might be nice to have.

Four rules are enough rules. Above all, *write about what got to you that day,* the way a parched John Barrymore did during a trip to Mexico in 1926 when he discovered a bar that to him was an oasis:

"The beer arrived—*draft* beer—in a tall, thin, clean crystal of Grecian proportions, with a creamy head on it. I tasted it. . . . The planets seemed to pause a moment in their circling to breathe a benediction on that Mexican brewer's head. . . . Then the universe went on its wonted way again. Hot Dog! But that *was* a glass of beer!"

That is the art of the diarist in its pure form, unafraid, intimate, important in its insignificance, ringingly free. Who can compare Barrymore's frothy recall with the insecure jottings-down of most of us on little expense ledgers?

Wish I still kept a diary. But you see, I get very tired at the end of the day, and besides, nothing interesting happens any more. And so to bed . . .

William Safire

TALK TO A FRIEND OR TEACHER

The carpenter who has trouble solving a problem in the construction of a roof consults a roofer or another carpenter. They talk about structure, look at plans, consider the design and the materials being used, and, finally, the carpenter is able to pinpoint the source of the problem. He can then attack his job with confidence, knowing that his problem was not a disgrace to be borne in silence but a working decision to be talked about with others.

In the same way, writers consult other writers without embarrassment or loss of face. One of the best ways to mobilize a topic before you write is to air your ideas with a fellow writer, a tutor, your teacher, or just a sincere and interested friend. Begin by telling your friend what you have been thinking of saying. Encourage your friend to ask you a number of questions that relate to your topic. Answer his questions, and see if he is satisfied. If he is not, tell him more. Describe as precisely as you can how you feel about your topic, what worries you about it, what seems unclear to you. Try to see your topic from your friend's point of view. Let him ask you questions about what is unclear to him, and be as precise as possible in your replies. Supply him with details. Answer questions like *when? where? what kind? then what did you say?* In particular, answer the question *why?* Tell him what you consider to be the single most important idea you have on this topic and tell him *why* it is important. Does he agree? State your attitude toward the topic in a single sentence. Ask one basic question about your idea, and then answer it.

It is also helpful to take along your freewriting or your focused freewriting and read it with your friend. Aloud, begin to shape your ideas. Are you making sense out of what you wrote? Are you groping for ways to rearrange the parts? If your friend seems confused, do you understand why? Can you eliminate that confusion? Do you see why your friend is skeptical? Have you found the heart of your interest in the subject?

If you have no friend or teacher you can discuss your writing with, try talking into a cassette recorder. If you're one of those students who say, "I can tell you my ideas. It's just when I get to writing them down, I freeze up," tell your ideas into the tape recorder. Talk in a relaxed conversational manner about what's on your mind. Then play your tape back and take notes as you listen. Jot down the important ideas and phrases.

Good conversation about writing may take place between friends in and out of the classroom or in a writing lab with a tutor. Remember to take all the help you can get. Listen to someone else's problem. It may be similar to your own.

At this point you will be ready for class discussion. Do not hesitate to join in. The best way to participate in class discussions about the next piece of writing is to spend a half hour the night before doing focused freewriting about it and underlining your important sentences. Even if you are out of habit a "nonparticipant," make yourself take part in these discussions because you stand to gain some first-rate advice on your paper. Begin by saying, "I have a lot of stories about times I went with my friends to the movies, but I am not sure what my main point is. Am I talking about the movies we saw or about the way I imagined myself to be the main character?" Trust yourself. Describe your doubts. Every writer has them, professional and beginner. And because your teacher and classmates have had similar doubts, they often can help you resolve your own. So when the occasion presents itself to talk about your writing, use it. If a teacher invites you to his office to talk about the assignment, go. If a friend asks what you think of her idea, tell her—and don't stop there. Ask her what she thinks of yours. But don't believe an answer without being given good reasons for that answer. Ask, *"Why* do you think so?" Then measure the answer you get against what you feel is true.

In short, corner someone you respect—a fellow writer, a wife, a good friend. Test your ideas on that person and offer precise responses that tell *why*. Try to enunciate a clear statement of why you are personally interested in your subject and what it is you want to find out about it.

DO SOME Even in your earliest papers, which depend for ideas on memory and **RESEARCH** personal observation, a very preliminary kind of research can often stimulate your writing. The process of writing today deals with the same concern it always has: getting hold of a reasonably good topic that can go somewhere as you find out more about it. If the subject of movies leads you to an interest in movie ratings or movie censorship, you may want to look up one of these topics in the *Reader's Guide to Periodical Literature* (see Chapter 18) or in the card catalog at your library and read one or two articles to gain an overview of the topic before you begin writing. One thing is certain: To write anything, you have to know what you are writing about. A writer who "throws the bull" is doomed. So is a lazy potato. If you need to read a magazine article or watch a TV documentary or talk to an expert to stimulate your thinking, do it. Simply keep track of the name of the article, the documentary, or the expert, and give credit when you incorporate anyone else's ideas among your own (see Chapter 18 on documentation). Every paper requires some kind of research: memory, observation, reading, talking with others, listening. Papers of personal experience rely on memory and observation; other types of papers often call for more extensive research, generally in a library. Your freewriting may constitute enough research for a start, but a library may yield a one-page magazine article central to your idea that can get your writing moving.

Research is an important prewriting strategy. Chapter 18 discusses another, more elaborate kind of prewriting that takes the form of more formal library research. For now it is important to know that the research you are doing for your early papers will differ only in degree from that described in Chapter 18. Its purposes are the same: (1) to identify a subject you know something about or can easily research further; (2) to limit your subject to one that is neither too small to be productive, nor too large to handle; (3) to discover a thesis that expresses your attitude to your subject (formulating a thesis is taken up in Chapter 3); and (4) to find out what you want to say about your subject so that you can present enough information to persuade your reader. Be on the alert for opportunities to do research easily. It need not be a tedious, dusty job. Talking to someone who knows about your topic, visiting a place you plan to write about, reading a short article or two on your topic need not take place in the stacks of your library. Research for your early papers can provide you with a quick burst of ideas reassuring you that you have a promising subject and are on the scent of a worthwhile topic.

WRITE A LIST Writing down a random list of ideas may be the most congenial way to get your writing started, particularly when ideas speed through your mind. The list may consist of single words or phrases that describe feelings, observations, incidents, facts, or attitudes relating to your subject. As in freewriting, your purpose is to put your ideas on paper as quickly as possible.

1. Write a freely associated list.

The list below shows another way that the writer of the paper about the movies might collect her thoughts on *Where the Lilies Bloom:*

afternoon	usher
trees	ratings
mountains	limitations
eldest sister	society
very pretty	simple lifestyle
burying father	envy
lots of villagers	my sister
barefoot	my dream
playing guitar	my home situation
picking flowers	my father
freedom	my mother
audience	hippie
escape	unacceptable to him
tears	unhappy
job	raining

2. Underline the items on your list that mean something important to you.

Here is the above list again. Notice the words the writer chose to underline because they seemed most important to her as she thought about the paper she would write.

afternoon	usher
trees	ratings
mountains	limitations
eldest sister	society
very pretty	simple lifestyle
burying father	envy
lots of villagers	my sister
barefoot	my dream
playing guitar	my home situation
picking flowers	my father
freedom	my mother
audience	hippie
escape	unacceptable to him
tears	unhappy
job	raining

Separate general and specific ideas Though general and specific ideas will be discussed more fully in the next chapter, for now remember that you need both kinds to organize your thinking. Some of the items in the list above about the movie *Where the Lilies Bloom* are general ideas and some are specific details or examples. For example, "freedom" is the broadest, most general term; "simple lifestyle" is less broad, and "picking flowers," "playing guitar," and "barefoot" are more specific details that illustrate "simple lifestyle." You should understand that no idea is absolutely general or absolutely specific. You can decide only what is more general or less general, more specific or less specific. Try to group your ideas by including certain specifics under larger, more general headings. For practice, look at a diagram of the first example in the exercise that follows:

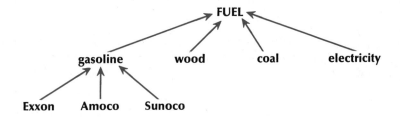

Fuel *includes* gasoline as one of many kinds of fuel. Gasoline *includes* Exxon as one of many brands of gasoline.

Most general		Fuel		Least specific
Less general	↓	Gasoline	↑	Less specific
Least general		Exxon		Most specific

In the exercises that follow, you will have a chance to test your ability to identify general and specific ideas.

Exercise 1 In each of the following groups, number the words to indicate the movement from general to specific. Use 1 for the most general, 3 for the most specific, and 2 for the item in the middle.

Example: Exxon __3__ fuel __1__ gasoline __2__

1 most general
3 most specific

a dessert _____ food __1__ ice cream __3__
b writer _____ poet __3__ profession __1__
c first baseman __3__ athlete __1__ ballplayer _____
d human being __1__ Roberta __3__ woman _____
e walk _____ move __1__ limp __3__
f soar _____ fly _____ move __1__
g temperature _____ 32° __3__ information __1__

h bitter __3__ painful __1__ distasteful _____
i artistic _____ talented __1__ musical _____
j assassinate __3__ kill __1__ murder _____

Exercise 2   Change the following general statements to specific ones:

Example: On holidays I love to do special things.

On the Fourth of July I love to go tuna fishing.

a That piece of furniture makes a funny noise. *when you set on it*

b Let somebody hold your book.

c The food my aunt served was not very good.

d Going out is important to most couples.

e That woman killed someone.

f I can see the stars tonight. *the sky is clear*

g Roberta's shoes looked odd. *on her feet*

h Put these papers together, please.

i Doctor, something is hurting me.

j The criminal was punished. *for stealing*

3. Now you are ready to see how the writer identified items on the list about the movies as specific details (*s*) or general ideas (*g*).

	s	eldest sister
	s	burying father
	s	barefoot
	s	playing guitar
	s	picking flowers
g		freedom
g		limitations
g		society
g		simple lifestyle
g		envy
g		my dream
g		my home situation
	s	my father
	s	hippie dress
g		unacceptable to him
g		unhappy
	s	job

The same principle of separating general from specific can be applied to other methods of getting started. The ideas contained in your focused free-writing on pages 16 and 17 can be separated into general and specific in the following way:

	s	The trees, the mountains, the girl singing that song as they buried her father.
g		It was more the feeling I had while watching it.
	s	I liked the sister the best, the eldest.
g		I sat and watched as if all the things I am, all the things I would really like to do were being viewed in front of me.
g		All the freedom I imagined was nothing more than imagination.
g		All the limitations being put on me by society.
g and s		I love simplicity, simple dress, living, everything down to earth.
	s	The girl dressed just the way I would like to dress.
	s	But I can't always be barefooted.
g		Or is it?
g		My father looks at that kind of dress as being hippie . . . not normal.

4. Once you've identified items as being general or specific, group the items that relate to one another. Begin each grouping with the most general "g" word that includes other "g" words and "s" words beneath it:

g	freedom		g	limitations
s	barefoot		g	my home situation
s	picking flowers		s	my father
s	simple dress		s	hippie dress
s	playing guitar		g	society
g	simple lifestyle		s	unacceptable to him
g	my dream		g	unhappy

Working toward an outline Not all of your items will lend themselves to grouping. Remember, your "g" and "s" labels are relative at best. But if you study your groupings, you can often detect a relationship between the groups as, say, between freedom and limitations on freedom in the example above. In working a freely associated list toward an outline, what you are actually doing is moving from a wide subject to a narrow topic and finally to the controlling personal thesis for your paper.

5. Narrow down your subject:

Subject: (Stage 1): movies (This is the large *subject* area.)

Topic: (Stage 2): "Where the Lilies Bloom"—free lifestyle of eldest sister (The free lifestyle seen in the movie is the *topic*.)

Thesis: (Stage 3): I believe that experiencing the freedom of the eldest sister in this film helped me see how limited my life has been by my father's old-world ideas. (The general statement that contains your own attitude toward the topic is your *thesis*.)

6. At this point you are ready to expand your thesis in Stage 3 by writing more specific statements that support your belief. These statements provide the skeleton of an outline:

Subheading: Seeing the film, I lived the sister's simple life vicariously.

Subheading: The next day I was unhappy and frustrated because I saw the impossibility of living that kind of life.

Subheading: I realized that my father's old-world ideas keep me from dressing simply and living the simple life that I prefer.

Spread your outline across a large sheet of paper and fill in the spaces below each subheading with details and specific supportive material from your list that will make your statements convincing: sandals, jeans, picking flowers, hippies, episodes from the film, your own explanations of your attitudes toward the film, your comparisons with other films or with your own life. Use all the skills at your command to convert your memory into a factory of ideas suitable for this paper: more freewriting, more talk with someone else who has seen the film, closer observation of your father, a longer list—any techniques along the way that will help you invent and relate ideas. Since this is a paper of personal experience, your memory is your chief research instrument. You will use it to dive into your mind frequently and poke around in the depths for usable debris.

A SPECIAL WORD TO DIEHARDS

Perhaps you are thinking that all this talk about getting started is not for you. Maybe you are a skeptic. Maybe freewriting, making lists, and keeping a journal seem gimmicky to you. You embarrass easily, or you are too self-conscious to undertake something as revealing as freewriting. You want to be very much on top of your writing. Sitting down to write the paper itself may be the only way you can comfortably get started. Well, even if you are convinced that it won't work, we suggest that every now and then you take another crack at freewriting. When you least expect it, you may find your freewriting pulling out the raw data stuck way back in your mind.

But when you wouldn't, won't, can't freewrite, begin by thinking a bit and then attempting to write an essay in one burst. Call it a crash-through draft, and crash on until it's finished. Then underline the best parts of what you've written, and distinguish the general ideas from the specific details. See if you can write a loose outline from your draft and a sentence describing how you feel about your topic. If starting on a rough draft seems too bland, too bloodless, too much of an undirected risk, put your crash-through into letter form. Write to someone real: Dear Professor Brewer, Dear Uncle Bert, Dear President Carter, Dear Billie Jean King. With such an immediate audience, you can often write with greater conviction. However you attempt your crash-through, it may only in its final sentence produce the idea you have been struggling to dislodge. Although most of the crash-through is thereby doomed to the wastebasket, writing it may have produced some valuable specific details you thought you had forgotten. Pay dirt sometimes lies at the end of a dig. A true first draft can then begin with a general idea that has evolved from the specifics in your crash-through. You are now ready to think seriously about general and specific ideas and to undertake the whole essay.

Chapter 3 / Reach for the Whole Essay: The Narrative Essay

TELLING AN EXPERIENCE From the start, it is important to reach for the whole essay. Then you can work on paragraphs, sentences, and words to make your whole piece of writing clearer and more effective. In Chapters 1 and 2, all our strategies for getting started took us finally in the direction of grouping specific details under more general ideas because that relationship—between the general and specific—provides the basic arrangement for the whole essay.

Although there are many natural channels of thinking along which essays can be shaped, the most ancient way human beings shape their experiences is to tell a story about them. As beginning writers, most of you can feel confident of your own story-telling ability because all your lives you have heard family anecdotes, read stories, and told jokes. Very likely you will remember, virtually word for word, certain specific details of stories repeated all through your childhood by a parent or grandparent. Besides having heard stories, you have gone to the movies and watched TV. You've listened attentively as your friends recited their experiences blow-by-blow, and you've cornered your friends to listen to your experiences as you told them, in detail, often blow-by-painful-blow. Narrating a story is the first writing form your essays will take because it is the form you naturally know most about.

Remember that the experiences you write about need not be earth-shaking. Beginning writers usually overlook everyday events as uninteresting and unworthy. But a good place to begin is with common ordinary experiences, especially those that, for some unaccountable reason, won't fade from memory but persist in your mind.

Exercise 1 In ten minutes of writing, tell the story of one memorable experience you had as a child. Here are a few ideas that might prompt you to recall one specific incident to tell about:

> getting lost
> performing in a school play or concert
> falling in love
> learning to swim
> seeing something you shouldn't have seen

Now read the following essay, which begins to grapple with a trivial, but unforgettable, experience a student had with a blow dryer:

THE BLOW DRYER AND ME

Learning lessons is a part of every person's life. I'm a very trusting person, often getting myself into scrapes I later realize I could have avoided. After one of my scrapes, I learned that a favor may not be a favor at all.

This past June, I went away for a weekend trip to New Jersey with a class from school. That Saturday, before dinner, I decided to wash my hair. Afterward, I went to a friend's room to borrow her blow dryer. She said she'd do me a favor, that she'd be happy to dry my hair for me. There were about five other people in the room sitting around talking and waiting for dinner. As my friend dried my hair, I was thinking how great it was that, for once, I didn't have to dry my own hair. Feeling like a prima donna, I closed my eyes and relaxed.

That is, I relaxed until half of the hair on my head got slurped into the blow dryer's motor. My "friend" had moved the blower too close to my hair, and some of it was actually inside of the blower. How nice. This monster had slurped down some of my hair from my split ends right down to my very scalp. Of course, everyone else in the room was doubled over with laughter, and the girl who had committed this mortal sin just kept saying, "Oh, Kathy, I'm so sorry." Her apologies did not console me. One guy finally managed to control his laughter and come to my aid. As he fumbled with the dryer, I picked up fragments of what was being said by the others, ". . . painful . . . all tangled up . . . she'll miss dinner . . . the expression on her face . . . it'll take a year to untangle . . . so funny . . . so many knots . . . unbelievable . . . worse than bubble gum . . ." Then I heard the ultimate horror, "scissors."

I adamantly told them that no one was coming near me with any pair of scissors. No way. Absolutely not. I told them I was willing to stay there all night to untangle myself and I would even eat my dinner with the dryer attached to my head if I had to.

By now, although I was extremely upset, I had to laugh at my predicament. It was a pretty funny situation. Finally the monster and I were untangled. I was so relieved. My friend was still apologizing, and I knew she felt terrible about the mess she had gotten me into. She said, "Listen, I have to make this up to you. I swear I'll be careful. Let me finish drying your hair, and I promise you it'll look beautiful." I gave her a long, hard look. This girl was my friend, and I wanted to show her that there were no hard feelings and that I still trusted her. Accidents happen, right? I smiled and said, "Okay." What a mistake. What a big mistake. You guessed it—my hair got caught again. This time not as many hairs got caught, but I was furious at myself. Boy, did I learn my lesson!

Another student has written an account of a love affair he had that proved to have some surprising risks. Read this "story" and see if it bears any resemblance to the "story" about the blow dryer.

RISKS

Risks are unavoidable. I've never met a person in my life who hasn't taken a risk. If you don't risk anything, you will never be able to gain anything. For all practical purposes, you would be living in limbo. Everything in life involves some kind of risk, and love affairs are no exception. Love affairs always involve the risk of getting hurt, but sometimes for reasons beyond love itself.

Two years ago I had an affair with a beautiful girl. We were about the same age and we shared the same interests, which enhanced our relationship. We were crazy about each other and we always hated to part company. I remember that I never had any difficulties with her or her parents, but I found out soon enough about the complications that would pop up. In the meanwhile, though, we continued to share a beautiful relationship. We were never closer. I think our relationship reached its peak because everything after was all downhill.

One Sunday I called for her at her home. It was the same procedure. Her parents greeted me. Then they asked me to sit down and have something to eat or drink. They were always very hospitable to me, and I always felt at home in their house. However, that particular day was different from any previous day. My girl and her mother left the room, and her father sat directly across from me. Usually we would all sit together, and her father would jokingly ask us when we were going to get married. But on that day, I sensed something strange because the stage had been set for a serious dialogue between her father and myself. At that moment, danger signals went off inside my head, and my hands became cold and clammy.

I knew that I was trapped, and I suddenly realized that these people had been planning this for some time. Her father looked at me and asked me about my job. He knew damn well that I hated my job because I always complained to his daughter about it. I said, "I'm tired of that place; I would really like to leave." This remark paved the way for my downfall. He owned a huge machine shop, and he didn't have any sons. The man was dying to have me in his family with the understanding that I would eventually run the business. He replied, "Well, then, why don't you come work for me?" All the color drained from my face and I almost fell off the sofa. He looked at me and asked if I was feeling all right. I said, "I'm all right. I'm just overwhelmed with your generous offer." At that point, he knew that he had me because there was no way I could back out.

His wife figured everything was over when she entered the room. She said, "Is everything OK?" Her husband insisted that I have a drink. He realized that I needed no coaxing because I could have finished off the bottle. After that day, my relationship with the girl was just about over because I used to get upset every time I saw her. I never went to her house any more, and our conversations always turned into arguments. I was torn apart inside and couldn't take this nonsense any more. Her father couldn't buy me, and it hurt to think that he thought he could. I had to be my own person and find my own way. I felt a lot of pain thinking about her. I know she was in a lot of pain, too. The affair had to end. We were both better off separated. We were both hurt, but I knew the hurt wouldn't last forever.

This was my first serious romance because it was the first time I had been so involved with another person's life. However, I knew from previous experiences that romances always involve a risk. People having romances can be hurt deeply in the end. I had taken the risk before, and I'll take it again in the future. There is really no escape from taking risks, especially in love affairs. Love affairs aren't any different from other experiences because everything we do in life involves some kind of risk.

STORIES AND NARRATIVE ESSAYS

Why do we call the pieces these two students wrote "essays"? Why not simply call them "stories"? What's in an essay that is not in a story?

Perhaps a closer look at stories will show us what is special about them. For one thing, the writer has *one* experience to relate, one string of events to put before the reader. Unrelated events and other experiences are omitted. The narrative essay is also single-minded because it is full of a single story. Certainly it makes use of the techniques of fiction—it has characters (you, among others) and a setting (your girl friend's house, your friend's dormitory room). It has snatches of what real people say to each other ("Well, then, why don't you come work for me?"), and, most important, it has a natural order: it unfolds events as they happen in time. What happened first is told first, what happened next is told next. Telling a story means relating a sequence of events that happened on a particular occasion to particular people. Events that occur day in and day out are, in themselves, never a story:

A person needs to start the day in solitude and privacy. I ride a bus to school daily. I have to stand all the way, since the stop before mine attracts a small mob changing from the intercity bus. I am jostled, though I always manage to study a minimal amount. I usually reach school frustrated and a little shop-worn.

A story happens only once. Notice in the previous examples the naturalness of the *once:* "The Blow Dryer and Me": *That Saturday;* "Risks": *One Sunday.* The paragraph above has no *once.* By contrast, the following sentences are a story because they are about one person on a specific bus *at a definite time.* The coming paragraph depends for its narrative force on stating when the events happened: *Last Tuesday.*

> A person needs to start the day in solitude and privacy. Last Tuesday, for example, I boarded the Q 72 bus, searched hopelessly for a seat, and as usual established myself midway up the aisle, clinging to an overhead strap. A man sitting nearby observed every move I made. I confess I felt awkward as I opened my Italian text. When he saw my book, he tapped my arm. *"Scusi,"* he said, *"per piacere,"* and he rose offering his seat. I would have grabbed it, but the woman standing next to me rushed forward, muttering something in a brisk Italian which instantly went beyond my Italian I, and plunged into the seat, shopping bag and all. By the time we reached the college, my new friend was talking, in English to be sure, about a local bar, and although I headed quickly for the door, he was holding one of my books. I turned to take it, annoyed at this daily kind of nuisance, annoyed that I couldn't have the space and time I needed to prepare myself for the day ahead.

But, as we will see, there is more to writing an essay than telling a story.

An essay is *more* than a story, though it may include a story. Nor is it, at the other extreme, a report bulging with facts and figures that can be checked out in a library, though essays may include some of that. Above all, an essay states an intelligent *idea* you have in your head about a real experience, a real problem, or a real person or place. In an essay you express your attitude about a specific experience or problem in a personal and interesting way. Even your earliest stories will hold an idea scrambling to get out. Notice how both "The Blow Dryer and Me" and "Risks" state an idea and an attitude in the very first paragraph. One writer wants us to know what she learned from her encounter with the blow dryer: "I learned that a favor may not be a favor at all." The other writer wants us to know what he learned from breaking up with his girl friend: "Love affairs always involve the risk of getting hurt, but sometimes for reasons beyond love itself." Your *thesis* is often stated in a sentence or two in the first paragraph of your essay. It is like having the address of your idea. You know where to find it.

**FORMULATING
A THESIS** Your thesis holds your personal idea about your experience. But the general truth of your idea will depend on how convincingly you illustrate it, defend it, or prove it in the remainder of your essay so that other people can say, "Yes. That statement is true. I have been in situations where it would also apply to me." A clearly stated idea that you understand helps you to *control* the rest of your essay because you can choose to include only those details that strengthen your thesis. In the same way, your thesis helps you to screen out details that have nothing to do with the idea that it expresses. The simple experience and the thesis are the two essentials of a narrative essay.

How does a writer formulate a thesis for an essay? *How do ideas take shape?* Consider the following passage about the murder of two teenage girls in Chicago a few years ago, which opened a longer essay by Philip Roth:

> Several winters back, while I was living in Chicago, the city was shocked and mystified by the death of two teenage girls. So far as I know, the populace is mystified still; as for the shock, Chicago is Chicago, and one week's dismemberment fades into the next's. The victims this particular year were sisters. They went off one December night to see an Elvis Presley movie, for the sixth or seventh time we are told, and never came home. Ten days passed, and fifteen and twenty, and then the whole bleak city, every street and alley, was being searched for the missing Grimes girls, Pattie and Babs. A girl friend had seen them at the movie, a group of boys had caught a glimpse of them afterward getting into a black Buick, another group said a green Chevy, and so on and so forth, until one day the snow melted and the unclothed bodies of the two girls were discovered in a roadside ditch in a forest preserve west of Chicago. The coroner said he didn't know the cause of death, and then the newspapers took over. One paper ran a drawing of the girls on the back page, in bobby socks and Levi's and babushkas: Pattie and Babs a foot tall, and in four colors, like Dixie Dugan on Sundays. The mother of the two girls wept herself right into the arms of a local newspaper lady, who apparently set up her typewriter on the Grimeses' front porch and turned out a column a day, telling us that these had been good girls, hard-working girls, average girls, churchgoing girls, et cetera. Late in the evening one could watch television interviews featuring schoolmates and friends of the Grimes sisters: the teenage girls look around, dying to giggle; the boys stiffen in their leather jackets. "Yeah, I knew Babs, yeah, she was all right, yeah, she was popular . . ." On and on, until at last comes a confession. A skid-row bum of thirty-five or so, a dishwasher, a prowler, a no-good named Benny Bedwell, admits to killing both girls, after he and a pal cohabited with them for several weeks in various flea-bitten hotels. Hearing the news, the weeping mother tells the newspaper lady that the man

is a liar—her girls, she insists now, were murdered the night they went off to the movie. The coroner continues to maintain (with rumblings from the press) that the girls show no signs of having had sexual intercourse. Meanwhile, everybody in Chicago is buying four papers a day, and Benny Bedwell, having supplied the police with an hour-by-hour chronicle of his adventures, is tossed in jail. Two nuns, teachers of the girls at the school they attended, are sought out by the newspapermen. They are surrounded and questioned, and finally one of the sisters explains all. "They were not exceptional girls," the sister says, "they had no hobbies." About this time, some good-natured soul digs up Mrs. Bedwell, Benny's mother, and a meeting is arranged between this old woman and the mother of the slain teenagers. Their picture is taken together, two overweight, overworked American ladies, quite befuddled but sitting up straight for the photographers. Mrs. Bedwell apologizes for her Benny. She says, "I never thought any boy of mine would do a thing like that." Two weeks later, maybe three, her boy is out on bail, sporting several lawyers and a new one-button-roll suit. He is driven in a pink Cadillac to an out-of-town motel where he holds a press conference. Yes, he is the victim of police brutality. No, he is not a murderer; a degenerate maybe, but even that is changing. He is going to become a carpenter (a carpenter!) for the Salvation Army, his lawyers say. Immediately, Benny is asked to sing (he plays the guitar) in a Chicago night spot for two thousand dollars a week, or is it ten thousand? I forget. What I remember is that suddenly, into the mind of the onlooker, or newspaper reader, comes The Question: is this all public relations? But of course not—two girls are dead. Still, a song begins to catch on in Chicago, "The Benny Bedwell Blues." Another newspaper launches a weekly contest: "How Do You Think the Grimes Girls Were Murdered?" and a prize is given for the best answer (in the opinion of the judges). And now the money begins to flow; donations, hundreds of them, start pouring in to Mrs. Grimes from all over the city and the state. For what? From whom? Most contributions are anonymous. Just the dollars, thousands and thousands of them—the *Sun-Times* keeps us informed of the grand total. Ten thousand, twelve thousand, fifteen thousand. Mrs. Grimes sets about refurnishing and redecorating her house. A stranger steps forward, by the name of Shultz or Schwartz—I don't really remember—but he is in the appliance business and he presents Mrs. Grimes with a whole new kitchen. Mrs. Grimes, beside herself with appreciation and joy, turns to her surviving daughter and says, "Imagine me in that kitchen!" Finally, the poor woman goes out and buys two parakeets (or maybe another Mr. Shultz presents them as a gift); one parakeet she calls Babs, the other Pattie. At just about this point, Benny Bedwell, doubtless having barely learned to hammer a nail in straight, is extradited to Florida on the charge of having raped a twelve-year-old girl there. Shortly thereafter I left Chicago myself, and so far as I know, though Mrs. Grimes hasn't her two girls, she has a brand-new dishwasher and two small birds.

This is a disturbing and ugly listing of details—from parakeets to appliances—in a hideously strange case. And you may well be uneasy about it. What is the point, after all?

If you had one comment to make about this whole passage, what would you say? Begin your comment with *I believe, I think,* or *I learned.* Remember that there is no right or wrong answer. In 1960, millions of readers read about the Grimes girls in the newspapers. Each reader's comment about the events would have been different according to his or her experience. Remember that people have different reactions to the same events. What you will be formulating is your own attitude toward these details about the Grimes girls.

I believe _____.

I think _____.

I learned _____.

Consider your own comment along with the following student comments:

1. I believe that living in the city is more dangerous than ever.
2. I believe that the Grimes girls were bad girls.
3. I think that what this piece says is that Americans react in strange ways to violence.
4. I learned that it is dangerous to see Elvis Presley movies at night.
5. I believe that a lot of people gave Mrs. Grimes money.
6. I think that Americans make heroes out of criminals.
7. I learned that the American media celebrate crime as if it were something great.
8. I believe that Benny Bedwell was a bum.
9. I believe that every American should own a parakeet.
10. I believe that any girl who gets into trouble is out there looking for it.
11. I believe that all men are potential rapists.

Now drop the words *I believe* or *I think* or *I learned* or any other words that don't relate to the events themselves:

1. I believe that living in the city is more dangerous than ever.
   Living in the city is more dangerous than ever.
2. I believe that the Grimes girls were bad girls.
   The Grimes girls were bad girls.
3. I think that what this piece says is that Americans react in strange ways to violence.
   Americans react in strange ways to violence.
4. It is dangerous to see Elvis Presley movies at night.
5. A lot of people gave Mrs. Grimes money.
6. Americans make heroes out of criminals.
7. The American media celebrate crime as if it were something great.
8. Benny Bedwell was a bum.
9. Every American should own a parakeet.
10. Any girl who gets into trouble is out there looking for it.
11. All men are potential rapists.

Notice that two of the comments merely restate the facts of the piece:

> Benny Bedwell was a bum.
> A lot of people gave Mrs. Grimes money.

Five of the comments express opinions that deal with only a small portion of the facts presented in the passage:

> It's dangerous to see Elvis Presley movies at night.
> Every American should own a parakeet.
> The Grimes girls were bad girls.
> Any girl who gets into trouble is out there looking for it.
> All men are potential rapists.

Two more sentences express opinions that deal with most of the facts in the passage but not all of the facts:

> Americans make heroes out of criminals. (Omits the fact that the mothers, who are not criminals, are also made into heroes and receive gifts of appliances and parakeets.)
> Living in the city is more dangerous than ever. (Omits the reactions of the public to the crimes and to the mothers.)

The remaining two sentences contain a personal idea that fits the whole passage. This idea is the thesis. The thesis statement serves the whole essay. It is an umbrella statement that covers the details of your subject as well as your attitude toward those details. The thesis must state the point of your essay. It must get to the one important thing that's on your mind—the idea that everything else spins out of. Either of the following sentences uses all the details in the "story" about the Grimes girls. Either one might express Philip Roth's attitude toward the details:

> Americans react in strange ways to violence.
> The American media celebrate crime as if it were something great.

But does it? What *was* on Philip Roth's mind? Why has he produced such a meticulous, relentless account? If you suspect a motive behind his work, if you suspect that he is working with great diligence to convince us of something, if you believe that he is trying to make a point about American life or American crime or American cities, if you are left wanting the reason for Roth's writing the story about the Grimes girls, you've picked up Roth's strategy. In the next paragraph of Roth's essay, he asks:

> And what is the moral of the story? Simply this: that the American writer in the middle of the twentieth century has his hands full in trying to understand, describe, and then make credible [make us believe] much of American reality. It stupefies, it sickens, it infuriates, and finally it is even a kind of embarrassment to one's own meager imagination. The actuality is continually outdoing our talents, and the culture tosses up figures almost daily that are the envy of any novelist.

Roth, who is a major American writer, has presented the stupefying, sickening, infuriating details of the Grimes case in order to show what is on *his* mind as a writer: how impossible it is for American writers to make up anything as bizarre as real-life events. In fact, this is only the beginning of Roth's essay "Writing American Fiction," which for several more pages goes on about American writers. His real interest is not the Grimes case at all, but what the case demonstrates about the infuriating ways Americans behave. He cites examples of several public events occurring in 1960 (the year the essay was written) whose actors are "the envy of any novelist." How many recent events can you name that would prove Roth's point is still valid? The kidnap and trial of Patty Hearst? Gary Gilmore's fight to die? Wouldn't you say, in fact, that Roth's general point might be valid at any time and that specific examples of a freshly infuriating, sickening, stupefying American event might be supplied for any year?

Usually you have experiences long before you reach an understanding of what they mean. The memory of some event buzzes around in your brain—a love affair, getting your hair snarled in a blow dryer, your first boring job in a restaurant, an ordinary experience that led you to a new insight into your parents as people. Out of the details of these experiences, you come to some general truth about them. The thesis statement is often called a *generalization* because it states an idea that the writer believes not only is true about his own experience but can be generalized to the experiences of others. In the following essay, Sherwood Anderson relates an experience from his childhood in which he "discovers" his father. Read the whole essay and see what Anderson generalizes from his experience that could apply to all of us:

I DISCOVER MY FATHER

You hear it said that fathers want their sons to be what they feel they cannot themselves be, but I tell you it also works the other way. A boy wants something very special from his father. I know that as a small boy I wanted my father to be a certain thing he was not. I wanted him to be a proud, silent, dignified father. When I was with other boys and he passed along the street, I wanted to feel a flow of pride. "There he is. That is my father."

But he wasn't such a one. He couldn't be. It seemed to me then that he was always showing off. Let's say someone in our town had got up a show. They were always doing it. The druggist would be in it, the shoe-store clerk, the horse doctor, and a lot of women and girls. My father would manage to get the chief comedy part. It was, let's say, a Civil War play and he was a comic Irish soldier. He had to do the most absurd things. They thought he was funny, but I didn't.

I thought he was terrible. I didn't see how mother could stand it. She even laughed with the others. Maybe I would have laughed if it hadn't been my father.

Or there was a parade, the Fourth of July or Decoration Day. He'd be in that, too, right at the front of it, as Grand Marshal or something, on a white horse hired from a livery stable.

He couldn't ride for shucks. He fell off the horse and everyone hooted with laughter, but he didn't care. He even seemed to like it. I remember once when he had done something ridiculous, and right out on Main Street, too. I was with some other boys and they were laughing and shouting at him and he was shouting back and having as good a time as they were. I ran down an alley back of some stores and there in the Presbyterian Church sheds I had a good long cry.

Or I would be in bed at night and father would come home a little lit up and bring some men with him. He was a man who was never alone. Before he went broke, running a harness shop, there were always a lot of men loafing in the shop. He went broke, of course, because he gave too much credit. He couldn't refuse it and I thought he was a fool. I had got to hating him.

There'd be men I didn't think would want to be fooling around with him. There might even be the superintendent of our schools and a quiet man who ran the hardware store. Once I remember there was a white-haired man who was a cashier of the bank. It was a wonder to me they'd want to be seen with such a windbag. That's what I thought he was. I know now what it was that attracted them. It was because life in our town, as in all small towns, was at times pretty dull and he livened it up. He made them laugh. He could tell stories. He'd even get them to singing.

If they didn't come to our house they'd go off, say at night, to where there was a grassy place by a creek. They'd cook food there and drink beer and sit about listening to his stories.

He was always telling stories about himself. He'd say this or that wonderful thing had happened to him. It might be something that made him look like a fool. He didn't care.

If an Irishman came to our house, right away father would say he was Irish. He'd tell what county in Ireland he was born in. He'd tell things that happened there when he was a boy. He'd make it seem so real that, if I hadn't known he was born in southern Ohio, I'd have believed him myself.

If it was a Scotchman the same thing happened. He'd get a burr into his speech. Or he was a German or a Swede. He'd be anything the other man was. I think they all knew he was lying, but they seemed to like him just the same. As a boy that was what I couldn't understand.

And there was mother. How could she stand it? I wanted to ask but never did. She was not the kind you asked such questions.

I'd be upstairs in my bed, in my room above the porch, and father would be telling some of his tales. A lot of father's stories were about the Civil War. To hear him tell it he'd been in about every battle. He'd known Grant, Sherman, Sheridan and I don't know how many others. He'd been particularly intimate with General Grant so that when Grant went East to take charge of all the armies, he took father along.

"I was an orderly at headquarters and Sim Grant said to me, 'Irve,' he said, 'I'm going to take you along with me.' "

It seems he and Grant used to slip off sometimes and have a quiet drink together. That's what my father said. He'd tell about the day Lee surrendered and how, when the great moment came, they couldn't find Grant.

"You know," my father said, "about General Grant's book, his memoirs. You've read of how he said he had a headache and how, when he got word that Lee was ready to call it quits, he was suddenly and miraculously cured.

"Huh," said father. "He was in the woods with me.

"I was in there with my back against a tree. I was pretty well corned. I had got hold of a bottle of pretty good stuff.

"They were looking for Grant. He had got off his horse and come into the woods. He found me. He was covered with mud.

"I had the bottle in my hand. What'd I care? The war was over. I knew we had them licked."

My father said that he was the one who told Grant about Lee. An orderly riding by had told him, because the orderly knew how thick he was with Grant. Grant was embarrassed.

"But, Irve, look at me. I'm all covered with mud," he said to father.

And then, my father said, he and Grant decided to have a drink together. They took a couple of shots and then, because he didn't want Grant to show up potted before the immaculate Lee, he smashed the bottle against the tree.

"Sim Grant's dead now and I wouldn't want it to get out on him," my father said.

That's just one of the kind of things he'd tell. Of course the men knew he was lying, but they seemed to like it just the same.

When we got broke, down and out, do you think he ever brought anything home? Not he. If there wasn't anything to eat in the house, he'd go off visiting around at farmhouses. They all wanted him. Sometimes he'd stay away for weeks, mother working to keep us fed, and then home he'd come bringing, let's say, a ham. He'd got it from some farmer friend. He'd slap it on the table in the kitchen. "You bet I'm going to see that my kids have something to eat," he'd say, and mother would just stand smiling at him. She'd never say a word about all the weeks and months he'd been away, not leaving us a cent for food. Once I heard her speaking to a woman in our street. Maybe the woman had dared to sympathize with her. "Oh," she said, "it's all right. He isn't ever dull like most of the men in this street. Life is never dull when my man is about."

But often I was filled with bitterness, and sometimes I wished he wasn't my father. I'd even invent another man as my father. To protect my mother

I'd make up stories of a secret marriage that for some strange reason never got known. As though some man, say the president of a railroad company or maybe a Congressman, had married my mother, thinking his wife was dead and then it turned out she wasn't.

So they had to hush it up but I got born just the same. I wasn't really the son of my father. Somewhere in the world there was a very dignified, quite wonderful man who was really my father. I even made myself half believe these fancies.

And then there came a certain night. He'd been off somewhere for two or three weeks. He found me alone in the house, reading by the kitchen table.

It had been raining and he was very wet. He sat and looked at me for a long time, not saying a word. I was startled, for there was on his face the saddest look I had ever seen. He sat for a time, his clothes dripping. Then he got up.

"Come on with me," he said.

I got up and went with him out of the house. I was filled with wonder but I wasn't afraid. We went along a dirt road that led down into a valley, about a mile out of town, where there was a pond. We walked in silence. The man who was always talking had stopped his talking.

I didn't know what was up and had the queer feeling that I was with a stranger. I don't know whether my father intended it so. I don't think he did.

The pond was quite large. It was still raining hard and there were flashes of lightning followed by thunder. We were on a grassy bank at the pond's edge when my father spoke, and in the darkness and rain his voice sounded strange.

"Take off your clothes," he said. Still filled with wonder, I began to undress. There was a flash of lightning and I saw that he was already naked.

Naked, we went into the pond. Taking my hand he pulled me in. It may be that I was too frightened, too full of a feeling of strangeness, to speak. Before that night my father had never seemed to pay any attention to me.

"And what is he up to now?" I kept asking myself. I did not swim very well, but he put my hand on his shoulder and struck out into the darkness.

He was a man with big shoulders, a powerful swimmer. In the darkness I could feel the movement of his muscles. We swam to the far edge of the pond and then back to where we had left our clothes. The rain continued and the wind blew. Sometimes my father swam on his back and when he did he took my hand in his large powerful one and moved it over so that it rested always on his shoulder. Sometimes there would be a flash of lightning and I could see his face quite clearly.

It was as it was earlier, in the kitchen, a face filled with sadness. There would be the momentary glimpse of his face and then again the darkness, the wind and the rain. In me there was a feeling I had never known before.

It was a feeling of closeness. It was something strange. It was as though there were only we two in the world. It was as though I had been jerked suddenly out of myself, out of my world of the schoolboy, out of a world in which I was ashamed of my father.

He had become blood of my blood; he the strong swimmer and I the boy clinging to him in the darkness. We swam in silence and in silence we dressed in our wet clothes, and went home.

There was a lamp lighted in the kitchen and when we came in, the water dripping from us, there was my mother. She smiled at us. I remember that she called us "boys."

"What have you boys been up to?" she asked, but my father did not answer. As he had begun the evening's experience with me in silence, so he ended it. He turned and looked at me. Then he went, I thought, with a new and strange dignity out of the room.

I climbed the stairs to my room, undressed in the darkness and got into bed. I couldn't sleep and did not want to sleep. For the first time I knew that I was the son of my father. He was a story teller as I was to be. It may be that I even laughed a little softly there in the darkness. If I did, I laughed knowing that I would never again be wanting another father.

From *Sherwood Anderson's Memoirs*

Exercise 2 Answer the following questions about "I Discover My Father."

1. Why does Anderson make a general statement about all fathers when he really wants to talk about his own father?

2. What do you believe caused Anderson to sit down and write this essay?

3. What words tell you when Anderson begins to tell a story about a specific event on a specific occasion? Give examples.

4. What techniques in this narration might lead you to think you are reading fiction? Be specific.

5. What does Anderson gain by devoting so much of his essay to a detailed account of the swimming episode?

Experiences like Anderson's may become a part of you long before something flashes and you see there is a general point to be made about them. You sense that the event stands out in your mind and you want to know why. Any experience that stands out from the crowds of others deserves your attention.

You might want to try this:

1. Think hard about one experience. Freewrite about it.

2. Try to recall details you may have temporarily forgotten.

3. If possible, talk to someone who was there with you.

4. Write down what you remember as you remember it.

5. Try to determine what the experience taught you. Write it down. Say, "I learned that ————."

Then, when you write your essay, your thesis and your experience will constantly reinforce each other. Most writers, especially beginners, should state their thesis first, although this in no way suggests that the general idea came before the experience. We carry our experiences and observations around with us indefinitely, seeing them somewhat veiled until an illuminating idea flashes and we *understand* how we feel about them.

Less often, as we saw in the Roth piece, writers allow the evidence to come first because the evidence is so powerful or their writing so artful that writers trust their readers will independently formulate the idea of the thesis as they read. Then readers feel gratified when their own sensible thinking is reinforced by the writer's statement of the thesis at the end.

Either way, in a narrative essay—the kind of essay you are beginning with—the arrangement is so visible as to *introduce* you to the basic essay rhythm. A narrative essay has two parts: you have one specific experience to tell, and that experience leads you to make a point—your thesis—from which the rest of your essay follows.

NARRATIVE ESSAY

Arrangement

Part I	One specific: your experience.	Blow dryer experience	Love affair	Swimming experience
Part II	One generalization: your point	A favor may not be a favor at all.	Love affairs involve the risk of getting hurt, sometimes for reasons beyond love itself.	A boy wants something very special from his father.

Or, as it usually appears in an essay, the reverse:

Arrangement

Part I	One generalization: your point	A favor may not be a favor at all.	Love affairs involve the risk of getting hurt, sometimes for reasons beyond love itself.	A boy wants something very special from his father.
Part II	One specific: your experience	Blow dryer experience	Love affair	Swimming experience

The hardest task— Writing the first draft may be your hardest task. Within five minutes, your
writing the mood varies from despair to sudden optimism and then to despair again.
first draft You had a clever way to begin, but now that you have it on paper it ?
Everyone you've spoken with says your idea is workable; yet
and nothing works.

Perhaps a few tips from other writers may help you get your first
draft moving:

> Think through your subject as much as possible ahead of time. Keep the
> underlined passages of your freewriting near you. Keep your specific
> experience and your generalization in mind: "I learned that ———," "I
> believe that ———," "I think that ———."

> Don't leave your work for the last minute. Allow a couple of days between
> your first draft and the time you want your writing ready.

> Writing requires energy. It is an active intellectual exercise. Begin to write
> when you feel your best.

> If you can't start with your generalization, start with your story. You can
> write the beginning later.

> If your hand gets tired of writing, stop for a while. Try to increase the
> amount you write at each sitting. With practice, you will be able to write a
> whole first draft at a sitting.

> Concentrate on what you are doing. Try to relive the experience you are
> recalling. Try to *feel* as you felt then. Ask yourself why the events that
> happened left you feeling that way.

> If your ideas are rushing you, write as quickly as you can. Abbreviate
> words. Use shorthand. But write in sentences so that later you can under-
> stand what you have written. You can edit later.

> Do not exclude doubtful items. It is easier to cut irrelevancies during a
> later revision than to pad a very meager first draft.

> If you pause in your writing, reread what you have already written. Think
> about the words in your sentences and allow them to suggest other ideas.
> Ask more questions about what you have already written. (See Chapter 9
> on modifiers, especially Exercises 1 and 2, pages 185 to 187.) If you can't
> think of anything to add, move on. You can go back later.

> Stop writing when you feel you have provided all the convincing details
> you can. Reread your opening paragraph and then write a conclusion,
> adjusting your opening so that the two are related.

Chapter 5, "Revising the Whole Essay," presents two drafts of two
student essays and goes into detail about how you move from a rough draft
to a more successful one. Meanwhile, remember to keep your progress
legible. If your first draft gradually comes to look like a maze of insertions,
arrows, crossings out, hysterical underlining, and exclamation points, copy
it over, preferably type it, so that you can see your progress clearly. An

TIPS FOR WRITERS—WRITING THE NARRATIVE ESSAY

1. Find out what experience interests you through freewriting, thinking, conversation, or reading.

2. Invention. Engage in one or more prewriting techniques: your writing cycle begins as you locate ideas through close observation. Record whatever you can remember about events, people, or objects. Recall an experience that interests you. Do a focused freewriting on that event, write an associative list, talk about it with a friend, do some brief research (talk to a person who shared the experience with you) or, if you have a tentative thesis in mind, do a crash-through of an essay, sometimes in letter form.

3. Separate general from specific. Mark your ideas which are more general "g" and the details which are more specific "s." It is a good idea to write the general ideas out in full sentences. Keep your details in words or phrases. Group specific details under a related general idea. Look for a connection between the groups.

4. Choose the groups that interest you.

5. Write a temporary thesis statement for the ideas suggested by this experience. Begin by saying the most significant thing you can about it. State your attitude toward your subject and what you learned from it. Write, "I think ———," "I believe ———," or "I learned ———."

6. Tell the personal experience. Be honest. Be vivid. Include the details that surfaced in your prewriting strategies.

7. Think of writing as a cycle of recurring acts. Turn your attention back and forth to the acts you need to repeat as you work out your thesis and your illustrative experience. At the end, mention again why your experience proves your thesis.

8. Get a reaction to what you have written from your class or from a friend.

9. Revise your essay.

BASIC ARRANGEMENT FOR A NARRATIVE ESSAY:

Part I: Generalization—your thesis

Part II: Your specific experience

already illegible paper inhibits you from making changes. Who wants to work with a mess like that? Remember that a revision of a first draft does not mean correcting only spelling and punctuation. It is a *re-vision*, a *seeing again* of your ideas. You must have a copy you can read, whose sentences and paragraphs you can easily enter and move about. You may want a pair of scissors handy to cut up your paper and reorganize. For this practical reason, write on only one side of the paper.

In all, a paper may need to be written out three times:

1. A first draft like the ones in Chapter 5, pages 92–94. You execute changes on this draft.
2. A legible working version of the first draft with some changes worked into it and with your thesis up front. You can read it aloud or have it dittoed for readers to comment upon.
3. A revised and proofread draft incorporating changes suggested by readers, neatly typed, double-spaced, on one side of the page, finished, and ready to be submitted. (See Chapter 5, pages 95 and 98–99.)

Exercise 3 Stand up in class and do any of the following exercises that interest you. Do *not* tell the "point" of your story.

1. Tell a joke.
2. Tell about something that happened to you in the last week.
3. Tell an anecdote you heard on a TV talk show.
4. Tell an anecdote about your mother, wife, sister, or girl friend.
5. Tell an anecdote about your father, husband, brother, or boyfriend.
6. Tell about an experience you had when you were a child.

Exercise 4 Stand up in class and do any of the following exercises that interest you. After you tell your story, tell the "point" of your experience. If you become interested in one of these exercises, write a brief account of the experience. Then write the point of your story or say what it taught you.

1. Tell about an experience you had getting your driver's license. What is the point of your story? Say it in a sentence.
2. Tell about an experience you had with extrasensory perception. What is the point of your story? Say it in a sentence.
3. Tell about an experience you had with a computer. In a sentence, tell what that experience taught you.
4. Tell about a *last* experience you had (the last time you saw someone dear to you, the last day of a job, the last day you lived in a place). In a sentence, tell what the experience taught you.

Exercise 5 Here are two brief personal anecdotes. Write a thesis for each one.

One day in May, my mother served us a big bowl of beautiful strawberries. I put a few on the edge of my plate to save while I ate my corn, pot roast, and string beans. Suddenly my brother Jack yelled, "Look out! There's a spider over you." I glanced up, and when I looked back down two of my strawberries were gone. I reached my left arm up around my plate and continued eating my pot roast. My brother Bert suddenly rolled his corn cob in my direction, and, without thinking, I brushed it back with my arm. Bert swiped the rest of my strawberries, and I had string beans for dessert.

One day I was driving my cab, and I picked up a fare who was cute and attractive. She didn't have a lot of make-up on, and she seemed pleasant. She asked me if she could sit up front. I said, "Sure." I pulled away, with no destination, and she started to talk. "My name is Cheryl." I paused and said, "Mine is Montgomery."

Cheryl: It's been a bad day.

Me: Yeah. It's been pretty cold.

Cheryl: I'm almost frozen stiff.

Me: Let me turn the heater up all the way. These cabs got some dynamite heaters.

Cheryl: Thanks, honey. You're nice.

Me: So are you.

Cheryl: You have to take a lot of garbage from people, don't you?

Me: Yeah, but it's part of the job. What about you?

Cheryl: That's different. I can pick my friends. You have to pick up anyone who waves a hand in the air, even me.

Me: Don't say that. You're all right. I'm not kidding. You're all right to me.

Cheryl: Well, thanks Dexter. That's the name on the license, isn't it?

Exercise 6 Use one of the following statements as a thesis for a brief essay.

Living in the city is more dangerous than ever.
Americans react in strange ways to violence.
Americans make heroes out of criminals.
The American media celebrate crime as if it were something great.

Before you write your essay do the following:

Freewrite for ten minutes, focusing on crime, violence, cities, or the media as you begin.

Underline passages in your freewriting that seem best to you. (Best written? Most interesting? Most provocative?)

Review the last few days' newspapers for details about a crime or a criminal case to support your thesis.

Change your thesis if you need to.

Begin to write:

Write an opening paragraph that contains your thesis.

In two or three more paragraphs, tell the story of one interesting crime you found in the papers. Include vivid details.

Remember: your essay will have two parts:

Your thesis.

A story about a crime from the newspapers to illustrate it.

Reach for the Whole Essay: Three More Arrangements

Chapter 4

Since business people and college students are dealers in information, much of your writing will need to explain and inform rather than tell stories about events that you experienced. Clear, exact writing is an indispensable skill to everybody, including college students. If you think "writing for college" must have an "intellectual" ring to it, if you think you must use four-syllable words in complicated sentences, forget it. Your job is to show as plainly as you can how much of a subject you understand.

But moving from writing about personal experiences to writing that explains is often a difficult leap for beginning writers. We hope you have spent many weeks writing narratives that prove a point by tapping the events of your own life. Establishing a thesis and telling in detail about some personal experience that proves your thesis will be the best preparation for the jump to explanatory writing you now face.

Your newest concern, as you attempt to explain ideas, is how to organize them. You began your work with narrative essays because a narrative usually organizes itself chronologically in a straightforward way. Events occur in time, and we tell about them as we always tell about our experiences: what happened first is told first, what happened second is told second, and so on. As a beginning writer, you were able to use energy you might have spent organizing or remembering events—recalling feelings, remembering details vividly, noting the sequence of happenings—without having to determine in what order to write them down. You organized them as they occurred, in chronological order. Except for rare strategies like flashbacks, where a writer "flashes back" to a previous episode and interrupts the time sequence to tell about it, narration runs chronologically.

In explanatory writing, sometimes called expository writing, you can no longer rely on chronology. It is true that some ideas and details can be organized around time, but others demand different principles, another kind of system *you* must consciously decide on. When you aren't telling stories, how can you organize your thinking? Are there a few other natural shapes for essays that will hold your thinking in an orderly way?

GENERAL AND SPECIFIC

The thesis and supporting ideas   The narrative essays you have been writing have followed a two-part arrangement:

Part I: Your thesis
Part II: Your specific experience

The following passages from a memoir by Claude Brown emphasize another kind of arrangement. (In a memoir, as its name suggests, a writer recalls experiences from memory, experiences he remembers from his own life.) Be assured that the writer, Claude Brown, has been through many drafts before his "arrangement" was published:

SATURDAY NIGHT IN HARLEM   *A Memoir*

Saturday night. I suppose there's a Saturday night in every Negro community throughout the nation just like *Saturday night in Harlem.* The bars will jump. The precinct station will have a busy night. The hospital's emergency ward will jump.

. . . .

To me, it always seemed as though Saturday night was the down-home night. In the tales I've heard about down home—how so-and-so got bad and killed Cousin Joe or knocked out Cousin Willie's eye—*everything violent happened on Saturday night.* It was the only time for anything to really happen, because people were too tired working all week from sunup to sundown to raise but so much hell on the week nights. Then comes Saturday, and they take it kind of easy during the day, resting up for another Saturday night.

. . . .

Saturday night down home was really something, but then Saturday night in Harlem was really something too. *There is something happening for everybody on Saturday night:* for the cat who works all day long on the railroad, in the garment center, driving a bus, or as a subway conductor. On Saturday night, there is something happening for everybody in Harlem, regardless of what his groove might be. Even the real soul sisters, who go to church and live for Sunday, who live to jump up and clap and call on the

Lord, Saturday night means something to them too. Saturday night is the night they start getting ready for Sunday. They have to braid all the kids' hair and get them ready. They have to iron their white usher uniforms and get pretty for Sunday and say a prayer. For the devoted churchgoers, Saturday night means that Sunday will soon be here.

. . . .

Saturday night has also been a traditional night for money to be floating around in places like Harlem. It's a night of temptation, the kind of temptation one might see on Catfish Row at the end of the cotton season, on the weekend. Most of the people got paid on Friday night, and Saturday they had some money. If they didn't get paid on Friday, there was a good chance that they'd be around playing the single action on Saturday in the afternoon. By the time the last figure came out, everybody might have some change, even if it was only eight dollars—one dollar on the 0 that afternoon. It was still some money.

. . . .

TIPS FOR READERS—FINDING THE THESIS

Although Brown never says it in so many words, the unmistakable point of the memoir is that *Saturday night in Harlem is the liveliest night of the week.* Every paragraph offers a specific idea or illustration to prove the broad assertion that Saturday night in Harlem is extremely lively. A realistic caution to keep in mind is that, although writers may state a thesis plainly, they may also, if they are experienced writers, imply it in an endless variety of artistic ways. While you may be required to include a clear thesis statement in every essay *you* write, you quite justifiably may feel at sea when you look for a thesis statement in the writing of professionals. Then you may ask, "Why should I write a thesis, when famous writers like X, Y, and Z don't?" and "How can I find the thesis when I read?"

The answers to these questions are related. For an inexperienced writer, it is useful to test the development of ideas against a plainly stated thesis. Writing a thesis and adjusting it to fit your ideas is the kind of shuttling practice that sharpens your thinking. The experienced writer has the knack of shuttling mentally between ideas and thesis. No matter how his essay digresses here and there, he always manages to pull it back to the single most important track laid down by the thesis he is carrying in his mind. Therefore, when you are reading, if you can't find the thesis in the opening paragraph, try reversing your method. Read the whole essay. By adding up all the points the writer makes in the entire piece of writing, you can figure out one idea they all point to. That point is the writer's thesis.

By reading all of Brown's paragraphs, you come to the logical realization of his thesis: *Saturday night in Harlem is the liveliest night of the week.* His actual opening is his own artistic way of beginning his essay.

It seemed as though Harlem's history is made on Saturday nights. You hear about all the times people have gotten shot—like when two white cops were killed on 146th Street a couple of years ago—on a Saturday night. Just about every time a cop is killed in Harlem, it's on a Saturday night.

. . . .

Harlem is full of surprises on Saturday night. I remember one in particular. I was down on 116th Street. I was going to visit someone, and I decided to call before I got there. I went into the bar on the corner to call. . . .

If Brown had to choose *one* thing to say about Saturday night in Harlem, it might be that violent things happen on Saturday night. But Brown has a second important thing to say about Saturday night: that there's something happening for everybody on Saturday night. And he has a third thing to say: he believes that Saturday night is a night for money to be floating around in Harlem. And a fourth: he thinks that Harlem's history is made on Saturday nights. And a fifth: he has learned that Harlem is full of surprises on Saturday nights.

Graphically, Brown's writing looks like the following scheme. The thesis at the top is the most general statement of all, and each of the supporting statements that follow is a degree more specific than the thesis.

I Thesis:	Saturday night in Harlem is the liveliest night of the week.
Opening statement:	There's a Saturday night in every Negro community throughout the nation just like Saturday night in Harlem.

Why is this a useful opening statement? For one thing, it centers the reader's attention on Saturday night in Harlem. Then, by relating Saturday night in Harlem to Saturday night in every Negro community in America, it justifies the reader's attention to Harlem, because if he knows what Harlem is like, he is going to know what every other Negro community in America is like. Finally, in the next three short sentences, the reader gets an early sense of how Harlem jumps on Saturday night so that he is curious to find out more about the liveliness of Saturday night in Harlem and thus about the liveliness of Saturday night in black communities all across America.

Brown's thesis occupies the highest level among the levels of generality. This means that it is the most general idea and includes all the other ideas in the essay.

| II Supporting idea: (topic sentence) | Everything violent happened on Saturday night. |

Now Saturday night in Harlem becomes more specific. Brown's statement focuses our view of Saturday night on violence and invites an explanation of violence, details of violence, or a story of a violent incident. This is the topic sentence of this paragraph. It is down one level of generality from the thesis. It says violence is one reason why Harlem is lively on Saturday night. It supports the thesis.

| III Supporting idea: (topic sentence) | There is something happening for everybody on a Saturday night. |

Saturday night in Harlem becomes more specific as Brown provides another point: something happens for everybody on a Saturday night. The reader knows another reason why Harlem, on a Saturday night, is lively and expects to hear an explanation of this point. The topic sentence of this paragraph is on the same level as the topic sentence on violence. This paragraph supports the thesis.

| IV Supporting idea: (topic sentence) | Saturday night has also been a traditional night for money to be floating around in places like Harlem. |

Again, Saturday night becomes more specific. The reader wants to know the amount of loose money in Harlem on a Saturday night: thirty-five bucks or a million? Where is it? Who has it? Where does it come from? Where does it go? This generalization is the topic sentence for the paragraph and sits on the same level as the sentence on violence. Then the paragraph supplies more specific details about money in Harlem. This paragraph supports the thesis.

| V Supporting idea: (topic sentence) | It seemed as though Harlem's history is made on Saturday nights. |

Saturday night becomes more specific through another topic sentence on the same level as those on
violence and money. Now Brown describes events of
consequence that have occurred on Saturday nights.
This point also supports the thesis.

VI Supporting idea: Harlem is full of surprises on Saturday night.
(topic sentence)

Brown begins to name one surprise and to narrate a
story that tells how it happened. Again, Saturday
night in Harlem is made more specific. This generalization is on the same level as those about violence, money, and Harlem's history. It forms the
topic sentence of this paragraph and of the one that
follows and supports the thesis.

A thesis is an umbrella statement for an essay.

*A topic sentence is an umbrella statement for a paragraph or a group of
paragraphs.*

*A topic sentence is more specific than a thesis statement, but it is more
general than the details that follow. It supports the thesis of the whole essay.*

*See Chapter 10 on paragraphs for a more complete discussion of topic
sentences.*

Without generalizations that are more and less specific than one
another, you would have no way of grouping all the details into an
organized essay that makes a point. Your readers would be out there on
their own, without anchor, and you would run the risk of allowing them to
float away. So, to keep from losing your readers, you throw them a rope.
You state, very plainly, what your main idea is, and you narrow the supporting ideas appropriately.

In your narrative writing, your thesis is the statement that tells what
you think is generally true about your experience. That statement accounts
for the details you include as you tell your experience. When you tell a
story, you make one generalization at the top of what you have to say.
Then you cite the one specific episode from your life that illustrates the
generalization. Remember, your narrative essay has two parts.

Now, in other kinds of writing there is an even greater interplay
between general and specific. That rhythm between general and specific
may be repeated several times. Instead of citing one specific episode in
your life to explain one general statement, you offer several specific ex-

amples or ideas to support one general statement. Your essay will be arranged in many parts:

Part I: Generalization—your thesis
   Part II: Supporting idea plus specifics
   Part III: Another supporting idea plus specifics
   Part IV: Still another supporting idea plus specifics
   Part V: And a fourth supporting idea plus specifics

Specific details bring each of the supporting ideas to life. Each idea and its own bundle of specific details form a paragraph to support your thesis. Each supporting idea is a little more specific than your thesis but less specific than the details that accompany it.

Levels of generality Our introduction to the concepts of general and specific in Chapter 2 stressed that the terms are relative. Look at page 27 to see how the word *fuel* includes *gasoline,* and the word *gasoline* includes *Exxon.*

Now let us consider sentences instead of words. Is the following sentence general or specific? *The cost of everything is inflated today.* Is it less specific or more specific than this sentence? *Canned fish has tripled in cost in the United States in the last five years.* Less specific or more specific? *The price of gold has risen sharply in the European market.* Less specific or more specific? *Japan has a 35 percent inflation rate.* Less specific or more specific? *Israel has a 37 percent inflation rate.* Less specific or more specific? *Real estate in Washington, D.C., has skyrocketed in cost.* Less specific or more specific? *The house former President Ford bought for $34,000 in 1957 was sold in 1977 for $137,000.* Less specific or more specific? *Mrs. Peggy Burdowski paid 99 cents for a can of tuna fish today at the Piggly Wiggly Market on School Street.*

The levels of generality for these statements look like this:

1 The cost of everything is inflated today.

2 Japan has a 35 percent inflation rate.

2 Israel has a 37 percent inflation rate.

3 Real estate in Washington, D.C., has skyrocketed in cost.

3 Canned fish has tripled in cost in the United States in the last five years.

3 The price of gold has risen sharply in the European market.

4 The house former President Ford bought for $34,000 in 1957 was sold in 1977 for $137,000.

4 Mrs. Peggy Burdowski paid 99 cents for a can of tuna fish today at the Piggly Wiggly Market on School Street.

Notice that both sentences marked 2 are at the same level because they make inflation more specific by telling where it occurs and at what rate. The three sentences marked 3 are at the next level because they tell what general groups of commodities have increased in cost and where. Both sentences marked 4 are at the most specific level because they name real people paying for specific items at specific times.

Writing a rough outline using general and specific statements

An informal outline using statements that are relatively general and specific may serve you better than a tight, formal outline full of headings, sub-headings, and Roman numerals. A rough outline, perhaps like the one that follows, will show you where to expand your ideas as you write and where to make them more specific. As you prepare an outline, bear in mind the levels of generality and see that the *thesis includes the main ideas marked A, B, C, and so forth.* (See Chapter 2 for the freewriting and lists of associated ideas for this outline on the movie *Where the Lilies Bloom.*)

Rough outline   Thesis: Experiencing the freedom of the elder sister in the film *Where the Lilies Bloom* helped me see how restricted my life is.

    A. Seeing the film, I lived the sister's simple life vicariously.
        barefoot
        simple dress
        played guitar
        picked wild flowers
        trees
        mountains
        father's burial—simple ceremony

    B. The next day I was unhappy and frustrated by the impossibility of my living that kind of life.
        reaction to film
       *society's limitations
        my job
        my home situation
        my father

    C. I realized that my father's old-world ideas keep me from dressing simply and living the simple life I prefer.
        in the U.S. seven years
        young people's ideas are unacceptable to him
        calls kids "hippies"
        says they are "not normal"
        my dream as shown in the movie
       *my struggle to fulfill my dreams

If an outline is too precise, it can lock you in a box and eliminate one of the great delights of writing: discovering as you write what you want to say and why you want to say it. The very material of writing—words—suggests more material—other words. That is, as you write, one word or phrase brings to mind another word or phrase or another train of thought. One sentence leads you to write the next sentence, and your thinking develops as you write. Try to work up some momentum as you go, and don't be afraid to follow your own developing train of thought. Keep one eye on your rough outline, but if what you're saying appears livelier than your outline, risk a departure.

If an outline is too vague, on the other hand, you may find, midway, that you are writing a boring paper because it lacks specifics. Stop. Revise your outline. Strengthen your vague statements by supplying details. In the outline above, for example, the starred items seem too vague. What about *society's limitations?* What are those limitations? Can they be made more specific? Add to the outline:

> living in the city instead of among mountains and trees
> wearing shoes
> dressing in "respectable" pants and skirts

What about *my struggle to fulfill my dreams?* What are those dreams? What is that struggle? Add to the outline:

> wanting to live in both worlds—my father's and the world of my American friends
> struggling to keep peace with my father although he objects to much of my behavior
> not lying but telling him only what is necessary; but feeling guilty

Such changes increase the usefulness of the outline because they make concrete details available to you as you write. *The more specific the details in your outline, the easier it is to write your sentences.*

In most writing, the writer moves between the general and the specific. That movement, back and forth and up and down the levels of generality, provides the basic rhythm for most writing. Beginning writers emphasize main points as generalizations and subordinate specifics as support. One of the writing skills called for in almost everything you write is the ability to move among sentences that are general in meaning and sentences that carry specifics. You strengthen your general statements by providing sentences rich with details, and you control your details by trimming your generalizations to the magnitude the details of your essay require.

Exercise 1 Practice moving between general statements and specific details in the following exercises.

    1. The following sentences describe Harry Truman in 1940 when he ran for reelection to the Senate. What's missing is an opening general statement describing Truman's condition at that time. Read the details and provide a suitable general statement to fill in the blank.

———————————————————————. His mother was eighty-eight years old, and they were threatening to foreclose the mortgage on her farm, which later, as you'll see, did happen. But Harry couldn't give her any financial help. Hell, at the beginning of the campaign he couldn't even afford stamps to write to people, old friends, asking for money. Later, he did manage to borrow $1,000 from a St. Louis contractor, which was repaid after the Democratic primary.

Merle Miller

2. The next two paragraphs about the Sun Myung Moon sect offer opposite points of view. Supply an opening general statement for each paragraph.

———————————————————————. Some parents have hired professional "deprogramers" to kidnap their children and free them from Moon's spell. Some have sued the Church for holding the youths against their will, a charge difficult and humiliating to prove when the kids swear they prefer Moon's Family to their own.

———————————————————————. Some feel it may be better than drugs or drifting aimlessly around the country. Others look with favor upon it as a Christian youth movement, without understanding exactly what the members do or believe.

Psychology Today, January 1976, p. 36

3. Charles Darwin describes in detail an unforgettable event that he experienced during his South American expedition on the ship the *Beagle.* Write a general statement that explains the entire passage.

———————————————————————. I happened to be on shore, and was lying down in the wood to rest myself. It came on suddenly, and lasted two minutes, but the time appeared much longer. The rocking of the ground was very sensible. The undulations appeared to my companion and myself to come from due east, whilst others thought they proceeded from southwest: this shows how difficult it sometimes is to perceive the direction of the vibrations. There was no difficulty in standing upright, but the motion made me almost giddy: it was something like the movement of a vessel in a little cross-ripple, or still more like that felt by a person skating over thin ice, which bends under the weight of his body.

Charles Darwin

4. This paragraph is an excerpt from Mary McCarthy's *Memories of a Catholic Girlhood.* Supply an opening general statement to prepare for the paragraph that follows.

———————————————————————. Protestants used to name their children out of the Old Testament and now they name them out of novels and plays, whose heroes and heroines are perhaps the new patron saints of a secular age. But with Catholics it is different. The saint a child is named for is supposed to serve, literally, as a model or pattern to imitate; your name is your fortune and it tells you what you are or must be. Catholic children ponder their names for a mystic meaning, like birthstones; my own, I learned, besides belonging to the Virgin and Saint Mary of Egypt, originally meant "bitter" or "star of the sea." My second name, Therese, could dedicate me either to Saint Theresa or to the saint called the Little Flower, *Soeur Therese* of Lisieus, on whom God was supposed to have descended in the form of a shower of roses. At Confirmation, I had added a third name (for Catholics then rename themselves, as most nuns do, yet another time, when they take orders) on the advice of a nun, I had taken "Clementina," after Saint Clement, an early pope—a step I soon regretted on account of "My Darling Clementine" and her number nine shoes.

5. Write a general statement about the practices of members of your own ethnic group when they name their children. Develop this statement with a paragraph.

Exercise 2   Supply specifics for the following general statements.

1. "Much is said about the pain of growing up in poverty, but not much about the pain of growing up rich."
   This is the opening statement of an impassioned letter to the editor of *Ms.* magazine. Even if you have never been "rich," write five sentences each of which gives a specific reason why growing up rich involves pain.

2. "The first in time and the first in importance of the influences upon the mind is that of nature."
   This general statement asserting the singular influence of nature on people was written by Ralph Waldo Emerson in 1837. Write three sentences supporting this statement, each of which suggests how a specific condition of nature shapes people's lives.

3. "From a very early age, perhaps the age of five or six, I knew that when I grew up I should be a writer."

   George Orwell

   This sentence was written by George Orwell, a writer known for his astute social views of the 1930s and 1940s. Other famous people have sensed the course of their lives from earliest childhood. Write a few sentences that concretely demonstrate how you know you are going to be a writer—or a dancer or a mechanic or a musician.
   Substitute any profession you choose for *writer*.

4. "My parents for as long as I have known them have been the most ideal couple I've ever seen."

   Robert W. White

   Write five sentences that give five reasons why you call your parents— or any other couple you know—an "ideal" couple.

THREE MORE ARRANGEMENTS

As human beings, we naturally think along certain channels. Even in our most disorganized thinking, there is often some method at work because our brains grope along familiar channels to sort out our ideas. We've seen that one way to organize our thoughts is to tell our experiences as stories. But our thoughts do not always have to follow the orderly progression of events as they occur in time. There are other ways that depend more heavily on *selection*. We can make a statement and prove it by *selecting details* from our experiences—as many vivid details as we need to convince someone else that our statement is valid. Or we can look at two objects, two events, two people and *compare* them because the similarity of their details is so striking that a comparison seems natural and inevitable. In the process, we may find that in spite of some fundamental similarities there are differences worth noting, and we note them. And, of course, we all struggle, however fumblingly, to *explain* why a condition exists, why an event occurred, why an action was taken, why we feel as we do; or, moving ahead, what the consequences of an action were, what a meeting between two people might lead to, what the effects may be of a certain process. We fight disorder by trying to see order wherever we can.

Thus, in addition to *telling our experiences in stories,* we can arrange the essays we write in three other shapes that follow the commonest ways our minds channel our thoughts: showing details, comparing and contrasting, and showing causes, reasons, and effects.

Writing a thesis and showing details

Describing One of the reasons people delight in coming together is to share experiences. But we don't all possess the same ability to tell the other person precisely what we've been through. Some people can describe a place so that it springs to life as they speak—what it looked like, what the weather was, how the light struck, how the air smelled, who was there, what they did, what the mood of the place was—while others simply say, "It was beautiful" or "I had a great time" and leave it at that.

Describing is a skill that engages us in the rigorous use of details. It requires that we observe what we see closely and intelligently. When we look at a small area of beach, for example, we make numbers of separate observations about the sand and what we see there:

rough sand	a container for suntan lotion
pebbles	clumps of feathers
dried seaweed	the rusted hook of a can opener
smooth piece of glass	a Kodak film roller
pale, smooth driftwood	shells

But the longer we look, the less satisfied we are with general observations. We soon discover that we need appropriate words to express the distinctions we begin to notice. Not all dried seaweed looks the same. We may eavesdrop on what people around us call the particular vegetation we are looking at. We may ask them, or we may get a book later that shows the difference between sea lettuce and sea moss. If we observe shells with enough interest and perception, we may see the rolling curves of a channeled whelk, the fan of a bay scallop, and the tiny mottled form of a periwinkle before we know their names.

The part of an essay or a paragraph that is richest in details is usually description. Writers may undertake whole essays of description to make a point, though more likely a descriptive passage is part of a narrative or an explanation. Examples and illustrations are often described so as to convey clearly and vividly their most outstanding features.

The following essay describes foods the writer remembers eating as she progressed through childhood colds and illnesses. It shows how a writer moves among general statements and specific details. The authenticity of these very personal details about food gives the description richness and accuracy. We *trust* writers who use details well because details verify that they know what they are talking about. The writers have been through the experience and remember the fine points. They are authorities. Read the essay below, and then read the thesis statement that follows.

OH, THOSE GRIPPES OF YESTERYEAR!
THAT CERTAIN SOUP . . . AND MOM'S T.L.C.

In our family, every occasion, sad or happy, had its own special menu and illness was no exception. It would all begin when my mother declared me officially sick—sick enough to stay home from school and, therefore, sick enough to stay in bed. Immediately the day took on a holiday air and I resigned myself to bedded-down luxury, helpless in the face of nature.

The illnesses I remember most were the head colds and grippes of winter and my progress in recovering could be measured by the food my mother served, for she always had strong ideas on exactly what one should eat when. Miraculously, her instinct seemed infallible, and, inevitably, when I did not know what I wanted, she did.

Meals always appeared on pretty trays, set with colorful mats, the best china and silver, and, when possible, a flower. In the earliest stages of an illness, the menus were based on what seemed to be an infinite variety of teas: plain, with lemon and sugar or honey, or with crystals of amber rock candy that slowly melted below the surface of the tea in tiny golden streams. Sometimes it was a flowery, rosey brew of dried raspberries, other times a clear, sunny, gently perfumed camomile, or bosky sassafras.

My favorite came in late afternoons or evenings, especially when I had the flu. It was steaming dark and strong tea spiked with Rock 'n' Rye and flavored with a clove-studded lemon slice. That, two aspirins, the sweet and exotic fumes of the camphorated oil on my chest and the candy-sweet scents of the tincture of benzoin being sent into the air from a nearby vaporizer sent me off in a drowsy torpor of half-dreams, three of which were recurrent and unforgettable.

In one dream, I was "Princess of Everything," a title I devised as being sufficiently all-inclusive. In another, I owned a bridge across the Atlantic Ocean, and had hotels and restaurants along the way, so travelers could drive to Europe in comfort as I became rich. A similar goal inspired my third dream, in which I had built a roof over the entire world so everyone, everywhere, had to pay me rent.

Such ambitious dreaming amid the insular warmth of flannel nightgowns, a floppy and scalding hot water bottle, bed socks, and drifts of blankets, left me pretty thirsty and there was always an assortment of fruit juices on hand when I awakened. Sometimes it was freshly squeezed orange juice, or orangeade chilled with cracked ice. Lemonade was served in a tall, icy glass, its rim frosted with sugar.

There might be fresh grapefruit juice, of which I was especially fond when the grapefruit was pink, or pineapple juice, with or without grape juice added to it. The tall fruit juice glasses always held a bent glass straw —the hospital kind—that allowed me to lean back on my mountain of pillows and sip at ease.

As I began to feel better and, therefore, more restless I called for hair ribbons and my mother's best silk bedjacket, and waited impatiently for alcohol rubdowns and dustings of perfumed bath powder. Radio soap operas filled the air and cutouts and coloring books cluttered the bed as the bedtrays became far more interesting.

Toast was a big item in my mother's culinary pharmacopeia. At first it was served plain and dry, but that was soon followed by crisp, sweet cinnamon toast, then baby-bland milk toast that tasted soothingly of fresh air. Thick slices of French toast, crisp and golden outside but moist and eggy within, would probably come next, always topped with a melting knob of sweet butter and a dusting of confectioner's sugar. I knew I was close to recovery when I got the toast I liked best—almost burned rye bread toast covered with salt butter.

Shortly after that, chicken soup would appear, first as a clear golden broth perfumed with knob celery, leeks, dill and the sweet root of parsley, petrouchka. Later it would be served adrift with bits of chicken, carrots and celery, sprinklings of parsley and rice or broad, buttery noodles.

Beef tea was an alternate soup, and to make it my mother put chunks of tough but juicy beef into a narrow necked glass milk bottle, which was then set in boiling water where it stayed for hours, until all of the beefy broth had been extracted. This was then salted and served in warm mugs, or poured over riced potatoes.

Eggs had a prominent place on these convalescent menus. Lightly poached, they would be served on toast or in the center of what my mother called a bird's nest of creamed spinach. They might be stirred into those tiny macaroni starlets, pastina, to which butter and grated cheese would be added, or scrambled with spicy caraway seeds. Finally, they arrived in my favorite guise—fried with crisp brown edges and a sprinkling of kosher coarse salt and black pepper.

It was only when my mother considered me more than half well that she began to serve milk. She and my grandmother were both of a mind that milk was bad for a fever or a cough, because, they said, it caused congestion, a view currently espoused by lacto-ova vegetarians. Once milk was permitted it came in thick, whipped egg nogs fragrant with vanilla and nutmeg. Or it was baked into custard in chocolate brown earthenware cups. Cinnamon-topped rice pudding studded with currants and warm baked apples with cream, cloudlike floating island pudding and pink junket were other standbys my mother used as "build-up" foods. So was red Jell-O, whipped when half-set to become a snowy mousse-like froth.

All of my childhood illnesses seemed to have a prescribed number of days in bed, and each had its own treatments and menus with the food geared to my rate of improvement. By the time I was able to have a full-scale meat and potatoes dinner, I was also able to be out of bed and dressed, and I knew the period of glorious luxury had ended.

Mimi Sheraton

THESIS   In our family, every occasion, sad or happy, had its own
STATEMENT: special menu, and illness was no exception.

Exercise 3 Our concern in this exercise is to experience the way a piece of writing *comes to life* as details are added to it. We have outlined the major ideas in support of the thesis and ask you to supply the specific details from the essay. The beginning is done for you. General statements are marked "g," and specifics are marked "s."

Supporting idea: The illnesses I remember most were the head colds and
                grippes of winter. (g)
Supporting idea: Meals always appeared on pretty trays. (g)
Specific details: colorful mats (s)
                best china and silver (s)
                a flower (s)
                In the earliest stages of an illness, meals included an
                infinite variety of teas. (g)
details: plain (s)
                with lemon and sugar or honey (s)
                with crystals of amber rock candy (s)

raspberry (s)

camomile (s)

sassafras (s)

My favorite tea came in late afternoons or evenings. (g)

details: steaming dark and strong (s)

spiked with Rock 'n' Rye (s)

flavored with clove and lemon (s)

Supporting idea: Tea and medications led to dreams. (g)

details: Princess of Everything (s)

owned a bridge across the Atlantic (s)

landlord of the entire world (s)

Supporting idea: Dreaming made me thirsty. There was always an assortment of fruit juices on hand when I awakened. (g)

Supply details:

Supporting idea: As I began to feel better I wanted more activities. (g)

Supply details:

Supporting idea: Toast was a big item in my mother's "pharmacopeia." (g)

Supply details:

Supporting idea: Soups would appear next. (g)

Supply details:

Supporting idea: Eggs had a prominent place on these convalescent menus. (g)

Supply details:

Supporting idea: It was only when my mother considered me more than half well that she began to serve milk. (g)

Supply details:

Conclusion: All of my childhood illnesses seemed to have a prescribed number of days in bed, and each had its own treatments and menus with the food geared to my rate of improvement.

How to order details   Noticing details is only half the skill involved in writing rich, detailed paragraphs and essays. Once you make your observations, you have to hit on some working purpose behind them so that you can judiciously select the details you want (see Chapter 9 on modifiers, page 182). Then you must deliver them, not haphazardly, but in an order that smoothly links the purpose of the paper to the effect you want your reader to experience. In your expository essays, three principles can help you arrange your details in an effective order. They are order of time, order of space, and order leading to a climax.

Order of time   Narrative is not the only form of writing dependent on time. In the essay you just read, the details are organized according to the progress of the writer's illnesses through time. As she improved, the menus, at first liquid and tea-like, expanded to include a variety of solid foods. The presentation of details clearly follows the progress of the writer's illnesses, as is apparent from her words:

> In the earliest stages of an illness . . .
> As I began to feel better . . .
> Shortly after that . . .
> Later . . .
> When my mother considered me half well . . .

Narrations, descriptions of events, explanations of how to do something, and any other writings dependent on time are organized by time words like these:

> First . . .
> Second . . .
> After that . . .
> Now . . .
> Next . . .
> Later . . .
> Then . . .
> Finally . . .
> The next evening . . .
> The following day . . .

Use these words to help you make transitions from one occurrence to the next. When you explain a process, it is essential to explain the steps in sequence. Notice how the time words in the following recipe organize the steps in the preparation procedure:

SKID ROAD STROGANOFF

4 servings

8 ounces uncooked noodles	2 teaspoons salt
1 beef bouillon cube	½ teaspoon paprika
1 garlic clove, minced	2 3-ounce cans mushrooms
⅓ cup onion, chopped	1 can condensed cream of
2 tablespoons cooking oil	chicken soup, undiluted
1 pound ground beef	1 cup commercial sour cream
2 tablespoons flour	chopped parsley

Start cooking those noodles, <u>first</u> dropping a bouillon cube into the noodle water. Brown the garlic, onion, and crumbled beef in the oil. Add the flour, salt, paprika, and mushrooms, stir, and let it cook five minutes <u>while</u> you light a cigarette and stare sullenly at the sink. <u>Then</u> add the soup and simmer it—in other words, cook on low flame under boiling point—ten minutes. <u>Now</u> stir in the sour cream—keeping the heat low, so it won't curdle—and let it all heat through. To serve it, pile the noodles on a platter, pile the Stroganoff mix on top of the noodles, and sprinkle chopped parsley around with a lavish hand.

Peg Bracken, *The I Hate to Cook Book*

Order of space When you write a description of a person, an object, or a scene, *space* can be your organizer: you describe a person from hair to sneakers, a museum building from front steps to rear parking lot, your bedroom from doorknob to the pile of books dumped under the window. You capture the view from your classroom window by detailing first what is nearest and gradually extending your observations to the horizon, or by beginning with what is out at the horizon (mountains?) and moving inward toward the man selling pretzels on the steps of the Humanities Building. *You* determine the order because you must decide emotionally and logically what you want your readers to "see" first. They can't read all your words at once, so they will follow the only possible order: the order of your sentences and the order of the details you choose to show them.

Organize your descriptions with words like these:

> Under . . .
> Above . . .
> To the left . . .
> On the right . . .
> Behind . . .
> In front of . . .

In the following paragraph, the student, who writes fondly about getting dressed while standing on the heater in his dining room, uses space signals to mark off the little area that was warmed by the heater (*to the right, behind, on the left*):

> On winter mornings, the heater in our dining room gave a cold kid a warm welcome. It was an old-fashioned kind that was just a grate in the floor, topping off a tube coming from the furnace. You didn't have to fool with gadgets, knobs, and thermostats; you just stood on it and felt great. The kitchen door was *to the right* of the grate and the light from that room let you see just enough to get your shoes on the right feet and shirt buttons in order. *Behind,* the warmed wall with its tiny dried drops of paint supported the dresser. *On the left* stood a small walnut desk and chair. By pulling the chair out in front of you, you would have a perfect three-sided dressing room. I think that just this feeling of being boxed in made you feel warmer. Today modern heating systems might be cleaner or safer or have some other glorious advantage. But for me they'll never replace that feeling as my cold toes stepped onto the warm squares of the heater back in our dining room.

Order leading In any kind of writing, you sort out the details available to you and seize
to a climax on the ones that best suit your purpose. Rarely are whole essays written to describe every aspect of a person or an object in its entirety. That completeness may be useful in a travel brochure, which makes available to the tourist complete information about every part of a country he may

be touring. You might also expect, and rightfully, a complete description of an item you wish to buy from a mail-order catalog. But in essays, such "molecular" descriptions offer excessive and unnecessary detail. Too much irrelevant information distracts a reader, often permanently. If you are describing a place, for example, study your reaction to it. Zero in on a single dominant impression you are left with. State that impression in your thesis. Then present your details in order of increasing importance, saving as the final crowning detail the one that will clinch it for the reader. For example:

Dominant impression: darkness

THESIS: My aunt's lonely life is reflected in her dark and gloomy living
room.

Details in order of increasing importance:

  chairs and sofa are upholstered in dark gray
  walls are papered with maroon trellises and maroon roses
  ceiling needs paint—is spidery gray
  heavy maroon draperies are always drawn
  aunt rarely puts on lamp at night
  when she watches TV, she sits alone in the gloom

Climax: The relationship of the aunt's emotional life to her dark living
room reaches a climax with the final detail that shows her sitting
alone in the gloomy living room watching TV.

  Dave Kilbourne, a pioneer sky sailor and kite builder from California, describes the experience of sky sailing through the singular effect it has on him—it allows him to feel free as a bird:

> I feel like I'm almost in a no man's land; like I'm really not supposed to be there. You're out in the open with nothing around you; sometimes you forget you even have a kite. You see many things—deer, and of course all the soaring birds. . . . Most of the small birds get out of the way, and the big hawks come over to look at you. . . . You know [they've got their] wings tucked in, running about one-tenth of their efficiency and you get a little annoyed after a while, so you'll yell at them or something and generally they'll peel off and really show you how to fly.
>
>   Quoted in Rick Carrier, *Fly: The Complete
>   Book of Sky Sailing*

A climax is reached as the sky sailor yells at real birds and tries to take a lesson from their airborne ballet.

  As a final example of the need to select details and build to a climax, let us say you want to describe your uncle. Your purpose is to prove that he is the grouchiest member of your family. The details you choose must therefore work toward that purpose. You exclude those that don't. You leave out the generous birthday presents he gives and the nifty clothes he wears. But you include the times he fails to smile at family jokes, the way he expects your aunt to clean up after him, the irritation in his voice when he speaks to his eight-year-old son. You include the evening your father had his heart attack and your uncle complained about trivia all night. You think, clearly, the last detail will be your clincher. Here's the brief essay:

> Uncle David is the grouchiest member of our family. Although we have some pretty comical relatives, Dave never cracks his face, not even at Thanksgiving dinner when the rest of us are laughing so hard that it's difficult to eat. Not Dave. He never loses the rhythm of putting sweet potatoes and turkey into his sour face.
>
> His son, Andrew, who is only eight, is often the target of his father's growling. Uncle David, who I suspect loves Andrew although all evidence points to the contrary, never lifts a finger to help the child or show him any affection. "Get it yourself" is the you-better-move-your-ass-without-bothering-your-old-man reply. Usually my Aunt Ada runs in to rescue Andrew, on the way wiping up around David if something has spilled and cleaning and serving without ever being thanked. My mother and father and I watch in perpetual disappointment.
>
> I still find it hard to believe the stories my mother tells about Uncle David the night my father had his coronary. David raced over to take my mother to the hospital, and then whined all the way there about his broken air conditioner and how expensive it would be to have it repaired. Then he spent the night out in the corridor with my mother, grumbling constantly about the nurses drinking Coca-Cola in the intensive care unit while his brother was lying there dying. David means well, and I know we'd probably miss him if he forgot to show up at one of our family get-togethers. Fortunately, he is the only grouch we have.

Exercise 4   In the description exercises that follow, be vivid. Use color, shape, motion, smell, heat, cold, texture, mood. Use organizing words—*first*, *second*, *above*, *below*, and the like—wherever they can help clarify your description.

1. Describe a place that is dominated by one of the following impressions. Include the physical details of the place, but make it clear that your sense of that place is dominated by one impression. Save the best details for last.

steamy	full of gadgets
noisy	glassy
full of books	crowded with trucks

2. Look through an upper-story window of a tall building and describe the scene as you see it. Begin with what is closest to you and move outward to the horizon.

3. Describe your closet from left to right, then from top to bottom.

4. Go to your college cafeteria. Describe a person you see there from his or her shoes up.

5. Describe a person who affects you in a particular way. Consider the following characteristics as possible themes to unify your description, or decide on your own. Save the best details for last.

saintly
sickly
philosophical
cheap
generous
paranoid
"out-to-lunch"

6. Describe a process you know well: how to play a game (tennis, poker, hockey, etc.), how to make a favorite dish (lasagna, egg salad, onion soup), or how to build something (a fire, a bookcase, a cocktail table out of a door and cement blocks).

7. Describe a process you engage in every day but rarely stop to think about: how to tie a shoe, start a car, brush your teeth, etc.

Defining   An additional skill that relies on accurate use of details is *defining*. In expository writing, you may have to start by telling your reader what your terms mean. If you are explaining financial aid at your college, for example, you must tell your reader what you mean by financial aid: "Financial aid at my school is monetary assistance granted to a student. It may come as a scholarship or as income that the student earns by working at campus jobs." The essay may then take up any number of questions: Who is entitled to financial aid? How many credits must a student be carrying to qualify? What is the role of the federal government? How can middle-income parents be helped to educate their children? Where do students work? Is this program typical? But the meaning of financial aid must be clear if the reader is to understand your discussion in the way that you intend it.

It is useful to see definition as an outgrowth of description. When you describe, you are singling out one individual object from the class of objects to which it belongs. *A description is specific,* in the same way that narratives are specific. Suppose you are asked to describe a chair. Your response might be, "Okay, which chair? I have to choose a specific chair and describe it." A description provides specific details that tell about a particular item at a particular time in a particular place (for example, the dark red armchair near your bed; the old brown leather chair your dentist had before he replaced it with a cool green plastic one). Your description of a chair distinguishes it unmistakably from every other chair because you emphasize the details that set it apart from every other chair.

A definition is general. A definition of a chair has to include all the details shared by every object we can call *chair.* How can you write a clear definition? You will discover what an interesting and demanding assignment that is if you try to take a simple term and define it without looking in a dictionary. Is it enough to say, "A chair is something a person can sit on"? What about a bed? Can't a person sit on a bed? What about a stool? Doesn't a person sit on a stool?

A definition serves two functions: (1) it places the object in a class of objects that are like it, and (2) it tells how the object is different from other members of the same class. For example, when you look for the word *chair* in your dictionary, you may find, "a seat, especially for one person, usually having four legs for support and a rest for the back and often having rests for the arms." (*American College Dictionary,* p. 244.) As definitions go, the details in this can't be rivaled for usefulness because they concisely separate *chairs* from all other *seats:* from *stools* (which have no back), *benches* (which are seats for more than one person), and *couches* (which are comfortable enough for reclining). How could a dictionary possibly offer *descriptions* of specific objects (for example, the dark red armchair near your bed)? Such a description would be useful only for the red chair near your bed and for no other chair. An artist always renders a specific object in a painting or drawing. A writer, on the other hand, must be prepared to do either, define or describe, depending on his purpose.

Exercise 5 Define and describe each of the following words. Remember, your definitions must include details that apply to all garbage, all food, etc. Your description must include details that apply to specific garbage (or specific food, etc.) in a specific place at a specific time.

1. Define *garbage.*   Describe garbage.
2. Define *food.*   Describe food.
3. Define *soldier.*   Describe a soldier.
4. Define *policeman.*   Describe a policeman.
5. Define *bed.*   Describe your bed.

Writing a thesis and comparing and contrasting Showing likenesses and differences is second nature to us. It is the route our minds take to explain the choices we make. In conversation, we run through comparisons very casually. Who hasn't compared summer with winter, husbands with wives, dormitories with apartments, Republicans with Democrats? But exactly how can we go about the acts required to compare items in order to make a point in an essay?

Choose
comparable items First, your choice of subjects must have enough in common to make a comparison possible. Comparing grapefruits to fur coats will drive you bananas. Contrasting the duties of the Supreme Court with the rules for playing hockey seems very far-fetched. You may, however, have a real need to compare two things to help you decide issues that are important to you. Usually, these two things have a common base. For example, should you live on the ground floor or live on the top floor? Should you travel in Europe or travel in the United States?

Look at the following list comparing the advantages and disadvantages of living on the ground floor of a dorm with living on the top floor.

	A **ground-floor room**	B **top-floor room**
Advantages:	easy access	provides exercise
	lots of company	no nuisance company
		no traffic in inquiries
	meet new people	close relationships with people on floor
	at the center of things	quiet—can study in room
	bring bicycle in	can't hear the gate at night
		excellent view of the campus
		no noises above
Disadvantages:	noisy	steps
	hear gate slamming all night	carrying books and packages
	noisy guys above	carrying laundry
	lots of interruptions for information	forgetting something
	too much traffic	"out of it"
	looks into back of bookstore	
	bathrooms are used by passers-through	can't bring up bike

The writer concludes that living upstairs is more serene and more congenial to working than living downstairs. Notice that the thesis in the following essay of comparison states the writer's preference, though not every comparison will lead to a preference. Essays of comparison can merely record differences, with the thesis generalizing about the significant difference. An essay of comparison can proceed along one of two strategies:

See the structure **1.** Tell all about A. Then tell all about B.
of your comparison **2.** Compare A and B point by point.

TELL ALL ABOUT A, THEN TELL ALL ABOUT B

Living on the ground floor of a dormitory has certain real advantages over living on the top floor, though for my part they are not advantages that improve my life. A ground-floor room, chiefly, has the special advantage of easy access. You can come in and out as often as you like without an expenditure of energy, and, for a student, that energy can mean the difference between staying up to finish an assignment and falling asleep over a book. That easy access is also tremendously inviting to other people. If you live downstairs, you are very much at the center of things, meeting new people all the time, never without company, never lonely. A minor advantage, but one important for a bike rider like me, is that if you keep a bike on campus, you can wheel your bike into your room without having to dismantle it or bang it up the steps. That is a personal advantage above and beyond the special ones that might make your life a little more convenient.

The disadvantages of living on the ground floor also have to do with its accessibility. The interruptions are everlasting. "Did you see Amelia?" "Which room is Twitch Lasky in?" "Do you happen to know where we sign up for the room lottery?" and on and on all day and far into the night. The noise is not only on your floor, but the guys upstairs thump around so that the noise comes at you in quadraphonic sound. Not only is the hall full of people, but passers-through tend to use your bathroom a lot. If you live downstairs, you lose privacy rapidly. And, finally, if you're interested in aesthetics, forget it. The view from your downstairs window is probably directly into the sox department of the bookstore.

The advantages of living on the top floor (which is the fourth floor in our dorm) center on the refinements of living. Nobody comes up without a special purpose. You don't have to spend your time getting rid of people in order to get a little work done, or, finally, in desperation, go to the library just to read your economics text. If you are lucky enough to have good people on your floor, you usually manage to make a few good friends. The floor is relatively quiet and private. No noise comes down on you from above. Nights are peaceful because you can't hear the gate slamming as residents come in and out. And the best reinforcement of peace and serenity is a pleasing view. Your view from the fourth floor is wide open. Your eye can move from the quad out to the foothills of the mountains. The seasons are quietly beautiful.

The disadvantages of the top floor all center on its location. No matter what you do, those long flights of steps are between you and your destination. It is a pain to carry books and packages and a particular pain to bring laundry up and down. But the biggest pain of all is forgetting something and having to dash back to retrieve it. For a freshman, the top floor may be too far "out of things," though after freshman year, the need for social traffic dwindles. And if you are a bike rider, you have to make other arrangements for your bike.

Weighing the advantages against the disadvantages, you may realize that privacy and quiet have a price. I did. I live on the top floor and hope I can stay up here for the next few years. Since I have more time to myself, I dig into my work, and my grades have improved. I am learning to turn the disadvantages of the steps to an advantage. I'm trying to become an efficiency expert and a master of my own memory. But when I fail and leave my glasses or my economics book back in my room, I climb back up, trying to smile, concentrating on the daily exercise I am getting.

COMPARE A AND B POINT BY POINT

Living on the ground floor of a dormitory has certain real advantages over living on the top floor, though not as many as you would think. On the ground floor, everything is readily accessible. You can come in and out as often as you like, whereas on the top floor you always have those long flights of stairs between you and your destination. On the ground floor you know what's going on. You're directly at the center of things, while on the top floor you're somewhat isolated. On the ground floor, you meet new people and move into more activities with them. On the top floor, you have just a few people on your floor, and if they are not your kind of people, you can be quite lonely. And, if you are a bike rider like me, you can wheel your bike into your room downstairs, whereas on the top floor you have to dismantle it, bang it up the steps, or, more likely, make other arrangements for locking it up somewhere.

The disadvantages of living downstairs may convince you that living upstairs, in spite of the steps, is a more agreeable way to live on campus. Downstairs is constant traffic; upstairs sees nobody who doesn't come up for a special purpose. Downstairs is constant noise: conversation, passers-through, and everlasting interruptions for information: "Did you see Amelia?" "Which room is Twitch Lasky in?" "Do you happen to know where we sign up for the room lottery?" The noise from the guys thumping around upstairs, of course, is totally eliminated if you live on the top floor. In your downstairs room you can hear the gate slamming all night, while upstairs you can't hear it at all. And your bathroom downstairs is usually full of strangers; upstairs you and your roommates have privacy. If you are interested in aesthetics, forget a downstairs room. The view from your window is probably directly into the sox department of the bookstore; upstairs your view is wide open. Your eye can move from the quad out of the foothills of the mountains. The seasons are quietly beautiful.

But most important of all, and the final reason for your choice, may be that upstairs you can get into your work without interruptions and that your grades reflect an improvement. I live on the top floor and hope I can stay up here for the next few years. I am learning to turn the disadvantage of the steps to an advantage. I'm trying to become an efficiency expert and a master of my own memory. But when I fail and leave my glasses or my economics book back in my room, I climb back up, trying to smile, concentrating on the daily exercise I am getting.

Exercise 6 Choose one of the following pairs and write two brief essays of comparison for the pair. Organize the first essay by telling all about term A and then telling all about term B. Organize the second essay by comparing A and B point for point. Begin both essays with the same thesis. State your preference toward one term in the comparison and give a general reason why you hold that preference.

A	B
1. marriage	living together
2. mother-in-law	father-in-law
3. dieting	eating
4. required courses	open curriculum
5. astrology	religion
6. sciences	liberal arts
7. my first impressions of _____	what I think of _____ now
8. my ambition five years ago	my ambition today
9. my conduct at parties when I was fifteen	my conduct at parties today
10. my belief in God when I was a child	my belief in God today
11. my relationship to my father as it was	my relationship to my father as it is
12. McDonald's	Burger King

Writing an analogy Another interesting form of comparison is *analogy*. An analogy is an extended and unusual comparison between two items. An analogy explains one thing by showing in vivid and unexpected detail how similar it is to another. Read the following paragraph, which presents an analogy between the reading tastes and the food tastes of children:

. . . A group of professors of education . . . recently proposed that the list of "required reading" in schools should be based upon a study which they have just sponsored of the tastes of school children. . . . Would any pediatrician base the diet which he prescribed for the young submitted to his care simply on an effort to determine what eatables they remembered with greatest pleasure? If he knew that the vote would run heavily in favor of chocolate sodas, orange pop, hot dogs and bubble gum, would he conclude that these should obviously constitute the fundamental elements in a "modern" child's menu?

Joseph Wood Krutch

Krutch goes on from this analogy to argue *against* letting children's tastes determine what they read, just as anyone with common sense would argue against letting children's tastes determine what they eat. He details the familiar junk-food favorites—chocolate sodas, hot dogs, and the like— as an unsatisfactory diet for a growing child, thereby suggesting that a child's selected reading menu would be equally unwholesome.

Analogies are often exciting to read because the unexpected and imaginative comparison of two things we had not thought similar gives us a surprising insight. Below is an exercise in analogy in which a student writer compares Thanksgiving dinner at his house to a free-for-all. Although he wrote this largely for the fun of it, it contains a semi-serious attempt to tell those of us who have never had Thanksgiving dinner at his house just how spirited the meal is, because we know that a free-for-all is a highly individualistic, competitive, and spirited brawl.

Notice that the student's title for the analogy that follows contains his thesis, as does his second sentence.

THANKSGIVING DINNER IS LIKE A FREE-FOR-ALL

On Thursday night, all my relatives gathered at my house for our annual rhubarb known as Thanksgiving. The rumble was over a cooked bird and all of its usual companions. The action began when my uncle plunged his fork into the midsection of the sweet potatoes. After that, everyone was going at it. A quick right and my little cousin started gnawing away at the drumstick. I decided to get in the action and threw a wild left. It connected against the lip of a glass from which a bloodlike substance emerged and bathed the tablecloth. My mother nursed the injury with a sponge. A few flurries were thrown, but more than not it was just talk. I was proclaimed champion when all the gladiators defaulted because of injuries, the most common ones being nausea and upset stomach. When cleanup time came, a few cousins engaged in their own donnybrook. They put their grasping hands all over each other's plates and silverware. The outburst was quickly resolved by allowing each opponent to place two items in the dishwasher. When it was time to depart, the combatants scurried away as if someone had screamed "Fire!" in the arena.

The success of the paragraph lies with the appropriateness of the comparison because there are so many elements of Thanksgiving dinner that are like a free-for-all:

> Getting at the food requires fighting skills.
> The excitement and energy of the struggle to eat cause minor injuries and spills among the participants.
> Cleaning up causes fresh outbursts and flare-ups.

But the success of the paragraph also comes from the vigor of the language. The specific words the writer chooses ring of the fight and tighten the analogy:

rhubarb	champion
rumble	donnybrook
a quick right	outburst
a wild left	combatants
connected against the lip	arena
nursed the injury	

Before you write an analogy, it is a good idea to remember that writing is a cycle of acts. Think back to the invention stage and outline in writing the similarities between your two items. Emphasize the similarities and omit differences. Be plain and systematic as you cite the similarities. Strengthen your language with the kinds of words pertinent to your comparison.

If an analogy forms your entire essay, your thesis will offer a statement that says *X is very much like Y—Thanksgiving dinner is like a free-for-all;* but you can use analogy as an element in a longer piece of expository writing when you want to argue for or against an issue vividly and also when you want to explain effectively or entertain. Many writers use an analogy to begin their essays because it is a fresh, unexpected attention getter that attracts readers.

Classifying A natural channel of thinking closely related to comparing is *classifying*. You can classify persons, things, or experiences according to principles of division you establish. When you write an essay of classification, you can feel the comparing process at work underneath all your decisions. For example, in a study of your telephone habits, you might sort out all the phone calls you receive into groups. You will be comparing and contrasting the calls to determine what they have in common and on what principles they differ. One principle might be *duration.* You ask, *How long do calls last?* On this principle, you find you have three kinds of calls:

> quick calls (one to three minutes) to deliver or obtain information
> conversational calls (four to thirty minutes) to keep in touch with friends and family
> interminable calls (longer than half an hour) to discuss, comfort, argue, or relate in excessive and repetitive detail

Your thesis might say:

> All telephone calls can be divided according to how long they last.

Another principle might be *callers:* You ask, *Who is calling and for what purpose?* On this principle you may again have three kinds of calls:

> nuisance calls from business advertisers, obscene or abusive callers, kids playing with the phone
> occasional calls from legitimate business people, infrequent calls from distant family or friends
> regular calls from close friends and family

Your thesis might say:

> All telephone calls can be divided according to who the caller is.

Suppose that for a study of the media you wanted to classify TV shows. What principles of division might you try? One principle might be the type of show. You ask, *What kinds of shows are on TV?* On this principle, you propose five types:

> talk shows
> situation comedies
> adventure series
> sporting events
> specials

Your thesis might say:

> *TV shows can be classified according to the kinds of entertainment they offer.*

Another principle might be *audience.* You ask, *Who watches the shows?* On this principle, you propose three types of shows:

> shows for children
> shows for general audiences
> shows of special interest for adults

Your thesis might say:

> *TV shows can be grouped according to the kinds of audience they attract.*

And another principle might be *scheduling.* You ask, *When are the shows scheduled?* On this principle you propose three basic time slots for TV shows:

> daytime shows
> prime-time shows
> late-night shows

Your thesis might say:

TV shows can be grouped according to the times they are scheduled.

Classification is neat and orderly. It can be used to develop an entire essay, with each division a paragraph, or it can simply help you with your thinking. As you classify, be careful of two things:

1. Keep your principles of division logical.
For example, if you divide TV into daytime, prime-time, and situation comedies, your classification will not be logical because the subgroups overlap. There are situation comedies during the day and during prime time.

2. Do not omit an important subgroup.
If you divide TV into daytime and prime time, your classification would be incomplete. A reader would immediately say, "What about late-night TV?"

Exercise 7 Practice classifying by completing the following exercises.

1. Choose five of the headings from the list below and classify each one into as many subgroups as you want according to at least two principles of division.

    Example: phone calls: duration   phone calls: callers
                    quick calls   nuisance callers
                    conversational calls   occasional callers
                    interminable calls   regular callers

2. Write a whole essay of classification. Break down one of the items from the list below into as many subgroups as you need. Begin your essay with a thesis statement that states your classification. Use as many paragraphs as your classification scheme requires.

    Example: Friends
    Thesis: When you live at the beach, you have all-year-round friends and fair-weather friends, who begin to show up around Memorial Day.
    Supporting paragraph 1: All year-round-friends
    Supporting paragraph 2: Fair-weather friends
    Conclusion: State your attitude toward these two types of friends, or the way you deal with the problem, or your reasons for putting up with it.

    List:

college teachers	relatives	hijackings	wars
college students	disc jockeys	weddings	terrorists
newspapers	musical groups	relationships	

TIPS FOR EXAM TAKERS

Use classification in your academic studies. It is a convenient way to frame answers to essay tests. A typical question in a history exam might be:

Describe the reasons for the rise of Cuban nationalism.

Your answer:
We can classify the reasons for Cuba's nationalism into three groups: geographic, economic, and political. Let us examine each one in turn.
Cuba's geographic position so close to the United States threatens the island's nationalism. . . .
You continue developing each paragraph with geographic, economic, and political details to support each classification.
See Chapter 20, "Practical Helps."

Writing a thesis and showing causes, reasons, and effects

Showing causes, reasons, and effects is another natural way of thinking. It is the route our minds take when we dig behind an event or a statement and ask, *What were the causes of such and such? Why did such and such happen? And it is the route we take when we ask, *What are the consequences of such and such? Something happened, and what were the effects?*

Suppose you get an A in a biology course. If you dig to find out why, you get to the causes or reasons why:

because you studied hard
because you studied the right materials
because your instructor liked you
because you benefited from studying with Jim
because you were a brilliant lab researcher
because your mother is a biologist

If you consider the consequences of getting an A in your biology course, you find the effects:

Your cumulative index will reach 3.0.
You'll become a biology major.
You'll get a summer job at the state biochemistry lab.
You'll make your mother happy.

If you were writing an essay on the causes or effects of your getting an A in biology, your thesis might look like one of these:

I got an A in biology because _____.

My getting an A in biology had the following results: _____.

There are several reasons why I got an A in biology this semester.

My getting an A in biology this semester had several consequences, some of them trivial, some of them important.

Sample essay showing causes and effects The following essay combines a narrative technique with an explanation of cause and effect. It was written by a student to show how a vacation caused a major change in his outlook on life. By going through the details of the vacation trip, the writer supplies the specific causes of his change in attitude.

THE SABBATICAL

It was twenty degrees when my friends and I boarded a jet at Kennedy airport. I felt vaguely good because I knew I was going to escape the cold, depressing atmosphere that plagues New York City in the winter. But I couldn't imagine how profoundly changed I would feel when I got back from my trip. I discovered that an eight-day trip to a faraway place in the sun can have effects that may last for months.

But the winter wasn't the only thing depressing me when I left. I was tired of my work in the factory, tired of going to school at night and feeling that everything I did took too long. It was such a tight squeeze going from work to school that I was doing everything like a robot, noticing nothing, just performing whatever was required of me mechanically, never doing a stroke more than I had to. When I did look around on my way home from school at night, the city looked like a place nobody could love.

Three hours and fifteen hundred miles after takeoff, our jet touched down in San Juan, Puerto Rico. I was overwhelmed by the warm tropical climate as soon as I got off the jet. It was only a trivial inconvenience, and I became accustomed to it in no time at all.

Not only was the climate warm, but the people were, too. They appreciated my feeble attempt to speak to them in Spanish and found it amusing. And they were always helpful in giving us directions. Their island was beautiful; the scenery was breathtaking; I opened my eyes and saw majestic palm trees, fishing boats cruising along in the warm turquoise waters of the Caribbean, and looking inland, the green-covered mountains towering over the tall hotels of the city.

One part of the island that put me in awe was the rain forest *El Yunque.* The rain forest is a jungle eternally covered by sinister-looking rain clouds. I had never walked around in a real jungle before, and this forest had all the makings of a real jungle. I mean, it had the dense tropical foliage, bamboo growing twenty feet tall, hidden waterfalls, and all kinds of wildlife. I was told that a tribe of people live up there in the mountains.

After the rain forest we split to St. Thomas for a couple of days. I loved the carnival atmosphere of St. Thomas, which was caused by the tourists and natives who crowded the small shops and narrow streets of the town.

After two days we flew back to San Juan. There wasn't much time left to our vacation. Our last day was spent in and about the apartment building, feeling sorry for ourselves because we knew the trip was over and we didn't want to leave.

I got back home the next day about five o'clock in the morning, and I was exhausted. When I finally came to, I realized what a fantastic time I had had. But it all seemed like a dream. I wanted to pinch myself to make sure it wasn't. However, I was sure that this trip changed my whole outlook on life.

Before I left I had felt tense and frustrated about everything I did. I was constantly worrying, but the sun and water eliminated those feelings that I had. All the beautiful sights I saw prepared me to see beauty everywhere, even in New York. The friendliness of the people returned my faith in my fellow citizens. I felt more alive than ever before, more aware of the present moment. The effect was so great that ten months later I still feel the same way today. I mean I feel like a kid all over again. Everything that used to be boring is now interesting, and everything that was bland is now exciting. It was as if I opened my eyes for the first time and learned how to see; I noticed people and objects that had been obscured to me previously. The city began to show me its friendliest bus drivers and its cleanest streets. When I came back, my friends at home thought I went mad because I seemed so loose. They still think I'm nuts, but one thing's for sure, they definitely saw a change in me they won't forget. I tell them, "Take a long trip, it's great therapy."

Sample essay showing reasons When we talk about causes, we can often point to something *specific* as a cause of something else: The lights in the house blew out *because* lightning struck the power station. Sometimes causes are not so obvious or definite, especially when we talk about feelings. When we discuss our feelings, we usually talk about *reasons* for those feelings: There are three reasons why Dr. Becker prefers to practice medicine in a small town.

In the following essay, Judy Syfers discusses the reasons *why* a wife is desirable, even to a wife. Notice that her title, "Why I Want a Wife," and the question in the second paragraph, *Why do I want a wife?* set us up for the reasons that follow.

WHY I WANT A WIFE

I belong to that classification of people known as wives. I am A Wife. And, not altogether incidentally, I am a mother.

Not too long ago a male friend of mine appeared on the scene fresh from a divorce. He had one child, who is, of course, with his ex-wife. He is looking for another wife. As I thought about him while I was ironing one evening, it suddenly occurred to me that I, too, would like to have a wife. Why do I want a wife?

I would like to go back to school so that I can become economically independent, support myself, and, if need be, support those dependent upon me. I want a wife who will work and send me to school. And while I am going to school I want a wife to take care of my children. I want a wife to keep track of the children's doctor and dentist appointments. And to keep track of mine, too. I want a wife to make sure my children eat properly and are kept clean. I want a wife who will wash the children's clothes and keep them mended. I want a wife who is a good nurturant attendant to my children, who arranges for their schooling, makes sure that they have an adequate social life with their peers, takes them to the park, the zoo, etc. I want a wife who takes care of the children when they are sick, a wife who arranges to be around when the children need special care, because, of course, I cannot miss classes at school. My wife must arrange to lose time at work and not lose the job. It may mean a small cut in my wife's income from time to time, but I guess I can tolerate that. Needless to say, my wife will arrange and pay for the care of the children while my wife is working.

I want a wife who will take care of *my* physical needs. I want a wife who will keep my house clean. A wife who will pick up after me. I want a wife who will keep my clothes clean, ironed, mended, replaced when need be, and who will see to it that my personal things are kept in their proper place so that I can find what I need the minute I need it. I want a wife who cooks the meals, a wife who is a *good* cook. I want a wife who will plan the menus, do the necessary grocery shopping, prepare the meals, serve them pleasantly, and then do the cleaning up while I do my studying. I want a wife who will care for me when I am sick and sympathize with my pain and loss of time from school. I want a wife to go along when our family takes a vacation so that someone can continue to care for me and my children when I need a rest and change of scene.

I want a wife who will not bother me with rambling complaints about a wife's duties. But I want a wife who will listen to me when I feel the need to explain a rather difficult point I have come across in my course of studies. And I want a wife who will type my papers for me when I have written them.

I want a wife who will take care of the details of my social life. When my wife and I are invited out by my friends, I want a wife who will take care of the babysitting arrangements. When I meet people at school that I like and want to entertain, I want a wife who will have the house clean, will prepare a special meal, serve it to me and my friends, and not interrupt when I talk about the things that interest me and my friends. I want a wife who will have arranged that the children are fed and ready for bed before my guests arrive so that children do not bother us. I want a wife who takes care of the needs of my guests so that they feel comfortable, who makes sure that they have an ashtray, that they are passed the hors d'oeuvres, that they are offered a second helping of the food, that their wine glasses are replenished when necessary, that their coffee is served to them as they like it. And I want a wife who knows that sometimes I need a night out by myself.

I want a wife who is sensitive to my sexual needs, a wife who makes love passionately and eagerly when I feel like it, a wife who makes sure that I am satisfied. And, of course, I want a wife who will not demand sexual attention when I am not in the mood for it. I want a wife who assumes the complete responsibility for birth control, because I do not want more children. I want a wife who will remain sexually faithful to me so that I do not have to clutter up my intellectual life with jealousies. And I want a wife who understands that *my* sexual needs may entail more than strict adherence to monogamy. I must, after all, be able to relate to people as fully as possible.

If, by chance, I find another person more suitable as a wife than the wife I already have, I want the liberty to replace my present wife with another one. Naturally, I will expect a fresh, new life; my wife will take the children and be solely responsible for them so that I am left free.

When I am through with school and have a job, I want my wife to quit working and remain at home so that my wife can more fully and completely take care of a wife's duties.

My God, who *wouldn't* want a wife?

Ms., December 1971

As Judy Syfers gives detailed, personal, knowing reasons why she would like to have a wife, she is also, quite intentionally, expressing her own feelings about a wife's role. Her thesis is *There are so many reasons why a wife is desirable that even I want one.* Is there an unstated thesis?

"Why I Want a Wife" suggests that a great deal of pleasure arrives for the reader in a flood of rich detail; but much of the pleasure depends on the orderly way the details are grouped. Each of Judy Syfers' reasons has its own bundle of details:

I want a wife who will work and send me to school.
My wife will arrange and pay for the care of the children.
I want a wife who will take care of *my* physical needs.
I want a wife who will not bother me with rambling complaints about a wife's duties.
I want a wife who will take care of the details of my social life.
I want a wife who is sensitive to my sexual needs.
I want the liberty to replace my present wife with another one.
And so on.

The importance In writing that explains, remember that *why* is your most important wedge
of asking why into conditions that seem impenetrable. When things happen to you that
you don't immediately understand, take them apart and ask yourself questions about them. Why? What are the reasons? How do I know? What are
the results?

TIPS FOR EXAM TAKERS
Essay exam questions are often written as cause or effect questions:

> Describe the causes of the American Revolution.
> Describe the effects of the American Revolution.

As you respond to the exam question, you think about the big question
why? Why did the Revolutionary War occur? What caused it? Gather all
the specifics you can, and then think about putting the specifics into some
order. These are the specific causes, and you end with the one you
consider most important:

> Great Britain exploited the colonies' natural resources.
> Great Britain discouraged the economic development of the colonies.
> Aristocratic Britons wanted the colonists to remain inferior.
> The Stamp Act stirred protests and boycotts.

The causes or the results can be *classified* according to several principles:

> We can classify the *causes* of the Revolutionary War into the pressing
> economic, political, and ideological *issues* of the time.

> or

> We can classify the *results* of the American Revolution into the effects
> it had on the *political, economic,* and *psychological framework* of
> the new American community.

> or

> We can classify *immediate* and *far-reaching effects* of the Revolution.

> or

> We can classify the *effects* of the war on the *young nation* or the
> *effects* on *Great Britain*.

Exercise 8   Choose two of the following occurrences. For each one, write three
or four sentences that state possible causes. Then, for each one, write
three or four sentences that state possible consequences.

1. getting an A in a course
2. getting a new job
3. skidding on the road

4. leaving school

5. disappointing a parent (or husband, wife, friend, or yourself)

6. gaining five pounds

7. improvement in your local bus service

Arguing   Since an explanatory essay requires that you move consciously back and forth between your point and your details, it is a particularly useful form for persuading. *Arguing* is persuading with exceptional care to logic and strategy. It is an extreme degree of persuasion, a very carefully arranged act of persuasion. Arguing in this sense does not mean yelling and quarreling. It means giving reasons for or against an idea. When you argue, you take a stand for or against an issue. For example, *All students ought to live in their own apartments*—for or against? *Students should be free to refer to textbooks during exams*—for or against? You state your commitment. You prepare to go all the way for the sake of your argument. Your essay gives the best reasons you can find for your position.

An essay of argument calls for several paragraphs. Each paragraph puts forth a piece of evidence to defend what you are proposing in your thesis—for example, *College students improve the quality of their lives and their studies when they move into their own apartments*.

The paragraphs of an argument will use all your writing skills: one paragraph may *describe* an apartment and *compare* it with a dormitory room; another paragraph may *tell* a brief *story* about a B— student whose grades rose to A— once he moved out of the dormitory and into his own quiet apartment; two more paragraphs may *explain* statistics or list approving parental opinions. Toward the end of your argument, you may need a clincher. You may therefore want to keep your best evidence—how your own life and studies have improved since you've had your own apartment—for the most strategic position of your argument. You don't want the points of your argument to bob randomly into view as they bobbed into

Argument is a decent and respectable way to develop ideas; what's more, it can be personal and move people to action. When you argue an idea you must put forward convincing and specific reasons not only logically but dramatically. The best oral arguers use all the skills at their disposal to convince you. They cite facts and figures and speak as logically as they can, but they do not stop there. You have heard the arguments of senators and Presidents. You have heard churchmen sermonize, and you have listened to politicians campaigning for office. They raise their voices, they smile, they gesture, they suddenly interrupt with an appealing story to illustrate their point, and before you know it you are nodding and agreeing with them. In the same way, the best writers of argument will advise you to make use of the most effective writing skills at your command in order to win your reader to your position. Your words and sentences must work for you on the page, where your voice, your smile, and your gesture cannot operate.

your head. Your talent as an essay writer will be measured as much by the deliberate *order* in which you arrange your evidence as by the choice cuts of evidence you select.

When your readers read your argument, they want to be appealed to fairly and logically. They don't want to be harassed. Using rash, questionable "facts" and sweeping statements to make a point can be just as aggressive as pushing and shoving. As an essayist you are not a rabble-rouser. You use sanity, reason, and charm. You move cautiously, step by step, and take your readers methodically along. You also assume that your readers are intelligent and will recognize a compelling argument. And because they are intelligent, your readers are as much on their guard in reading as in any other transaction. They do not want to be swindled. They can smell a phony. Lacking another defense, they apply skepticism and a "show me" attitude.

Here are some guidelines for writing an honest and effective argument:

1. Choose evidence carefully. Don't overuse facts and figures, but check the ones you do use.
2. Arrange your evidence in a convincing and dramatic order.
3. Don't offer an opinion as if it were a fact.
4. Don't generalize excessively. Don't say "all" when you mean "most." Don't say "will" when you mean "may."
5. Don't ignore the objections your reader will inevitably raise. Try to disarm your reader near the beginning of your argument.
6. Keep calm. Don't appeal to your reader through emotions alone. Emotional energy should supplement reason.
7. Don't assume that since A came before B, A therefore caused B.
8. Don't oversimplify. An event may have many causes, not simply the one you are discussing.
9. Keep your argument on course.

BASIC ARRANGEMENT FOR WHOLE ESSAY THAT EXPLAINS:

Part I: GENERALIZATION—your thesis

Part II: First supporting idea plus specifics

Part III: Second supporting idea plus specifics

Part IV: Third supporting idea plus specifics

Part V: Fourth supporting idea plus specifics

TIPS FOR WRITERS—EXPLAINING AND INFORMING

1. Identify a large subject area. Find out what interests you through freewriting, thinking, conversation, reading and/or by suggestion from a teacher.

2. Invent or locate ideas. Engage in one or more prewriting techniques. Your writing cycle begins by locating ideas through close observation, focused freewriting on your subject area, writing an associative list, talking with a friend, doing some brief research (book, magazine article, interview), or writing a crash-through draft, sometimes in letter form. Underline ideas that matter to you.

3. In your prewriting materials, separate general ideas from specific details. Mark general ideas "g" and specific details "s." Write the general ideas out in full sentences. Group related details under the general idea that seems to include it.

4. Study the groups. Get a sense of a natural channel of thinking that is appropriate to these ideas. Will your thesis be supported by details or examples? Are you comparing two things? Are you explaining why? Are you showing effects?

5. Write a temporary thesis statement that follows the appropriate channel of thinking and includes the details you have. Write *I believe* . . . State your attitude toward your subject, and be sure you know *why* you feel that way. For a comparison you may want to write:

> I believe X is like (or different from) Y.
> I believe X is more (or less) _____ than Y. I prefer X (or Y).

For a cause/effect essay, you may want to write:

> I believe X was caused by _____.
> I believe the consequences of X are _____.

6. Set up an outline with your thesis at the top. Under it write the main headings that are somewhat more specific than your thesis. Jot down details under each heading. Adjust your thesis as you add or subtract details.

7. Write a first draft. Move back and forth between your general statements and specifics. Understand your principle of organization. Time? Space? Climax? Keep the best details for last. Keep writing. You can make changes later.

8. Reread your draft and make the immediate changes that *you* feel are necessary.

9. Recopy your draft if you need to. Get a reaction from a friend or fellow writer.

10. Go back for more ideas, a clearer outline, a better thesis. Cut irrelevancies. Expand the most important sections. Think. Make details as vivid as you can.

11. Revise.

Chapter 5

Revising the Whole Essay

You begin to reread what you have written while you and your essay are still honeymooning. The first rosy glow of success persists. You wrote it. It's yours. And you know you're going to cherish it, immediately raising your defenses to guard your hard work against any doubts that are already seeping in at the edges of your confidence. Your stubborn impulse is to resist those doubts, resist tampering with any line of that page in front of you. After all, you planned on being finished by now. And haven't you had that experience before: pull one thread and the whole essay begins to unravel? You can't change just *one* word. One word leads to another . . . and another . . . and another.

When you think of writing as a cycle of repeatable acts, revision is in your plans from the start. By the second or third essay you write, the barrier you have always felt between writing and revising weakens. Writing, you discover, *is* revising. Instead of condemning yourself to a first draft forever, you know that the writing process puts you in charge of improving your essay. You keep writing, keep clarifying, keep adding details, keep deleting what doesn't belong, keep finding out what you mean. You make more lists, reread your freewriting, weigh your general statements against the specific details that support them. And you try to write your way out of strained, cramped sentences into a simple clarity.

Your outline may help you. Keep it nearby, checking what you have written against your plan. If you have no outline, a good time to formulate one is after you've written your first draft. At least, try to extract your thesis and your main subheadings of thought. Then examine the structure of your logic as you see it, perhaps more distinctly, in outline form.

After carefully studying the logic of your main ideas, do a quick proofreading—supply missing words, repair faulty sentences, and be on the lookout for misspelled words. Then recopy your draft so that you can ask friends to read what you have written without handicapping them with the messy insertions and corrections of your first revision.

GIVING AND GETTING REACTIONS

When you hand over a piece of writing to a friend for a reaction, you should request in return the most constructive, concrete reaction he can give you. Similarly, when *you* give a reaction to someone else's writing, be precise enough to help the writer put his finger on the very sentences and words that need rewriting. A teacher need not see everything you write. Writers can learn from each other. Your friend may hand your work back saying, "I think this is terrific. One or two weak spots but, on the whole, terrific." Your heart is lighter. Sometimes, however, you sense something fishy. Your friend avoids your eye. "I guess you're not through working on it yet," he says. You snatch it back, muttering. In either instance, your friend's responsibilities as a reader have collapsed because his comments are too indefinite. They leave you stranded. But if you secretly arm yourself with the right questions, you can convert your helpless friend (or yourself) into a useful critic. First of all, no matter how vague his first reaction, don't let him get away. *You* can help him be more precise. It won't matter whether you've written an essay, a letter to the Chairman of the Board of the Volkswagen Company, a paragraph about a poem, or a recommendation to your boss about locking up late at night. You can use some or all of the following questions to guide a reader into revealing what you've actually said. Is your reader saying, "It's not here on the page. I don't see it"? You may have *intended* to say a lot of things, but you may have missed. Try out these questions:

1. What's in this piece of writing? Which parts absolutely have to remain? Why?
2. Do the essential parts get enough attention?
3. Can any part be eliminated? Why?
4. Is there anything you want to hear more about? Why?
5. What do you remember as outstanding? Why is it outstanding?
6. Is the outstanding feature important to the whole piece of writing? In what way?
7. Can the best part go last?
8. Does any part jar you? Does the paper change course?
9. Do you feel any part can be shortened? Which part and why?
10. Can any dialogue be added? Does the included dialogue sound natural?

11. Do any parts seem unclear to you? Which?

12. Is the beginning effective? Does it attract you to read what follows?

13. Does the essay satisfy you? Does the ending, in particular, satisfy you? Does it relate sensibly to the beginning?

14. Without looking at the piece of writing, can you state its thesis?

FIRST SAMPLE ESSAY AND REASONS FOR REVISING

Here is the first draft of the essay about the blow dryer. Many of the changes have been written right on the page itself. Since some of the changes affect more than a word or a line, the facing pages show whole passages that were rewritten. Notice, however, that all revisions are numbered and that reasons for each change are given. Read the revisions and reasons carefully, and compare the new version to the original underlayer. Then read the revised whole draft, which includes all the changes you see in handwriting plus an additional few that seemed inevitable on the way to the typewriter.

An early draft

1   The Blow Dryer and Me
      ~~Feeling Like A Prima Donna~~

2   Learning lessons is a part of every person's life. I'm a very trusting person, often getting into scrapes I later realize I could have avoided. After one of my scrapes I learned that a favor may not be a favor at all.

3   This past June I went away for a ~~trip~~ weekend to New Jersey with a class from school. That Saturday, ~~in the afternoon,~~ before dinner I decided to wash my hair. Afterward ~~After doing so, I remembered that my~~

4   ~~friend Lois had brought a lot of stuff with her including a bag of rollers and her blow dryer. I wondered if she would lend it to me.~~ I went into a friend's room to borrow her blow dryer. ~~which was down the corridor that had a window at the end and she~~ She said she'd do me

5   There were about five other people in the room sitting around talking and waiting for dinner. favor, that ~~a favor. She told me that~~ she'd be happy to dry my hair for me. As my friend dried

6   my hair, I was thinking how great it felt not to dry ~~your~~ my own hair. Feeling like a prima donna, I closed my eyes and relaxed.

7   That is, I relaxed until half of the hair on my head got slurped into the b.d.'s motor. My "friend" had moved the blower too close to my hair and some of it was actually inside the blower. How nice. This monster had slurped down some of my hair from my split ends right down to my very scalp!

8,9   ~~Suddenly I felt my hair caught in the b.d.'s motor.~~ ~~Lois~~ said how sorry she was and I was sorry we had ever come on the trip. Other people in the room were laughing. I could hear the comments they were making. Boy, did I feel ridiculous and annoyed. One guy finally came to my aid, he worked hard at trying to diconnect me ~~from the b.d.~~

10   When someone said to cut me free, I told ~~them~~ her No way, absolutely not. save Although

Reasons for revisions

1. Make title more specific. Get people's attention. Mention *blow dryer* in title.
2. Start with general statement of what I learned. *Say* what I learned. Move last sentence up to top.
3. Add information. Use more details to set scene, give background of trip, tell time was before dinner when people were hanging around.
4. Cut out unimportant details about Lois's stuff, the corridor, the windows, etc. They have no bearing on the episode.
5. Take another look at freewriting for more details. Tell more about other people in room. Do another focused freewriting.
6. Good. Keep. Tells how I felt. Change "your" to "my." Keep first person consistent.
7. Tell why hair got caught. Go into more detail. This is important. Remember, this "story" is about the blow dryer and me. Use word "slurp" from freewriting.
8. Give Lois's exact words. Hear Lois's voice. Use quotation marks.
9. Maybe take out Lois's name. Just call her "my friend." Adds sarcasm?
10. Rewrite big scene. Expand. Tell about *this moment* in detail. Tell what people said. Use quotation marks for their exact words. Mention "bubble gum"?

Rewrite: (8, 9, 10)

...to my very scalp! Of course everyone else in the room was doubled over with laughter. The girl who had done it just kept saying, "Oh, Kathy, I'm so sorry." Her apologies did not console me. One guy finally managed to control his laughter and come to my side. As he fumbled with the dryer, I picked up what was being said by the others, "painful... all tangled up... she'll miss dinner (and I was getting very hungry)... the expression on her face... it'll take a year to untangle... so funny... so many knots... unbelievable... worse than bubble gum..." Then, the ultimate horror," scissors." I adamantly told them that no one was coming near me with any pair of scissors. No way. Absolutely not. I told them I was willing to stay there all night. I would even eat my dinner with the dryer attached to my head. Although

11 I was extremely upset, I had to laugh at my predicament. I thought about a lot of

12 other predicaments I got into. Like the one when my sneaker got caught in the

Finally the monster and I were
untangled. Thank God! I was so relieved.

13 fence at the zoo. With me in it. ~~Anyway Lois kept~~ *My friend was still* apologizing and begged[*save*] me to[*expand*]

14 let her finish drying my hair. ~~I knew how good she was at hair she always looks~~

15 ~~nice and groomed.~~   So I figure[*save*] accidents happen and I tell her to go ahead. What[*save WHAT A*]

This time not as many hairs got caught but I was
furious at myself. Boy, did I learn my lesson!

16 *big mistake!* a mistake! My hair got caught again. ~~Well, learning lessons may be a part of~~

~~every person's life and I learned mine that Saturday.~~

11. Start new paragraph.

12. Cut out zoo. Zoo is distraction. And another predicament makes me sound like a jerk, as if incident was my own fault, as if I'm always getting into scrapes.

13. Say in a sentence that I finally was untangled.

14. Hear "friend" pleading. Use quotation marks.

15. Cut out. Her talents with hair are irrelevant. Besides, my lesson is "a favor may not be a favor at all." If I let her try again because of her talents, then I sound vain. Keep sympathy with *me*.

16. Say how furious I was with myself. Keep past tense throughout. Say, "I told her to go ahead."

Rewrite: (11–16)

By now, although I was extremely upset, I had to laugh at my predicament. It was a pretty funny situation. Finally the monster and I were untangled. Thank God! I was so relieved. My friend was still apologizing, and I knew she felt terrible. She said, "Listen I have to make this up to you. I swear I'll be careful. Let me finish drying your hair, and I promise you it'll look beautiful." Now it was my turn to feel troubled. This girl was my friend, and I wanted to show her that there were no hard feelings and that I still trusted her. Accidents happen, right? I smiled and told her to go ahead. What a mistake! What a big mistake! You guessed it — my hair got caught again. This time not as many hairs got caught, but I was furious at myself. Boy, did I learn my lesson!

The revised essay

The Blow Dryer and Me

Learning lessons is a part of every person's life. I'm a very trusting person, often getting myself into scrapes I later realize I could have avoided. After one of my scrapes I learned that a favor may not be a favor at all.

This past June, I went away for a weekend trip to New Jersey with a class from school. That Saturday, before dinner, I decided to wash my hair. Afterward, I went into a friend's room to borrow her blow dryer. She said she'd do me a favor, that she'd be happy to dry my hair for me. There were about five other people in the room sitting around talking and waiting for dinner. As my friend dried my hair, I was thinking how great it was that, for once, I didn't have to dry my own hair. Feeling like a prima donna, I closed my eyes and relaxed.

That is, I relaxed until half of the hair on my head got slurped into the blow dryer's motor! My "friend" had moved the blower too close to my hair and some of it was actually inside of the blower. How nice. This monster had slurped down some of my hair from my split ends right down to my very scalp! Of course everyone else in the room was doubled over with laughter and the girl who had committed this mortal sin just kept saying, "Oh, Kathy, I'm so sorry." Her apologies did not console me. One guy finally managed to control his laughter and come to my aid. As he fumbled with the dryer, I picked up fragments of what was being said by the others, "painful . . . all tangled up . . . she'll miss dinner . . . the expression on her face . . . it'll take a year to untangle . . . so funny . . . so many knots . . . unbelievable . . . worse than bubble gum . . ." Then, the ultimate horror, "scissors." I adamantly told them that no one was coming near me with any pair of scissors. No way. Absolutely not. I told them I was willing to stay there all night to untangle myself and I would even eat dinner with the dryer attached to my head if I had to.

By now, although I was extremely upset, I had to laugh at my predicament. It was a pretty funny situation. Finally the monster and I were untangled. I was so relieved. My friend was still apologizing, and I knew she felt terrible about the mess she had gotten me into. She said, "Listen I have to make this up to you. I swear I'll be careful. Let me finish drying your hair, and I promise you it'll look beautiful." I gave her a long, hard look. This girl was my friend, and I wanted to show her that there were no hard feelings and that I still trusted her. Accidents happen, right? I smiled and said, "Okay." What a mistake. What a big mistake. You guessed it -- my hair got caught again. This time not as many hairs got caught, but I was furious at myself. Boy, did I learn my lesson!

SECOND SAMPLE ESSAY

The early draft of the next essay, "Verbalizing Thoughts," does not show revisions because the changes required additions of whole paragraphs, shifts of parts, expansions, and extensive rewriting. But just as for the preceding essay, the facing page lists reasons for every change, numbered to match the problem as it appears in the early draft. See how these changes respond to some of the questions in the guidelines on pages 91 and 92 of this chapter. The final draft follows on pages 98 and 99.

An early draft

1   Verbalizing Thoughts

2   In the past I would listen to a conversation about the weather and suddenly a

3 thought about Einstein's theory of relativity would pop into my head. Instead of
waiting for my turn to speak, I would interrupt the person who had the floor. But

4 people were turned off by me. They did not listen to what I had to say. I'm human

5 like everybody else, and after a while I finally picked up the hint.

6   Another problem I faced was taking sides. Someone was always displeased with me.

7   I would hear some gossip and since I was always quick to open my mouth, I was
soon a gossip myself. When I heard some gossip about someone I knew I would just
spread it. I didn't realize that the news invariably got back to the person being
talked about. I also soon discovered that the news never came back to them without

8 changes and elaborations. One day I heard news about myself and I realized that my
road to change was longer than I had originally thought.

9   Lately, I have been working at solving some of my problems. There is one major

10 cause of my changed ways of handling my thoughts. I was led to this change by
realizing that once you've verbalized a thought it's too late to take it back.
This had a beneficial effect on me, because I found myself putting my foot in my
mouth much less often than before.

11   When a controversial topic arises now, I attempt to remain neutral if I don't
know much about it. When in doubt, I say nothing. With this philosophy, the worst
that I can be accused of is being neutral. It also prevents you from arguing when
you know there really isn't one <u>right</u> answer.

12   Believing that "empty heads have long tongues" caused me to learn to be silent
when I had nothing to say. I learned this through reading books on Eastern
philosophy, particularly books on meditation and Hatha Yoga. Greater knowledge
may be obtained by listening than by speaking.

13   Reading these books led me to try meditation. Now I can hear and listen
better to my thoughts while I'm silently in meditation.

14

Reasons for revisions

1. This beginning is too specific. Write a new opening paragraph. Thesis should mention both the problem and the solution. It should generalize about how talking "off the top of my head" got me into problems with people. Mention a solution, but don't give it away.

2. Supply a topic sentence about interrupting others. Important idea. Be sure to keep.

3. Einstein's theory sounds like a put-on. It jars me. Eliminate. Use a more believable example, a subject I would be more likely to have on my mind than relativity.

4. Explain *why* people were turned off by me, *why* people did not listen to me. Important.

5. Drop final sentence—it sounds like a cliché. Don't move toward the solution quite yet.

6. This is a good idea. Expand into a full paragraph.

7. This concrete talk about gossip is OK but needs an example and maybe a word or two of transition from the preceding paragraph.

8. Unclear connection between "news about myself" and "my road to change" being so long.

9. Major transition is OK. Structure of paper seems clear. Now entering second major part: the solution to the problem. But need a topic sentence that clearly covers the new few paragraphs. Try introducing Eastern philosophy here, since changes began to happen once I began to meditate.

10. Seems obvious and repetitious here. Save for end?

11. Paragraph needs some tightening, maybe a convincing example. Look up day I wrote in journal on thinking about putting blind children in regular classes. (Change "you" to "me.")

12. Change order. Put this paragraph after one ending "my road to change was longer than I had originally thought." Expand because this is the most outstanding feature of the essay; is the *cause* of all the changes.

13. Move this paragraph along with one above. Add details about procedures in meditating. Add analogy to river and leaf.

14. Need an ending. Should deal with improvement in quality of thoughts since I started to meditate. That is the best, most significant effect. Would be a direct comment on a thesis about talking without thinking.

Verbalizing Thoughts

Many of the problems people have with other people can be traced to what they say to each other. I used to have serious problems in getting along with people because of the way I verbalized my thoughts. I would verbalize <u>all</u> of my thoughts, even the ones "off the top of my head" that I hadn't thought much about at all, and I would do it instantly. I now get along better with people because I have found a way to deal with my thoughts without having to verbalize all of them.

In the past, one of my worst habits was interrupting other people. I would listen to a conversation about a movie, and suddenly a thought about a basketball game would pop into my head. Instead of waiting for a lull in the conversation, I would interrupt the person who had the floor. People were turned off by me. They did not listen to what I had to say because it was usually unimportant and irrelevant and I made no attempt to work it into the conversation.

Another problem I faced was taking sides. If two people were debating a topic, I always found myself agreeing with one of them. The reason for my support usually had nothing whatever to do with the merits of the argument. I might know one of the speakers, or maybe one was a girl I was trying to impress, or maybe I could sense someone having the edge in the argument, because the speaker had either a louder voice or a more spirited vocabulary. As usual, I would speak first and think second. The result was that someone was always displeased with me.

Occasionally I would hear some unpleasant gossip about people I knew, and since I was always quick to open my mouth, I soon became a gossip myself. I didn't realize that the news invariably got back to the people being talked about. I also soon discovered that the news never came back to them without changes and elaborations. I learned this when I heard people saying I had hepatitis when actually I had only sprained my wrist. Such nonsense made me realize the potential danger in talking without thinking.

Lately, I have been working at solving some of my problems. There is one major cause of my changed outlook on verbalizing my thoughts. I learned through reading books on Eastern philosophy, particularly books on meditation and Hatha Yoga, that "empty heads have long tongues," that greater knowledge may be obtained by listening than by speaking. Reading these books led me to try meditation.

Meditation quiets your mind so that your thoughts eventually become clearer. The method is to concentrate on a series of meaningless sounds called your <u>mantra</u>. You say, for example, "Om-m-m, om-m-m," and think only of this sound. When you direct your conscious thoughts towards your <u>mantra</u>, your other, semiconscious, thoughts can flow freely and express themselves.

It is like the way a river will let a leaf flow along with the river until the leaf eventually finds a place to rest on one of the river's banks. In the same way, your thought finally comes to rest in a place in your mind where you can observe it clearly. Meditation gave me the effect I wanted. Now my thoughts have a new outlet for expression. .I am able to hear and listen to my thoughts while I am silently meditating. My thinking is clearer, and I verbalize only my best thoughts.

When a controversial topic arises now, I attempt to say nothing if I don't know much about it. In a discussion last week about whether blind children should go to school in the same classes with sighted children, I kept quiet because I had never thought about it before. But my meditation has been helping me think about it in the sensitive way such a subject deserves.

Although I talk less now, I enjoy people more. I'm not always feeling bad because I just put my foot in my mouth. My thoughts have greater sharpness and I perceive when I can make a contribution to a conversation. Interruptions, gossip, and taking sides are no longer instant ways for me to get attention. Instead, people are beginning to pay attention to what I say.

Remember that writing *is* revising. You are always free to enter your composition at any point and change order, add sentences, delete sections, or change emphasis. You are continually discovering what you *really* want to say. Sometimes you may not find out until you have progressed into your next piece of writing. In any case, don't be tyrannized by your own words. Don't cherish them unduly. You made them up. They belong to you. On another try, you might even do better.

PROOFREADING Once you've written your essay and revised it to your satisfaction, you will want to prepare a final copy to give to your reader. Sometimes your reader is a teacher, but by no means will you go through life preparing final drafts only for teachers in classes. Business letters, letters of complaint or request, reports for a supervisor on a job, or important personal letters that you want to be perfect all require that special and patient attention to the final draft that we call *proofreading*. Reading *proof* means checking copy for errors and making the needed corrections. In the same way, a photographer shows you proofs of photographs that can be touched up to correct the flaws and blemishes you notice. Your final draft, remember, represents *you* and deserves a special, intense final reading to make sure you are represented at your best.

Proofreading is hunting for mechanical errors that can be corrected "locally," and, usually, without further changes in the surrounding context. Proofreading means that you do for yourself what editors do before a manuscript by a professional writer is published. That is not to suggest that professional writers do not proofread their own work. They certainly do; but a publisher's job is to guarantee that no accidental errors exist to distress readers, and so the publisher provides expert backup people, editors and proofreaders, to check every letter and every mark of punctuation on every page. Spelling mistakes, common errors like *there* for *their, to* for *too, its* for *it's, -ie* for *-ei* become a nuisance to a reader. The repetition of a word, an omitted word, half of a set of quotation marks left out, a single mark of parenthesis, a misplaced comma or period, a typographical error, a wrongly used capital letter, or the absence of a capital distracts your reader's attention vrom the meaning of the sentence to the curious look of a word by itself (*vrom?*). And you ought to remember that certain grammatical problems discussed in Part Four of this book —like the *-s* ending or the *-ed* ending—can sometimes be overlooked until you are ready to proofread because matters of correctness can never be at the center of your mind as you put your ideas down on paper.

If careless errors in writing call the reader's attention to a word instead of to an idea, then perhaps the problem itself tells you how to solve it. Looking carefully at every word and at every letter of every word may be the best way to spot careless errors. The technique of proofreading requires you to change your usual way of seeing your work. Some people suggest reading out loud; others say read your writing from the end to the beginning, sentence by sentence. In any case, you've got to slow your reading speed to a crawl. Youve got to look at the makeup of word in in a way that you have not occupy yoursef with in the first heet of writint.

STOP. Did you notice any errors in the preceding sentence? Were you able to catch typographical or spelling errors in the normal pace of your reading? There were seven errors in all:

Youve	for	*You've*
word	for	*words*
occupy	for	*occupied*
yoursef	for	*yourself*
heet	for	*heat*
writint	for	*writing*

plus a repeated *in* at the beginning of a line.

If you caught all seven errors, you are already a skilled proofreader. But if you did not, you might profit from proofreading your work several times, each time on the hunt for one type of mistake. As you write more often, and as other people comment on your work, you will come to know the mistakes you most frequently make. If *-s* endings are your problem, you should proofread one time exclusively for them. If bad spelling is your affliction, then you should proofread once through, word by word, with a vigilant eye for possible spelling devils (see Chapter 17 on spelling). If your typing is shaky, proofread once for typos and correct them carefully with a correction device or in ink. With practice, you will not need to proofread so many times, but you *must* proofread every page, whether handwritten or typed, before you can consider it ready for a reader. And if you write your papers in longhand, be sure to form your letters clearly. Do not conceal your uncertainties about spelling or punctuation behind a smokescreen that will make even those words you are sure of unreadable

Exercise 1 Proofread the following passages carefully. Correct all the errors you find, such as incorrect spellings, punctuation errors, omitted *-s* and *-ed* endings, and omitted words.

1. Many of the problem people have with other people can be trace to what they say to each other. I use to have serous problem in getting along with people because of the way I verbalized my thoughts. I would verbalize *all* of my thought, even the one "of the top of my head" that I hadnt thought much about at all, and I woul do it instantly. I now got along better with people because I hav vound a way to deal with my thoughts without hafiing to verbalize all of then.

2. Learning lessons is a part of evry persons life. Im a very trustinb person, often geting mysef into scraps I later realize I could of avoided. After one of my scraps I learn that a favor may not be a favor at all.

3. Disasters are things that you can read about in the paper everyday. A funny thing about them is that their is nothing real about them I mean I realiz that they realy did happen but not to my little world. Disaster is something that only really bother me when its a disaster effecting my life. When I read in the news paper about a familly dyeing in a fire. I think about it for a minute but then quickily forget it. However if the fire, was on my block, or in my neihborhood, then it would be, a personel disaster. Personel disaster, make me think of God right away and pray for help. Tears usualy acompany my prayers along with steps to remeday the situation. However cruel it may seam I think disaster, ony really effects people when it hit home.

4. Although you have made an apointment with a tutor in the Writin Skills Workshop, you may not aware that you are particapating in a nation wide movment to improfe the writing skill of colege student by inivisual peer instruction. Like, the other srudents in writing workshops around the country, you have come either on your own or at the suggeshun of your instructor. In either case you, will probly agree their is no time to loose. You've decide to invest sometime out of a crowded week and you want you're investment to paid off. The tips that follow will help you make the most of this timely oportunity with a privat teacher. If, you have problems in scheduleing or in working with an assign tutor do not hesitate to see a supervisor and request a change, you are therefore encouraged to keep all your appointments regular.

Part Two

Seeing Sentences

Chapter 6

Finding the Verb and Subject

As we turn now to Part 2, you may feel that you are taking a step backward. If you have tried your hand at essay writing (and we hope you have), you may wonder why you need to work on sentences.

We recently overheard a teacher announce to his students: "Now it's time to study grammar. Ugh." It is no secret that both students *and* teachers often dread the study of grammar, seeing it as a painful enterprise, unrelated to anything in the real world. Many teachers in fact have thrown out the study of grammar, using as their argument several studies suggesting that learning grammar has little to do with improving writing.

The study of grammar alone does not improve writing. *Only writing improves writing*. We have observed, however, that writers who understand the principles of grammar can more easily *control* their writing. Students quietly admit that they are tired of not understanding what fragments and run-ons are; they want to know about sentences because they feel powerless in their writing.

In this book, you can turn to a review of grammmer wherever you need to—in Chapters 6 and 7, which deal with the subject-verb unit and basic patterns, or Chapters 8 and 9, which emphasize combining sentences. We know of an *advanced* writing course where students turned to the material in Chapter 6 because they wanted to know, once and for all, what a sentence was. The point is that inexperienced and advanced writers often do not know what they need to know about sentences. We hope that you will use the chapters in this section as you and your instructor see fit and that you will feel the strength all writers feel as they get grammar under control.

Can you unscramble these sentences?

nut Brazil a I'm

SELL WANT CARS TO WE

personal needs he attention

Can you place each of the following words into one blank in the next sentence?

race   racer   racing   raced

That _____ in the silver _____ car _____ in the last _____.

Why is it that you came up with these results?

I'm a Brazil nut.
We want to sell cars.
He needs personal attention.
That *racer* in the silver *racing* car *raced* in the last *race*.

Why didn't you write this?

That racing in the silver raced car racer in the last race.

YOU HAVE THE GRAMMAR The answer is that you have a *grammar* that insists you turn up precisely these results. With this grammar, you are able to unscramble sentences because you intuitively know how sentences in your language are put together. The grammar requires one kind of word for each slot, and you have a natural feel for fitting that kind of word into its place in the sentence.

You've had this grammar for a long time. By the time you reached first grade, you were already an expert in your language. You had absorbed a grammar, that is, a way of creating and understanding English sentences. And now, as you continue to create sentences, each one will be brand new, but each one will be understandable to other speakers of the language. That's quite amazing, when you stop to think about it.

This chapter will tell you what you need to know about sentences so that you can *see* sentences in your writing. Seeing sentences in your writing involves two things. First, it involves avoiding nonsentences—fragments—in your writing. Second, it involves actually trying your hand as a writer of sentences. You may be like many students who write short, abrupt sentences most of the time because you don't want to make mistakes. You play it safe, but your sentences are "Dick and Jane" sentences. You're not sure what a *fragment* is, but you think that writing short sentences will help you avoid them. The "labels" of grammar are mysterious to you. *Subject* and *verb, phrase* and *clause* have fuzzy meanings. Sometimes they mean one thing, and sometimes they mean another. Worse, now that you're in college, your confusion about sentences worries you because you know that your writing somehow depends on understanding sentences.

MUHAMMAD ALI'S OWN STORY

THE GREATEST   Love at first sight

Soviets demand Mideast talks

THE GREATEST BOOKS
EVER WRITTEN

The words on this page were taken from the media—from newspaper headlines and magazine advertisements—from the language you see all around you. Which of these illustrations are sentences, and how do you know? Is "Love at first sight" a sentence? Why or why not? Is "Soviets demand Mideast talks" a sentence? Why or why not?

The language you see and hear all around you is filled with bits and pieces of sentences as well as with sentences. In college writing, the accepted grammatical unit is the sentence. Fragments will not do; you are expected to write complete sentences. So, even though you've been speaking sentences for years, you need to *see* sentences and to understand what makes up sentences in order to write them.

For a moment, let's compare speaking and writing. When you speak, you rely on gestures and pauses, intonations and inflections to get your message across. If someone dashes in front of a car, you might scream, "Hey!" or "Look out!" or you might push the person out of the way of the oncoming car. Your actions are not limited to words on paper. When you speak, you can change your mind in the middle of a sentence; you can smile or wink or cough or emphasize a particular word by raising your voice. You often use very few words to communicate with others:

"Did you see the game last night?"
"Yeah."
"Good, huh?"
"Terrific."

In writing, since you can't rely on gestures or screams or shoves to convey your message, you need to spell out your ideas in sentences, which are relationships between ideas. The simplest sentence relates two ideas in a subject-verb unit. For example, an idea of fish and an idea of swimming produce this sentence:

Fish swim.

Or the idea of the Giants and the idea of winning produce this sentence:

Giants win.

These are sentences because each contains a *subject-verb unit.* Every sentence must contain a subject-verb unit.

Any two words strung together do not produce a sentence:

fish dogs
Giants winning
boys girls
is are
finally faithfully
into on

Only when two words together make up a subject-verb unit is there the possibility of a sentence. In the section beginning on page 108, we will look specifically at how to *find* these subject-verb units.

Throughout the next few chapters, we'll be looking at the grammar of the sentence—how words are put together to form sentences. We'll be moving toward a *working definition* of a sentence, that is, a definition that will *work* for you when you need to test your own writing for sentence completeness according to standard English grammar.

But *finding* subjects and verbs is not the whole story; you need to *write* sentences and believe in your potential to create sentences in endless combinations, in endless shapes and sizes. You can write very short sentences:

Groucho snickered.
Harpo smirked.

You also can write sentences that go on and on as you add to the few basic sentence patterns. The *Guinness Book of World Records* tells us that:

A sentence of 958 words appears in *Cities of the Plain* by Marcel Proust and one of 3,143 words with 86 semicolons and 390 commas occurs in the *History of the Church of God* by Sylvester Hassell of Wilson, North Carolina, c. 1884. . . . A report of the President of Columbia University, 1942–43, contained a sentence of 4,284 words.

Guinness does not report a sentence by James Joyce, in his novel *Finne-gans Wake,* that goes on for twenty-eight pages. Here is a fairly "short" sentence by Herman Melville of only ninety words or so:

Whenever I find myself growing grim about the mouth; whenever it is a damp, drizzly November in my soul; whenever I find myself involuntarily pausing before coffin warehouses, and bringing up the rear of every funeral I meet; and especially whenever my hypos get such an upper hand of me, that it requires a strong moral principle to prevent me from deliberately stepping into the street, and methodically knocking people's hats off—then, I account it high time to get to sea as soon as I can.

Moby Dick

WHAT'S IN A SENTENCE? If you're not sure how to find the subjects and verbs in sentences, the following pages offer you a way to locate them. At the start, remember that every sentence has two grammatical requirements: a subject and a verb. Every sentence can be thought of as having a *subject slot* and a *verb slot*. These slots must be filled. Because the subject and verb act together as a unit, once you find one part of the unit, it's usually not difficult to find the other part. Keep in mind as you begin your search into the sentence that the subject slot can be filled by *one or more words* and that the verb slot can be filled by *one or more words*.

Finding the verb Every verb in a sentence is connected to time—the past, present, or future. Since verbs have this special quality of showing time, you can find the verb by changing the time in a sentence.

Rich Kids Have Problems, Too

Change time: Rich kids *had* problems, too.
Change time: Rich kids *will have* problems, too.

The word that changes as you change the time is the verb: *have/had/will have.*

Let's look at this more slowly. In a sentence a one-word verb always shows time:

One-word verb	*Sentence*	*Time*
did	Harry *did* it.	past
feel	I *feel* miserable.	present
followed	They *followed* your advice.	past

In a sentence a verb that is more than one word also shows time:

Verb of more than one word	*Sentence*	*Time*
will do	Harry *will do* it.	future
was feeling	I *was feeling* miserable.	past
have followed	They *have followed* your advice.	past

Verbs show different times by changing form. Every verb has several forms. By looking at the following sentences, you can see that all the sentences contain a form of the verb *snicker:*

Groucho *snickers* in all his movies. (present)
Groucho *snickered* yesterday. (past)
Groucho *will snicker* tomorrow. (future)
Groucho and Chico *snicker* frequently. (present)
Groucho *is snickering* right now, wherever he is. (present)

Look at the four forms that come from *snicker:*

snickered

snickers

snicker

snickering

Each of the verbs in the above sentences contains one of the four forms of *snicker:*

snickers

snickered

will snicker

snicker

is snickering

Like *snicker,* most verbs have four forms:

roar	smile	smirk
roars	smiles	smirks
roaring	smiling	smirking
roared	smiled	smirked

(See Chapter 13 for complete lists of verb forms.)

Notice that three of the above sentences contain a one-word verb (*snickers, snickered, snicker*). In the other two sentences, the verb is two words (*will snicker, is snickering*). In each sentence, the verb is connected to time. Since every sentence contains a verb connected to time, *change the sentence time to find the verb.*

1. Read the sentence.

   The ungreening of America begins with careless fire.

2. Change to future time.
   If the sentence is not in the future, change it to future time. Add the word *will* to the sentence. Add the word *tomorrow* to signal the time change:

   (Tomorrow) The ungreening of America *will begin* with careless fire.

3. Change to past time.
   To make certain that you've found the verb, change to a one-word past. Use the word *yesterday* to signal this change:

   (Yesterday) The ungreening of America *began* with careless fire.

4. Find the verb.
   The word that changes is the verb:

   begins
   will begin
   began

Everybody came for a last drink

1. Read the sentence.

   Everybody came for a last drink.

2. Change to future time.
   If the sentence is not in the future, change it to future time. Add the word *will* to the sentence. Add the word *tomorrow* to signal the time change:

   (Tomorrow) Everybody *will come* for a last drink.

3. Change to past time.
   To make certain that you've found the verb, change to a one-word past. Use the word *yesterday* to signal this change.

   (Yesterday) Everybody came for a last drink.

   (The sentence is in the past.)

4. Find the verb.
   The word that changes is the verb:

   came
   will come

You'll be a better person for it.

1. Read the sentence.

   You'll be a better person for it.

2. Change to future time.

   (The sentence is in the future.)

3. Change to past time.

   (Yesterday) You *were* a better person for it.

4. Find the verb.

'll be (will be)
were

The following description, taken from Ernest Hemingway's story "Big Two-Hearted River," is written in past time. The events have already occurred:

Nick laid the bottle full of jumping grasshoppers against a pine trunk. Rapidly he mixed some buckwheat flour with water and stirred it smooth, one cup of flour, one cup of water. He put a handful of coffee in the pot and dipped a lump of grease out of a can and slid it sputtering across the hot skillet. On the smoking skillet he poured smoothly the buckwheat batter. It spread like lava, the grease spitting sharply. Around the edges the buckwheat cake began to firm, then brown, then crisp. The surface was bubbling slowly to porousness. Nick pushed under the browned under surface with a fresh pine chip. He shook the skillet sideways and the cake was loose on the surface. . . .

When it was cooked Nick regreased the skillet. He used all the batter. It made another big flapjack and one smaller one.

By acting as fortuneteller, as one who will predict Nick's actions, you can change the sentences to future time:

(Next summer) Nick will lay the bottle full of jumping grasshoppers against a pine trunk. Rapidly he will mix some buckwheat flour with water and will stir it smooth, one cup of flour, one cup of water. He will put a handful of coffee in the pot and will dip a lump of grease out of a can and will slide it sputtering across the hot skillet. On the smoking skillet he will pour smoothly the buckwheat batter. It will spread like lava, the grease spitting sharply. . . .

The word that changes in the Hemingway description, in each case, is the verb:

Past time	*Future time*
laid	will lay
mixed	will mix
put	will put
dipped	will dip
slid	will slide
poured	will pour
spread	will spread

As you see, in changing a sentence to future time, the spelling of the verb itself may change (*laid* becomes *will lay*), or, the spelling of the basic verb may stay the same (*put* becomes *will put; spread* becomes *will spread*). In each case, however, the word *will* has been added. When you change the sentence time by moving from *past time* to *future time,* the verb shows up. To find the verbs in the rest of Hemingway's sentences, follow the same procedure: change from the one-word past to the two-word future with the word *will:*

Past time	*Future time*
found	will find
sliced	will slice
peeled	will peel
cut	will cut

This contrast between the one-word past and the two-word future (with *will*) should help you find the verb in every sentence.

If a sentence doesn't seem to be in the past time, then shift the sentence to the past. Now you are ready to shift the sentence to the two-word future with *will.* Don't worry about identifying the time of the given sentence, *just make a move.* As long as you change the time, the verb will change also.

Sometimes a part of the whole verb can help you identify it. Remember that the verb slot in a sentence can be filled by a one-word verb or by a group of words called a *verb phrase.*

> One-word verbs: sign, signs, signed
> Verb phrases: will sign, could sign, should have signed, might have signed, must sign, ought to sign

Words like *should, can, could, may, might, ought to, must, have to,* and *need to* are important signals to finding the verb. Whenever one of these words appears in a sentence, you can expect another part of the verb to follow:

> I *should have called* him.
> I *must find* her.
> He *needs to talk* to me.

These words, with meanings of their own, are part of the verb. They signal that more of the verb is to follow. Together with the rest of the verb, they make up the whole verb in a sentence.

Other signals to finding the verb may be less reliable. *Do, does,* and *did; am, is, are, was,* and *were; has, have,* and *had* may be part of a whole verb phrase.

> I *did spend* that money today.
> I *am looking* for work.
> I *have asked* for your help.

But they can also appear in sentences alone as verbs:

> I *did* it.
> I *am* a friend of his.
> I *have* green eyes.

Whether the verb is one word or several words, you can always find the verb by changing it to a one-word past or to a two-word future with *will*.

> Example A I *should have called* him.
> I *called* him.
> I *will call* him.

Should have called is the verb in Example A.

> Example B I *must find* her.
> I *found* her.
> I *will find* her.

Must find is the verb in Example B.

Exercise 1 Find the verbs in the following sentences.

> Example: Soviets demand Mideast talks.
> (Tomorrow) Soviets will demand Mideast talks.
> (Yesterday) Soviets demanded Mideast talks.
> The verb in the example is *demand*.

1. Expos blankety-blank Mets, 7–0, 7–0.
2. The ungreening of America begins with careless fires.
3. TV sets caused 196,000 home fires in the United States in 1974.
4. Little Maria had been hungry all her life.
5. She will never forget the pain of poverty.
6. Market rises sharply during light trading.
7. My daddy's richer than your daddy.
8. Here comes the bride.
9. I lost 7 pounds and 5½ inches off my waist in nine days.
10. Along came the little people.
11. Sailing in the Arctic is a new challenge for a yachtsman.
12. The essence of a well-attired gentleman lies somewhere between his unmistakable style and unerring taste.
13. Getting it together also means keeping it together.

Exercise 2 Change each verb in the following sentences to a one-word past and a two-word future with *will*.

> Example: Steel union accepts contract.
> Steel union accepted contract.
> Steel union will accept contract.

1. Storm toll rises to twenty-six.
2. Everybody came for a last drink.
3. Planes nearly collide.
4. Big plane dives to avert crash.
5. Suspect escapes from hospital.
6. Father knows best.
7. They danced till dawn.
8. Life begins at fifty.
9. You're not getting older. You're getting better.
10. Crime rate spurts in nation.
11. Companies report sales and profits.
12. Ohio State defeats Illinois.

Exercise 3 The following paragraph expresses past time through a single word, the verb *got*. *Got* is such a useful word that it is often overused. Practice working with verbs by replacing each *got* in the paragraph with another verb that expresses a more specific action. Keep the time in the past, and try not to repeat any verbs.

> Example: I got up this morning, got dressed, and got my instant breakfast.
> I awoke this morning, dressed, and drank my instant breakfast.

A Lot of Got

I got up this morning, got dressed, and got my instant breakfast. I got my coat and hat and got the elevator. I got a newspaper at the corner store and got the train. I got to my office and got the morning mail. I got an overdue bill from Con Edison. I got the adjustment manager on the phone and got the matter straightened out. At 10 o'clock, I got a cup of coffee and a doughnut. At 10:15, I got back to work. I got a call from my supervisor. We got together for lunch. I got a tuna sandwich and a cup of coffee. I got back at the office at 1:30 and got caught up on a lot of work. At 5 o'clock, I got my coat and got the elevator and got the train and got home by 6 o'clock. All in all, I got a lot done today.

Exercise 4 After you have rewritten "A Lot of Got," change the time of the paragraph to the future. The sentences will require *will* plus the verb ("I *will awake* tomorrow morning, *will dress*, and *will drink* my instant breakfast"). When there are several verbs connected to one subject, it is all right to carry over the *will* from the first to following verbs ("I *will awake* tomorrow morning, *dress*, and *drink* my instant breakfast").

Verbs and -ing words

In 1903, Wilbur and Orville Wright Were In North Carolina Looking For A High Old Time. They Found It.

The British Are Coming!

Some writers mistake an *-ing* word by itself for the verb in a sentence. An *-ing* word alone is never the verb in a sentence. The verb in every sentence must connect to time—the past, present, or future.

> It *rained.* (past)
> It *is raining.* (present)
> It *will rain.* (future)

The *-ing* word, however, does not specify the past, present, or future. It is a word that suggests continuation, and it must be combined with a time word (*is, was, will be, are, were,* and the like) if it is to be connected to the past, present, or future.

> It *is raining.*
> It *was raining.*
> It *will be raining.*

When the *-ing* word is connected to the past, present, or future, it is part of the verb phrase of a sentence.

Remember: The *-ing* word alone cannot be used as the verb.

NO:	YES:
It *happening* right now.	It *is happening* right now.
She *sailing* in the bay.	She *was sailing* in the bay.
The Yanks *coming.*	The Yanks *are coming.*

An *-ing* word may have nothing to do with the verb in a sentence. Try the test for a verb on this sentence:

1. Read the sentence.

   Toby walked down the street, eating a salami sandwich.

2. Change to future time.

   (Tomorrow) Toby will walk down the street, eating a salami sandwich.

3. Locate the verb.

   walked
   will walk

But what about *eating? Eating* and the words that follow it provide more information about the basic sentence ("Toby walked down the street). The *-ing* word is not part of the verb in this sentence. Connected to a time word, *eating* could be part of a verb in another sentence:

Toby *was eating* a salami sandwich.

Here *eating,* combined with the time word *was,* is the verb in the sentence. In the original sentence, the *-ing* word combined with other words to make Toby more specific—"Toby walked down the street (eating a salami sandwich)."

Test these sentences for the verb:

1. Read the sentence.

   The ungreening of America begins with careless fire.

2. Change to future time.

   (Tomorrow) The ungreening of America will begin with careless fire.

3. Locate the verb.

   begins
   will begin

1. Read the sentence.

   Clutching her shopping bag, the old woman climbed into the bus.

2. Change to future time.

   (Tomorrow) Clutching her shopping bag, the old woman will climb into the bus.

3. Locate the verb.

   climbed
   will climb

You
start
slowly,
gliding easily,
breaking the silence
with the soft "shhh....shhh...." of your skis
as they sweep up sprays of powder
at each turn.
Here and there,
the sun catches snow crystals,
turning them to diamond dust.
Ever so gently
the slope steepens,
drawing you into widening, flowing, sensuous arcs.
And suddenly, magically,
you've found the mountain's rhythm!
You're flying, soaring, feeling your spine tingle, seeing the trees
rush by in a blur, laughing inside at the incredible feeling
of freedom and beauty and speed,
laughing because you just can't believe anything in this world
could be
so
much
fun.

This is skiing—and in less time than you think, you can be doing it!
The Killington Accelerated Ski Method makes it as easy as learning
to fox trot. And this is Killington—52 fantastic trails on 4 separate
peaks, a full 6-month season, heaps of beautiful snow, hosts of lodges,
restaurants, night spots, a super ski school...and the inspiration for
the sentiments expressed above. For more details on the Killington
ski scene, send for our 36-page booklet. Write: Killington Ski Resort,
147A Killington Road, Killington, Vermont 05751.

For reservations, call us TOLL FREE between October 1 and April 1
800-451-4221 if you live in New England or New York (except 802 and 716 area codes)
800-451-4281 if you live in any other state east of the Rockies.
802-422-3333 if you live in any area not included above: this is a toll call.
Or ask your travel agent about Killington Travel 7-day IT (inclusive tour) travel plans.

WATCH OUT FOR FRAGMENTS

REMEMBER: The *-ing* word is a major cause of sentence fragments.

NO:	YES:
Here and there the sun catches snow crystals. *Turning them into diamond dust.*	Here and there the sun catches snow crystals, turning them into diamond dust.
You're flying, soaring, feeling your spine tingle. *Seeing the trees rush by in a blur. Laughing inside at the incredible feeling of freedom. Laughing because you just can't believe anything in the world could be so much fun.*	You're flying, soaring, feeling your spine tingle, seeing the trees rush by in a blur, laughing inside at the incredible feeling of freedom, laughing because you just can't believe anything in the world could be so much fun.
Toby walked down the street. *Eating a salami sandwich.*	Toby walked down the street, eating a salami sandwich.
In 1903, Wilbur and Orville Wright were in North Carolina. *Looking for a high old time.*	In 1903, Wilbur and Orville Wright were in North Carolina looking for a high old time.

Exercise 5 Locate the verbs in these sentences, which were taken from the skiing advertisement on page 118.

1. You start slowly, gliding easily, breaking the silence with the soft "shhh . . . shhh . . ." of your skis.
2. Ever so gently the slope steepens, drawing you into widening, flowing, sensuous arcs.
3. You're flying, soaring, feeling your spine tingle, seeing the trees rush by in a blur, laughing inside at the incredible feeling of freedom and beauty and speed, laughing because you just can't believe anything in this world could be so much fun.
4. This is skiing.
5. The Killington Accelerated Ski Method makes it as easy as learning to fox trot.

Exercise 6 The following sentences are taken from Ernest Hemingway's story "Big Two-Hearted River." Determine in which sentences the *-ing* word is part of the verb and in which sentences the *-ing* word is not part of the verb.

1. The tent was starting to get hot.
2. The grasshoppers were already jumping stiffly in the grass.
3. In the bottle, warmed by the sun, they were jumping in a mass.
4. Nick laid the bottle full of jumping grasshoppers against a pine trunk.
5. He slid the grease sputtering across the hot skillet.
6. On the smoking skillet he poured smoothly the buckwheat batter.
7. It spread like lava, the grease spitting sharply.
8. The surface was bubbling slowly to porousness.
9. Nick took it from his hook book, sitting with the rod across his lap.
10. He tested the knot and the spring of the rod by pulling the line taut.
11. It was a good feeling.
12. Rushing, the current sucked against his legs.
13. He floated rapidly, kicking.
14. In a quick circle, breaking the smooth surface of the water, he disappeared.

Exercise 7 The following groups of words are fragments—bits and pieces of sentences. The *-ing* word cannot be used alone as a verb; it must be used with a form of the verb *to be* (*is, are, were, was, will be,* and the like) or it must be turned into a one-word form of the verb that is itself a time word (*raced, jumped*). Rewrite each fragment so that it is a sentence.

Example: Dominick racing for the streetcar.
          Dominick was racing for the streetcar.
                            or
          Dominick raced for the streetcar.

1. Jack and Jill kissing passionately on the bus.
2. The playground swarming with children.
3. The policeman dodging a bullet.
4. The old man chasing a young girl.
5. Vivian crying in her bedroom.
6. Walter tickling her toes.
7. Sara staring at the television set.

Exercise 8 Add a sentence before or after each group of words below. The group of words should make the meaning of the added sentence more specific.

Example: Carrying a striped umbrella.
Before: Seymour strolled down the avenue, carrying a striped umbrella.
After: Carrying a striped umbrella, Seymour strolled down the avenue.

1. crashing through the picture window
2. pinching her rosy cheeks
3. zipping her dress
4. curling up on the sofa
5. making a toasted cheese sandwich
6. waltzing into the room
7. racing for a taxi
8. leaning on the counter

For more exercises on sentence fragments, see Chapter 8.

Verbs and adverbials

WATCH OUT FOR ADVERBIALS

Other words in sentences designate time, but they are *not* verbs. Do not mistake words like *now* and *then* and *tomorrow* for verbs. As you have seen, verbs usually change form to show time:

**They satisfied then.
They satisfy now.**

New Chesterfield Filters.

       v
They *satsify* now.
        v
They *satisfied* then.
         v
They *will satisfy* tomorrow.

Words like *now, then,* and *tomorrow* do not have different forms. These words, called *adverbials,* narrow down the time of the verb. You make the time of your sentence more specific when you use an adverbial. In the following sentences, the verb phrase *will land* designates future time. By adding adverbials, you make the time in the future more specific.

      We will land on Mars.
      We will land on Mars tomorrow.
      In a few days we will land on Mars.
      We will land on Mars by the year 2000.
      We will land on Mars within the next century.

The following adverbials all relate to time:

sometimes	yesterday morning
always	three seconds ago
later	then
tomorrow	usually
yesterday	in the meantime
in six months	last week

Other adverbials designate place (*nearby, there, here*) or manner (*slowly, quickly, peacefully*). See Chapter 9 for a discussion of adverbials as modifiers.

Finding the subject   The same word does not necessarily function in the same way in every sentence. A word that is a verb in one sentence may be a subject in another. Consider these lines by Elizabeth Barrett Browning, from her poem "How Do I Love Thee?":

	S-V UNIT
How do I love thee? Let me count the ways.	I do love
I love thee to the depth and breadth and height	I love
My soul can reach, when feeling out of sight	
For the ends of Being and ideal Grace.	
I love thee to the level of every day's	I love
Most quiet need, by sun and candle-light.	
I love thee freely, as men strive for Right;	I love
I love thee purely, as they turn from Praise;	I love
I love thee with the passion put to use	I love
In my old griefs, and with my childhood's faith.	
I love thee with a love I seemed to lose	I love
With my lost saints—I love thee with the breath,	I love
Smiles, tears, of all my life!—and, if God choose,	
I shall but love thee better after death.	I shall love

Throughout the poem, the word *love* is used as a verb (except in the line "I love thee with a love . . ." where the first *love* is used as a verb and the second is used as a noun). In most cases, the subject-verb unit is *I love*. In the following sentences, the word *love* is used as the *subject* of each sentence:

	S-V UNIT
Love is blind.	Love is
Love is love's reward.	Love is
Love is the salt of life.	Love is

The subject-verb unit is a grammatical requirement of every sentence. Every sentence must contain both a subject and a verb. But what is a subject and how do you find it in a sentence? The beginning of this chapter states that the subject-verb unit is a relationship between two ideas. One idea is expressed as a verb, a time word, and the other is expressed as a subject:

birds	and	flying	= birds fly
fish	and	swimming	= fish swim

Connecting ideas means connecting subjects to verbs. Because every subject is connected to a verb, one way to find the subject of a sentence is first to locate the verb—as you did in the preceding section. Once you locate the verb, you can track down the subject by finding the idea that connects to the verb. You do this by setting up a *who* or *what* question:

1. Read the sentence.

   Rich kids have problems, too.

2. Locate the verb.

   have

3. Ask *who* or *what?*

   Who or what have?

4. The subject fills the *who* or *what* slot.

   Rich kids   have

1. Read the sentence.

   Nothing slows you down.

2. Locate the verb.
   slows

3. Ask *who* or *what?*

   Who or what slows?

4. The subject fills the *who* or *what* slot.

   Nothing   slows

1. Read the sentence.

   Expos blankety-blank Mets.

2. Locate the verb.

   blankety-blank

3. Ask *who* or *what?*

   Who or what blankety-blank?

4. The subject fills the *who* or *what* slot.

   Expos   blankety-blank

   In most sentences, the subject comes before the verb. This is the usual English word order. Once you've found the verb, the subject generally will come before it. Occasionally, however, the subject follows the verb; in *there* and *here* sentences, the subject always follows the verb.

HERE COMES THE BRIDE...

Consider this sentence:

ALONG CAME THE LITTLE PEOPLE

Once you've found the verb, *came,* you then ask, who or what came? *Along* is not the idea that tells who or what came. *Along* cannot come. You must look to the other side of the verb for the answer:

SUBJECT	VERB
The little people	came.

Phillies Defeat Pirates

The subject-verb unit is a logical unit with its meaning largely determined by word order. In the sentence "Phillies defeat Pirates," *Pirates* could not be the subject because of its *position* in the sentence. If you want *Pirates* to be the subject, your sentence would have to read like this:

Pirates defeat Phillies.

The subject in the following sentence is *man:*

Man Bites Computer

If the computer were the subject, the sentence would read:

Computer bites man.

Whatever the subject of a sentence is, it can be connected to its verb by asking a *who* or *what* question. In the sentence, "Down fell the rain," the verb is *fell.* To the question "Who or what fell?" the answer is *rain.*

To double-check that the subject you find is correct, you can also:

Look for logical units of meaning in the sentence.

or

Look at the word order in the sentence. The subject almost always comes before the verb.

Exercise 9 Write sentences in which you use each of the following words as verbs. Use any form of the verb you wish. Then write a second set of sentences, using these *same* words as subjects.

Example: The Rolling Stones often *play* at the coliseum.
The *play* attracted huge crowds.

1. love	8. saw
2. hate	9. cut
3. scratch	10. cheat
4. laugh	11. burn
5. flower	12. run
6. crash	13. milk
7. fly	

Exercise 10 Find all the subject-verb units you can in this table-of-contents page.

January 19, 1976   Vol. 5 No. 2

4 | **Mail**

6 | **Up Front**
Lt. Kenneth O'Neil dogs the trail of a mystery bomber——Henry Wynberg's vision of his lost love, Elizabeth Taylor——Sen. James Abourezk, a South Dakota Arab, speaks for the Indians——Dallas quarterback Roger Staubach points toward the Super Bowl showdown

19 | **Lookout**
Artist Guy Peirce——Equities analyst Denise Selden

20 | **Couples**
If Lee Majors is worth $6 million, Farrah is priceless

24 | **Arts**
Red and Mimi Grooms convert Manhattan into 3-D Pop art

29 | **In His Own Words**
Psychiatrist Robert Coles views a generation of troubled kids

39 | **For a Song**
Soft rockers Seals & Crofts sing for gold records and God

42 | **People Puzzle**

Exercise 11 Find all the subject-verb units you can in these television-page cutouts.

10:00 a.m. ⑨ Creature From The Black Lagoon Richard Carlson, Julia Adams. Originally produced in 3-D, this better-than-average science fiction tale has more than its share of visual gimmicks. The plot, complete with bewildered scientists and love interest, appears no innovation, but fans of this genre will enjoy it. (1954) ☆☆☆

1:00 p.m. ⑤ World Without End Hugh Marlowe, Nancy Gates. An interesting premise makes this sci-fi tale a bit more absorbing than some comparable films. A space flight intended for Mars goes through the time barrier and ends up on Earth during the 26th century. (1956) ☆☆

④ Lifestyles With Beverly Sills — "The Alcoholics." Miss Sills' guests include two reformed alcoholics: actor Patrick O'Neal and Rebecca Sanchez, director of the Alcoholic Program at Prospect Hospital in the Bronx.

8:30 p.m.
⑬ Best of Ernie Kovacs — (Repeat) The entire program will be a collage of some of the off-beat musical interpretations of the late comic, Ernie Kovacs.

10:00 p.m.
② Miss USA Beauty Pageant — Fifty-one beauties vie for the coveted title of "Miss USA 1977."

11:30 p.m.
④ Saturday Night — Actress Shelley Duvall is guest host and the Not Ready for Prime Time Players put on their hilarious skits.

Chapter 7

Seeing Sentence Patterns

SENTENCE PATTERNS

Every sentence must contain at least one subject-verb unit. But sentences, as you know, are made up of more than subjects and verbs. Look at this sentence:

Every sentence has room for expansion. The subject can be expanded, the verb can be expanded, and the whole sentence can be expanded. Every sentence, regardless of how long or complex it is, falls into one of the basic English sentence patterns. Seeing sentences means knowing the basic patterns so that you can see the structure of an English sentence.

Seeing sentences also means understanding that the basic patterns can be developed and that the slots in each sentence can be filled by one word or by a group of words. You saw in Chapter 6 how the verb can be one word:

> Alex *telegrammed* Loretta.

or a verb phrase:

> Loretta *will telegram* Alex.

Now you'll see that the subject can also be one word or a group of words.

The command pattern There are two required slots in every sentence: the subject slot and the verb slot. The words that fill these two slots form the subject-verb unit. In one sentence pattern, the *command,* the verb slot is filled, but no word fills the subject slot. This does not mean that a command has no subject; rather, the subject is said to be "implied," which means that it is not stated but understood. The command orders someone to do something, but the someone is not named:

> Watch out!
> Close the door.
> Don't do that.

If you were in a room with a friend, and part of the ceiling started to fall, your friend might scream, "Watch out!" You'd know, without question, that your friend was speaking to you. Like "Watch out!" every command speaks to "you"—to one person or to a group of people. This is what is meant by the implied "you" in the command.

The command qualifies as a sentence because it has the two required sentence elements—a subject and a verb—even though the subject is not stated. Commands are commonplace, especially in advertisements that invite you to buy something or mail something or save something. "You" in the subject slot is understood in the following advertisements:

Exercise 1 Find as many subject-verb units as you can in this letter. List the commands.

*   *   *

DEAR ABBY: When does a mother say no? I am 77, have worked in factories for 44 years and have raised three sons alone after an early divorce. Two of my boys are fine. The youngest is my problem.

Mel, now 50, was in the Navy and graduated from college under the G.I. bill, but his big dream was getting into show business. (He is a good musician but not good enough to work the big time, which is all he will settle for.)

I have lost track of all the money Mel has cost me. It seems like all I do is draw money out of the bank for him. My income is only $260 a month, and I am eating up my nest egg.

My other sons tell me I am a fool and that Mel can work if he wants to. (They have both sent him money but gave up.) Mel can sell, but he hates to get up in the morning and work a regular routine. He still thinks he can make it in show business.

How can a mother refuse her son? I love him so much. He never married. What am I to do?   **—MOTHER LOVE**

DEAR MOTHER: Don't send Mel another penny! He probably never stuck with a job because he knew he didn't have to—Mother would support him. Tell him that you are all tapped out.

Not everyone can do what he wants to do for a living, in which case he does what he can. At 50, it's time Mel became a man. And at 77, you've earned a rest.

*   *   *

Exercise 2 Record ten bumper-sticker slogans you have seen on passing cars. Identify which are sentences and which are not. Identify those sentences that are commands.

Subject-verb pattern

SUBJECT	VERB
Groucho	snickered.
Harpo	smirked.

Grammatically, the subject-verb unit stands as a sentence. Notice how often newspaper headlines use this basic sentence pattern:

Agatha Christie   dies

Musicians   return

Planes   Collide

Storm Toll   *Rises*

Subject–linking verb–completer pattern

SUBJECT	LINKING VERB	COMPLETER (COMPLEMENT)

Seymour is my brother.
Seymour looks angry.

LOVE IS MONEY

Linking verbs are forms of the verb *be: am, are, is, were, was, have been, will be, can be, should have been:*

I *am* hungry.
Bill *was* thirsty.
Mary *has been* sick.
Lunch *will be* ready soon.

Linking verbs are also verbs that express feeling, growing, sensing, tasting, becoming, and the like:

I *am getting* tired.
He *felt* energetic.
Her perfume *smells* terrible.
She *looked* doubtful.
He *seemed* angry.
The milk *tasted* sour.

Every sentence containing a linking verb has a *sentence completer*. A completer is a word or group of words that follows the verb to complete the meaning of the S-V unit. The completer of a linking verb always refers back to the subject, telling us something about the subject:

S	LV	C
Seymour	is	my brother.

(*My brother* tells who Seymour is.)

S	LV	C
Seymour	looks	angry.

(*Angry* tells how Seymour looks.)

Caroline is a princess.
Money is the root of all evil.
The price is right.

A linking-verb sentence is like an equation in which the verb acts as an equal sign.

Caroline is a princess.
Caroline = a princess.

WATCH OUT FOR <u>THERE</u> AND <u>HERE</u>

The words *there* and *here* are never subjects. They are words that point to the subject, which comes after the verb:

There is *my friend.*
Here comes *the bride.*
There goes *my dear wife.*
There are *my brothers.*

Subject–action verb–completer pattern

SUBJECT	ACTION VERB	COMPLETER (DIRECT OBJECT)
Blast	**rips**	**oil tank**
Martha	**leaves**	**hospital**
Rangers	Conquer	Bruins
Babies	*need*	*shoes*
Companies	*Report*	*Sales*
Ohio State	Defeats	Illinois
Eastham college student	receives	his BA
Alabama	*Tops*	*L.S.U.*

The direct object In this pattern, the completer that follows the verb refers to something other than the subject. This completer, which introduces a new element into the sentence, is called a *direct object,* and the verb in this pattern is often called an *action verb.*

Compare these patterns:

Subject-verb:	The Red Sox won.
Subject–linking verb–completer:	The Red Sox are the winners.
	The Red Sox $=$ the winners.
Subject–action verb–completer:	The Red Sox beat the Pirates.
	The Red Sox $\neq$ the Pirates.

The subject-verb pattern relates two ideas in the subject-verb unit:

    S   V
The Red Sox won.

In the subject–linking verb–completer pattern, the verb links the subject and a completer that identifies or describes the subject. The verb in this pattern is similar to an equal sign:

      S   LV   C
The winners are the Red Sox.
The winners = the Red Sox.

      S   LV   C
The Red Sox are the winners.
The Red Sox = the winners.

The subject–action verb–completer pattern calls for a different kind of completer:

      S   V   C
The Red Sox beat the Pirates.

This completer, *the Pirates,* is not equivalent to *the Red Sox. The Pirates* adds a new element to the sentence.

    The Red Sox ≠ the Pirates.

This completer, called the direct object, does not refer back to the subject. See Chapter 13, p. 340, for a discussion of the way verbs work in sentences.

The indirect object A second object, called the *indirect object,* can come between the action verb and the direct object. The indirect object tells to whom or for whom something is done:

SUBJECT	ACTION VERB	INDIRECT OBJECT	DIRECT OBJECT
Felix	gave	Oscar	a Rolls Royce.
Lucy	offered	Desi	a ride.
Ethel	made	Fred	a pie.

You can tell if a word or phrase is an indirect object by turning it into a *to* or *for* phrase following the direct object:

Felix gave a Rolls Royce *to Oscar.*
Lucy offered a ride *to Desi.*
Ethel made a pie *for Fred.*

The passive The *passive* is a transformation of an action-verb sentence. Watch the shifts in these sentences:

Active: A lion bit the trainer.
Passive: The trainer was bitten by a lion.

The object of an active sentence becomes the subject of a passive sentence:

Active: A lion bit *the trainer.*
Passive: *The trainer* was bitten by a lion.

And the subject of the active sentence becomes part of a by-phrase in the passive:

Active: *A lion* bit the trainer.
Passive: The trainer was bitten *by a lion.*

See Chapter 13, page 341, for a discussion of the verb in the passive.

WATCH OUT FOR PUNCTUATION AND CAPITALIZATION

Every sentence must begin with a capital letter. Every sentence must end with a period, question mark, or exclamation point. Make sure to punctuate each of your sentences as a sentence.

For statements, use a period:

Giants live here.

For questions, use a question mark:

Why do you smoke?
When are you going to quit smoking?

WHAT KIND OF NUT ARE YOU?

For exclamations, use an exclamation point:

You must be kidding!

Perk up!

Exercise 3 Write sentences using these words as verbs. Use any form of the verb you wish, and punctuate each sentence appropriately. Once you've written your sentences, identify which pattern each falls into: command, subject–verb, subject–linking verb–completer, or subject–action verb–completer.

1. speak
2. listen
3. cry
4. die

5. live
6. believe
7. give
8. build

9. smack

10. hit

11. drive

12. is

13. become

14. feel

15. taste

16. smell

Exercise 4   Using the words listed below as subject, write a sentence for each of the three patterns.

Example: man
Subject–verb: The man tripped.
Subject–linking verb–completer: The man is a photographer.
Subject–action verb–completer: That man lost his umbrella.

1. woman

2. lasagna

3. skunk

4. snake

5. trombonist

6. motorcycle

7. hi-fi set

8. shoe

9. conductor

ADDING ADVERBIALS TO THE BASIC PATTERNS

THIS
SENTENCE
GOES ON
AND ON
AND ON
AND ON
AND ON
AND ON
AND ON
AND ON
AND ON
AND ON
AND ON
AND ON
AND ON
AND ON
AND ON
AND ON
AND ON
AND ON

Although subjects, verbs, and completers make up the basic sentence patterns, you aren't limited to speaking or writing sentences like these:

Groucho snickered.
I'm spoiled.
Babies need shoes.

Sentences can go on and on and on as you add to the patterns, often by using *adverbials*. Adverbials are single words (adverbs) or groups of words that answer such questions as *when? where? how? why? how much?* or *how often?* in a sentence.

Note where the adverbials are placed in the following sentences and how they develop the basic patterns:

      s   **v**
Groucho snickered.
Groucho snickered *on my birthday*.
Groucho *often* snickered.
Only three seconds ago, Groucho snickered.
Groucho snickered *playfully*.
Groucho snickered *like a little kid*.
Groucho snickered *in the back of the recording studio*.
Groucho snickered *at the bar of Snickers*.

Some adverbials can be shifted from one part of the sentence to another:

Groucho *often* snickered.
Often Groucho snickered.
Groucho snickered *often*.

"I lost 7 lbs. and 5¾ inches off my waist in only 9 days!"

In only 9 days I lost 7 lbs. and 5¾ inches off my waist.

When you write, you aren't limited to writing simple S-V units; you can expand your ideas in various ways. Note how the adverbial in the following sentence develops the S-V unit, *Guadalupe died*.

       S   V

Guadalupe died *as she had lived, without medical care, in unrelieved pain, in hunger, worrying about how to pay the rent or raise money for the bus fare for a trip to the hospital, working up to the last day of her life at the various pathetic jobs she had to take to keep going, leaving nothing of value but a few old religious objects and the tiny rented space she had occupied.*

Oscar Lewis

There is room in *each* of the basic patterns for the adverbial. (Chapter 9 on modifiers discusses the adverbial, as well as other ways to develop the basic sentence patterns.)

FILLING THE SUBJECT AND COMPLETER SLOTS

Look again at the basic sentence patterns:

subject–verb:	S V The Red Sox won.
subject–linking verb–completer:	S LV C The Red Sox are the winners.
subject–action verb–completer:	S V C The Red Sox beat the Pirates.

In each of these patterns, the subject and completer slots can be filled by a single word or by a group of words:

          S   V
The first baseman   screamed.

          S
The first baseman, clutching
his empty mitt,   V
                                     screamed.

	S		V
	The first baseman, clutching his empty mitt and hanging on to the leg of the umpire,		screamed.

	S	LV	C
	The woman	is	my grandmother.

	S	LV	C
	The woman serving the sandwiches	is	my grandmother.

	S	LV	C
	The woman in the yellow bikini serving the sandwiches	is	my grandmother.

	S	LV	C
	My favorite activity	is	sleeping.

	S	LV	C
	My favorite activity	is	sleeping in the afternoon.

	S	LV	C
	My favorite activity	is	sleeping on the job behind the meat refrigerator in the back of the A&P in the afternoon.

	S	V	C
	The man	entered	the room.

S		V	C
The man, carrying a box of chocolate-covered cherries,		entered	the hospital room.

S		V	C
The rain-drenched man, carrying a dripping box of chocolate-covered cherries,		entered	the empty hospital room.

As a writer of sentences, you have the power to expand the sentence slots by adding words that convey your meaning more precisely. Although in this chapter we are concerned with the basic patterns and with the opportunities that exist to expand the slots in sample sentences, keep in mind the sentences you will write. The possibilities discussed here are also opportunities for your own sentences. In the remainder of this chapter, we will look more closely at the subject and completer slots.

Nouns Single words that fill the subject and completer slots are often *nouns*. All the words on the following page are nouns and can function in sentences as subject or completer. Typically, nouns are defined as *names*—of persons, places, things, ideas, and qualities. A practical test for a noun is to see how it behaves.

power

Ideas

Lemon

people

authority

JAPAN China

Canadian

inspiration

SAVINGS

improvement

Doris Lessing

things

Europe

AMERICA

mover

Rabbit

THOMAS JEFFERSON

RAINBOW

Eve

1. Most nouns change their spelling to show a change from one to more than one (from singular to plural):

thing	things
authority	authorities
improvement	improvements
woman	women

2. Most nouns change their spelling to show possession:

Japan	Japan's
rabbit	rabbit's
woman	woman's

3. A noun can always be introduced by *a, an,* or *the:*

thing	a thing
authority	the authority
improvement	an improvement

4. *This, that, these,* and *those* often signal a noun:

thing	these things
woman	that woman
rabbit	those rabbits

Pronouns   Pronouns are words like *I, you, he, she, it, we, they, him, her,* and *them.* Certain pronouns, called *subject pronouns,* fill the subject slot:

Subject pronouns

I	we
you	you
he, she, it	they

> *He* needs personal attention.
> *I* also need personal attention.
> *We* all do.

We've got a secret!

Other pronouns, called *object pronouns,* fill the direct object slot:

Object pronouns

me	us
you	you
him, her, it	them

> Roger hit *him* again.
> Will you leave *her* alone?
> Pauline missed *them* for the second time.

See Chapter 15 for a full discussion of pronouns and the ways they are used.

Noun phrases   A *phrase* is a group of related words that does not contain a subject-verb unit. Once you surround a single word (such as a noun) with words that make it more specific, the single word becomes part of a phrase. Watch how that happens.

Noun: woman
Noun phrase: the woman in the yellow bikini serving the sandwiches

Like a noun, a noun phrase can fill the subject or completer slot:

s	v	c
The woman	is	my grandmother.

s	v	c
The woman in the yellow bikini serving the sandwiches	is	my grandmother.

s	v	c
My grandfather	is	that man.

s	v	c
My grandfather	is	that man in the tan swimsuit serving the beverages.

Watch how the subject slot expands:

	S	V	C
Noun:	Any person	has	one of these.

Noun phrase: Any well-heeled, self-made, sophisticated, uninflated, pompous, narcissistic, quixotic, average, elegant, down-home person

	S	V	C
	Any person	has	one of these.

Prepositional phrases Prepositions—words like *up, on, in, at, from, of,* and *with*—connect a single word or a group of words to another part of the sentence. The preposition and the words it connects are called a *prepositional phrase.* Remember, a phrase is a group of words with *no* subject-verb unit. A prepositional phrase often accompanies the noun in the subject or completer slot:

	S	V	C
	The man	entered	the room.

S		V	C
The man			
in the purple striped		V	C
pajamas		entered	the room
prepositional			*at the top of the stairs.*
phrase			prepositional phrases

	S	V
	The woman	fainted.

S		V
The woman *in front of me*		fainted.
prepositional		
phrase		

	S	V	C
	Seymour	followed	the woman.

	S	V	C
	Seymour	followed	the woman *of his heart.*
			prepositional phrase

Prepositional phrases also work as adverbials to describe the verb.

I was reading.
I was reading *at the kitchen table.*

See Chapter 9 for a fuller discussion of prepositional phrases as modifiers.

The following is a list of familiar prepositions:

aboard	besides	on
about	between	over
above	beyond	per
across	by	round
after	concerning	since
against	despite	through
along	down	throughout
alongside	during	till
amid	for	to
among	from	toward
around	in	under
as	inside	until
at	into	up
before	like	upon
behind	near	via
below	of	with
beneath	off	within
beside	onto	

Here is a list of combinations of words used as prepositions:

ahead of	in front of
according to	in place of
apart from	in spite of
because of	in view of
contrary to	on account of
up to	out of

Sometimes prepositions function as part of the verb and are called *particles.*

Verbs with particles

drop off	The mailman *dropped off* the package.
call up	We *called up* for an appointment.
look over	I *looked over* the checkbook.
think through	You need to *think through* the problem.

See how these words can be used as prepositions in prepositional phrases:

The pencil dropped *off the table.*
Ross called *up the stairs.*
Sharon looked *over the wall.*
I thought about Bess *through the night.*

Verbals and verbal phrases   A verbal may look like a verb (*seeing, covered, to stay*), but it does not behave like a verb in a sentence since it does not connect to time.

A verbal can work in a sentence in the following ways:

1. By filling the subject and completer slots
2. By describing the subject and completer

Verbal

seeing
believing

s	v	c
Seeing	is	*believing.*

to love

s	v	c
To love	is	all.

recycling

s		v
Recycling		**works.**

screaming

	s	v
The	*screaming* woman	burst into the room.

covered

s	v	c
Henry	brought	a *covered* casserole to the dinner.

See Chapter 13, page 345, for a discussion of verbs and verbals.

A verbal works along with the words that follow it to form a *verbal phrase.* Like a verbal, a verbal phrase can fill the subject and completer slots:

Verbal phrase

being a kid   ***Being a kid again isn't always funny!***

to get the facts   **Our job is to get the facts**

Verbal phrases can also work as modifiers:

Verbal phrase

covered with mud   The children, *covered with mud,* burst into the kitchen.
seeing the accident   The woman, *seeing the accident,* called the police.

For a fuller discussion of verbals as modifiers, see Chapter 9.

Exercise 5   Expand each noun below by adding a prepositional phrase to it. Use the expanded unit as a subject or a completer in a sentence.

Example: man
Subject: *The man in the grey flannel suit* jumped onto the train.
Completer: My father is *the man in the grey flannel suit.*

1. dog
2. table
3. pipe
4. hands

5. conversation
6. corner
7. tray
8. flashlight

Exercise 6   Use each of the following verbals or verbal phrases as subjects or completers in your own sentences.

Example: combing
Subject: *Combing his beard* is Brian's favorite pastime.
Completer: Brian enjoys *combing his beard.*

1. recycling
2. seeing
3. being a kid again
4. to visit Paris

5. to get the facts
6. relaxing after dinner
7. to win the race
8. smoking his pipe

To summarize, there are two important things to remember about phrases:

1. A phrase is a group of words that does *not* contain a subject-verb unit:

the lost child
the man in the grey flannel suit
to get the facts
smoking a cigar
Paul Newman's big blue eyes

2. Any phrase can become a part of a sentence:

Phrase	*Sentence*
the lost child	The salesman comforted *the lost child*. (S) (V) (C)
the man in the grey flannel suit	*The man in the grey flannel suit* tripped. (S) (V)
to get the facts	My job is *to get the facts*. (S) (V) (C)
smoking a cigar	*Smoking a cigar* was Groucho's trademark. (S) (V) (C)
Paul Newman's big blue eyes	*Paul Newman's big blue eyes* are color-blind. (S) (V) (C)

WATCH OUT FOR FRAGMENTS

When phrases are punctuated like sentences, they are called *fragments*. Watch out for prepositional phrases and verbal phrases that are lopped off a sentence and punctuated like separate sentences.

NO:	YES:
Henry visited his mother. *During the mid-semester break.* (prepositional phrase)	Henry visited his mother during the mid-semester break.
Caroline watched her brother play tennis. *In the afternoon.* (prepositional phrase)	Caroline watched her brother play tennis in the afternoon.
Charlie watched the woman. *Running for her bus.* (verbal phrase)	Charlie watched the woman running for her bus.
Lauren ate a thick pancake. *Covered with maple syrup.* (verbal phrase)	Lauren ate a thick pancake covered with maple syrup.
Wilbur and Orville Wright were in North Carolina. *Looking for a high old time.* (verbal phrase)	Wilbur and Orville Wright were in North Carolina looking for a high old time.

If you have a problem with fragments, see Chapter 8, page 176.

Exercise 7 Turn these phrases into sentences.

Example: the tall woman in the black suit
The tall woman in the black suit is an investigative reporter for her college newspaper.

1. wishing you were here
2. bumping her head
3. the setting sun
4. in spite of his misery
5. up, up, and away
6. blue suede shoes
7. tumbling out of bed
8. to go to the store
9. flashing lights
10. was driving down the street
11. down by the river
12. after the dance
13. star-crossed lovers
14. running for the bus
15. eating a nectarine
16. killed a spider
17. painted a room
18. to win the game
19. until the end of my shift
20. my grandmother's candlesticks

Clause A *clause* is a group of related words that contains at least one subject-verb unit.

Each of the following clauses contains a subject-verb unit. These clauses work as sentences:

s   v
Time flies.

s   v
Final exams are scheduled for next week.

s   v
I'll be studying all weekend.

Other clauses, although they contain a subject-verb unit, cannot work as sentences:

when time flies
although final exams are scheduled
because I'll be studying the whole weekend
whoever passes the test
whatever he pleases

Clauses that begin with words like *although, because,* and *when* cannot work as sentences. They will be discussed in Chapter 8. Here we are interested in clauses that begin with words like *whoever, whatever, who,* and *what,* for these clauses can fill the subject and completer slots:

        s   v   c
    Whoever passes this test   passes the course.

The subject of the sentence is:

    Whoever passes this test

                                    s   v
The subject is itself a clause: whoever passes this test

        s   v   c
    Jeffrey   always   does   whatever he pleases.

The completer of the sentence is:

    whatever he pleases

                                    s   v
The completer is also a clause: whatever he pleases

Inflation may sometimes be what's needed

SUBJECT	VERB	COMPLETER
		s v
Inflation	may be	*what's needed.*

'Propaganda' Is What You Don't Agree With

SUBJECT	VERB	COMPLETER
		s v
Propaganda	is	what *you don't agree with.*

Exercise 8 The following are bits and pieces of sentence patterns. Taken from newspapers, they reflect much of the language that you see all around you. By adding any words you need, change these pieces of sentences into sentences.

Example:

Flu absenteeism on the rise

Flu absenteeism on the rise is a piece of a sentence; it needs a verb, a time word, to qualify as a sentence:

Flu absenteeism *is* on the rise.

Sharing a Swamp With the Gators

Bus shelters? Yes

Wholesale prices stable

LOW COST ALTERATIONS OUR SPECIALTY.

GRAND OPENING

A happy marriage of career and family

Workshop for crafts

Different strokes for different folks.

Hate to have breakfast alone?

Complete satisfaction

Experience recommended

Meeting special needs

Making Connections

Chapter 8

English offers you a variety of ways to make connections among your ideas so that you aren't limited to delivering your ideas one by one in short, disconnected sentences. Instead, your writing can show exactly how your ideas relate to one another. What you write can reveal the fascinating processes of association that go on, sometimes at breakneck speed, as you think.

But when you speak and when you write, you often depend on different ways to join your ideas. Observe the connectors you use in speech by listening as you and your friends talk. For example, do you hear many *and*'s? Notice how the telephone operator, whose talk about her job is recorded below, links her ideas:

> Say you've got a guy on the line calling from Vietnam, his line is busy *and* you can't interrupt. God knows when he'll be able to get on his line again. You know he's lonesome *and* he wants to talk to somebody, *and* there you are *and* you can't talk to him. There's one person who feels badly *and* you can't do anything. When I first started, I asked the operator *and* she says, "No, he can always call another time."
>
> One man said, "I'm lonesome, will you talk to me?" I said, "Gee I'm sorry, I just can't." *But* you can't. I'm a communications person *but* I can't communicate.
>
> I've worked here for two years *and* how many girls' first names do I know? Just their last name is on their headset. You might see them every day *and* you won't know their names. At Ma Bell they speak of teamwork, *but* you don't even know the names of the people who are on your team.

It's kind of awkward if you meet someone from the company *and* say
"Hi there, Jones," *or* whatever. It's very embarrassing. You sit in the
cafeteria *and* you talk to people *and* you don't even know their names.
I've gone to a lot of people I've been talking to for a week *and* I've said,
"Tell me your name."

Studs Terkel

This is speech, with its abundance of *and*'s. One sentence adds to another,
creating a flow of ideas that threatens to keep on going. You could add on
to any of her sentences:

You know he's lonesome and he wants to talk to somebody and there you
are and you can't talk to him and you feel really bad and then you remember that that's the way things go and that makes you even sadder and
then . . .

In your speech you often add one sentence to another, one thought to another by the use of words like *and, but,* and *or.*

Without these connectors, you might be limited to speaking short,
monotonous sentences like these:

Albert loves Myrtle. Myrtle is beautiful. Myrtle is wealthy. Myrtle owns
her own stables. Albert doesn't even own a pair of shoes. Albert wants to
marry Myrtle. Albert lives on a farm. Myrtle lives in town. Albert wants
to raise chickens. Myrtle is attracted to Raymond. Raymond loves Sybil.
Sybil loves Walter. Raymond is attracted to Myrtle's wealth.

Monotony isn't the only problem in these sentences; they're also confusing
because the relationships among ideas are fuzzy. You must hunt for connections. Does Albert want to marry Myrtle *because* she is beautiful or *because*
she is wealthy or *because* he needs a pair of shoes? Will Myrtle consider
Albert *when* she is attracted to Raymond? Will Raymond pursue Myrtle
although he loves Sybil? And what about Walter?

Fortunately, you don't always create such havoc in your sentences,
even when you speak, for you connect your ideas through two important
thinking processes—*coordination* and *subordination.* You use these processes unconsciously in your speech. The telephone operator in describing
her job didn't say to herself, "Now I'm going to use a subordinator in this
sentence," or "This sentence calls for a coordinator." In writing, however,
where you can't let your sentences drift on and on, where they can't hang
next to each other like wash on a line, you need to become conscious of
your thinking processes so that you can choose the connectors that get
closest to the heart of your meaning.

Let's stop for a moment to define these two words. *Coordination*
means putting together ideas or things or people that are of equal rank or
importance—policemen, cabinet members, professors, and so forth. *Subordination,* on the other hand, means putting ideas or things or people into
positions where one is of greater rank or importance than another. Police-

men are subordinate to the chief of police; cabinet members are subordinate to the President; professors are subordinate to the dean.

In speech we often coordinate ideas by putting one idea right next to another, joining them with an *and*. We treat these ideas equally. We also use subordinators, words like *because, although,* and *if,* to give some ideas more emphasis than others. In writing, we are often more deliberate about our choice of connectors than we are in speaking. As writers, we become more aware of our options for making connections. As you think about making connections among ideas in sentences, keep in mind that these natural thinking processes work similarly in the whole essay.

Consider an essay that you are writing. In your essay, some ideas are more important to your thesis than others. Your thesis is the *primary* idea, the one big idea that controls the whole essay. The rest of your ideas are subordinate—or of secondary importance—to that thesis. These subordinate ideas are usually the supporting examples and details that you use to explain your thesis.

Thesis—primary idea
Supporting ideas—secondary ideas that are subordinate to the thesis. They support the main idea and make it more specific.

If you are writing an essay about childhood injustice, you may develop four paragraphs about how young children are treated unjustly. The plan for your essay may look like this:

Thesis: Young children are often unjustly treated by adults.

> Paragraph 1: Parents spank children.
> Paragraph 2: Parents don't listen to children.
> Paragraph 3: Parents don't take children seriously.
> Paragraph 4: Parents make decisions without consulting children.

These four examples are subordinate to the thesis. But, individually, the four examples are coordinate to each other because they depend equally on the main idea, the thesis. They are all of equal rank, and together they all stand in a subordinate way to the big idea, your thesis.

On a smaller scale, a sentence can be similar to an essay because, in addition to the one big idea expressed by the subject, verb, and completer, a sentence can add other subordinate ideas. Such a sentence is said to have a main idea and *subordinate* ideas.

But there are also some sentences that differ from essays because they can add another big idea of equal rank to the first. Such a sentence expands by a different process. It is said to have two (or more) *coordinate* ideas. As we examine these two processes in the sentence, keep in mind that subordination and coordination make use of different connectors:

thoughts are of equal value

one thought is more important than others

Coordinators		*Subordinators*	
and	as	if	
but	before	unless	
or	because	since	
nor	although	when	
for	until	who	
yet	so that	which	
so	that	while	

Exercise 1 Record a conversation between two people (between your friends or members of your family or two characters in a television program). Note the words that hold ideas together. Are they coordinators or subordinators or both?

COORDINATION Coordination is the linking of similar sentence parts or similar whole sentences of equal rank. Since there are few coordinators in the English language, it's a good idea to memorize them so that you'll become aware of how and when you're making connections in your own sentences. These are the coordinators:

and	for
but	yet
or	so
nor	

Coordinating words and phrases in a series

Petunias, begonias, ferns, cucumbers, and your family will enjoy outdoor living more under a Howmet Domed Skylight patio cover.

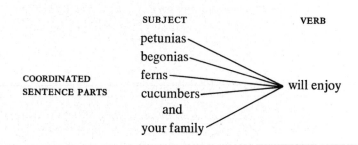

COORDINATED
SENTENCE PARTS

SUBJECT
petunias
begonias
ferns
cucumbers
and
your family

VERB
will enjoy

Wheaties® suits you, courts you and keeps you hopping.

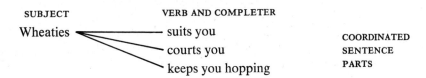

SUBJECT

Wheaties

VERB AND COMPLETER

suits you

courts you

keeps you hopping

COORDINATED
SENTENCE
PARTS

Read the following fable, "The Bear Who Let It Alone," and notice how often sentence parts are coordinated:

THE BEAR WHO LET IT ALONE

In the woods of the Far West there lived a brown bear who could take it *or* let it alone. He would go into a bar where they sold mead, a fermented drink made of honey, *and* he would have just two drinks. Then he would put some money on the bar *and* say, "See what the bears in the back room will have," *and* he would go home. *But* finally he took to drinking by himself most of the day. He would reel home at night, kick over the umbrella stand, knock down the bridge lamps, *and* ram his elbows through the windows. Then he would collapse on the floor *and* lie there until he went to sleep. His wife was greatly distressed *and* his children were very frightened.

At length the bear saw the error of his ways *and* began to reform. In the end he became a famous teetotaller *and* a persistent temperance lecturer. He would tell everybody that came to his house about the awful effects of drink, *and* he would boast about how strong *and* well he had become since he gave up touching the stuff. To demonstrate this, he would stand on his head *and* on his hands *and* he would turn cartwheels in the house, kicking over the umbrella stand, knocking down the bridge lamps, *and* ramming his elbows through the windows. Then he would lie down on the floor, tired by his healthful exercise, *and* go to sleep. His wife was greatly distressed *and* his children were very frightened.

Moral: You might as well fall flat on your face as lean over too far backward.

James Thurber

The following sentence demonstrates coordinated verbs:

He would reel home at night, kick over the umbrella stand, knock down the bridge lamps, and ram his elbows through the windows.

SUBJECT	VERB
he	would reel
	kick over
	knock down
	ram

All of the actions in this sentence belong to the bear (*he*), but you don't need to repeat *the bear* or *he* each time you connect a verb to him, nor do you have to repeat *would* each time you add another verb.

Just as you can attach a number of verbs to one subject, you can also attach a number of subjects to one verb:

His wife, his son, his daughter, his mother-in-law, his first-grade teacher, and his dog were greatly distressed by his behavior.

SUBJECT	VERB
his wife	
his son	
his daughter	
his mother-in-law	were distressed
his first-grade teacher	
his dog	

In the same way, you can write compound subjects (more than one subject) and compound verbs (more than one verb):

His wife, son, daughter, and mother-in-law stood on their heads, turned cartwheels, kicked over the umbrella stand, knocked down bridge lamps, and rammed their elbows through the windows.

COMPOUND SUBJECT	COMPOUND VERB
his wife	stood
son	turned
daughter	kicked over
mother-in-law	knocked down
	rammed

Coordination offers you shortcuts and helps you eliminate unnecessary words. The Dale Carnegie Course advertisement on the next page combines two sentences:

The Dale Carnegie Course helps you manage your job more effectively.
The Dale Carnegie Course helps you manage your life more effectively.

**The Dale Carnegie Course
helps you manage
your job and your life
more effectively.**

The Dale Carnegie Course helps you

your job   *and*   your life.

Notice the coordination of sentence parts in this Subaru advertisement; one subject is connected to three verbs:

THE SUBARU 4 WHEEL DRIVE WAGON CLIMBS LIKE A GOAT, WORKS LIKE A HORSE AND EATS LIKE A BIRD.

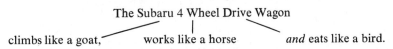

climbs like a goat,   works like a horse   *and* eats like a bird.

When you coordinate ideas, you make connections among ideas that you think are related as equals. The same subject repeated in several sentences may not advance your writing and often becomes tedious to read:

> He would reel home at night.
> He would kick over the umbrella stand.
> He would knock down the bridge lamps.
> He would ram his elbows through the windows.

But a swift act of coordination brings these ideas together in the same sentence and allows your reader to see how all the verbs are, in fact, connected to the same subject:

> He would reel home at night, kick over the umbrella stand, knock down the bridge lamps, and ram his elbows through the windows.

When you coordinate sentence parts, be careful to combine similar grammatical structures:

> The bear enjoyed *drinking* and *lecturing*.

> The bear loves to *drink* and *lecture*.

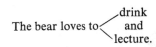

If you mix up grammatical structures, you jolt your reader:

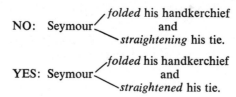

NO: Seymour *folded* his handkerchief and *straightening* his tie.

YES: Seymour *folded* his handkerchief and *straightened* his tie.

When coordinated sentence parts have the same grammatical structure, they are said to be *parallel.*

Nonparallel: Sharon needs *a coffee break* and *resting for fifteen minutes.*

Parallel: Sharon needs *a coffee break* and *a fifteen-minute rest.*

Nonparallel: *In the morning, in the afternoon,* and *when it's evening,* Henry races his German shepherd around the block.

Parallel: *In the morning, in the afternoon,* and *in the evening,* Henry races his German shepherd around the block.

When you coordinate sentence parts, your reader expects to see similar grammatical patterns. Once you set up an "in the morning" phrase, your reader naturally looks for other "in the _____" phrases. That is what is meant by parallel construction.

TIPS FOR WRITERS—PARALLELISM

Note the power of this coordinated sentence by Antoine de Saint-Exupery:

> A pilot's business is *with the wind, with the stars, with night, with sand, with the sea.*

Saint-Exupery uses a writing technique called *parallelism.* He selects coordinated sentence parts that are not only close in grammatical structure and meaning but also close in length. He does this with the repetition of *with,* which slows you down and makes you consider each of the coordinated parts:

> with the wind
> with the stars
> with night
> with sand
> with the sea

Without the *with*'s, we would rush right through the sentence:
A pilot's business is with the wind, the stars, night, sand, the sea.

Study the passage; begin to recognize your options for repeating a word like *with,* choosing commas or coordinators, adding or deleting a final *and.* Saint-Exupery omits the final *and* to guarantee identical emphasis in all. Try yourself out as a writer.

Exercise 2   In each of the following exercises, follow the directions for connecting sentence parts:

1. **a.** Using a sentence in one of your recent essays, write a sentence in which you connect at least six verbs to one subject. Or write a new sentence using these verbs: *work, scrimp, save, bank, invest, worry.*
   b. Revise a sentence in one of your recent essays so that you connect at least six subjects to one verb.
   c. Revise a sentence in one of your recent essays so that you write a sentence with multiple subjects and multiple verbs.

2. Imitate Saint-Exupery's sentence on page 154 by connecting six similar phrases that begin with *with.*

3. Using the following sentence as a model, write a sentence that connects several phrases beginning with an *-ing* word.

   He would turn cartwheels in the house, kicking over the umbrella stand, knocking down the bridge lamps, and ramming his elbows through the windows.

4. Using the following sentence as a model, write a sentence that connects several phrases beginning with the word into:

   Alice fell into the rabbit hole, into the world of Wonderland, and into trouble.

5. Coordinate the parts within a long sentence in an essay you have written. Be sure to use parallel grammatical structures.

Exercise 3   The following sentences, taken from student writing, all contain non-parallel grammatical structures. Rewrite each sentence so that the coordinated parts are parallel.

1. She was an awkward student and never paying attention to class assignments.

2. The four of us were just happy, innocent young girls with our only objective being to relax and having a good time.

3. I feel that the three reasons I have mentioned—profitable to advertisers, pressure from women's groups, and acceptance by the public of women's changing roles—have all contributed equally in bringing about the change in television commercials.

4. Women are presented as passive, submissive, vain, empty-headed creatures who either belong in the kitchen or mothering children.

5. Women buy the food, the detergent, the soaps, the Charmin.

6. Men fly the airlines, take the vacations, buy the cars, use the credit cards, and are responsible for writing the checks.

7. In every show there is a winning debate between Archie and his son-in-law, Mike (who is of Polish descent, long-haired, and a liberal).

Combining whole sentences by coordination   Combine whole sentences into one coordinated sentence when you want to give them equal emphasis. Remember, a sentence is a group of words that contains at least one subject-verb unit. A clause that can stand as a sentence is called an *independent clause.*

1. Join independent clauses with a comma plus a coordinator:

Drivers shout, dogs bark, and the race is on!

_____, and _____
_____, but _____
_____, or _____
_____, nor _____
_____, for _____
_____, yet _____
_____, so _____

He hit a home run, and the crowd went wild.

2. Join independent clauses with a semicolon and omit the coordinator when you want to show a *close* connection between the clauses.

_____; _____

He hit a home run; the crowd went wild.

When you combine whole sentences, you tell your reader that these sentences belong together. The period separates one sentence from another, but the comma and coordinator allow your reader to see how the ideas in the sentences are connected. If you string one sentence to another, you give *all* of your sentences equal emphasis:

He hit a home run, and the crowd went wild, and I was at the refreshment stand buying popcorn, and I missed the excitement.

The reader of this sentence would conclude that the batter's hitting the home run, the crowd's cheering, and your buying popcorn and missing the excitement are on the same level in your mind, that they are all of the same importance to you. Don't string your sentences together with *and*'s unless you want to emphasize them all equally.

You also need to consider *why* you combine two sentences. There must be some relation between their ideas. In the following sentence, it would be difficult for your reader to understand why these two clauses are connected:

I like chocolate-covered raisins, but Albert was reading a book.

What do these two activities have to do with each other? Your reader could make more sense out of the following connections:

I like chocolate-covered raisins, but Albert prefers coconut patties.

I tried to speak to Albert, but he was reading a book.

Similarly, when you use semicolons to join sentences, you must be sure that the sentences are *closely* connected. If you use too many semicolons, your reader will have difficulty seeing the relationship among your ideas:

He hit a home run; the crowd went wild; I was at the refreshment stand buying popcorn; I missed the excitement.

Use the semicolon only when you want to add a brisk, forceful connection between two sentences. The semicolon doesn't slow your reader down as the period does. Rather, it acts like a weak period, signaling to your reader that two sentences are so closely connected that they should be read together:

He hit a home run; the crowd went wild.
The bomb exploded; the bridge collapsed.
He fell from the ladder; his knee split open.

In each of these sentences, the semicolon indicates the close connection that exists between the two combined sentences.

As a writer, remember that you have options in punctuating sentences. A period stops your reader. A semicolon invites your reader to see a close connection between two sentences. A comma and coordinator show your reader that you are combining sentences containing related ideas. To make your sentences varied and interesting, use all three options in your writing:

_____. _____.
_____; _____.
_____, and _____.

Study the effective use of coordination in the following passages:

Everybody's got a Helene Tucker, a symbol of everything you want. I loved her for her goodness, her cleanliness, her popularity. She'd walk down my street, and my brothers and sisters would yell, "Here comes Helene," and I'd rub my tennis sneakers on the back of my pants and wish my hair wasn't so nappy and the white folks' shirt fit me better. I'd run out on the street. If I knew my place and didn't come too close, she'd wink at me and say hello. That was a good feeling. Sometimes I'd follow her all the way home and shovel the snow off her walk and try to make friends with her Momma and her aunts. I'd drop money on her stoop late at night on my way back from shining shoes in the taverns. And she had a Daddy, and he had a good job. He was a paper hanger.

Dick Gregory

WATCH OUT FOR COMMAS WITH COORDINATION

Use commas between words, phrases, or short clauses in a series. A series is more than two items.

Series: *apples, peaches, pears,* and *plums*

Words: Steven loves *apples, peaches, pears,* and *plums.*
a, b, c, and d

Phrases: A pilot's business is *with the wind, with the stars, with night, with sand, with the sea.*
a, b, c, d

Short clauses: *Drivers shout, dogs bark,* and *the race is on.*
a, b, and c

Do not use a comma every time you use an and.

Do not use a comma between two words or two phrases joined by a coordinator.

NO:	YES:
a, and b	a and b
Steven loves apples, and pears.	Steven loves apples and pears.
Harriet signed, and delivered the letter.	Harriet signed and delivered the letter.
A pilot's business is with the wind, and with the stars.	A pilot's business is with the wind and with the stars.

Use a comma and a coordinator between independent clauses.

_____, and _____ .

His wife was very distressed, and his children were very frightened.

He couldn't promise to change his behavior, but he promised to try.

He hit a home run, and the crowd went wild.

If you have problems with run-on sentences, see pages 173–176.

Do not use a comma when the and combines the elements of a compound subject or a compound verb:

The crowd *went* wild *and rushed* onto the field.

Do not begin a new line with a comma.

NO:	YES:
Seymour loves apples, peaches , pears, and plums.	Seymour loves apples, peaches, pears, and plums.
His wife was very distressed , and his children were very frightened.	His wife was very distressed, and his children were very frightened.

TIPS FOR WRITERS—USING <u>AND</u> AND <u>BUT</u> EFFECTIVELY

1. Coordinators link sentences, even when they're separated by a period. At one point or another, you may have been told that you can't begin a sentence with *but* or *and*. But that isn't so. Begin a sentence with *and* to emphasize the addition of an idea; begin with *but* to emphasize contrariness.

You can make mistakes with any typewriter.
But this one can also erase them.

2. A writer may use *and* between combined sentences for special effects. Combining sentences with *and* creates the effect of conditions co-existing or events happening all at the same time. Consider these coordinated sentences by Ernest Hemingway:

> It was morning and had been morning for some time and he heard the plane. It showed very tiny and then made a wide circle and the boys ran out and lit the fires, using kerosene, and piled on grass so there were two big smudges at each end of the level place and the morning breeze blew them toward the camp and the plane circled twice more, low this time, and then glided down and leveled off and landed smoothly and, coming walking toward him, was old Compton in slacks, a tweed jacket and a brown felt hat.

Use a series of *and*'s deliberately when you want to create these special effects.

I was not a dull or energyless child, or neglected by my parents. Our house was full of books and paints, and sometimes I did choose to draw or ride my bike. But the picture of my childhood that comes to mind is one of a dimly lit room in a small New Hampshire town and a girl listening, leaden-eyed, to some talk-show rendition of "I Left My Heart in San Francisco." It is a picture of myself at age 8, wise to the ways of "Vegas," the timing of stand-up comics, the marriages of Zsa Zsa Gabor, the advertising slogans of Bufferin and Fab.

Joyce Maynard

SUBORDINATION Subordination is the placing of one sentence part in a position where it depends on another sentence part and makes that part more specific. A subordinated part never stands alone as a sentence.

You only ride like a Pacer if you're wide like a Pacer.

Knicks Are Ousted in Playoffs As Rockets Post 118-86 Victory

If You Like Fresh Herring, Your Ship Is In

All of the above sentences contain subordinated parts:

if you're wide like a Pacer
as Rockets post 118–86 victory
if you like fresh herring

Words like *if, because,* and *when* are subordinators when they precede the subject in a subject-verb unit. A subordinator introduces an incomplete expression that is connected in a sentence to an independent clause:

If you smoke menthol, you're still subjecting yourself to some of the dangers of tars and nicotine.

No matter how brief or incomplete an expression seems, if it has a subject-verb unit and no subordinator, it qualifies as a sentence:

The sun sets.
It's there.

A sentence may take on meaning from sentences before and after it:

Are you looking for the shoe horn? I just saw it. *It's there.* It's next to the clothes brush.

Out of context, *It's there* has little meaning. But it is a sentence, nonetheless, because it has a S-V unit and no subordinator introducing it. But if a subordinator introduces the clause, the clause is *dependent:*

WHEN THE SUN SETS

The subordinator always signals that the dependent clause connects in a specific way to another clause that has no subordinator. In such a sentence, the clause *without* the subordinator is an independent clause:

DEPENDENT   INDEPENDENT
CLAUSE   CLAUSE

When the sun sets, I feel romantic.

BECAUSE IT'S THERE

DEPENDENT   INDEPENDENT
CLAUSE   CLAUSE

Because it's there, *I feel better.*

If you want to reach me you'll find me reading

COSMOPOLITAN®

DEPENDENT CLAUSE   INDEPENDENT CLAUSE
If you want to reach me   you'll find me reading *Cosmopolitan.*

It's tough to cut a whisker when it's down.

INDEPENDENT CLAUSE   DEPENDENT CLAUSE
It's tough to cut a whisker   *when* it's down.

Hobbies Boom As The Economy Fizzles

INDEPENDENT CLAUSE   DEPENDENT CLAUSE
Hobbies boom   *as* the economy fizzles.

The power of subordinators The following words are subordinators when they are used to introduce a dependent clause:

after	unless	whom
before	as	whose
when	if	which
until	as if	that
since	so that	whoever
while	in case	whomever

as soon as	how	whichever
once	what	whenever
by the time	where	whatever
because	who	wherever
although		

Each word establishes a different relationship or a different connection between ideas.

When you coordinate ideas, you *add* one idea to another, giving equal emphasis to all your ideas. One thing happens and then another and then another:

> I was in a wretched mood last night, and I went to the movies and saw a mystery, but in the last five minutes the projector broke, and I don't know "who dunnit," but I can't go back tonight, and I'll have to find someone who knows the ending, and by the end of the film I was in a vile mood.

When you subordinate one idea to another, you relate them by showing the specific connection between them in your sentence. You can, for example, make one activity the *cause* of another:

> Because I was in a wretched mood last night, I went to the movies.

You aren't adding one thought to another; you're establishing a cause-and-effect relationship between the two ideas. This is a much more complex thought process than adding.

Different subordinators produce different connections:

Subordinator	*Purpose*
Although I was in a wretched mood last night, I went to the movies.	Writer implies that he doesn't enjoy going to the movies if he's in a wretched mood, but he went anyway.
Whenever I'm in a wretched mood, I go to the movies.	Writer asserts that the movies is where he goes when he's in a wretched mood. This mood may be a recurring event.
If I'm in a wretched mood, I go to the movies.	Writer asserts that he goes to the movies on the condition that he's in a wretched mood. The suggestion is that the mood is not habitual.
Because I was in a wretched mood, I went to the movies.	Writer now makes his going to the movies a result of his wretched mood.

As a writer, think about your connectors and search for the particular connector that expresses precisely the way one idea relates to another in your sentence.

By changing *if* to *because* or *since*, you can move from uncertainty to certainty:

If you're considering college, you should consider how "Army Officer" would look on your job application.

Certainty: Because you're considering college, you should consider how "Army Officer" would look on your job application.

Uncertainty:

If you love to think...wrestle with great ideas... become outraged occasionally... laugh out loud...and–above all– be informed...you are invited to enter a trial subscription to *Saturday Review*

Certainty: Since you love to think . . . you are invited to enter a trial subscription to *Saturday Review*.

You can express time relationships by choosing subordinators that convey time:

Phillies Sink Reds As Schmidt Stars

Hobbies Boom As The Economy Fizzles

Exercise 4 Combine each of the following pairs of sentences into one sentence containing an independent clause and a dependent clause. Emphasize the ideas you think are important, and choose appropriate subordinators.

Example: **a.** I slept ten hours last night.
   b. I'm still tired.
   Although I slept ten hours last night, I'm still tired.

1. **a.** I was taking a bath.
   b. The phone rang.
2. **a.** Henry's shoelace broke.
   b. He was late for work.

3. **a.** I had to walk to the train station.
   b. The car wouldn't start.

4. **a.** I adore her.
   b. She is witty.

5. **a.** I stayed up until three o'clock in the morning.
   b. I couldn't sleep.

6. **a.** The Education Department fired four instructors.
   b. The Education Department suffered a budget cut.

WATCH OUT FOR COMMAS WITH DEPENDENT CLAUSES

When you begin a sentence with a dependent clause, the clause is usually followed by a comma.

1. *Until you do it,* you'll never know how much good you can do.
2. *When a whisker is down,* it's tough to cut it.
3. *Because I was in a wretched mood last night,* I went to the movies.

Often, when the introductory dependent clause is short, there is no comma after it.

Whenever it rains the streets get wet.
After he died they sold the house.

The comma is usually not used when the dependent clause follows the independent one.

1. You'll never know how much good you can do *until you do it.*
2. It's tough to cut a whisker *when it's down.*
3. I went to the movies last night *because I was in a wretched mood.*

Who, *whom*, *whose*, *which*, *that*   These five connectors also work as subordinators. They differ from other subordinators, however, in that they stay close to the word or words they describe.

He is a man *who* needs a vacation.
Millie visited Pauline, *whose* house is near the bay.
This is the house *that* I want to rent for the summer.
Allan gave Janet an emerald, *which* is as big as half a dollar.

THE MAGAZINE THAT WINS
52 PRIMARIES A YEAR IS THE ONE
THAT REACHES THE PEOPLE WHO LISTEN.

The magazine *that wins 52 primaries a year* is the one *that reaches the people who listen.*

                     s   v   c
Basic sentence: The magazine is the one.

In each case, a dependent clause is connected to a word and makes its meaning more specific. (See Chapter 9 for additional discussion of clauses as modifiers.)

CHECK LIST FOR A SENTENCE This check list for a sentence summarizes the materials in Chapters 6, 7, and 8. Use the check list when you are proofreading your essays to make certain that you've written whole sentences.

1. A sentence must contain at least one subject-verb unit:

Johnny Bench whacked a home run.

To find the subject-verb unit, locate the verb by changing the sentence time:

Johnny Bench whacked a home run.

(Tomorrow) Johnny Bench will whack a home run.

Verbs: *whacked, will whack*

Then connect the subject to the verb:

Who whacked?

s   v

Johnny Bench whacked.

WATCH OUT FOR <u>WHO</u>, <u>WHICH</u>, AND <u>WHOSE</u>

Who, which, and *whose* function as subordinators when they begin a dependent clause.

He is a man *who needs a long vacation.*

Sharon played her clarinet loudly, *which annoyed her sister, who was trying to practice the piano.*

Fragments—which are only parts of sentences—occur when a dependent clause is disconnected from its related independent clause.

NO: *He is a man.* Who needs a long vacation.
NO: Sharon played her clarinet loudly. *Which annoyed her sister. Who was trying to practice the piano.*

See the discussion of fragments on pages 176–178.

Who, which, and *whose* can also begin questions.

Whose scarf is that?
Which course are you taking?
Who won the election?

Distinguish between these words when they are used as subordinators and when they are used as question words.

2. **The verb cannot be an -*ing* word alone:**

> Not a sentence: the crowd screaming

Connect the -*ing* word to a time word:

> The crowd was screaming.

Or connect the phrase containing the -*ing* word to a sentence with a time word:

> The crowd screaming, Bench whacked a home run.

3. **A subject-verb unit introduced by a subordinator (*when, because, if, since*, and the like) is not a sentence but a dependent clause:**

> Not a sentence: when Bench whacked a home run

Connect the *when* clause to its related independent clause:

> INDEPENDENT CLAUSE
> When Bench whacked a home run, the crowd went wild.

4. *Who, which, whose,* **or** *whom* **cannot be the subject of a sentence unless the sentence is a question. A subject-verb unit introduced by these words is not a sentence but a dependent clause:**

> Not a sentence: Which made the crowd go wild.

Connect the *who* or *which* clause to its related independent clause:

> INDEPENDENT CLAUSE
> Johnny Bench whacked a home run, which made the crowd go wild.

Exercise 5   Which of the following clauses are independent and can stand alone as sentences? Which of the clauses are dependent? Punctuate those that are sentences.

1. whenever I feel bored
2. she proposed to me
3. I hate to write
4. although I am her cousin
5. Charles Smith and I love each other
6. if I were king
7. before the semester began
8. while I was sitting on that park bench
9. I intend to finish college
10. after Arlene left for Los Angeles

Exercise 6 Dependent clauses must be connected to independent clauses; otherwise, dependent clauses are sentence *fragments*. Write your own sentences in which each of these dependent clauses is connected to an independent clause.

1. whenever I feel bored
2. although she proposed to me
3. because I hate to write
4. if I were king
5. while I was sitting on that park bench
6. because I can't stand subways
7. wherever you go
8. when I sleep late in the morning
9. before you leave
10. after the movie ends

Exercise 7 Rewrite the following paragraph so that you use subordinators to show the connections among the ideas.

Example: John, who is nineteen years old, was speeding down the expressway on his motorcycle.

John was speeding down the expressway. John is nineteen years old. He was riding his motorcycle. It was a beautiful day. The sun was shining. Suddenly a Dodge Dart was upon him. The car rammed into John. His motorcycle was wrecked. An ambulance arrived within minutes. The driver of the Dodge was concerned. John was rushed to Los Angeles Medical Center. The nurses and doctors were very kind to him. They were competent. He needed forty-three stitches in his left leg. He didn't complain. He didn't press charges.

Exercise 8 Choose an appropriate subordinator to complete each of the following sentences.

Subordinators:

although	whenever	unless
because	until	in order that
since	wherever	after
when	if	
where	as	

1. _____ it is warm, I am heading for the beach.
2. _____ I love my brother, I argue with him.
3. I visit the White House _____ I am in Washington, D.C.
4. _____ you give me back my passport, I'll call the police.

5. _____ I wrote a magnificent anthropology paper last night, I did not sleep very well.

6. _____ I wrote a magnificent anthropology paper last night, I stayed up for the midnight movie.

7. _____ we eat at the Servery, we'll run into Professor O'Connor.

8. _____ there has been rain in the sub-Sahara, the threat of starvation has lessened.

9. _____ there's smoke, there's fire.

10. "Goodnight, Mrs. Calabash, _____ you are."

11. I couldn't read the bottom line _____ I had my glasses on.

12. _____ you like Etruscan art, I'll give you this bronze horse.

13. _____ people seem to like me, I have few friends.

14. _____ people seem to like me, I plan to become a social worker.

15. _____ the snake crept toward us, our eyes searched for a pointed stick.

16. The musicians gathered _____ there was a good piano.

17. I don't leave my house _____ my astrologer says my aspects are poor.

18. _____ my girl friend and I have made up, my life is sweet and serene.

19. _____ you like nuts, you won't like this cake.

COORDINATION AND SUBORDINATION WORKING TOGETHER

Coordination and subordination work together as processes for relating ideas. As a writer, you have the options of coordinating ideas when you want to show equal emphasis or of subordinating one idea to another for varied emphasis.

The following selections provide models of subordination and coordination working together in longer pieces; you are invited to read, study, and think about the ways writers use these processes:

> My father's business seems to have been one of slow but steady growth. He and his local partner, Llewelen Tozer, had no vices. They were devoted to their families and to "the store," which grew with the town, which, in turn, grew and changed with the State (California) from a gambling, mining, and ranching community to one of farming, fruit-raising, and building. Immigration poured in, not gold-seekers now, but farmers, business-men and home-builders, who settled, planted, reaped, and traded in the natural riches of the State, which prospered greatly, "making" the people who will tell you that they "made the State."
>
> Lincoln Steffens

In an age where there is so much talk about "being yourself," I reserve
to myself the right to forget about being myself, since in any case there
is very little chance of my being anybody else. Rather it seems to me
that when one is too intent on "being himself" he runs the risk of imper-
sonating a shadow.

Thomas Merton

Easterners commonly complain that there is no "weather" at all in
Southern California, that the days and the seasons slip by relentlessly,
numbingly bland. That is quite misleading. In fact the climate is characterized by infrequent but violent extremes: two periods of torrential
subtropical rains which continue for weeks and wash out the hills and send
subdivisions sliding toward the sea; about twenty scattered days a year of
the Santa Ana, which, with its incendiary dryness, invariably means fire.
At the first prediction of a Santa Ana, the Forest Service flies men and
equipment from northern California into the southern forests, and the
Los Angeles Fire Department cancels its ordinary non-firefighting routines.
The Santa Ana caused Malibu to burn the way it did in 1956, and Bel Air
in 1961, and Santa Barbara in 1964. In the winter of 1966–67 eleven
men were killed fighting a Santa Ana fire that spread through the San
Gabriel Mountains.

Just to watch the front-page news out of Los Angeles during a Santa Ana
is to get very close to what it is about the place. The longest single Santa
Ana period in recent years was in 1957, and it lasted not the usual three
or four days but fourteen days, from November 21 until December 4. On
the first day 25,000 acres of the San Gabriel Mountains were burning,
with gusts reaching 100 miles an hour. In town, the wind reached Force
12, or hurricane force, on the Beaufort Scale; oil derricks were toppled
and people ordered off the downtown streets to avoid injury from flying
objects. On November 22 the fire in the San Gabriels was out of control.
On November 24 six people were killed in automobile accidents, and by
the end of the week the Los Angeles *Times* was keeping a box score of
traffic deaths. On November 26 a prominent Pasadena attorney, depressed
about money, shot and killed his wife, their two sons, and himself. On
November 27 a South Gate divorcee, twenty-two, was murdered and
thrown from a moving car. On November 30 the San Gabriel fire was
still out of control, and the wind in town was blowing eighty miles an
hour. On the first day of December four people died violently, and on the
third the wind began to break.

It is hard for people who have not lived in Los Angeles to realize how
radically the Santa Ana figures in the local imagination. The city burning
is Los Angeles's deepest image of itself: Nathanael West perceived that,
in *The Day of the Locust;* and at the time of the 1965 Watts riots what
struck the imagination most indelibly were the fires. For days one could
drive the Harbor Freeway and see the city on fire, just as we had always
known it would be in the end. Los Angeles weather is the weather of

catastrophe, of apocalypse, and just as the reliably long and bitter winters of New England determine the way life is lived there, so the violence and the unpredictability of the Santa Ana affect the entire quality of life in Los Angeles, accentuate its impermanence, its unreliability. The wind shows us how close to the edge we are.

Joan Didion

Exercise 9 Read the following sentences, and determine the relationship between the parts. Fill each empty slot with either a semicolon, a coordinator (*and, but, or, nor, for*), or a subordinator (*although, because, since, when, as, after, before, until, wherever, unless, while, in order that*) to show the clearest connection of ideas. Add whatever punctuation is necessary.

1. Research papers demand a lot of time _____ they must be accurate.

2. Many children are still in need of homes _____ foster parents receive a stipend for providing them with a family.

3. Foster parents receive a stipend _____ many children need homes.

4. From his father, William received a sound Methodist upbringing _____ his mother was more concerned with the welfare of the neighborhood poor.

5. From his father, William received a sound Methodist upbringing _____ from his mother he inherited an almost congenital concern for the problems of the poor.

6. The money, the thousands and thousands of unsought dollars, fell into their lives without rippling their stride _____ even their children were scarcely aware of any change.

7. They took our seats _____ we left.

8. We left _____ they took our seats.

9. Does your mother still have your baby curls _____ does your father tell you tales of your first howling haircut?

10. Does your mother still have your baby curls _____ your father saves nothing but his memories?

11. **a.** _____ my father was angry with me, he remained silent for days.
    b. My mother screamed at me for every wrongdoing _____ she just as quickly forgave me.
    c. _____ I had to choose, I'd rather have the outbursts than the silence.

12. _____ James took an accounting course, he couldn't manage his finances.

13. _____ he took an accounting course, he became a financial whiz.

14. He took an accounting course _____ he could manage his finances.

Exercise 10 Read the following groups of sentences. Rewrite each group in as many sentences as you need to show relationships between ideas. Use coordinators when you want to give equal emphasis to ideas and subordinators when you want to show one idea as more important than another.

Example: The school budget lost. Programs will be seriously cut again this year. Teachers will lose their jobs. The children will suffer in crowded classrooms. More families will move out of the area.

Because the school budget lost, programs will be seriously cut again this year. More teachers will lose their jobs, more children will suffer in overcrowded classrooms, and more families will move out of the area.

1. Fashions change. Hemlines go up. Hairstyles go down. People stay the same.

2. Americans take to their wheels in the summer. The country is a stream of motorcycles. The country is a stream of cars. The country is a stream of campers. The country streams with smoke.

3. The cities are dirty. The suburbs are bursting. Americans are returning to the country.

4. Sally overdresses. Her friends turn up for their parties in jeans and T-shirts. Sally glitters in long, sequined dresses.

Exercise 11 Read the following passages from an essay on television by Joyce Maynard. Fill each empty slot with one of these connectors:

so	if
but	which
and	when

We got our TV set in 1959 _____ I was 5. _____ I can barely remember life without television. I have spent 20,000 hours of my life in front of the set. Not all of my contemporaries watched so much, _____ many did, _____ what's more, we watched the same commercials, were exposed to the same end-of-show lessons. So there is, among this generation of television children, a shared history, a tremendous fund of common experience. These massive doses of TV have not affected all of us in an identical way, _____ it would be risky to draw broad conclusions. _____ if a sociologist were—rashly— to try to uncover some single most important influence of this generation, _____ has produced Patty Hearst and Alice Cooper and the Jesus movement and the peace movement; _____ he were searching for the roots of 1960's psychedelia _____ 1970's apathy, he would do well to look first at television.

who	when
because	or
and	but
that	

My strongest memories are of one series and one character. Not the best, _____ the one that formed me more than any other, _____ haunts me still, _____ left its mark on a goodsized part of a generation: *Leave It To Beaver*. I watched that show every day after school (fresh from my own failures) _____ studied it, like homework _____ the Cleaver family was so steady and normal— _____ my own was not _____ the boys had so many friends, played basketball, drank sodas, *fit in*. Watching that series _____ other family situation comedies was almost like taking a course in how to be an American.

I loved my father _____ I longed secretly for a "Dad" like Ward Cleaver, _____ puttered in a work shed, building bookcases _____ oiling hinges, one _____ spent his Saturday afternoons playing golf _____ mowing the lawn _____ dipping his finger into cake batter whipped by a mother in a frilly apron _____ spent her time going to PTA meetings _____ playing bridge with "the girls." . . .

Occasionally I go to college campuses. Some student in the audience always mentions Beaver Cleaver, _____ _____ the name is spoken, a satisfied murmur can be heard in the crowd.

Exercise 12 Rewrite the following monotonous sentences by coordinating and/or subordinating those ideas you want to connect.

I shot out of bed. I grabbed my clothes. I dashed out of the house. At the corner store, I swiped the *Times*. I hijacked a cab. The cab driver looked surprised. I left him standing on the street corner.

At my desk in the office, I opened the morning mail. I glared at a bill from Con Edison. I had already paid it. I screamed at their adjustments manager on the phone. He apologized. He offered to send me $100 for my inconvenience. At 10:00 I drank a cup of coffee. I savored three glazed doughnuts. My superior called at 10:30. We met leisurely for two hours. I finally told him that I disagreed with his office tactics. He was an ineffective administrator. He let the department go to pot. He didn't know how to handle his underlings. He thanked me for my honesty. He gave me a $50-a-week raise.

At 12:30 my day was over. I gathered my swim clothes. I headed for the beach. I lay on the sand the whole afternoon. The day was perfect. The sky was clear. The ocean breeze was cool. Suddenly, I felt a strong tug at my foot. I opened my eyes. My wife was pulling my leg in my own bed. "You're late," she said. "Get up and get going."

PROBLEMS WITH CONNECTORS   Two sentence errors, *run-ons* and *fragments,* are the most troublesome sentence faults for inexperienced writers. Usually they occur not because you can't arrange words in sentences but because you have trouble punctuating the words as sentences. Correct punctuation is the key to eliminating run-ons and fragments. A misplaced comma or period often results in run-ons and fragments. To confront these sentence demons head-on, use your understanding of sentences along with the sentence check list on pages 165-166. The following pages offer instructions for eliminating run-ons and fragments along with exercises in which to practice your sentence skills.

Run-ons   There are two types of run-on sentences.

1. When two or more sentences are written without any punctuation mark between them, the error is known as a *fused sentence:*

> We were glad to leave Kansas it was too hot.
> Colorado was nice I was surprised to see snow in July.
> The next day we drove to the Grand Canyon the first day we were there we had to wait till noon to get a campsite.

2. When two or more sentences are written with only a comma as a connector, the error is known as a *comma splice* or a *comma fault:*

> The state of Kansas felt like one big farm, we drove for six hours through the same wheat field.
> We had to wait till noon to get a campsite, we had to put our names on a waiting list.
> The next day we drove to the Grand Canyon, it was spectacular.
> The shower went off, luckily I had another quarter.

Runs-ons often cause readers difficulty because it is not clear where one sentence ends and another begins.

Eliminate run-ons   First, using the sentence check list on pages 165-166, determine that you have two sentences. Then, use the options for separating, coordinating, or subordinating sentences.

1. Use a period:

_____. _____.

The shower went off. Luckily I had another quarter.

2. Use a semicolon:

_____; _____.

The shower went off; luckily I had another quarter.

3. Use a comma plus a coordinator:

_____, but _____.

The shower went off, but luckily I had another quarter.

4. Subordinate one clause to another:

When _____, _____.

_____ when _____.

When the shower went off, I luckily had another quarter.

I luckily had another quarter when the shower went off.

Run-ons	*Correcting run-ons*
We were glad to leave Kansas it was too hot.	We were glad to leave Kansas. It was too hot.
	We were glad to leave Kansas, for it was too hot.
	We were glad to leave Kansas because it was too hot.
	We were glad to leave Kansas; it was too hot.
The shower went off, luckily I had another quarter.	The shower went off. Luckily, I had another quarter.
	The shower went off, but luckily I had another quarter.
	When the shower went off, I luckily had another quarter.

Exercise 13 Read the following passage, which was adapted for this exercise from Muhammad Ali's book, *The Greatest*. Place punctuation marks wherever they are needed to end or coordinate sentences. Capitalize words as necessary.

I hit Ernie Terrell until I knew he was out on his feet his eyes were puffed his nose bleeding lips cut and swollen but the referee egged us on I knew that unless I held back he would be injured for life it's against the rules but I began to pull my punches the crowd wanted more blood and those against me hoped he could come up with a miraculous counterattack but he was beaten and there was no point in pounding him anymore he had a family sisters brothers and parents just like I had why should I maul him just to satisfy some of the screamers.

Exercise 14 The following selections are taken from a student journal. If the student were to move beyond this spontaneous writing, he would have to think about sentence structure. Edit his writing—separating, coordinating, or subordinating sentences wherever you choose. Decide which sentences you want to emphasize equally and which you want to subordinate. Omit any word you think unnecessary.

As I start this journal I hope I am spelling journal right, later on I will look it up in a dictionary. I've been starting this journal for about two or three days. But I finally started it. This notebook has a surplus of twenty pages, I doubt that I will use those extra pages.

As my alarm clock rang I jumped out of bed and gathered my bags it was five o'clock in the morning and it was still dark, within twenty minutes we were ready to go I quickly said good-bye to my parents who slipped me a twenty dollar bill for food as I kissed my mother good-bye and walked out the door I knew I would enjoy myself and not miss home Chris met me in his driveway the car was packed the tank was full and we were on our way.

After dinner Chris and I went down to the cliffs of the canyon I saw the most intense sunset I've ever seen, there was a rainbow of colors upon the red and grey shale and the sun sank into the canyon.

The next day we got up at eight o'clock and started walking into the canyon we brought a knapsack with a camera and three cans of beer, as we walked down in the early morning heat we met people coming up who had slept in the canyon over night and were now walking up. All the people we met told us to turn around and go back up, but not us, we said if you could walk down we could so we kept walking down.

On the way down we met a guy and his wife walking up about ten in the morning. The walk down was about eight miles we made time walking down. We reached the bottom about eleven so it took about three hours to walk, there was a river at the bottom everybody was swimming it was so hot I had to go in the water, it was so hot that when my shirt fell in the water it dried in about two minutes.

We swam around for about a half hour and decided to start back up. We started walking at noon by three we were only a third of the way up and had nothing we had drunk all the beer and had nothing to eat, the heat was starting to get to us.

Walking straight up the canyon walls was very tiresome, we had to stop and rest every five minutes. While walking up we met the same people we had met in the morning, we couldn't believe we passed them going up. Each step we took was harder and harder. We reached the top at eight-thirty, when we got to the top we were glad to be at the top, the first thing we did was to run to the snack bar and ate three hamburgers and five beers each.

It took us three hours to walk down and eight and a half to walk up.

Fragments   Fragments are bits and pieces of sentences that are punctuated as whole sentences. Most often fragments are phrases and dependent clauses that are disconnected from their independent clauses.

Phrases as   Remember: a phrase is a group of words without a subject-verb unit. The
fragments   phrase must be connected to an independent clause, or it will be considered a fragment. The following italicized phrases are fragments:

> The man was racing. *Down the street. Tripping on a curb. Running down the street.* He was late. He was a tall man. *Thin, pale, and tired.* He ripped his pants. *And scraped his knee.* He felt like a fool. *A child.* He had been on his way to the co-op. *To buy a dictionary. For his English class.* Now he wasn't sure what he would do. *Go home to change his trousers? Or go to class?* He liked to be punctual. *And meticulous.* He hated to miss class. They were discussing run-ons. *And fragments.*

To eliminate fragments, connect them to nearby independent clauses, or rewrite the fragments as parts of new sentences:

> The man was racing down the street. He tripped on a curb. He shouldn't have been running down the street, but he was late. He ripped his pants and scraped his knee. He felt like a fool, a child. He had been on his way to the co-op to buy a dictionary for his English class. Now he wasn't sure what he would do. Should he go home to change his trousers? Should he go to class? He liked to be punctual and meticulous. He hated to miss class because they were discussing run-ons and fragments.

Dependent   Remember: dependent clauses cannot stand alone as sentences; they must
clauses as   be connected to independent clauses. Memorize the list of subordinators on
fragments   pages 161-162 so that each time you use a subordinator you can anticipate at least two parts to the whole sentence, a dependent part and an independent part. Make certain that you are not cutting the whole sentence short, as in the following examples:

> The man was racing down the street. *Because he was late.*
> He ripped his pants. *Which weren't even paid for.*

To eliminate fragments, connect the dependent clause to the independent clause:

> The man was racing down the street because he was late.
> He ripped his pants, which weren't even paid for.

Another good way to catch run-ons and fragments is to read your writing aloud. Your voice will automatically drop at the end of a sentence. Notice the subordinators and coordinators. Catch the places where you have written a period. Does the period cut off a piece of a sentence? Whenever your voice drops, make certain that a sentence either ends or is connected properly to the following or preceding sentence.

If you're having difficulty with run-ons and fragments, there's usually a pattern to your problems. You may be disconnecting *when* or *although* clauses, or using *-ing* words as verbs, or running your sentences together with commas and no *and* or *but*. Don't shelve your papers. Look over past papers and study those that are returned to you. If you rewrite nothing else, rewrite sentence errors correctly. Your sentence problems will begin to diminish if you practice seeing where your sentences begin and end.

Eliminate fragments First, using the sentence check list on pages 165-166, determine that you have a subject-verb unit in every sentence. Then, follow these guides.

1. Watch out for *-ing* words.

The *-ing* word cannot stand alone as the verb in a sentence. Make certain that it is fastened to a time word:

Fragment	*Sentence*
Henry *eating* a slice of pizza.	Henry was eating a slice of pizza.

Do not cut off an *-ing* phrase from its sentence:

Fragment	*Sentence*
Henry walked down the street. *Eating a slice of pizza.*	Henry walked down the street, eating a slice of pizza.
Being an only child. Charles was pitifully spoiled.	Being an only child, Charles was pitifully spoiled.

2. Watch out for prepositional phrases.

Do not punctuate a prepositional phrase as a sentence:

Fragment	*Sentence*
Suzanne visited her parents in Switzerland. *In the summertime.*	Suzanne visited her parents in Switzerland in the summertime.
Ross ate a frozen yogurt. *During his break between classes.*	Ross ate a frozen yogurt during his break between classes.

3. Watch out for subordinators:

because	when	after	unless	whose
although	if	until	who	which
since	before	while	whom	that

Do not disconnect a dependent clause from the sentence it belongs to:

Fragment	*Sentence*
I admire Henry. *Because he is sensitive.*	I admire Henry because he is sensitive.
He disliked the man. *Who wanted to marry his daughter.*	He disliked the man who wanted to marry his daughter.
Although Lauren never studied the piano. She plays like a professional.	Although Lauren never studied the piano, she plays like a professional.

4. Watch out for these words:

especially	except	such as
instead of	including	for example

Do not disconnect a phrase or clause that begins with one of these words:

Fragment	*Sentence*
Jennifer enjoys mint julep. *Especially when she's relaxing on a hot summer day.*	Jennifer enjoys mint julep, especially when she's relaxing on a hot summer day.
Sam bought his stereo at Gimbels. *Instead of Macy's.*	Sam bought his stereo at Gimbels instead of Macy's.
I enjoy traveling to new places. *Such as the Grand Canyon, Yellowstone, and Niagara Falls.*	I enjoy traveling to new places, such as the Grand Canyon, Yellowstone, and Niagara Falls.
We bought tickets for the whole family. *Except Edna and Elmer.*	We bought tickets for the whole family, except Edna and Elmer.

Exercise 15 You write fragments when you punctuate phrases and dependent clauses as sentences. Turn the following fragments into sentences.

1. Who was using this towel.
2. Falling off a wild bronco.
3. To love all mankind and to search for the truth.
4. Before she was graduated from college.
5. Drinking a cup of black coffee.
6. The tears streaming down his face.

7. While whistling a tune.

8. Bitten by a mosquito.

9. All through the night.

10. The motorcyclist in his crash helmet.

11. Through the dark alley.

12. Whenever I'm sleepy during my math class.

13. Although I know him well.

14. Strawberries and cream for dessert.

15. Who ripped open the envelope.

16. After payday.

17. If ever I should leave you.

18. Singing in the rain.

19. Raindrops falling on my head.

20. That was on the table.

Exercise 16 Read the following advertisements, which have been adapted for this exercise. Each advertisement contains phrases and dependent clauses that are punctuated as whole sentences. Find all the fragments and either connect them to the sentences they belong to or turn them into new sentences.

1. Advertisement for Volunteers

You can help people. In fact, there's a crying need for you. Your talents. Your training. Your concerns. They can make you priceless. As a volunteer in your community.

Take a moment to think of all that can be done. For children. The environment. Sick people. Old people. People who just need someone behind them.

Then take another moment to think of what you can do. Perhaps by applying your job skills. Or personal interests to voluntary action.

There are probably several organizations hard at work in your town. Doing things you'd be proud to be part of. We'll put you in touch with them. Join one. Or, if you see the need, start a new one.

If you can spare even a few hours a week, call your local Voluntary Action Center. It'll do you good. To see how much good you can do.

2. Advertisement for Coca-Cola

If you'll stop and think for just a moment. You'll find more of the good things in this country. Than anywhere else in the world. Think of this land. From the surf at Big Sur. To a Florida sunrise. And all the places in between. The Grand Canyon. The wheat fields of Kansas. Autumn in New Hampshire. You could go on forever. But America is more than a place for good times. It's Saturday night. It's a trip down a dirt road in a beat-up old jalopy. It's your team winning. It's a late-night movie. You could enjoy a thousand times. And, yes, when you're thirsty. It's the taste of ice-cold Coca-Cola. It's the real thing. In fact, all of the good things in this country are real. They're all around you. Plainly visible. We point to many of them in our advertising. But you can discover many, many more. Without ever seeing a single commercial for Coke. So have a bottle of Coke . . . and start looking up.

Exercise 17   Read the following unpunctuated advertisement, which has been adapted for this exercise. Find the sentences, and then separate them, coordinate them, or subordinate them. Capitalize words wherever necessary.

If the Harley-Davidson man seems overly protective there's a good reason for it apparently there's something irresistible about the Harley-Davidson you see it's one of the most ripped-off motorcycles in the country so you can't blame the Harley-Davidson man for taking an extra precaution or two what is it about this machine that attracts such a dedicated following among enthusiasts of every type the answer of course is that the Harley-Davidson occupies a special place among people who know and love motorcycles after seven decades it is still recognized as the ultimate achievement in quality-built precision motorcycles a product of this heritage is the electric start XL-1000 shown here (also available with kick start) the styling and overall beauty of this 1000cc 4-stroke v-twin are timeless the unique ride the spectacular torque and the deep distinctive sound of the powerful engine are pure Harley-Davidson the other members of this family of superbikes include the FX and FXE-1200 and the FLH-1200 all are available for a limited time only with our special "Liberty Edition" option—metal-flaked black finish with full color tank insignia celebrating our country's bicentennial you'll find these superbikes along with our . . . line of classically styled 125cc 175cc and 250cc street and on-off road motorcycles at your AMF Harley-Davidson dealer stop by it's a great way to learn about these superb machines and best of all it's legal.

Exercise 18   Read the following unpunctuated paragraph to determine which sentences belong together. Think about your options for coordinating and subordinating sentences, and then rewrite the paragraph by changing some sentences into dependent clauses or phrases and by coordinating other sentences. You may need to add subordinators and coordinators. Punctuate appropriately.

I think back on my years growing up in a small Pennsylvania town I feel nostalgic now for those times people cared for each other there they accepted the poor the old and the disabled women in the community baked bread on the weekends they shared it with the poor and sick they invited them to Sunday dinner people grew old they lived with their children no one went to an old age home or a nursing home many of my friends had their grandparents or an aunt living with them the disabled and even the retarded lived with their families too they were part of the community I can never return to that small town I would like to recapture some of the qualities of small-town life.

Exercise 19 Using the following facts as the beginning of a news story, finish the story by writing several paragraphs. Connect the ideas by means of varying techniques. Add coordinators and subordinators. Edit for run-ons and fragments.

It was 11:00 P.M. It was raining. A woman was walking down Jefferson street. She was alone. She always walked that street at night. Suddenly out of the darkness appeared a . . .

Exercise 20 Edit the following piece of student writing for fragments and run-ons.

Once you've gotten into a habit good or bad it's hard, or close to impossible to break. I have a very good example. I started smoking in junior high school. I'm not sure but I think it was in ninth grade. My brother and I were in the same grade so we bought one pack of cigarettes a week. He smoked ten and I smoked ten. It was always cheaper that way.

Because if I were to go out and buy a pack a week. By the end of the week the cigarettes that were left would all be stale. Four years and a pack a day of cigarettes later. I decided that I had to quit. I wrote away to the American Cancer Society. For tips on quitting. After looking at that book filled with pictures of cancerous lungs. Anybody would stop smoking. I stopped smoking the same day I got the booklet in the mail. I followed their tips of drinking water whenever I had the urge to have a cigarette. Also drinking a lot of V-8 juice. For about a week or so it worked until one Friday night I went out to a bar with my friends. Of course everybody knows that if you're going to drink you're going to smoke.

Well you guessed it on Saturday morning I was smoking again. So much for will power. Another year had passed and I was still smoking but by now I really hated it I kept switching from one brand of cigarettes to another. Finally I figured if I must smoke I might as well smoke a cigarette which wasn't as harmful but after a while I got sick of sucking air. So one day I woke up and said that's it and went cold turkey. It's hard to believe but that was a year and a half ago and I feel I will never smoke again.

Chapter 9 / Modifying

Drawing by Dedini; © 1977 The New Yorker Magazine, Inc.

Which words make "fried chicken" more specific?

MODIFIERS—WHAT THEY ARE AND WHAT THEY DO

Your grasp of general and specific ideas in the whole essay prepares you to understand what a modifier is and how it functions in a sentence. Here is an example of one of the basic sentence patterns reviewed in Chapter 6:

PATTERN: subject–linking verb–completer

       S   LV   C
That woman   is   my grandmother.

Although you understand that *woman* is a more specific word than, say, *person* (as in *That person is my grandmother*), you may wish to make *woman* even more specific. You can add a modifier in the subject slot to accompany *that woman:*

    S + MODIFIER   LV   C
    That beautiful woman   is   my grandmother.

If you wish to make *that woman* still clearer to the reader, you can add another modifier in the subject slot:

    S + MODIFIER + MODIFIER   LV   C
    That beautiful woman who is serving sandwiches   is   my grandmother.

If you wish to make *that woman* clearer yet to the reader, you can add still another modifier in the subject slot:

    S + MODIFIER + MODIFIER + MODIFIER   LV   C
    That beautiful woman in the yellow bikini who is is   my grandmother.
    serving sandwiches

Similarly, you can make *my grandmother* more specific by adding a modifier in the completer slot:

    S + MODIFIER + MODIFIER + MODIFIER   LV C + MODIFIER
    That beautiful woman in the yellow bikini   is   my maternal
    who is serving sandwiches   grandmother

These examples and the cartoon about fried chicken tell us that a modifier is a word or group of words that make the meaning of another word or group of words more specific. A modifier can be a single word *(beautiful),* a phrase *(in the yellow bikini),* or a clause *(who is serving sandwiches).* It can be an adjective *(maternal* grandmother), the name of something *(Alabama* fried chicken), or other words. Modifiers help writers make ideas more specific and less general within the few basic patterns of English sentences. Words, phrases, or clauses move into the subject, verb, or completer slots next to the words they belong to.

PATTERN: subject-verb

    S   V
    Groucho snickered.

    S + MODIFIER   V
    Groucho, flicking his cigar ashes, snickered.

    S + MODIFIER   V + MODIFIER
    Groucho, flicking his cigar ashes, snickered playfully.

    S + MODIFIER + MODIFIER   V + MODIFIER + MODIFIER
    Groucho, flicking his cigar ashes   snickered   playfully
    and rolling his eyes,   into the contestant's ear.

PATTERN: subject–verb–completer

S	V	C
Johnny Bench	hit	a home run.

S + MODIFIER	V	C
Johnny Bench, the Reds' catcher,	hit	a home run.

S + MODIFIER	V	C + MODIFIER
Johnny Bench, the Reds' catcher,	hit	a towering home run.

S + MODIFIER	V + MODIFIER	C + MODIFIER
Johnny Bench, the Reds' catcher,	smoothly hit	a towering home run.

As you can see, modifiers make the elements of all the basic sentence patterns more specific.

SEEKING MODIFIERS

Invention When you find yourself stalled in your writing, you may be experiencing a crisis that is related to your ability to use modifiers: you simply can't come up with enough ideas to keep on fueling your writing. You've written only three or four sentences, but these seem to have exhausted your ready supply of ideas. An hour before, you would have sworn your head was full of ideas, but now that the writing is in progress, just a few ideas slip out, one by one. The clock ticks. You wait. Those ideas you have seem detached, abrupt, and threaten to give out entirely. Although you have in mind the basic scheme of what you want to say, your writing is skeletal and bare. You wonder how professional writers manage to have so much to say. How do they produce such richness and texture? Where do all those specifics come from?

For the answers to these questions, we must look to the act of composing sentences. You may be a writer who writes very minimally at first. You may have a clear notion of your point and a carefully thought-out thesis. You may be able to rattle off the essential features of an experience you plan to relate in your writing. But too often you express all that in a few sentences at most. What you may not do is make the most of these sentences. You haven't searched the sentences you've already written for hints of more ideas hidden there. The sentences you write often themselves suggest the details that they lack. Another way to say this is that *every sentence asks implicit questions,* or that you can enlarge your ideas by thinking of questions to ask about the key words in your sentences.

Consider this sentence:

My pockets were loaded.

To discover implicit questions in *My pockets were loaded,* decide which are the key words:

Probable key words: *pockets, loaded*

Here is one possible question this sentence might suggest. The question grows out of the key words:

What were my pockets loaded with?

One way you can answer this question is by supplying details in the next sentence:

My pockets were loaded. I had shells and polished sea glass in them, as well as a few dimes, a Band-Aid, and a generous supply of sand that had spilled in to weigh me down.

Here is another possible question the sentence might suggest:

Why were my pockets loaded?

This question, too, can be answered by supplying details in the next sentence:

My pockets were loaded. Since my hands held tightly to the twins' rafts, I let them stuff all the treasures they found on the beach into my pants pockets.

Here is a third possible question the sentence might suggest:

Where were the pockets?

Here is the sentence sequence which answers this question:

My pockets were loaded. In the pocket of my new denim jacket I had the keys to the Chevy and to Jake's car; in my blouse pocket I had the slip of paper on which I'd scribbled the address of the party I planned to go to that night; in my pants pockets I had Jake's old biology test, which he had brought along for me to look at; and in my rear pants pocket I had my rain hat and a ten-dollar bill tucked way down.

Every sentence you write can be the source of more ideas. By raising questions about the key words of your sentences, you can refuel your writing.

Exercise 1 For each of the following sentences, decide on an implicit question that it suggests. Then rewrite the given sentence, and add the next sentence that answers the question.

Example: My files contain dozens of letters from people who used my diet.

Implicit question: *What kind* of people were the letters from?

Sentence sequence: My files contain dozens of letters from people who used my diet. They were from seriously overweight people who lost seventy-five pounds or more.

1. He was often short with her.

2. The days were long and monotonous.

3. Most of the young people sat in the back of the bus.

4. The champion raised doubts about the fight.

5. In a dozen parts of the city, bombs went off.

6. I fell into his lap and covered him with kisses.

7. Sometimes a person has a grudge against his neighbor.

8. "The Graduate" made Dustin Hoffman a star.

9. He knocked me down, grabbed my pocketbook, and ducked around the corner out of sight.

10. Every evening after nine, the class gathered with Professor Loomis on the observatory roof to watch for the comet.

11. President Lincoln was shot at Ford's Theatre.

12. It wasn't Scottie we saw with her, going into the Palm Room.

13. I do not mean by these comments to ridicule the zookeepers.

Sentence combining Now we are drawing closer to modifiers. But modifiers are not extra sentences, as the preceding discussion may have led you to believe. Rather, they are parts of sentences—words, phrases, and clauses—that we slip into the basic sentence patterns to provide concrete details. Ideas for modifiers are often hidden in the sentences you write. You simply have to discover them and expand your sentences to make room for them.

Sentence:	That woman is my grandmother.
Implicit question:	What does that woman look like?
Sentence sequence:	That woman is my grandmother. She is beautiful.
Sentence with modifier:	That beautiful woman is my grandmother.

Implicit question:	What is she doing?
Sentence sequence:	That woman is my grandmother. She is beautiful. She is serving sandwiches.
Sentence with modifiers:	That beautiful woman who is serving sandwiches is my grandmother.

Sometimes the sentences you write already include modifiers as you compose them. The modifiers are there in your first draft. On other occasions you compose skeletal sentences. You go back to ask questions and put the details you discover into separate sentences. The boundaries between what should be a separate sentence and what should be a modifier may seem to blur. Look again at your sentences. When you have several short sentences in a row, combine them, cutting out excess words and embedding the essential ideas from one sentence into another as modifiers:

beautiful ⟵

That woman is my grandmother.   ̶S̶h̶e̶ ̶i̶s̶ (beautiful.)

Exercise 2 In Exercise 1, you asked questions about a sentence and then answered them by writing the next sentence. For this exercise, ask an implicit question about each of the following sentences, but answer the question by including modifiers in the subject, verb, or completer slots of the original sentence.

Example:	My files contain dozens of letters from people who used my diet.
Implicit question:	*What kind* of people were the letters from?
Sentence with modifiers:	My files contain dozens of letters from seriously overweight people who used my diet and lost seventy-five pounds or more.

Example:	The snowplow moved down the street.
Implicit question:	*How* did the snowplow move down the street?
Sentence with modifier:	The snowplow moved clumsily down the street.

1. I admired Greg's hair.
2. The explorer landed at the North Pole.
3. Larry's squash won first prize at the fair.
4. Driving can be fun.
6. The prime minister called an election.
5. The plane crashed.
7. My camp experience depressed me.
8. Iris and I wrote letters.
9. The lake froze.
10. Mr. Perdue roasted a chicken.
11. The singer fainted.

What do modifiers do? They tell why, where, when, in what manner. They offer details of color and sound, of mood and attitude, of location and size. In fact, the more you write, the more you associate one idea with another and the wider the range of modifiers that becomes available to you. If your problem is writing sentences that look like bare bones, then you must think again of writing as a cycle of acts, some of which you need to repeat to put some flesh on those bones. One act is to observe your own life carefully. (You may want to follow the suggestions in Chapters 1 and 2.) A second act—if you can't think of a way to include the details from your life—is to make the most of the sentences you have already written. Remember, you can refuel your writing by asking questions about the key words in your sentences. In the same way, you can always go back to ask questions about your thesis statement. By underlining the key words in it, you can generate ideas for the topic sentences of your remaining paragraphs.

Learn to take all your sentences seriously; every one can be the source of new ideas.

SELECTING MODIFIERS A second crisis you may face when you are composing sentences is the opposite of a lack of ideas. Not a problem of scarcity, nor of invention, this one is a problem of plenty. You have too many ideas, all of them buzzing around in your mind, demanding your attention at once. Experienced writers will admit that modifiers are at the heart of good writing, but they will hurry to raise a note of caution: however tempting a modifier may be, use it only if it helps you move your writing forward. Good writing contains a range of sentences—long ones streaming with modifiers as well as short, tight ones without a single unnecessary modifier. Composing a sentence, therefore, may demand your sharpest powers of selection. It may test your skill in sifting among the many ideas that seem to flutter in your head simultaneously. For in all this wealth of ideas, there is a risk. When your head swarms with details, you can easily become distracted from your thesis. The best way to keep your writing focused is to select for your sentences only those details that contribute to your thesis.

Modifiers and your purpose The two news headlines below dramatize the importance of selecting details that are most useful to your purpose. The writers of these headlines chose modifiers that would not fail to involve their readers in the tragedy of the event.

Plane With 243 Orphans Crashes Near Saigon

Saigon—A giant U.S. Air Force C-5 Galavy cargo plane carrying 243 Vietnamese orphans and 50 American and Australian relief workers crashed shortly after taking off from Saigon's Tan Son Nhut air base today, authorities said.

This news event occurred shortly after the Vietnam war. Why did the writer of this headline choose to say *Plane With 243 Orphans Crashes Near Saigon?* He might have chosen several alternate headlines from the information given in the first paragraph of the news article:

1. Giant Plane Crashes Near Saigon

2. Cargo Plane Crashes Near Saigon

3. U.S. Air Force Plane Crashes Near Saigon

4. Plane Carrying Relief Workers Crashes Near Saigon

The modifier *With 243 Orphans* helps convey the tragedy of the crash, and perhaps the tragedy of the war, most directly to the reader. *Giant Plane, Cargo Plane, U.S. Plane, Plane Carrying Relief Workers* would not have conveyed the tragedy as effectively as *Plane With 243 Orphans*.

WRECKAGE AT RUSH HOUR

A packed electric rapid-transit train crashed into the rear of another train parked in a station along the median strip of the Kennedy Expressway in northwest Chicago yesterday morning, injuring more than 400 of the 600 passengers. No deaths were reported.

Why did the writer of this headline choose to say *Wreckage at Rush Hour?* He might have chosen several alternate headlines from the information included in the first paragraph:

Rapid-Transit Trains Crash

Wreckage at Chicago Station

Wreckage with No Deaths

Just as in the first headline, the chosen modifier (head word, *Wreckage;* modifier, *at Rush Hour*) attempts to involve the reader in the potential tragedy of this accident. The writer is confident that readers will relive their own rush hours—the monotony of the daily routine, the jamming crowds, the mindlessness of a city's entire work force heading home after a day on the job, and, finally, the sudden and terrifying possibility of mass death.

TIPS FOR WRITERS—MODIFIERS AND ECONOMY

You select the modifier that makes another word more specific in a way that best serves your purpose. Sometimes you can provide as many modifiers as you need for a full-blown description. More frequently, to avoid taking your writing on a detour, you must be economical and single out the one or two most useful details as modifiers.

Modifiers are words that are closely connected to the bones of your sentences—to the nouns and verbs—because ideas for writing arise in your head in connected clusters that need sorting out according to the purpose of your work. Rarely does an idea arrive without bringing with it a trail of associations: a person and his looks, a meal and its taste, a game and its action. Sometimes the sorting is instantaneous. You know immediately, even intuitively, what to let in and what to keep out. Other times you write down more than you need. But there's no sense holding back ideas in the early stages—let them come. Later, once you've written a couple of pages and finally discovered what it was you meant to say all along, you may want to scratch out three-fourths of those pointless modifying ideas that were part of the original gush. Still other times you may leave space in your writing for a detail that you know will fit your subject to a "T," though you simply cannot come up with it. If only you can. Consciously or unconsciously, the hunt is on. The detail may suddenly, miraculously materialize as you write, or that space may go unfilled or inadequately filled and nag at you for a long while.

But let us return to *Wreckage at Rush Hour*. The scheme below attempts to analyze what happens when you select a modifier. The writer of this headline had to sort through all the possible details yammering for her attention at *A* in order to select the single detail that would connect most persuasively with her point at *B*—a train wreck involving 600 passengers:

A	*B*
packed trains	
electric trains	injures more than
wreckage at Chicago	400 of the 600
wreckage at rush hour	passengers.
morning wreckage	

Pruning the possibilities at *A* results in *Wreckage at Rush Hour,* because it is the *rush hour* detail that explains the numbers of passengers injured and arouses the greatest anxiety in readers, as well as the greatest likelihood that they will read the news.

So, the present emphasis on modifiers does not mean that you should use a $20 adjective next to every noun or that you should trade short sentences for long, embroidered ones. Instead, you need to take a kind of X-ray look at the process you go through as you compose sentences. When ideas crowd you, the *impulse* to write a sentence is very strong, but it can be as disorderly as an unmade bed. In the confusion, you must never let the ideas get away. The *act* of writing requires a little preliminary housekeeping, not with word choices on the first draft, but with purposes. You need an instant to pull your overall purpose straight before you climb in. After all, if you think of writing as a cycle of acts, you can constantly reevaluate your thesis. And with your thesis always in mind, you will select details that deliver the heart of your meaning.

The examples below show that modifiers are not just so much decoration. Modifiers can be as important to the writer's *purpose* as subject and verb:

S-V unit *without modifiers*	*S-V unit* *with modifiers*
Nick lost buckle.	Nick lost his 14K gold buckle, which was an heirloom given to him by his Hungarian great-grandfather.
Meet Me in St. Louis (MGM) is musical.	*Meet Me in St. Louis* (MGM) is a musical that even the deaf should enjoy. They will miss some attractive tunes like the surefire "Trolley Song," the graceful "Have Yourself a Merry Little Christmas," the sentimental "You and I" and the naively gay title waltz. But they can watch one of the year's prettiest pictures.
	James Agee

Note that words such as *a, an, the, that, this, these, those, his* are all modifiers.

In the first example, the loss of the buckle is underscored by its history, which is described by the modifiers. In the second example, the modifiers hold the real surprise of this movie review. Agee's startling observation begins in the modifier—a dependent clause—*that even the deaf should enjoy* this musical. Agee delivers this ironic insight at the outset: imagine a musical so graceful and handsome to look at that even people who can't hear the songs will find something in it to enjoy. Without modifiers, both examples have little impact.

Remember that a *dependent clause* (see Chapter 8) is a grammatical term that means the clause cannot stand as a sentence. For this reason, you might say that a dependent clause is *grammatically* less important than an independent, or main, clause. But this does not necessarily mean the dependent clause is less important in *meaning* than the main clause. In a

---

TIPS FOR WRITERS—CHOOSE MODIFIERS THAT WORK FOR YOU

It is pointless to say *female* women because all women are female. *Female* does not narrow the meaning of *women* and serves no purpose at all in your writing. Here are a few more examples of combinations that would contribute nothing to your work but a dreary wordiness:

> *unimportant* trivia
> *sorrowful* grief
> to succeed *well*
> to assemble *together*
> a *good* benefit

The italicized modifier does nothing to advance your job. Instead it repeats a quality you already know exists in the head word. It becomes deadwood.

Consider this example:

> Wordy: Eating out was a *pleasurable* delight.

If you flinch and say, "Show me a delight that isn't pleasurable," you understand why an effective writer often prefers no modifier at all to a repetitious one.

> Preferred: Eating out was a delight.

Still, this may be the place where you can flash the experience of eating out to your reader exactly as it struck you.

Interesting possibilities of modifiers:

> Eating out was a *luxurious* delight.
> Eating out was an *unexpected* delight.
> Eating out was a *congenial* delight.

thesis statement, a dependent clause often introduces the point of the essay. Agee's review does not dwell on the general fact expressed in the main clause, that *Meet Me in St. Louis* is a musical, but on the specific idea expressed in the *dependent* clause, that even deaf people can watch and enjoy this musical.

The decision as to which details are crucial confronts painters and photographers as well as writers. What should you include? What can you leave out? Which details will best convey to your audience your message— the crucial thing you want them to know about an event or a scene or a person? In short, which details will unmistakably deliver your point? An analogy from photography might be useful here. Imagine that you are at a golf tournament and have the opportunity to take a picture of your friend Scott wearing Jack Nicklaus's personal golfing cap. Scott, who is a golfing freak, wants this picture for his memory book. But when the snapshot is developed, Nicklaus's cap is cut off the top of the picture. Old Scott goes bananas and you run for your life. The photograph is missing its most telling detail and is worthless.

A well-composed sentence is like a well-composed photograph. It must include only the essential details you need to keep your prose compact, vigorous, and purposeful.

MAKING MODIFIERS FOR NOUNS AND VERBS

Modifiers of nouns can be single words, phrases, and clauses:

Single words: fat, skilled, kitchen, holy, hidden, embarrassing

THE FAT CATS

Holy War

Hidden Treasure

Kitchen Cabinet

skilled hands

embarrassing moment

Phrases: with a future, of beer

A Job With a Future

can of beer

Clauses: that's as adult as you are

A COLLEGE DEGREE PROGRAM THAT'S AS ADULT AS YOU ARE.

Modifiers of verbs can be single words, phrases, and clauses:

Single words: out, over, now, completely, vertically

Move Over

Call now

Cool completely

Hang vertically

Phrases: by the foot, into your living room

Success can also be measured by the foot.

Invite America's greatest theater companies into your living room.

Clauses: because he's the best operator on the court

They call Julius Erving "The Doctor" because he's the best operator on the court.

Forms of modifiers   What form should your modifier take? If you want to say, for example, that Albert is worried, there is no single correct way. Although you can express approximately the same idea in a variety of ways in English sentences, you will learn, perhaps unconsciously, to choose one over another for reasons of emphasis, compactness, or sentence rhythm.

The rest of this chapter will explore the choices that are open to you and discuss options like the following in greater detail. Notice that each modifier is a single word, a phrase, or a clause:

Sentence		Modifier
Albert is a *worried* man.	single word (verbal)	worried
Albert is a man *with worries*.	phrase	with worries
Albert is a man *who has worries*.	clause	who has worries
Albert is a man *who is worried*.	clause	who is worried
Albert is a man *worried about his job and his family*.	verbal in a phrase	worried about his job and his family
The bomb squad handled the attaché case *carefully*.	single word (adverb)	carefully
The bomb squad handled the attaché case *with care*.	phrase	with care

Single-word modifiers

Adverbs The most frequent modifiers of verbs are single words called adverbs.

DRIVE CHEERFULLY.

Cheerfully tells specifically how you should drive.

Adverbs also modify adjectives:

Strangely beautiful   "AND NOW FOR SOMETHING COMPLETELY DIFFERENT"

They modify other adverbs:

very slowly
exceptionally quickly

And they modify whole sentences:

<u>Finally</u>, it's your turn for some applause.

Finally, it's your turn for some applause.

Adverbs have few identifying marks, though many can be formed by adding -*ly* to the adjective:

slow	+	ly	=	slowly
secret	+	ly	=	secretly
premature	+	ly	=	prematurely

Add -*ly* even when the adjective ends in -*l*.

final	+	ly	=	finally
cheerful	+	ly	=	cheerfully
real	+	ly	=	really

A few short, common adverbs can be used with or without the -*ly* ending:

Short adverb	Long adverb (*with -ly*)	Both correct
slow	slowly	Drive slow. Drive slowly.
wrong	wrongly	Albert directed us wrong. Albert directed us wrongly.
tight	tightly	Pull the shoelace tight. Pull the shoelace tightly.

Other short adverb forms are *bright, cheap, close, deep, loose, smooth, quick, loud.*

WATCH OUT FOR SPELLING OF ADVERBS

Write the full form of adverbs ending in -*ly*. Unlike slow/slowly, most adverbs have only the -*ly* form. Without -*ly*, the word is an adjective:

NO: She was *considerable* delayed in traffic.
YES: She was *considerably* delayed in traffic.

NO: Albert's wife sings *different* in church.
YES: Albert's wife sings *differently* in church.

NO: We were *horrible* disappointed by the game the Astros played last night.
YES: We were *horribly* disappointed by the game the Astros played last night.

See Chapter 17, page 429, for a discussion of spelling rules.

Exercise 3   Some of the following sentences require an adjective and some an adverb. Fill in each blank with the correct form of the word.

1. Mounds chocolate bars are _____ delicious. (indescribable/ indescribably)

2. I arrived here yesterday after a _____ rough voyage. (real/ really)

3. The sky turned _____ in the afternoon. (dark/darkly)

4. He is unhappy with an _____ buzzing sound in the new piano. (occasional/occasionally)

5. Please speak _____ to Uncle Hugo. (loud/loudly)

6. Walk _____ along the edge of the wall. (steady/steadily)

7. I see everything in a _____ light. (different/differently)

8. Albert went _____ after the collision to the Motor Vehicles Bureau. (immediate/immediately)

9. Ravel _____ felt _____ about reports of a misunderstanding with Toscanini. (sure/surely) (bad/badly)

10. The young Liszt had a _____ precocious imagination. (terrible/terribly)

Adjectives   That *beautiful* woman is my *maternal* grandmother.

FAST FOODS *good reason*

Free Spirit   **a clean ashtray**

The word that makes the meaning of a noun more specific is an adjective:

beautiful	clean
maternal	good
fast	free

Adjectives are descriptive words that usually go before the noun they modify. You can spot certain adjectives by their endings:

-ous	marvelous
-al	maternal
-ful	beautiful
-ic	realistic
-ive	descriptive

Exercise 4 Rewrite the following sentences so that the italicized words can be used in adjective form. Use a dictionary if you need help.

Example: You are a *marvel.*
You are *marvelous.*

1. Pierre shows a lot of *aggression* when grades are due.
2. His parents *permit* him to do anything he wants.
3. Pierre's new car is the color of a blue *metal.*
4. It has many gadgets that are a *wonder.*
5. Pierre has become an *authority* on rear window defoggers.
6. He showed a lot of *skill* when he installed his tape deck.
7. Pierre has a lot of *curiosity* about the mileage he will get.
8. His ideas about motorcycle motors reveal his *concern* with progress.
9. Once he acquired his own car, his popularity shot upward like a *meteor.*
10. When he talks about his car, he is full of *emotion.*

Modifiers as Modifiers can occur as completers in the sentence pattern that uses linking
completers verbs (subject–linking verb–completer):

The champion looked *punchy.*

The heiress to the pantyhose fortune was *barelegged.*

. Modifiers can also occur following direct objects of other verbs:

You make me *sick.*

They found the bank guard *bleeding.*

In sentences using linking verbs (such as *seem, look, appear, feel,* and forms of *to be*), use an *adjective* to show that the completer refers to the subject.

Linking verb: Albert's wife is thoughtful.
(*Thoughtful* describes Albert's wife.)

Linking verb: Albert's wife feels bad.
(*Bad* describes Albert's wife.)

Linking verb: Albert's wife looks eager.
(*Eager* describes Albert's wife.)

In other sentences, use an *adverb* to describe the action of the verb.

Not linking: Albert's wife looked eagerly through the microscope. (In this sentence, what follows the word *looked* does not describe Albert's wife. It describes the action of looking through the microscope, and takes the form of an adverb.)

WATCH OUT FOR <u>GOOD</u> AND <u>WELL</u>, <u>BAD</u> AND <u>BADLY</u>, <u>REAL</u>, AND <u>SURE</u>

1. *Good* and *well* can both be used as adjectives.

    Linking pattern:

    YES (Adjective):   She feels *good* when she raises money.
    (happy, satisfied)

    YES (Adjective):   She feels *well* when she gets enough sleep.
    (in good health)

    Only *well* can be used as an adverb.

    Not a linking pattern:

    NO (Adjective):   She works *good* with children.

    YES (Adverb):   She works *well* with children.

2. Many speakers overcorrect their speech and say, "I feel badly about . . ." instead of "I feel bad about . . ."

    Linking pattern:

    NO (Adverb):   I feel *badly* about Albert and his wife.

    (To *feel badly* means to do a bad job of experiencing something through your sense of touch—for example, *We felt our way badly through the tunnel*.)

    Yes (Adjective):   I feel *bad* about Albert and his wife.

3. *Real, sure, good,* and *bad* are inappropriate as adverbs in written English:

    NO: We *sure* waited a long time.

    YES: We *surely* waited a long time.

    NO: The chicken with artichokes was *real* special.

    YES: The chicken with artichokes was *really* special.

    NO: Albert doesn't cook *bad*.

    YES: Albert doesn't cook *badly*.

    NO: Albert's wife plays tennis as *good* as Arthur Ashe.

    YES: Albert's wife plays tennis as *well* as Arthur Ashe.

Comparing Adjectives and adverbs can be compared to show greater or lesser degree.
adjectives and They change form according to the following system:
adverbs

6 soft, softer, softest 9

Most adjectives of one syllable:

Positive	**Comparative**	**Superlative**
(Describe *one*)	(Compare *two*)	(Compare *three* or *more*)
Kleenex is *soft*.	Kleenex is *softer* than other tissues.	Kleenex is the *softest* tissue in the world.
strong	stronger (than . . .) less strong	the strongest (in the . . .) the least strong

Longer adjectives:

suspicious	more suspicious less suspicious	the most suspicious
economical	more economical	the most economical

Adverbs:

tightly	more tightly	the most tightly
suspiciously	more suspiciously less suspiciously	the most suspiciously the least suspiciously

Irregular words:

good, well	better	the best
bad, badly	worse	the worst

Other single-word modifiers of nouns are not adjectives and cannot be compared. They are (modifiers in italics):

1. Numbers
   28 flavors, *fifty* stars

2. Possessives
   Robert Redford's career, *Colorado's* mountains, *your* headache (See Chapter 17 for a discussion of possessives.)

3. Other nouns
   kitchen cabinet, *chocolate* milk, *milk* chocolate, *hotel* room, *overcoat* weather

4. Names of people, places, institutions, or things (written with an initial capital letter)
   an *IBM* mind, a *Beatles* tune, my *Chicago* relatives, *Rolls Royce* economics, the *Yale* game, *Alabama* fried chicken

One of the pleasant characteristics of English is that you can move a noun into the position of an adjective to do the work of an adjective without changing the ending of the noun (*kitchen* cabinet, the *Yale* game). This easy transfer adds color to your writing without adding unnecessary words. *Her IBM mind,* for example, consists of three snappy words. In some contexts, that can be a real economy compared with the eight words of *She had a mind like an IBM machine.*

WATCH OUT FOR TOO MANY NOUNS IN A ROW

Try not to put more than two nouns together. Phrases like the following suffocate meaning and force your readers to slow down as they sort out ideas. Remember that modifiers should clarify, not confuse.

CONFUSING:	CLEAR:
career educator workshops	workshops for career educators
railroad timetable improvement	improvement of the railroad time-table
high school athletics committee money problems	money problems of the high school athletics committee

Note: In the *confusing* column, the noun being described (for example, *workshops*) comes last after a string of modifiers. In the *clear* column, this noun comes first and is followed by phrases or clauses in explanation.

Readers frequently trip on sentences that contain too many nouns in a row. Bombarded with noun forms, they have no signals that say which of the nouns are modifiers:

High school athletics committee money problems will be discussed at the next Board of Education meeting.

Readers stumble along thinking each of those first four nouns is about to tie to a verb, only to encounter still another noun along the way. The fifth noun, *problems,* finally ties to the verb *will be discussed.*

---

*Superlative
adjective forms
from the* Guinness
Book of World
Records

Weight

Lightest Humans. The lightest recorded adult was Lucia Zarate, born in San Carlos, Mexico, on January 2, 1863. At birth she weighed 2½ lbs. This emaciated ateliotic dwarf of 26½ inches weighed 4.7 lbs. at the age of 17. She "fattened up" to 13 lbs. by her 20th birthday. She died in October, 1889.

The thinnest recorded adults of normal height are those suffering from Simmonds' disease (Hypophyseal cachexia). Losses up to 65 per cent of the original body weight have been recorded in females, with a "low" of 45 lbs. in the case of Emma Shaller (1868–1890) of St. Louis, Missouri, who stood 5 feet 2 inches tall. In cases of anorexia nervosa, weights of under 70 lbs. have been reported.

It was recorded that the American exhibitionist Rosa Lee Plemons (born 1873) weighed 27 lbs. at the age of 18. Edward C. Hagner (1892–1962), *alias* Eddie Masher, is alleged to have weighed only 48 lbs. at a height of 5 feet 7 inches. He was also known as "the Skeleton Dude." In August, 1825, the biceps measurement of Claude-Ambroise Seurat (born April 10, 1797, died April 6, 1826), of Troyes, France, was 4 inches and the distance between his back and his chest was less than 3 inches. He stood 5 feet 7½ inches and weighed 78 lbs., but in another account was described as 5 feet 4 inches and only 36 lbs.

Heaviest Man. The heaviest medically weighed human was the 6-foot-0½-inch tall Robert Earl Hughes (born 1926) of Monticello, Illinois. An 11¼-lb. baby, he weighed 203 lbs. at 6 years, 378 lbs. at 10, 546 lbs. at 13, 693 lbs. at 18, 896 lbs. at 25, and 945 lbs. at 27. His greatest recorded weight was 1,069 lbs. in February, 1958, and he weighed 1,041 lbs. at the time of his death. His claimed waist of 122 inches, his chest of 124 inches and his upper arm of 40 inches were the greatest on record. Hughes died of uremia (condition caused by retention of urinary matter in the blood) in a trailer at Bremen, Indiana, on July 10, 1958, aged 32, and was buried in Benville Cemetery, near Mount Sterling, Illinois. His coffin, as large as a piano case measuring 7 feet by 4 feet 4 inches and weighing more than 1,100 lbs., had to be lowered by crane. It was once claimed by a commercial interest that Hughes had weighed 1,500 lbs.—a 40 per cent exaggeration.

Races

Tallest. The tallest race in the world is the Tutsi (also called Batutsi, Watutsi, or Watussi), Nilotic herdsmen of Rwanda and Burundi, Central Africa, whose males *average* 6 feet 1 inch, with a maximum of 7 feet 6 inches. A tribe with an average height of more than 6 feet was discovered in the inland region of Passis Manua of New Britain in December, 1956. In May, 1965, it was reported that the Crahiacoro Indians in the border district of the States of Mato Grosso and Pará, in Brazil, are exceptionally tall—certainly more than 6 feet. A report in May, 1966, specifically attributed great stature to the Kran-hacacore Indians of the Xingu region of the Mato Grosso, whose adult males reputedly averaged more than 6 feet 6 inches. In December, 1967, the inhabitants of Barbuda, Leeward Islands, were reported to have an average height in excess of 6 feet.

WATCH OUT FOR COMPARISONS

Unnecessary repetitions

1. Do not put *more* or *most* before adjectives of one syllable to which you have already added -*er* or -*est:*

NO:	YES:
more better	better
more tighter	tighter
most greenest	greenest
most worst	worst

2. Do not add -*er* or -*est* to adjectives of one syllable when they are preceded by *less* or *least:*

NO:	YES:
less smarter	less smart
least strongest	least strong

Worse and worst

Do not use *the worse* when you mean *the worst:*
  NO: That is *the worse* city in the world.
  YES: That is *the worst* city in the world.

When you compare *two* of anything, use *worse:*
The smog in L.A. is *worse* than it is in Pittsburgh.

When you compare *three or more* of anything, use *the worst:*

That city has *the worst* smog in the world.
    (More than two cities in the world have smog.)

Exercise 5 Write ads for the five possessions listed below. Be sure to spell *than* (as in *sexier than*) with an *a. Then* with an *e* means *at that time* (as in *Then I walked out).*

Example: My underwear is _____ than Raquel Welch's.
    My underwear is *sexier* than Raquel Welch's.

    My electric typewriter runs more _____ than a Rolls Royce.
    My electric typewriter runs more *quietly* than a Rolls Royce.

1. My jacket
2. My stereo
3. My wristwatch

4. My bed
5. My telephone directory

Exercise 6

THE MOST EXTRAVAGANT $17⁵⁰ PIECE OF JEWELRY EVER MADE.

The smallest present might just be the biggest gift.

Write your own sentences using each of the following adjectives in the superlative degree.

Example: strategic
superlative: most strategic

The *most strategic* mind in the world probably belongs to a chess champion.

1. liberal	**6.** puzzling
2. impressive	**7.** tireless
3. low	**8.** unscrupulous
4. staunch	**9.** sly
5. milky	**10.** comical

Exercise 7 Read aloud the following phrases, which have been taken from textbooks, magazines, and newscasts. Notice what a mouthful each is. Rewrite each phrase for greater clarity, using no more than two nouns in succession.

Example: theater performance training
Rewritten: training for performance in the theater

1. state unemployment committee research
2. childhood personality growth graph
3. family vacation country
4. pocket camera film
5. television program options smorgasbord
6. sewage storage tank explosion

Exercise 8 In the following movie reviews, fill in each blank with a modifier that narrows down, identifies, or explains the noun that follows. Be daring.

1. [Jean Simmons] is a(n) _____, _____, _____ girl and unquestionably a(n) _____ one; she also has the makings of a _____, _____ movie star. She already gets _____ fan letters a week. Among them there have already been _____ proposals of marriage and a proposition from a (n) _____ chiropodist which is the ultimate sort of accolade a _____ star must get used to. Would Miss Simmons be so kind, the _____ fan asked, as to send him a photograph of her feet, and a sliver of toenail?

James Agee

2. Benjamin is a _____ _____ graduate who returns to his parents' _____ home and flops—on his bed, on the _____ raft in the pool. Politely and dispassionately, he declines the options thrust at him by _____ society. The _____ wife of his father's _____ partner seduces him. Benjamin is increasingly _____ in the continuing affair, for _____ reasons. . . . (The _____ scene in which Benjamin tries to get her to *talk* to him is a jewel.) The woman's daughter comes home from college, and against the _____ wishes, Benjamin takes her out. He falls in love with the girl—which is _____ but entirely _____. He is blackmailed into telling her about his affair with her mother, and in revulsion, the girl flees—back to Berkeley. Benjamin follows, hangs about the campus, almost gets her to marry him, loses her (through her _____ interference), pursues her, and finally gets her. For once, a _____ ending makes *us* feel _____.

Stanley Kauffmann

Exercise 9 Think of a restaurant you know well (the college cafeteria, McDonald's, a local diner, or the like). You may have to revisit the restaurant to observe the place more purposefully. Using fifteen of the categories in the review on the next page, write a three-paragraph review of your restaurant. Rate your restaurant on a scale of forks, one to five with five forks being an outstanding eating establishment. Justify your rating with convincing details. Be vivid and truthful.

Restaurant Reviews

The Best and Worst, the Most and Least In 20 Star-Filled Months of Dining Out

By JOHN CANADAY

In an idle hour one day last week we thumbed through our card file of 208 starred restaurants visited during the last 20 months and jotted down a few retrospective mosts, leasts, bests and worsts, as follows:

Best meal in a major French restaurant: La Caravelle.

Worst meal in a major French restaurant: Le Manoir.

Best service in a major French restaurant: Le Cygne.

Worst service in a major French restaurant: Le Mistral.

Most attractive quarters, major French restaurant: Lutèce.

Most surprising clatter and stacking of dishes in otherwise elegant quarters, **major** French restaurant: Lutèce.

Handsomest ethnic restaurant: Tandoor.

Most sensational restaurant interior of any kind in New York: Maxwell's Plum.

Most unexpectedly excellent food in New York: Maxwell's Plum.

Most satisfactory continued performance in small restaurant following enthusiastic review: Parioli Romanissimo.

Most satisfactory continued performance in large restaurant following enthusiastic review: Il Monello.

Most embarrassing deterioration in restaurant of any kind following enthusiastic review: Il Rigoletto.

Most inexcusable rudeness to customers and disregard of reservations following favorable review: Nicola's.

Favorite pub: Billy's.

Most precious atmosphere: The Box Tree.

Topnotch restaurant least frequently recognized as topnotch: Chalet Suisse.

Pleasantest intimate Village restaurant: Charlie & Kelly.

Best rabbit: Chez Napoleon.

Best steak: Christ Cella.

Most interesting limited menu: Coriander.

Most arrogant captains: Orsini's.

Most indifferent captains: Barbetta's.

Most disappointing performance under pressure: De Cuir's.

Most eager to please: La Toque Blanche.

Least Japanese Japanese restaurant: Inagiku.

Most Japanese Japanese restaurant: Kitcho.

Best Japanese proof that East is East and West is West but harmoniously the twain may meet: Saito.

Most effusive host-proprietor: El Parador.

Host-proprietor most closely resembling Henri Matisse: Ballato.

Most patrician host-proprietor: Giovanni.

Most authentic small Spanish restaurant: El Rincon de España.

Most attractive presentation of dishes, small restaurant: Gavroche.

Silliest name: Genghiz Khan's Bicycle.

Personal over-all favorite, Italian: Isle of Capri.

Most welcome newcomer, Chinese: House of Tu.

Most genuine Bohemian atmosphere: Inca Bar and Restaurant.

Small Indian Restaurant most neglected by public: India Pavilion.

Best Turkish food in simplest quarters: Istanbul Cuisine.

Most for your money: La Bonne Soupe.

Inspiration of largest number of letters complaining of ill treatment of female guests unaccompanied by males: Le Chambertin.

Worst restaurant in proportion to its popularity: Le Cirque.

Most inexplicably popular restaurant: Le Moal.

Most disastrous and unnecessary remodeling of what was one of the coziest restaurants in town: Le Steak.

The New York Times/Stan Mack

Most habitually overrated restaurant, French: Veau d'Or.

Most habitually overrated restaurant, other: Lüchow's.

Prettiest Japanese appointments: Yoshi's.

Most sinister atmosphere: Ponte's.

Most crowded tables at the price: Café Argenteuil.

Most crowded tables at any price: Nodeldini's.

Most nostalgic recall of pre-World War II New York, midtown: Algonquin.

Most nostalgic recall of pre-World War II Greenwich Village: Portofino.

Most nostalgic re-creation of classy Parisian bistro: La Goulue.

Most curious hybrid: Bernstein-on-Essex Kosher Chinese Delicatessen **and** Restaurant.

Steamiest: Cabana Carioca.

Most beautiful flowers: La Grenouille.

Waitresses most resembling flowers: Arirang House.

Highest decibel count: One If by Land, Two If by Sea.

Saddest demise: Mandarin East.

Least regretted demise: La Croisette.

Most welcome return from the dead: Grand Central Oyster Bar.

Least worth the trouble: "21."

Verbals Many modifiers of nouns are formed from verbs:

sagging	guaranteed
moisturizing	limited
laughing	skimmed

-ing *Verbals* Use *-ing* modifiers to add immediacy to your writing. The *-ing* form gives the sense that an action is continuing to happen:

a competing airline

flying insects

enchanting places

embarrassing moment
enchanting places
sagging sofa

Use *-ing* forms in any sentence slots that contain nouns:

s + MODIFIER	LV	C
That *laughing* woman	is	my boss.

-ed *Verbals* Use *-ed* modifiers when the action expressed by the modifier has already been completed:

Regular forms	*Irregular forms*
skimmed milk	*hidden* treasure
limited time	*ground* pepper
	frozen yogurt

for a limited time only   selected theatres

Broken Pipes

FROZEN YOGURT   proven performance

Limited Edition

NEEDED IMPROVEMENTS   Marked improvement

Use -ed forms in any sentence slots that contain nouns:

S   V   C + MODIFIER
I drank the *skimmed* milk.

Condensed Books   **United States**

DIGNIFIED PERSONAL SERVICE   DISTINGUISHED BOARD

United Artists   ***Unadvertised Specials***

sweetened concentrate

WATCH OUT FOR OMITTED -ED ENDINGS

The final -*ed* has come to be a sign of competence in written English. Read the examples on this page aloud, emphasizing the final *d* sounds. If you know you have a problem with endings, always proofread your work once exclusively to check for -*ed* endings.

Notice how the following sentences are changed to form phrases with verbals.

The sofa sags.   the *sagging* sofa
Hair is unwanted.   *unwanted* hair
Time is limited.   *limited* time
The lotion moisturizes.   the *moisturizing* lotion
The milk is skimmed.   the *skimmed* milk
The woman is laughing.   the *laughing* woman

Use verbals to combine sentences:

The sofa sags. It needs repair.   The sagging sofa needs repair.

Hair is unwanted. Hair is removed by electric tweezers.   Unwanted hair is removed by electric tweezers.

See Chapter 17 to find out how to form -*ing* and -*ed* verbals.

Exercise 10 Combine each of the following pairs of sentences into one sentence that contains an -*ing* modifier.

Example: I listened to the traffic light for an hour.
           The traffic light was clicking.
Combined: I listened to the *clicking* traffic light for an hour.

1. I invited the professor to the Spanish Club.
   The professor was visiting.
2. Stars warn us of catastrophe.
   Stars shoot.

3. The snow will freeze tonight.
   The snow is melting.

4. The students are highly vocal.
   The students attend the law school.

5. Amy was the only contestant who wrote the words and the music.
   Amy was among the contestants who were winners.

Exercise 11 Combine each of the following pairs of sentences into one sentence that contains an -ed (-en) modifier.

Example: The turkey was in the refrigerator.
           The turkey was stuffed and roasted.
Combined: The *stuffed* and *roasted* turkey was in the refrigerator.

1. The sentence was unnecessary.
   The sentence was deleted.

2. Stephanie tiptoed up the steps.
   The steps had carpeting on them.

3. The page had a lot of errors.
   The page was typewritten.

4. The dollar bill split in half.
   The dollar bill was taped.

5. The house shone in the sun.
   The house was freshly painted.

Exercise 12 Expand the following sentences by adding adjectives, verbals, or other single-word modifiers to the subjects or completers.

Example: The pilot and the stewardess were married.
         The *balding TWA* pilot and the *unforgettable Lufthansa* stewardess were married.

1. The elevator crashed.
2. The accountant caught a fish.
3. Citizens bought guns.
4. Monet painted snowstorms.
5. The sign said, "For Sale."
6. Indians hunted game.
7. The child looked for her parents.
8. The oboist played Bach.
9. Soybeans are food.

Modifiers in phrases Adjectives, verbals, and other single-word modifiers usually go *before* the nouns they describe—*black* hair, the *laughing* woman. Sometimes, however, you need more than one word to express all the ideas you have in mind about a noun. You can make your modifier more precise by expanding it into a longer, more specific unit. Modifiers expanded into phrases go *after* the nouns they describe—her hair, *black as her heart;* the woman, *laughing at the elephants*.

Whenever a single-word modifier doesn't express your idea with sufficient detail, extend it into a phrase. Then move the longer modifier into position *after* the noun.

WATCH OUT FOR COMMAS

If a sentence does *not* depend on the modifier for its meaning, separate the modifier from the sentence with commas:

> Lenore's hair glittered under the moon.
> Lenore's hair was black as her heart.

> Lenore's hair,   , glittered under the moon.
> Lenore's hair, black as her heart, glittered under the moon.
> s-v: *hair glittered*

> These men are actually members of the police department's decoy squad.
> These men are dressed in shabby and disheveled clothing.

> These men,   , are actually
> members of the police department's decoy squad.
> These men, dressed in shabby and disheveled clothing, are actually
> members of the police department's decoy squad.
> s-v: *men are*

Note: In the preceding example, commas help the reader to avoid misreading the sentence. Without commas, the s-v might be misread as *men dressed:*

No comma: These men dressed in shabby and disheveled clothing are actually members of the police department's decoy squad.

If a sentence *does* depend on the modifier for its meaning, do not separate the modifier from the sentence with commas:

> Hot dogs steamed in beer have a gourmet flavor.

> (It is not true that *hot dogs have a gourmet flavor.* Only hot dogs steamed in beer have that flavor.)

> This bakery specializes in cakes decorated the way you want them.

> (It is not true that *this bakery specializes in cakes.* This bakery's specialty is cakes decorated the way you want them.)

Writer's purpose

Adjective: black	Lenore's *black* hair glittered under the moon.	To show that the color of Lenore's hair is black.
black extended into a phrase	Lenore's hair, *black as her heart*, glittered under the moon.	To add evil to Lenore's character.
	Lenore's hair, *black as a bear's*, glittered under the moon.	To add wildness to Lenore's character.
Verbal: laughing	The *laughing* woman carried a tape recorder.	To show that the woman was laughing.
laughing extended into a phrase	The woman, *laughing at the elephants*, carried a tape recorder.	To explain specifically what the woman was laughing at.
	The woman, *laughing behind her note pad*, carried a tape recorder.	To show precisely how the woman is concealing her laughter.

TIPS FOR WRITERS—IMAGES

By extending adjectives into figurative language (for example, *clear as the sun, fair as the moon*) you can produce specific and powerful emotions in your reader. Writers and poets use images to get a lot of mileage out of a few words. By *comparing* something we don't know (his beloved) to something we do know (the moon), the writer speeds our grasp of his specific feelings, attitude, and purpose. Professor Leslie Brisman of Yale University has said that an image is like a Mack truck. It has the power to move a huge, complex idea forward in a single vehicle. (Professor Brisman's idea itself arrives as an energetic image.)

The beloved is (from *Song of Solomon*):	WRITER'S PURPOSE
fair as the moon	To show that the beloved is lovely because of a pale remoteness such as the moon has.
clear as the sun	To show that the beloved is vivid and intense.
terrible as an army with banners	To show that the beloved is fearsome, bold, and triumphant.

(See Chapter 12 for fuller treatment of figurative language.)

Single-word modifiers go before the noun

Modifiers in phrases go after the noun

**WORLD FAMOUS
HOT DOGS
STEAMED IN BEER**

steamed hot dogs

hot dogs *steamed in beer*

**machines matched
to your job**

matched machines

machines *matched to your job*

CAKES DECORATED
The Way You Want Them

decorated cakes

cakes *decorated the way you want them*

Exercise 13 In each of the following sentences, expand the italicized one-word modifier into a phrase and move the phrase to its clearest position in the sentence. Use commas where appropriate.

Example: No one comforted the *defeated* American skater.
No one comforted the American skater, *defeated by a seventeen-year-old Japanese girl who had never competed before.*

1. The President appealed to a *divided* Senate.
2. The *redesigned* gardens became an outdoor salon for all the dogs of Bedford Heights.
3. The Napoleonic Wars were a *prolonged* struggle that profoundly taxed Western Europe.
4. Social workers provide juvenile addicts with *needed* strength.
5. "Stompin' at the Savoy" is one of the greatest *recorded* swing numbers of all time.
6. The *stolen* Toronado turned up near the docks.
7. Science has impact because of its *validated* conclusions.
8. The *scattered* homes are for small groups of Georgia youngsters who cannot live in their own homes.
9. Beethoven was suspicious of the *corrected* manuscripts.
10. We tutored three classes of *underprepared* pilots.

Exercise 14   In each of the following sentences, expand the italicized one-word modifier into a phrase and move the phrase to its clearest position in the sentence. You may want to consider converting some of the modifiers into images. Use commas where appropriate.

Example: I was startled by her *white* face.
I was startled by her face, *white as a handkerchief.*

1. The farmer picked the *tiny* green tomatoes.
2. Look out for *sharp* edges.
3. Help! I see a *drowning* man.
4. No one knew what to do with the *crying* baby.
5. Alexander brought the *covered* pot to the dinner table.
6. We left the *surprised* biology teacher in the laboratory.
7. Who likes the *woven* tapestry?

Exercise 15   Read the following poem. Why does the poet repeatedly use *-ing* modifiers to convey her experience at the movies? What is the force of the *-ing* in the final use of the word *wedding*?

The Fact of the Darkness

The fact of the darkness may account for it,
the fact of my shape filling the darkness
with the seat to the left of me empty
may account for it, for my quiet tragedy
in the widowing darkness
on the aisle
with the seat to the left of me empty.
You know how we end up
holding hands, or touching knees
at the occasion
of the good parts.
Tonight everything is framed
as an occasion
here in the no-smoking darkness
where I wait with the outrage
of a bereaved,
invisible as a tree
dying in the forest,
my feet tapping in the litter of earth,
the popcorn of the man behind even now
(now as the air conditioning cools me)
spilling itself on my leg.

The eyes of couples move everywhere
past me like dogs
on their way to the screen
trained in the matinees of their youth
to find their rewards.
No one is aware of my credits.
My laughter, my sighs, the formality of my eyes
shining in the darkness
speak to no one of my taste,
how it runs to art, to spies
and sentimentality. Tonight
the lovers will take over the world
and I will have to put up with it
as they ask once again for those few
final words, *Darling, at the end,*
what was it she said?
In the darkness there is no one to tell me.
Outside, the clamminess stays in my sandals,
the lights of the shopping center fall
through the haze of the heat wave,
I run to my car, to my bed
and ask you in the wedding darkness
how it will end.

                              Sandra Schor

Prepositional phrases as modifiers Prepositional phrases also specify the meanings of nouns and verbs. (See page 140 for a list of prepositions.) Their use in English is everywhere— even in this sentence. Like other phrases, they always follow the nouns they modify:

Nouns	Prepositional phrases
Jazz	*at noon*
Joy	*of cooking*
Letters	*to the Editor*
Winner	*of six Academy Awards*

CHAMPION   **OF THE WORLD**

Parking	*in Rear*
the Gulf	*of Mexico*

Solutions   **to Last Week's Puzzles**

Plane   *With 243 Orphans*

Prepositional phrases function as adjectives:

Albert is a student *with worries*.	Albert is a *worried* student.
He wrote an essay *of distinction*.	He wrote a *distinguished* essay.
His teacher found an error *of importance*.	His teacher found an *important* error.

Prepositional phrases also function as adverbs:

The bomb squad handled the attaché case *with care*.	The bomb squad *carefully* handled the attaché case.
The police chief recommended the promotion *in a hurry*.	The police chief *hurriedly* recommended the promotion.

Exercise 16   Restrict the meaning of each italicized noun in the following sentences by adding a modifier.

Example: *Life* is difficult.
　　　　Life *during a blizzard in Buffalo* is difficult.

1. *Income* has risen sharply in the last five years.
2. I fear the dangers of *television*.
3. If you study changes in *education,* you will realize how far behind we lag.
4. Robert's *cooking* makes him the envy of all the *men*.
5. *Smoking* can be hazardous to your health.
6. Your *promise* should be appreciated by the neighbors.
7. The *law* requires that the body be disposed of overboard.
8. *Honesty* follows a special code.
9. Her *success* led to a *contract*.
10. *Humiliation* is particularly distressing.

Exercise 17   Rewrite the following sentences so that the prepositional phrases are transformed into one-word adverbs.

Example: The middleweight champion drank the Coke *with eagerness*.
　　　　The middleweight champion drank the Coke *eagerly*.

1. *With vigor* the masseur worked on the boxer.
2. Sid the Kid smiled *in gratitude*.
3. He could now move his left shoulder *without pain*.
4. The reporters remained outside so the Kid could recover *in privacy*.

5. Sometimes they hollered his name *in familiarity*.

6. Sid the Kid answered *without cheer*.

7. *In desperation* he thought that he had fought his last fight.

8. *In misery* he remembered dreams of glory.

9. The masseur patted the Kid *with confidence*.

10. Sid the Kid rose from the table and *with great caution* said farewell to the reporters.

Clauses as modifiers Most of the modifiers we have looked at in this chapter are in reality reductions of longer modifiers:

Clauses as modifiers of nouns

Reduced modifier	*Longer modifier*
I like *black* hair.	I like hair *that is black*.
We were passengers on the train during the wreckage *at rush hour*.	We were passengers on the train during the wreckage that *occurred at rush hour*.
Lenore's hair, *black as her heart*, glittered under the moon.	Lenore's hair, *which was as black as her heart*, glittered under the moon.
The *tallest* race in the world is the Watussi.	The race *that is the tallest* in the world is the Watussi.

Streamlining these long clauses produces concise, lean writing. But good writers know that it is neither always possible nor always desirable to reduce all clauses to single words or phrases. Sometimes, to be clear, a clause must be written out fully.

Like all clauses, a clause that modifies a noun has its own subject and verb. It goes after the noun and begins with the word *who, which, that, why, when,* or *where* (sometimes *whose* or *whom*).

Examples: He gave a reason why his child was late.
That is the corner where we met.

Use *who* when the clause modifies a noun that refers to a person:

THE MAN WHO CAME TO DINNER

Use *which* or *that* when the clause modifies a noun that refers to something other than a person:

A CAR THAT'S OVERLY LUXURIOUS COULD LITERALLY BORE YOU TO DEATH.

WATCH OUT FOR <u>THAT</u> AND <u>WHICH</u>

The air conditioners that drip/The air conditioners, which drip,

1. When a clause gives a noun a special qualification necessary to the understanding of the sentence, use *that* to introduce the clause:

    The air conditioners *that* drip should be reported to the Maintenance Department.

That drip identifies those air conditioners to be reported. If *that drip* were omitted, the sentence would change its meaning to the sense that all the air conditioners would need to be reported. (*The air conditioners should be reported to the Maintenance Department.*) Notice that no commas are required in the sentence because *that drip* belongs to the idea of the whole sentence. The sentence says that only air conditioners that drip should be reported. It implies that other air conditioners need not be reported.

2. When a clause does not give the noun a special meaning and is therefore unnecessary to the meaning of the whole sentence, use *which*, never *that*:

    The air conditioners, which drip, should be reported to the Maintenance Department.

The clause, *which drip,* is not essential to the meaning of the sentence. If *which drip* were omitted, this sentence would retain its original meaning. (*The air conditioners should be reported to the Maintenance Department.*) The sentence says that all air conditioners should be reported because they all drip. *Which drip* needs punctuation because it is not essential to the meaning of the whole sentence but is a parenthetical comment. This sentence might have been written, *The air conditioners (which drip) should be reported to the Maintenance Department.*

Here are two more examples:

    The mistakes *that* resulted from poor copying are being corrected by the typist.

Only mistakes in copying are being corrected by the typist. The implication is that other mistakes—perhaps those of substance—must be corrected by someone else.

    The mistakes, *which* resulted from poor copying, are being corrected by the typist.

All the mistakes resulted from poor copying, and they are all being corrected by the typist.

Sometimes modifying clauses appear without *that, who,* or *which.* The object of the clause (*that* or *whom*) is omitted.

We loved the drinking songs   the chorus sang.
We loved the drinking songs *that* the chorus sang.

The mugger resembled a man   we had seen on Broadway.
The mugger resembled a man *that* (*whom*) we had seen on Broadway.

In the last sentence, *that* is used informally instead of *whom.*

Exercise 18 Expand the following sentences by adding modifying clauses in the subject and completer slots. Use commas where appropriate.

Example: The students picketed outside the school cafeteria.
The students, *who were sick and tired of eating mashed potatoes and spaghetti,* picketed outside the school cafeteria.

1. Women have power.
2. The Exxon station ordered a sign.
3. The Queen can help you find a plumber.
4. The inspector closed Mario's souvlaki parlor.
5. Goya used the same model twice.
6. The veteran raised a flag.
7. An earthquake killed 700 persons.
8. The students threw a party for their professor.
9. Transistor radios are a blessing.
10. My grandmother has fifty-eight bankbooks.

Exercise 19 In one of your recent essays, find five nouns that you might expand by adding a modifier. Rewrite the sentences containing those nouns, adding the modifier with appropriate commas. Do you like your essay better with the modifier or without them? Explain.

Appositives An appositive is a noun that comes immediately after another noun that explains it and can act as its substitute. In the sample, *Rubinstein* is the appositive for hero.

This ageless hero, Rubinstein

Appositives may also be clauses, phrases, or other words that behave like nouns.

my favorite sport, *swimming* (appositive identifies my favorite sport)
the racer's fear *that he would die violently* (appositive restates the racer's fear)
her wish *to visit Hawaii* (appositive identifies her wish)

Appositives are reductions of longer forms. Consider the following:

Koko, who is a gorilla	Koko the gorilla
Dennis, who is a menace	Dennis the Menace
Otto Soglow, who was a cartoonist	Otto Soglow, the cartoonist,
my favorite sport, which is swimming	my favorite sport, swimming,

---

TIPS FOR WRITERS—SAVE WORDS BY COMBINING RELATED SENTENCES

You can move an extra idea into a sentence by adding an appositive to explain or identify a noun:

My favorite sport is fun all year.
My favorite sport is swimming.
My favorite sport,   , is fun all year.
My favorite sport, swimming, is fun all year.

Her wish finally came true.
Her wish was to visit Hawaii.
Her wish   finally came true.
Her wish to visit Hawaii finally came true.

WATCH OUT FOR COMMAS WITH APPOSITIVES

When an appositive is part of a title, do not use commas:

The explorers Lewis and Clark
My cousin Ellen

When an appositive is not part of a title and is not essential to the meaning of a sentence, use commas:

Otto Soglow, the cartoonist, died.
My favorite sport, swimming, is fun all year.

When an appositive is essential to the meaning of a sentence, do not use commas:

Her wish to visit Hawaii finally came true.
The racer's fear that he would die violently made him give up racing.

Obituaries make frequent use of the appositive.

Otto Soglow, <u>Cartoonist</u>, Dies; Creator of 'Little King' Was 74

By WILLIAM M. FREEMAN

Otto Soglow, the cartoonist who created "The Little King" and other characters, was found dead yesterday in his apartment at 330 West 72d Street. Death was ascribed to emphysema or a heart attack. He was 74 years old.

Otto Soglow

Giancana, <u>Gangster</u>, Slain;

Groucho Marx, <u>Film Comedian and Host of 'You Bet Your Life</u>,' Dies

Exercise 20 Combine each of the following pairs of sentences into one sentence containing an appositive. Underline the appositive. The sentences are adapted from an article called "Sharks" by Elizabeth Keiffer (*New York Times*, May 4, 1975).

Example: Sharks are set apart from all other fishes except their relatives. Their relatives are the skates and rays.

Appositive: Sharks are set apart from all other fishes except their relatives, *the skates and rays.*

1. John G. Casey got hooked on sharks some 12 years ago. John G. Casey is the 41-year-old director of the research project.

2. Wesley Pratt is interested in the reproductive cycle of the blue shark. Wesley Pratt is a 30-year-old underwater photographer.

3. Charles Stillwell is making a study of what sharks eat. Charles Stillwell is an experienced diver.

4. Americans never lack for protein. Americans are notoriously finicky fish eaters.

5. Some species of shark provide juicy white steaks. These species are notably the mako and the sandbar.

PROBLEMS WITH MODIFIERS

Remember that you use modifiers to improve the way your sentence expresses your idea. Modifiers must help your sentence clarify your idea. Though you are free to move certain modifiers to different positions in your sentence, each modifier must *clearly* refer to the term it describes. Two problems may result when modifiers do *not* clearly refer to the terms they describe.

Misplaced modifiers   A misplaced modifier is one that is placed near a term the writer does not intend to describe. Faulty placement clouds meaning, causing confusion and often unintended humor.

		Confused effect
Misplaced modifier:	*Stewed in brandy,* Uncle Albert served the peaches.	Uncle Albert, not the peaches, appears to be stewed in brandy.
YES:	Uncle Albert served the peaches stewed in brandy.	
Misplaced modifier:	Lenore's hair glittered under the moon, *black as night.*	The moon, not Lenore's hair, appears to be black as night.
YES:	Lenore's hair, black as night, glittered under the moon.	
Misplaced modifier:	*Ill-housed, ill-clad, ill-nourished,* I see one-third of a nation.	The speaker, not the nation, appears to be ill-housed, ill-clad, and ill-nourished.
YES:	I see one-third of a nation ill-housed, ill-clad, ill-nourished.	

Franklin Delano Roosevelt,
Second Inaugural Address,
January 20, 1937

Consider Groucho Marx's famous quip:

"One morning I shot an elephant in my pajamas. How he got into my pajamas, I don't know. Then we tried to remove the tusks but they were embedded so firmly that we couldn't budge them. Of course, in Alabama the Tuscaloosa. But that's entirely irrelephant . . ."

A modifier that falls between two terms may require your reader to guess which term the modifier describes. To take the guesswork out of your reader's decision, move the modifier to a position in which your meaning is unmistakable, as in the first example below:

		Confused effect
Misplaced modifier:	The solutions that the students discovered *immediately* impressed their teacher.	Did the students discover them immediately or was the teacher immediately impressed?
YES:	The solutions that the students *immediately* discovered impressed their teacher.	
	The solutions that the students discovered impressed their teacher *immediately*.	
Misplaced modifier:	The teller said *on Friday* the bank would be closed.	Did the teller say this on Friday or will the bank be closed on Friday?
YES:	The teller said on Friday *that* the bank would be closed.	
	The teller said *that* on Friday the bank would be closed.	

Dangling modifiers A modifier is said to dangle when the term being described does not appear in the sentence. When readers see a modifying phrase, they expect it to describe the noun closest to it. But when the intended noun is omitted, the modifier will appear to lean toward the nearest noun in the sentence, creating uncertainty for the reader and, frequently, unintended humor.

		Confused effect
Dangling modifier:	Looking out the window, a horse came down the street.	Was the horse looking out the window?
Improved:	Looking out the window, I saw a horse come down the street.	
or:	As I was looking out the window, a horse came down the street.	
or:	I looked out the window and saw a horse come down the street.	

Dangling modifier:	At the age of seventeen, a car is a challenge.	Is the car seventeen years old? (It is true, of course, that a seventeen-year-old car *would* be a challenge.)
Improved:	To a seventeen-year-old, a car is a challenge.	
or:	When you are seventeen, a car is a challenge.	
Dangling modifier:	Soft and mushy, Albert baked a banana cake.	Was Albert soft and mushy?
Improved:	Albert used the soft, mushy bananas in a banana cake.	
or:	Since the bananas were soft and mushy, Albert baked a banana cake.	
Dangling modifier:	Buried under mulch for the winter, Jerry settled down to wait for spring.	Was Jerry buried under mulch for the winter?
Improved:	With next spring's lilies buried under mulch for the winter, Jerry settled down to wait for them.	

Exercise 21 Ambiguities can result from awkward placement of modifiers. Revise these sentences by repositioning the modifier or rewriting the sentence completely. In your own writing, make revisions like these as you edit your first draft.

1. The woman with the baby who was complaining about the perfume called the manager.
2. A man rode a horse in swim trunks.
3. After opening the oven door, the chicken cooked more slowly.
4. Pregnant and en route to the hospital, a traffic cop told Mrs. Rogers to pull over.
5. Taking a bath, the water stopped.
6. Members of the Club Español sold tickets for the car wash in their Cervantes class.
7. Blowing through the trees, we pulled on our sweaters.
8. Strolling through the park, a stone lion suddenly appeared.

9. Being a good dancer, Sally entered her brother Curtis in the dance contest.

10. By rewiring the telephone lines on the main road, service was finally restored.

Exercise 22 Rewrite this tragic headline so that the unfortunate and unintended humor is eliminated.

Girl, 13, Found Slain by Road

Exercise 23 Rewrite the following sentences so that the misplaced or dangling modifier clearly refers to its noun.

Example: Private art collections often are amassed and kept unavailable to scholars *in virtual secrecy*.
(Which are in virtual secrecy, the scholars or the private art collections?)
Improved: Private art collections often are amassed *in virtual secrecy* and kept unavailable to scholars.

1. The handsome display was approved by the curators in a separate gallery.

2. One bronze bracelet was guarded by security men in the main showcase.

3. The guide said the unusual pieces of Greek jewelry reflect the taste of the people who owned them on the tour.

4. One of the tourists, herself a jeweler, offered to make Greek-style earrings for my friends with screws in them.

5. The exhibition was sponsored by a local Greek nightclub on the third floor of the museum.

6. Craftsmen came to study the ancient designs from all over the state.

7. Working in silver, the craftsmen's imitations were excellent.

8. Sketching a second-century anklet, the facing lion's heads met above the ankle bone.

9. Guards passed among the visitors charged especially with the security of a rare bronze head of Hadrian.

10. Viewing those ancient personal treasures, my own necklace felt like a mark of royal identity.

**WATCH OUT FOR SUBJECT-VERB AGREEMENT
WITH INTERVENING MODIFIERS**

A modifier that comes between a subject and its verb may seem to disconnect the subject from its verb and lead you to make errors in subject-verb
agreement.

AGREEMENT ERROR:	The *price* of eggs *are* high.
CORRECT:	The *price* of eggs *is* high.

s-v: *price is*

When you add the modifier *of eggs,* you do not change the s-v unit of the
sentence. *Price* is still the subject, and *price* is still a singular noun requiring
a singular verb. You can add a great variety of modifiers without changing
the s-v of the sentence:

	S-V
The price of an egg is high.	PRICE IS
The price of watermelon is high.	PRICE IS
The price of movie tickets is high.	PRICE IS
The price of polyester pants is high.	PRICE IS
The price of fish is high.	PRICE IS
The price in Mexico is lower.	PRICE IS
The price in the West Indies is higher.	PRICE IS
The price in the department stores is higher.	PRICE IS
The price in the discount stores is lower.	PRICE IS

For a full review of agreement problems and exercises on agreement, see
Chapter 14.

Part
Three

Choosing
Effectively

Chapter 10

Writing Convincing Paragraphs

unified
coherent
complete

You might say that your writing has been going forward in two arenas, one inside of the other. Right from the start, you have been thinking big, reaching for the whole essay, rounding up your ideas and arranging them in a few basic ways to form wholes. At the same time, you have been taking an inside look at the grammar of sentences because good sense tells you how impossible it is to write long pieces without some precision in the smaller units that form them. So your twin efforts call for practice in strengthening the larger form—the essay—and the smaller form—the sentence and its parts.

Every time you write a clear sentence, you are nailing down the meaning of your whole essay. That is one of the pleasures you have been working toward in your frequent writing practice. Your meaning shows itself, not in one dandy, well-written sentence, but as you chase it along in sentence after sentence, refining it and developing it. The clearer each sentence, the easier the task of presenting your whole message becomes. Now that you are gaining confidence in your writing skills, you may feel a mounting need to organize the sentences that make up the body of your essay. You want to relate them to one another and group them into bundles that "interpret" what you are saying. And just as you understand what your point is when you arrange the subsections of your essay in a clear design, so the reader also has a chance to consider your whole meaning through the orderly, reasonable, and always visible presentation of its parts. These subsections in the thinking of your whole essay are the units of control we call *paragraphs*.

WHAT DO PARAGRAPHS DO?

The following examples show the history of one piece of writing from its earliest glimmers in ten minutes of freewriting to a fairly solid essay with paragraphs. It is entirely possible that you may rely on other methods to get your writing started, but, whatever your method, your swing toward writing convincing paragraphs will be similar to what follows.

Freewriting

Gotta go to work soon. Wonder if Pete will be there. Pete is the kind of guy who borrows a dollar and then eats your lunch. But when he isn't there I miss him. He's smart and keeps me entertained. Gotta make some money. Want to pay for the bracelet for Marjorie. Wonder where she is now. I have to work or I don't get any money. Too hard at home. Won't ask. Gotta help myself. God helps those etc. Not even a living wage but I get to learn a lot about the public. About Pete, and his kid and his old lady. And about customers that eat bleu cheese ice cream. Wonder when this will be over over over over over. I feel like I'm wasting time. I gotta go to work. What is everybody in here writing about? Better keep writing. Maybe I'll find an idea for my assignment. I work until 10:30 tonight. Not much time left at the end of the day. Hope Pete is there or I'll lose my mind mind mind mind.

Underlined sentences

When he isn't there I miss him.
Gotta make some money. Gotta help myself.
Too hard at home.
Want to pay for the bracelet for Marjorie.
I get to learn a lot about the public.
About Peter. And about customers.
Not much time left at the end of the day.

Outline

I have to work while I go to college.
    I don't earn much money.
      Enough for pocket money, extras, gifts.
I learn a lot from the interesting/strange people I meet.
    Customers have strange habits.
    Peter is an interesting guy.
I don't have much time left at the end of the day.

Rough first draft

I have to work while I go to college. This year I have a job as a counterman at a Baskin-Robbins ice cream store.

My job gives me money I wouldn't otherwise have. I don't earn very much, but it is enough for pocket money, to buy some extras like a book or a hamburger, or gifts when an occasion for a gift comes up, and even when there's no special occasion.

I learn a lot from the interesting and strange people I meet. Customers are a group who have strange habits. They buy weird flavors and then are sorry. Peter, the guy I work with, is an interesting person. He knows about international affairs, is married, has a kid, goes to school, and has two jobs. I learn a lot at my job.

But I don't have much time left at the end of the day.

As you read over the stages of this piece of writing, you may make a few observations: for one thing, the freewriting sounds much more natural than the rough first draft. That is because the rough first draft is not very different from the outline—jerky, sketchy, telegraphic, and not fully developed. It leaves you dissatisfied because it doesn't flow the way a relaxed, fully developed piece of writing should. Its sentences are not fluent. They are abrupt and contain few details. No sooner do you meet an idea than it's behind you. On the whole, the piece of writing leaves you with a lot of unanswered questions.

The difference between an outline and a fully developed essay lies in the expansion of each subsection into a paragraph. In a paragraph, you play out your ideas. You grab hold of an idea and elaborate it, inviting the reader to follow the steps in your thinking. In this rough first draft, the headings of the outline have merely been included in sentence form, without much further development. The essay remains essentially an outline. However promising the ideas in this outline, the "writing up" has taken them no further.

Since this is a rough first draft, the next action on the writing cycle is for the writer to reenter the piece of writing, to work it through again in an effort to expand the ideas and show the reader plainly how he moved from one thought to the next.

Suppose you are the writer of this essay. What are some of the thoughts that go through your mind as you try to enlarge the sentences of this draft into fuller paragraphs?

Sentence:	*I have to work while I go to college.*
Key words:	have to work
	college
Ask questions:	Why do I have to work? What do I need money for? What expenses do I have because I go to college?
Give examples:	With seven kids in the family, I can't expect my parents to have any money left over for the "extras" I need. I need to buy books for classes, but I also like to have a little pocket money for a hamburger, a record, a pair of pants, or a date with my girl. Sometimes I like to buy her a present. The other day I bought her a thin silver bracelet.
Comment on it:	My job at Baskin-Robbins gives me cash to stay afloat. If I didn't make any money, I would have to live like a grind while I was in school. I don't think I could

live without some money in my pocket. I'd probably quit school if I couldn't work. I'm not the type to just study and do without the things I want.

Sentence:	*I learn a lot from the interesting and strange people I meet.*
Key words:	learn a lot interesting people strange people
Ask questions:	Who is interesting? What, specifically, makes him interesting? Who is strange? What, specifically, makes him strange? What do I learn?
Give examples:	Peter is an interesting guy. He borrows money and eats my lunch. He is married, has a kid, goes to college. He is interested in everything. Talks to me about his other job, his motorcycle, his classes, his wife, his kid, India. He meditates and sells alfalfa sprouts. Customers are strange. They read all the flavors and then some of them always order vanilla. Others order the worst flavor going just because it sounds different. For example, bleu cheese ice cream. Ugh! The flavor of the month?
Comment on it:	How do I feel about these people? about my job? Do I have good or bad feelings? My job gives me a chance to learn how disconnected people can be, how much they daydream and don't hear what the next guy says. But I also know that there are young people like Pete and his wife who care about each other and work hard to take care of their future.
Restate it:	Can I say that in any other way? Try to make it still clearer. Tell what I believe, what I learn. I learn as much about human psychology at Baskin-Robbins as I do in my abnormal psych class.
Sentence:	*I don't have much time left at the end of the day.*
Key words:	not much time
Support it:	I go to classes, study, work, then study some more.
Ask questions:	How do I feel about not having much time? Do I manage to have any fun? Do I ever get free time? How?
Give examples:	I go to classes from 9:00 A.M. to 2:00 P.M., study from 3:00 P.M. to 7:00 P.M., work from 7:00 P.M. to 10:30 P.M., and finish studying after 10:30 P.M.
Comment on it:	Every now and then the schedule gets to me. I try to cut free by taking a whole day off: no classes, no

work, no studying. Then I'm okay again for a few weeks. I just need to break the routine when I feel I absolutely must loosen up.

Comment generally on whole paper. Begin with:

> *I believe* _____.
>   or
> *I learned* _____.

Write my thesis. What can I say generally about my job?

I believe that without my job I might have more time, but I'd also have less independence. It would be almost impossible for me to enjoy myself, and it would be a lot harder on my family.

Can I restate my thesis? Can I extend it? What can I generalize about people who work while they go to college?

I learned that working while you go to college, even when there may not be any choice about it, can extend your education.

See Chapter 3 for a discussion on developing a thesis.

FROM HEADINGS TO PARAGRAPHS

Notice how different you may feel as you read the following revised draft of the essay. You will probably say that now you know more about the writer, his job, and his attitude toward working while going to college. The paragraphs in the essay provide the space for the writer not only to explore his ideas and spell out their implications but to show how he goes from one idea to the next. As you read the essay, you get a view inside the writer's mind; the steps in his thinking become visible. The beginning and ending of the essay say something that is true for this writer and that can also be true for other people.

A revised draft

WORKING AND STUDYING

Working while you go to college, even when you have no choice about it, isn't all bad. It is a way of extending your education. In my family, if you want to go to college, you have to go out and get a job. With seven kids, my parents don't have enough money to take care of food and bills, much less the expenses of a college student's books, clothes, and a steady girl friend. I feel morally responsible to help out and do my share.

This year I have a job as a counterman at Baskin-Robbins, the ice cream store. My job gives me the cash I need to be somewhat independent. I don't earn very much, but it is enough for pocket money. I can get a coke and a hamburger without feeling guilty. I can buy books for my courses and I can go out with my girl friend or buy her a present when I feel like it. Last night, for no reason, after I got paid, I bought Marjorie a bracelet because I know she likes thin silver bracelets and I saw one that I thought would look nice on her. I don't make what you would call a "living" wage, but without it I would have to live like a grind while I was in school. I don't think I could go on living without some money in my pocket. I'd probably quit school if I had no job. I'm not the type who just studies, and I can't do without things for long. I'm too proud.

But my job also gives me some things money can't buy. It gives me a chance to learn about the public. I work with some strange and interesting people. Peter, the guy who manages the store when I'm on duty, has a positive outlook on life. He spends twenty minutes every morning and every night meditating. He says it relaxes him and gives him energy. And he needs energy because he has two jobs and a wife and kid, plus he goes to college full time. His other job is selling alfalfa sprouts to health food stores. He is interested in everything, knows what's in the papers, has opinions about the President and foreign affairs, especially India. The best thing is that he talks to me about whatever is on his mind: recent political changes in India, his wife, his political science classes, nutrition, being a father, overpopulation.

My customers are interesting, too, but usually a little strange. They take ten minutes to read all the flavors and then order vanilla. Or they order the worst flavor on the list just to be different. For example, the other day two people ordered bleu cheese ice cream. It was a guy and a girl. They stood there reciting the 31 flavors and then dared each other to try the most bizarre flavor. People were looking at them. When they ate that bleu cheese ice cream, they both sat in their seats, expressionless. I wonder about people like that who will do anything to stand out and be noticed. But I am also impressed by people like Pete and his wife who care about each other and about the world and work hard to take their place in it.

Because I am under considerable pressure, I try to take time out occasionally. Unfortunately, I don't have much time left at the end of the day, because I often study after I get home from work at 10:30. Every now and then, I cut free by taking a whole day off: no classes, no work, no studying. Then I'm okay again for a few months. I allow myself to break the routine when I feel I absolutely must. I think I've found what a lot of college students have found, that without my job I might have more time, but I'd have less independence. It would be almost impossible for me to go out and enjoy myself, and it would be a lot harder on my family. I also learn as much about the range of human psychology at Baskin-Robbins as I do in my abnormal psych class.

As you read the revised essay, you get a feeling of the strength and conviction of the writer. You say, "This writer has given his subject some thought, and he has his subject under control." Preparing his final draft should not take long because he has grouped his ideas in well-developed paragraphs.

The paragraphs of the essays you write allow you space:

1. To control your ideas
2. To provide concrete examples, reasons, and illustrations that strengthen your ideas
3. To comment on your ideas and tell how you feel about them
4. To state your main point again in other ways
5. To generalize for other people by stating what you believe or what you learned

If your writing is thin and needs development, you may not be taking advantage of the space that paragraphs offer. Keep these five purposes in mind as you think through your ideas and work them out patiently and convincingly in paragraphs.

Exercise 1 Before you write your next essay, go through these preliminary steps as a help to writing convincing paragraphs.

1. Do a focused freewriting (See Chapter 2).
2. Write a brief sentence outline and a trial thesis statement. Consider each sentence as a topic sentence for a paragraph.
3. Underline the key words in each sentence.
4. Raise questions about the key words in each topic sentence. Be sure to write the questions.
5. Write answers to the questions you raise.

WHAT DOES A PARAGRAPH LOOK LIKE?

As a reader, you recognize a paragraph because its first line is indented from the left margin and forms a solid clump of print with space around it. Paragraphing helps you read because it permits you to absorb writing in comfortable gulps and pause before the next gulp, though the length of these unbroken gulps is by no means uniform. Paragraphs can be a skinny line or two or go on without relief for fat pages of unbroken text. In newspapers, for example, because of the narrowness of the columns and the nature of the "news," paragraphs often are a single sentence in length. Such very brief paragraphs have a purpose—they enable you to speed your eye down through the day's news. In books and essays, paragraphs have undergone many changes over the years. A hundred years ago, it was fashionable to write paragraphs three times longer than we do now, and long before that, there were no paragraphs at all. Today, five to eight sentences generally clump together to form a paragraph averaging between 150 and 200 words. This modern paragraphing offers a reader another important advantage. Besides helping your eye, paragraphing supplies your mind with the sections of thought into which a writer's work effectively divides.

How do you know when to indent for a paragraph? Indentations for paragraphs generally follow *shifts* in thought, changes from one part of a topic to another, changes from the general idea to the specific case, or shifts in place, time, or speaker. These are natural movements in thinking that you signal when you write, often intuitively, by beginning a new paragraph. For example, in the following excerpts from narrative essays, new paragraphs show changes in place and time. The first two examples are from Sherwood Anderson's "I Discover My Father":

> He had become blood of my blood; he the strong swimmer and I the boy clinging to him in the darkness. We swam in the silence and in silence we dressed in our wet clothes, and went home.

Change of place
> There was a lamp lighted in the *kitchen* and when we came in, the water dripping from us, there was my mother. She smiled at us. I remember that she called us "boys."

> . . . Somewhere in the world there was a very dignified, quite wonderful man who was really my father. I even made myself half believe these fancies.

Change of time
> And then there came *a certain night*. He'd been off somewhere for two or three weeks. He found me alone in the house, reading by the kitchen table.

Notice that in the next examples, the writer indents to show that he is getting down to specific cases. A new paragraph often shows the change from a general observation to a specific event or occasion.

The following paragraphs are from the student essay entitled "Risks" (see Chapter 3):

> Risks are unavoidable. I've never met a person in my life who hasn't taken a risk. If you don't risk anything you will never be able to gain anything. For all practical purposes, you would be living in limbo. Everything in life involves some kind of risk, and love affairs are no exception. Love affairs always involve the risk of getting hurt, but sometimes for reasons beyond love itself.

Change to a specific case
> *Two years ago* I had an affair with a beautiful girl. We were about the same age, and we shared the same interests, which enhanced our relationship. We were crazy about each other, and we always hated to part company. I remember that I never had any difficulties with her or with her parents, but I found out soon enough about the complications that would pop up. In the meanwhile, though, we continued to share a beautiful relationship. We were never closer before. I think our relationship reached its peak because everything after was all down hill.

Change to a more
specific time
> *One Sunday* I called for her at her home. It was the same procedure. The parents greeted me. Then they asked me to sit down and have something to eat or drink. . . .

When you write dialogue, indent to show a new speaker:

Change of speaker

"Listen, Charles, when you were in high school, did *you* know exactly what your interests were?"

"Yes," I said. "Girls."

She turned over on her side so we could really talk this out head on. I stooped to meet her. She smiled. "Charles, I'm almost finished with school and I can't even decide what to take in college. I don't really want to be anything. I don't know what to do," she said. "What do you think I should do?"

I gave her a serious answer, a handful of wisdom. "In the first place, don't let them shove. Who do they think they're kidding? Most people wouldn't know if they had a million years what they wanted to be. They just sort of become."

Grace Paley

In narrative writing, you use certain words or phrases to help signal a new place or a new time, and you indent to begin a new paragraph:

In the morning – – – – – – –
– – – – – – – – – – – –.

One Sunday – – – – – – – –
– – – – – – – – – – – –.

By the next spring – – – – – –
– – – – – – – – – – – –.

On the other side of town – – –
– – – – – – – – – – – –.

Outside my window – – – – – –
– – – – – – – – – – – –.

In St. Louis – – – – – – – – –
– – – – – – – – – – – –.

In writing that is not storytelling, other purposes press you to indent for a new paragraph. Again, certain introductory words or phrases will signal the new paragraph. One such purpose is a change from one specific reason to another:

First, – – – – – – – – – – –
– – – – – – –.

Second, – – – – – – – – – –
– – – – – – –.

Finally, – – – – – – – – – –
– – – – – – –.

A change from one example to another also calls for a new paragraph:

For example, – – – – – – – –
– – – – – – –.

Another example is – – – – –
– – – – – – –.

Indent to show the progress of a comparison or contrast:

X, as we know, is – – – – – –
– – – – – – –.

In the same way, Y is also – –
– – – – – – –.

X has always struck me as – –
– – – – – – –.

Unlike X, Y strikes me as – –
– – – – – – –.

Other pairs of words work together to begin new paragraphs. Here are a few examples:

A few writers – – – – – – – –
– – – – – – –.

Most writers, however, – – – –
– – – – – – –.

On the one hand – – – – – –
– – – – – – –.

But on the other hand – – – –
– – – – – – –.

In this climate – – – – – – – –
– – – – – – –.

In hotter climates – – – – – –
– – – – – – –.

The earliest records show – – –
– – – – – – –.

Later records show – – – – –
– – – – – – –.

Look again at the essay "Why I Want a Wife" (Chapter 4, page 83) and notice that each new reason why Judy Syfers wants a wife begins a new paragraph. Even though, in most cases, *I want a wife who* is repeated, the specification of each new reason—the specific thing a wife will be able to do—shifts the meaning and requires indentation to signal a new idea. Each of the following sentences is the first sentence of a new paragraph:

I want a wife who will work and send me to school.
My wife will arrange and pay for the care of the children.
I want a wife who will take care of *my* physical needs.
I want a wife who will not bother me with rambling complaints about a wife's duties.
I want a wife who is sensitive to my sexual needs.
I want the liberty to replace my present wife with another one.

In the essay on page 63, notice that paragraph indentations again mark the shift from one idea to another that supports the thesis. Each of the specific foods on the writer's convalescent menu has its own collection of specific details and requires a new paragraph:

> Toast was a big item in my mother's culinary pharmacopeia.
> Shortly after that, chicken soup would appear.
> Beef tea was an alternate soup.
> Eggs had a prominent place on these convalescent menus.

In a paragraph for each, toast, chicken soup, beef tea, and eggs get the full and leisurely attention of the writer.

Exercise 2   Indicate where in the following passage you would indent for a new paragraph. For each new paragraph, tell what changes occur in the text that suggest a new paragraph is necessary. If a word or phrase signals such a change, identify that word or phrase.

> Three passions, simple but overwhelmingly strong, have governed my life: the longing for love, the search for knowledge, and unbearable pity for the suffering of mankind. These passions, like great winds, have blown me hither and thither, in a wayward course, over a deep ocean of anguish, reaching to the very verge of despair. I have sought love, first, because it brings ecstasy—ecstasy so great that I would often have sacrificed all the rest of life for a few hours of this joy. I have sought it, next, because it relieves loneliness—that terrible loneliness in which one shivering consciousness looks over the rim of the world into the cold unfathomable lifeless abyss. I have sought it, finally, because in the union of love I have seen, in a mystic miniature, the prefiguring visions of the heaven that saints and poets have imagined. This is what I sought, and though it might seem too good for human life, this is what—at last—I found. With equal passion I have sought knowledge. I have wished to understand the hearts of men. I have wished to know why the stars shine. And I have tried to apprehend the Pythagorean power by which number holds sway above the flux. A little of this, but not much, I have achieved. Love and knowledge, so far as they were possible, led upward toward the heavens. But always pity brought me back to earth. Echoes of cries of pain reverberate in my heart. Children in famine, victims tortured by oppressors, helpless old people a hated burden to their sons, and the whole world of loneliness, poverty, and pain make a mockery of what human life should be. I long to alleviate the evil, but I cannot; and I too suffer. This has been my life. I have found it worth living, and would gladly live it again if the chance were offered me.
>
> Bertrand Russell

CHIEF SKILLS IN PARAGRAPHING

Paragraphing is an important technique to master because through paragraphs you control the design of your whole essay. As you write, you move back and forth between general ideas and specifics, taking pains to support your general idea with interesting specifics or rephrasing a general idea to show the limits of the details you include. Paragraphs show these moves. Each of the specific details or experiences you think of to support, prove, or illustrate the general idea of your essay will get a paragraph of its own and sometimes more. These paragraphs give you the space to carry out the promise of your ideas and display their importance to your thesis. You can improve your ability to write convincing paragraphs by sharpening the following skills:

1. *Finding the subdivisions suggested in your thesis.*
> Use an outline or a rough draft.
> Mark general statements "g" and specifics "s."
> Underline your important statements.
> Group the specifics under the more general or abstract statements.

2. *Providing support* for each important subdivision in your thesis to make your ideas convincing and clear.
> Provide examples.
> Provide illustrations.
> Tell an experience that relates to your idea. Compare your idea to something else. Tell how your idea came about. Tell what it leads to. Restate an idea to make it clearer.
> Comment on your statement. Tell how you feel about it.
> Tell what you believe or learned from an experience or a way of thinking that would be generally useful to other people.

Follow the same procedure for each major subdivision.

> Write in paragraphs.
> Carry out your ideas fully.
> Don't worry about writing too much. You can cut later.
> (See pages 245–252 in this chapter for a discussion of paragraphs of support.)

3. *Writing a sentence that tells the topic of your paragraph.* Topic sentences control your essay. They outline the major subdivisions of your thesis and guide you in writing paragraphs according to your purpose and plan. Since a topic sentence expresses the most important idea of your paragraph, it helps you decide which details to include. On the contrary, a topic sentence also helps you to identify details that are not relevant in a paragraph and eliminate them. A topic sentence does for a paragraph what a thesis statement does for a whole essay because it concisely expresses the meaning of all the details in the paragraph just as the thesis

statement expresses the essential meaning of all the ideas in the whole essay.

The topic sentence in each of the following paragraphs is italicized:

I may have been the best fighter, but I was also the poorest. I owned one T-shirt, two pairs of pants, several pairs of shoes with holes in them. My jackets were torn and patched, and hardly a day went by when my pants didn't split somewhere. And although I had won nearly all my fights, and was on the verge of turning professional, I had never been able to afford a first-class mouthpiece to protect my teeth. I had to wait until the other fighters finished so I could borrow their headgear, or their trunks or bandages. I wanted my own training gloves, my own gear.

Muhammad Ali

In this paragraph, Muhammad Ali proves that, despite his ability as a fighter, he was very poor. He supplies details about his success along with examples of his limited wardrobe and examples of equipment that he couldn't afford to own.

Remarkable as it may seem, Wednesday night, while the whole city crashed and roared into ruin, was a quiet night. There were no crowds. There was no shouting and yelling. There was no hysteria, no disorder. I passed Wednesday night in the part of the advancing flames, and in all those terrible hours I saw not one woman who wept, not one man who was excited, not one person who was in the slightest degree panic-stricken.

Jack London

Every sentence in London's paragraph supports the idea expressed by the topic sentence—that, remarkably, the Wednesday night of the San Francisco earthquake was "a quiet night."

Now notice how each italicized topic sentence in Claude Brown's memoir "Saturday Night in Harlem" (see page 52) specifically supports the point Brown is making, that *Saturday night in Harlem is the liveliest night of the week.* Remember that there are occasions when an author never states his thesis explicitly but implies it. Brown's thesis, that *Saturday night in Harlem is the liveliest night of the week,* is implied in every italicized topic sentence.

USE A PARAGRAPH BLOCK WHEN YOU NEED TO EXTEND YOUR THOUGHT

Once you've decided on your thesis and the main subsections in support of your thesis, you have other decisions to make about paragraphing. In your early outlines, each heading may become a topic sentence and signal the start of a new paragraph. The topic sentence says what the paragraph will be about. But as you develop flexibility and control, that arrangement may be too mechanical for you. You may want to give more than one paragraph to an idea and its development. The same topic sentence can promise two or three paragraphs to come. It's entirely possible that, as you progress through your piece of writing, rewriting and unraveling your ideas, you'll need to expand a heading into two or three paragraphs. You may want to convey the importance of a section by writing about it in greater detail—giving it a greater proportion of details, examples, and explanations. When this happens, your topic sentence at the beginning of one paragraph may also govern the next paragraph of examples or explanations.

The following paragraphs begin with a general statement about the manner in which one's parents grow old. The first paragraph includes the example of the writer's mother (the writer is Margaret Mead, the anthropologist). But the example of her father requires several paragraphs:

> The way in which one's parents grow old matters a great deal. My mother had a severe stroke and had to learn to talk and walk and relate to the world again. It took her a year to do it, and once she had fully recovered so that she could find any book in the house and locate any name we wanted to know, she died. Her death left my father free because he would not have wanted her to make the long, weary recovery again.
>
> Although he was now alone, he stayed on in the little house into which they had moved on his retirement and in which the rooms were too small for committee meetings. He was as forgetful and as careless of material things as he had always been, but as he did not smoke and the furnace had an automatic fire arrangement, the principal hazards were to himself and not the neighbors in whose children he was deeply interested and for whose sake he had taken down the fence so that they would have more room to play. My youngest sister thought he ought to live in a home for the elderly. She feared that he might fall down the steep little staircase or be run over when he absentmindedly crossed a street against the light. But I stood out against this. I believed he had a right to run risks in his own way.
>
> As my father grew older he became more eccentric. He became parsimonious, where once he had been openhanded, and complained about the bills run up by the students who sometimes lived with him. He often woke up at four in the morning and started to go out of the house. And he mislaid things, but he had never in his life had to find anything or file anything. He told the same stories, but he had always repeated stories, absorbed in the telling and unaware of the listener's expression of recognition or boredom. Now he had fewer stories to tell and told them oftener.
>
> But the structure of his personality remained intact and his mind was as keen and fresh, as alert to anything new and interesting as it had ever been. The spring before he died I gave a seminar to a group who thought of themselves as avant-garde, but his were the most searching questions.
> . . . Watching a parent grow old is one of the most reassuring experiences anyone can have, a privilege that comes only to those whose parents live beyond their children's early adulthood.
>
> Margaret Mead

KNOW WHAT EACH PARAGRAPH DOES FOR
THE WHOLE ESSAY

Paragraphs in short essays perform many functions. They can open your essay, close your essay, line up support for your thesis, develop ideas, provide transitions between ideas, and single out an important sentence or two for special emphasis.

Opening *paragraphs* An effective opening paragraph works in two ways at once: it attracts the attention of your reader, and it launches the main ideas of your essay without delay.

Attracting your *reader* The opening paragraph must grab your reader's attention and hold it for those first important moments while he's deciding whether to give your essay a chance or turn you down cold.

Here are a series of opening paragraphs (some with closing paragraphs from the same essay) that demonstrate the range of possibilities:

1. Point an arrow at the heart of a universally accepted truth. (Imagine anyone saying we don't need a physical once a year.)

Opening:

Health maintenance has become our national obsession. Logic suggests that in order to maintain health, we must prevent disease, and that this is best accomplished by eating balanced meals, exercising regularly—and seeing the doctor once a year for a check-up. This latter ritual, the annual physical, has been extensively promoted by physicians and enthusiastically accepted by patients as an effective means of maintaining health. But is it?

Closing:

Perhaps future developments will allow us to be more optimistic. For the present, it must be concluded that the annual physical examination has proved to be little more than an elaborate and expensive ritual that has not fulfilled its promise. ■   Richard Spark, M.D.

2. Startle your reader with bizarre or alarming information. (Who isn't morbidly interested in the remembrances of someone pronounced dead who unexpectedly recovers?)

Life After Death?

The experience is a familiar one to many emergency-room medics. A patient who has been pronounced dead and unexpectedly recovers later describes what happened to him during those moments—sometimes hours—when his body exhibited no signs of life. According to one repeated account, the patient feels himself rushing through a long, dark tunnel while noise rings in his ears. Suddenly, he finds himself outside his own body, looking down with curious detachment at a medical team's efforts to resuscitate him. He hears what is said, notes what is happening but cannot communicate with anyone. Soon, his attention is drawn to other presences in the room—spirits of dead relatives or friends—who communicate with him nonverbally. Gradually, he is drawn to a vague "being of light." This being invites him to evaluate his life and shows him highlights of his past in panoramic vision. The patient longs to stay with the being of light but is reluctantly drawn back into his physical body and recovers.

Newsweek, July 12, 1976, p. 41

3. Use a strikingly fresh analogy in your opening sentences. (See the discussion of analogy in Chapter 4.)

Opening: Discovering backpacking is a bit like leaving home for the first time. There's a mixture of pain and new freedom, and your family is not sure it approves. The comparison is imperfect, of course; the pain of the hike is only physical, and from backpacking you always return. But there's a root similarity. In wilderness, as in that first apartment, you find independence that you didn't know was there.

Michael Parfit

4. Open with an anecdote or brief narrative. In a few sentences, make it vivid.

> Twenty-one years ago, on September 30, 1955, a young American was killed while driving a car. His name was Pablo Efran Pizarrow of 218 East 95th Street, New York City. He and three friends were on their way home from a movie when a stranger ran to the car window, shouted "Are you Demons or Dragons?" and then shot Pizarrow through the head. The film that the dead boy had just seen was *East of Eden.* On the same day, at the very same hour (5:45 P.M. Pacific time), at the intersection of Routes 466 and 41 near Paso Robles, California, the driver of another car, a silver Porsche Spyder, ended his own life at 86 miles an hour in a crash that almost severed his head from his body. The driver was the star of *East of Eden.* His name, James Dean.

Derek Marlowe

5. Use a striking quotation (preferably by an authority) that points directly to your main idea.

In this excerpt, William F. Buckley points to the gap between the time twenty years ago when scientists might have gone to the moon and the time they actually did go in 1969:

> As a freshman at college seeking grist for the undergraduate newspaper, I approached a famous astrophysicist, Lyman Spitzer, and asked if it was true that he intended to fly to the moon. He replied frostily, "I shouldn't know what to do if I got there."

William F. Buckley, Jr.

6. Refer to a common condition. (Almost everybody knows somebody in a second marriage living with someone else's children.)

Opening:

> Every year at least half a million Americans marry someone who is a parent already. When people go into a second or subsequent marriage, they are full of great hopes of improving on the past. Unfortunately, these do not always turn out to be realistic—especially when children are involved.

Brenda Maddox

Keep the language of your opening paragraph direct and simple. Avoid a lot of words that don't move fast. If you have to write effectively anywhere in your essay, you have to do it right here up front, where the life of your essay depends on it.

Launching your In addition to attracting your reader's attention, your opening paragraph
essay must launch your topic and send your essay specifically and immediately on its way.

1. Don't start too far back from your thesis. If your thesis is *Most summer camps are a waste of time,* say so. Don't go back to the founding of the Boy Scout movement in 1908 by Lord Baden-Powell, who was chief scout of the world.

2. In a short essay, don't write a general and abstract opening paragraph that fails to mention your specific subject area. If your subject is *flying* and you think your thesis will be, *If you really want to, you can overcome your fear of flying,* then don't open with a paragraph like the following. No one could possibly tell what your subject and thesis are from this much too general opener:

> Almost everybody has some deep and secret fear. Sometimes a fear so handicaps people that they spend a large share of their energy trying to go on with their lives normally in spite of that fear. It is not unusual to find people living lives of mounting personal and business difficulties because they never squarely and honestly try to locate the source of their fear and fight back.

3. Avoid a dull opening paragraph that repeats itself and says nothing new. The following paragraph, for example, contains three sentences, but all three say the same old thing:

> People spend a lot of money on clothes because styles change every year. If designers didn't dress their models differently every season, you and I would save a pile. We are the losers while the designers and manufacturers laugh all the way to the bank.

4. Avoid "old reliable" beginnings like the dictionary definition ("Webster defines *fear* as . . .") and the familiar quotation. One beginning writer, for example, whose topic was fear of flying, turned President Franklin Roosevelt's much-quoted statement into an opening cliché:

> Franklin Roosevelt once said, "The only thing we have to fear is fear itself."

Closing Use your closing paragraph primarily to satisfy your reader that you have
paragraphs made the point your opening paragraph promised you would make. Your essay should clearly be finished and your reader not left "hanging" or

abandoned. You may want to close—as many writers do—with a powerful final observation, one that leaves a particularly strong impression on your reader.

Your closing paragraph should keep the whole essay visibly before the reader. Perhaps some of the closing paragraphs that follow will illustrate the merits of keeping the whole essay in mind as you write the conclusion.

Opening:

> Being a black "conservative" is perhaps not considered as bizarre as being a transvestite, but it is certainly considered more strange than being a vegetarian or a bird watcher. Recently a network television program contacted me because they had an episode coming up that included a black conservative as one of the characters, and they wanted me to come down to the studio so that their writers and actors could observe such an exotic being in the flesh.

Closing:

> So being a black "conservative" is not quite as distinctive as it might seem. ■
>
> Thomas Sowell

Opening:

> Every year at least half a million Americans marry someone who is a parent already. When people go into a second or subsequent marriage, they are full of great hopes of improving on the past. Unfortunately, these do not always turn out to be realistic—especially when children are involved.

Closing:

> While there are special tensions in stepfamilies, there are many advantages. Stepfamilies are often less claustrophobic than ordinary families. They offer more diverse ties to people outside the immediate family circle, which can be a great help to children as they make the transition to independent adulthood. Stepfamilies can be just as happy as other families, even happier. It just takes more work, and an acceptance of a hard fact of life—that while spouses are replaceable, parents are not. ■

1. Write a final paragraph that logically fulfills the expectation set up in the opening paragraph.
2. Echo the tone and language of the opening paragraph in the closing paragraph. If you used a metaphor, go back to it. Pick up the thread of an analogy, or recapture in different words the tone of the assertion you made in your opener. See that the final paragraph relates in spirit to the opening paragraph.

3. Speculate freely about what your opening generalization implies for the future or end with your own general evaluation of the points you have made.

4. Close with a convincing quotation, a clever anecdote, a twist of irony, or a humorous remark that directly illuminates your discussion.

In writing the closing paragraph of your essay there are certain things to avoid:

1. Avoid summarizing in 1, 2, 3 fashion your main points. Why bore a reader who has just been through them and needs no reminder of the outstanding points?

2. Avoid introducing something new in the closing. It would be pointless to conclude the essay on physical examinations (page 240) by suddenly stating your outrage about increased rates for Blue Cross/Blue Shield.

3. Avoid a sudden irrelevancy. In an essay on sanitation workers, don't conclude with a remark about the good work done by your local police department.

4. Avoid a sudden reversal:

> While all these facts warn us that annual physical examinations are un-necessary and may be dangerous, I advise you to keep going down to your doctor annually because there are always new and baffling diseases around.

5. Avoid a final apology:

> I know this argument is not too convincing, but it's the best an amateur like me can do.

6. Avoid a final complaint:

> This was a tough assignment and there wasn't much information to be found on it, nor do I know personally any sanitation workers who would let me interview them.

7. Avoid a final, rash promise or impossible claim:

> In conclusion, I can swear that private garbage trucks will soon be rolling down the avenues in your neighborhood.

Paragraphs of support What do paragraphs in the middle section of your essay do? They achieve the enormously important work of supporting your thesis by treating the rest of your ideas fully and reflectively. As you formulate your thinking about your topic and let your ideas roll forward, you'll discover ideas in your essay that you'd like to expand—by adding examples, reasons, causes, consequences—the life-signs that your writing is authoritative and solid. Remember that readers are reading to find out something new, something they don't already know. The information your readers must have is generated in the paragraphs of support. That information is critical: it makes your essay unique and worth reading.

Kinds of support Four arrangements of the whole essay were discussed in Chapters 3 and 4—essays that tell a story, essays that present examples, essays that compare, and essays that show causes and consequences. These four arrangements apply to the paragraph as well. Although a whole essay may develop along a single channel (for example, an essay-length comparison), it normally develops along several channels, one after the other. These different channels of thinking show up in your paragraphs. Your subject naturally maneuvers you into the kinds of development that are most appropriate—telling an anecdote, offering an explanation, formulating a definition, or whatever. In your first draft, you won't be thinking consciously about the kind of paragraph you're writing, but you must later be constantly aware of your thesis as you check each paragraph that you've written against your plan for the whole essay and test whether the details you've arranged in paragraphs really back your thesis statement.

Here are some sample paragraphs that supply support in recognizable patterns.

1. General statement followed by details

Soap operas are a consolation to the lonely and the frustrated. Their audience consists mainly of women, women of all ages, who are at home, either pursuing the eternal routine of household chores, or those who do not have much to occupy them and sit there alone. As a matter of fact, the soap opera addicts are mostly people who are alone either for the day, until the husband and children come home, or forever. They turn on the television and are turned on themselves because here are the well-known voices which speak to them, not of cleaning the refrigerator or doing the ironing, although these will also be dealt with in well-spaced advertisements, but of the infinite situations, exciting adventures, romantic entanglements of TV fiction. The soap opera takes the viewer out of the drab predictable, everyday world into a life of possibility.

All the details in this paragraph develop the key words of the topic sentence, the first sentence in the paragraph:

consolation

lonely

frustrated

The details explain who the lonely and frustrated are and how soap operas console them.

In the next paragraph, the general statement appears after a few sentences of introduction. It serves as the topic sentence of the paragraph and is followed by examples. The sentence is italicized:

Most people have the popular misconception that all the bait you need for fishing is a rusty can of worms. They think that the lowly worm will lure anything from a one-pound flounder to a hundred-pound shark. This, however, is not the case. *There are many fish in the ocean that wouldn't give a worm a second glance.* The mighty cod, for example, will reject anything but large chunks of clam belly. Fluke prefer a thin strip of squid that's tapered at the end. Weakfish seem to gorge themselves on grass shrimps, and striped bass rarely reject live eels. Remember this the next time you go fishing so that you won't waste your day drowning worms.

The examples of "many fish that wouldn't give a worm a second glance" are cod, fluke, and weakfish. The details included in the examples testify to the writer's experience as a fisherman.

2. Telling the story before you make the point

Why tell the story first? A vivid anecdote leading to a generalization attempts to persuade the reader subtly. This paragraph, from George Orwell's *Homage to Catalonia,* is such an episode from his description of the grim and ironic conditions during the Spanish Civil War. The topic sentence is italicized:

Towards the end of March I got a poisoned hand that had to be lanced and put in a sling. I had to go into the hospital, but it was not worth sending me to Sietamo for such a petty injury, so I stayed in the so-called hospital at Monflorite, which was merely a casualty clearing station. I was there ten days, part of the time in bed. The *practicantes* (hospital assistants) stole practically every valuable object I possessed, including my camera and all my photographs. *At the front everyone stole, it was the inevitable effect of shortage, but the hospital people were always the worst.* Later, in the hospital at Barcelona, an American who had come to join the International Column on a ship that was torpedoed by an Italian submarine, told me how he was carried ashore wounded, and how, even as they lifted him into the ambulance, the stretcher-bearers pinched his wrist-watch.

Notice Orwell's final "chaser." The closing example of the wristwatch being stolen is a rather sophisticated maneuver. We suppose that most beginners would either start with the topic sentence or lead up to it and end with it. Orwell, who is one of the most effective prose writers in English, amuses us by giving us this detail as a sensational encore.

3. Details leading to a general statement

As you read the following paragraph of student writing, notice that the writer waits until the last sentence to reveal what the details in the paragraph mean:

The library was packed with students. Every table and chair was occupied with someone intently studying or frantically poring over books and articles. A feeling of concentration and tension came from every corner.

Crowds clustered at the card catalogue, and the two Xerox machines were so overworked they were literally heating the space around them. It was obviously exam time at the college.

4. Cause and effect

A paragraph in which a condition leads to an effect explores the results of that condition. In the following paragraph, for example, the opening statement generalizes that a lack of interest among businessmen in hiring liberal arts majors leads to certain consequences:

> It is among undergraduates that the business bias against the liberal arts sets up the most far-reaching chain of consequences. When the upperclassman finds at first hand that the recruiters prefer [people] with the technical specialties, the word gets around the campus very quickly indeed. To the freshmen and sophomores who are pondering a choice of major, this is the real world talking. Why, then, the liberal arts? Sales work, they hear, is about the only slot they would qualify for if they took English or history or politics or such, and they have the strong feeling, not entirely erroneous, that the offer is made only because the recruiters can't interest the preferred ones in sales. So they listen politely when an occasional alumnus or speaker at a career-counseling meeting speaks glowingly of the liberal arts and the full man, the need for culture, and so on. Then they go sign up for something practical.
>
> William H. Whyte

The consequence, or effect, stated in the final sentence is that students avoid majoring in the liberal arts and enroll instead in "practical" courses.

5. Exploring a condition for reasons why it exists

A paragraph that explores a condition for its causes begins with the condition and then examines the reasons why the condition exists. In this paragraph from Sir Thomas More's famous *Utopia* (published in 1516), the visitor to Utopia gives reasons why it makes sense for people who marry to examine each other naked before they marry. Note that More's most convincing reason is presented in the form of a comparison:

> In choosing their wives they use a method that would appear to us very absurd and ridiculous, but it is constantly observed among them, and is accounted perfectly consistent with wisdom. Before marriage some grave matron presents the bride naked, whether she is a virgin or a widow, to the bridegroom; and after that some grave man presents the bridegroom naked to the bride. We indeed both laughed at this, and condemned it as very indecent. But they, on the other hand, wondered at the folly of the men of

all other nations, who, if they were to buy a horse of a small value, are so cautious that they will see every part of him, and take off his saddle and all his other tackle, that there may be no secret ulcer hid under any of them; and that yet in the choice of a wife, on which depends the happiness or unhappiness of the rest of his life, a man should venture upon trust, and only see about a hand's breadth of the face, all the rest of the body being covered, under which there may lie hid what may be contagious, as well as loathsome. All men are not so wise as to choose a woman only for her good qualities; and even wise men consider the body as that which adds not a little to the mind: and it is certain there may be some such deformity covered with the clothes as may totally alienate a man from his wife when it is too late to part with her. If such a thing is discovered after marriage, a man has no remedy but patience. They therefore think it is reasonable that there should be good provision made against such mischievous frauds.

6. Defining

A paragraph of definition presents *your own* clear definition of a term as it suits the purpose of *your* essay. Don't quote a dictionary. Wayne Booth, in the following paragraph, defines the word *rhetoric* classically as "persuasion" and then brightens the definition by restating it in the colloquial language of a student:

I suppose that the question of the role of rhetoric in the English course is meaningless if we think of rhetoric in either its broadest or its narrowest meaning. . . . But if we settle on the following, traditional, definition, some real questions are raised: "Rhetoric is the art of finding and employing the most effective means of persuasion on any subject, considered independently of intellectual mastery of that subject." As the students say, "Prof. X knows his stuff but he doesn't know how to put it across." If rhetoric is thought of as the art of "putting it across," considered as quite distinct from mastering an "it" in the first place, we are immediately landed in a bramble bush of controversy. Is there such an art? If so, what does it consist of? Does it have a content of its own? Can it be taught? Should it be taught? If it should, how do we go about it, head on or obliquely?

7. Likenesses and differences (comparison and contrast)

You can often explain something by showing, in a paragraph, how it is like or unlike something else. Both items usually have some element in common—remedies for illness in the following paragraph about acupuncture and women in the life of Lyndon Johnson in the next paragraph about Lady Bird Johnson.

Likenesses

In comparing the mysteries of acupuncture to the mysteries of aspirin, the writer of the following paragraph hopes to justify the use of acupuncture since the success of both is based on clinical observation rather than medical theory:

> Some doctors or patients may indeed wonder how one can practise a form of medicine where the theories on which that practise is based are possibly suspect. Just as a doctor will prescribe aspirin because he knows what are its effects in the body of a patient, so an acupuncturist will needle a certain acupuncture point because he knows what the consequent reaction of the body will be. It is of secondary importance to the doctor to know just why it is that aspirin has its specific effects, no matter how intellectually interesting such knowledge might be. At the time of writing little is understood of why the known effects of aspirin take place, yet aspirin, with its simple chemical formula, is the most commonly used drug in the world.
>
> Felix Mann

Differences

Notice how the following contrast between Lady Bird Johnson and her mother-in-law begins in a methodical, point-by-point fashion, moving back and forth from Lady Bird to Rebekah, from Rebekah to Lady Bird on every point discussed. But midway, we understand that the point of the paragraph is to convey the character of Lady Bird. Lady Bird is the center, and the contrast with her mother-in-law serves to enhance her portrait:

> To both mother and wife Lyndon Johnson would always ascribe a scarcely credible perfection. But it is evident that they were crucially different women. The mother's inordinate passion for her son had been employed to spur achievements which she herself had determined. The wife endeavored to sustain and better organize the energy which Rebekah had been instrumental in setting loose. Where Rebekah withdrew into a stony anger over her husband's spontaneity, Lady Bird gracefully hosted unexpected throngs, welcoming the political friends Lyndon perpetually invited to their house. Where the mother confided her severest disappointments to her son, Lady Bird complained to no one. Amid the most complicated intrigues and struggles of her husband's career she remained outwardly composed and reasonable. If his incessant demands and orders (he instructed her to avoid full skirts and low shoes; often picked out her clothes; depended on her not only to manage the house but to lay out his clothes in the morning, fill his pens and his lighter, put the correct pocket items in place, pay his bills—in short, to manage him) or his occasional abuse in front of company became too much for her to bear, she possessed, or soon developed, a strange ability to take psychic leave. "Bird," Johnson

would call out at such moments, "are you with me?" And straight off, her accustomed alertness and competence reappeared. Without such devotion and forbearance, without a love steadily given and never withdrawn, the course of Lyndon Johnson's continuing ascent in the world of politics becomes inconceivable.

Doris Kearns

You can develop a great range of subjects, both personal and public, by contrasting a situation with a corresponding one at an earlier point in history or by speculating on what changes might evolve by a future date. Here is a paragraph that contrasts the arrival of a relief pitcher today to the arrival of a relief pitcher on the baseball field years ago. Notice that this contrast is not accomplished point by point. Instead, a description of the relief pitcher as he used to arrive is rendered in its entirety, and then a complete description of the modern relief pitcher arriving in a golf cart follows:

When the bullpen gates open, just about everyone in the ball park peers across to watch the relief pitcher step out of the enclosure. He used to come to the pitcher's mound by foot, his warm-up jacket hung loosely off his pitching shoulder, walking with the slow stride of a man with a lot on his mind, and sometimes he had a word to say as he passed one of his outfielders, and you could see him look back up at the scoreboard to check what the situation was; he had a long way to go, and there was plenty of time to sit there and relish the awful responsibility facing this man. Nowadays, the pitcher travels from the bullpen in a mechanical conveyance (back in 1960 all the parks were supplied with electric golf carts shaped like baseball caps), and some of his dignity—the sense of being the lone warrior sent to patch things up—is obviously diminished by being driven to the mound in this monstrous toylike gadget, sitting next to the driver with his glove in his lap like a rather embarrassed guest being delivered up to a fancy-dress party.

George Plimpton

8. Classification

See Chapter 4, pages 84–85, for a full discussion of classification.

9. Analogy

The subject of your essay can be unexpectedly spotlighted by the use of analogy, a vivid comparison that springs from the writer's imagination. When you write an analogy, you draw an extended comparison between what you wish to explain and somethig else that your reader is likely to consider a rather unexpected object of comparison. Analogy often carries the pleasure of luminous surprise, even shock, because your reader might never in a thousand years have hit on the one connection that has jumped out of your imagination. (See Chapter 4, page 82, for more discussion of analogy.) Here Peter Elbow, in *Writing Without Teachers,* draws an analogy between writing without getting feedback from readers and being blind and deaf:

> Imagine you are blind and deaf. You want to speak better. But you are in perpetual darkness and silence. You send out words as best you can but no words come back. You get a few clues about your speaking: perhaps you asked for something and didn't get it; or you got the wrong thing. You know you did something wrong. What you aren't getting is the main thing that helps people speak better: direct feedback to your speech—a directly perceived sense of how different people react to the sounds you make.
>
> This is an image of what it is like when you try to improve your writing all by yourself. You simply don't know what your words make happen in readers. . . .

Another writer, James Thurber, uses an analogy to show an odd similarity that struck him: that his editor went to work on a manuscript the way a skilled mechanic goes to work on a car:

> Having a manuscript under Ross's scrutiny was like putting your car in the hands of a skilled mechanic, not an automotive engineer with a bachelor of science degree, but a guy who knows what makes a motor go, and sputter, and wheeze, and sometimes come to a dead stop; a man with an ear for the faintest body squeak as well as the loudest engine rattle. When you first gazed, appalled, upon an uncorrected proof of one of your stories or articles, each margin had a thicket of queries and complaints—one writer got a hundred and forty-four on one profile. It was as though you beheld the works of your car spread all over the garage floor, and the job of getting the thing together again and making it work seemed impossible. Then you realized that Ross was trying to make your Model T or old Stutz Bearcat into a Cadillac or Rolls-Royce. He was at work with the tools of his unflagging perfectionism, and, after an exchange of growls or snarls, you set to work to join him in his enterprise.

Paragraphs of transition In examining the pattern paragraphs make on a given page of print, your eye may detect some that are not very long at all, more like indented sentences or questions than full-length paragraphs. These are very often paragraphs of a single sentence or two that signal a sharp shift in the writer's thinking. In an essay about hairdressing, for example, sentences such as "Let us now turn our attention to men's hairstyles" or "But what does the return of femininity mean to the future of unisex hair salons?" might stand alone as paragraphs of transition.

You may indent such sentences or questions to slow the reader down and emphasize that you're now asking him to shift his attention away from one line of thinking and toward another. In an essay that's only four or five paragraphs long, however, a whole paragraph of transition may be an extravagance.

Graphically, a paragraph of transition may look like this on a page:

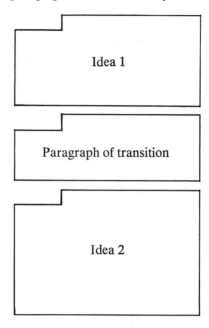

In his famous essay about boys in English public schools, "Such, Such Were the Joys . . . ," George Orwell writes the following paragraph of transition between the detailed and tender description of his humiliating ordeals as a young boy at school and his view of changing attitudes toward education:

> . . . Failure, failure, failure—failure behind me, failure ahead of me —that was by far the deepest conviction that I carried away.

Paragraph of transition

> All this was thirty years ago and more. The question is: Does a child at school go through the same kind of experiences nowadays?

> The only honest answer, I believe, is that we do not with certainty know. Of course it is obvious that the present-day *attitude* towards education is enormously more humane and sensible than that of the past. . . .

Paragraphs of special emphasis   For special effect, a writer may isolate a detail or observation and bring it into prominence in a paragraph of its own to emphasize it for the reader. The paragraph needs no other reason to justify its existence. If you want to attract very special attention to an idea, you may wish to try this, but use such paragraphs sparingly and only for a good reason.

In the following news item from the "Welcome Freshmen" issue of the Yale *Daily News,* the effect of the second paragraph may be horror and fear, but because it is separated from the gentility of the first paragraph, it delivers a sardonic humor.

On the first day of their arrival in the 18th century, incoming freshmen would line up solemnly against a wall in the old chapel. Facing them would stand a parallel line of seniors, well seasoned in the rigors of college life. At a pre-arranged moment, one of the seniors, a man chosen for his gravity and weight of character, would step forward and explain to the novices the peculiar customs of the University. He gave the lesson, by all reports, with dignity and kindness. Most of the freshmen, as befitted their station, received and regarded his advice in the proper spirit.

Those who didn't were paddled, stripped naked, and tossed out on Elm Street.

Paragraph of emphasis

COHERENCE IN THE TOTAL ESSAY

Link ideas between paragraphs Keep your paragraphs in touch with the main idea of your essay so that the whole essay holds together. Learn to provide connections from one paragraph to the next so that the main idea is visible from beginning to end.

Paragraphs have been said to "interpret" your thinking to your reader; that is, paragraphs help your reader understand what your writing means because every paragraph indentation makes another step of your thinking visible:

The first example is . . .
Another example is . . .
A final example is . . .

One reason for this is . . .
A second reason to consider is . . .
A third reason, and one no less important, is . . .

Let us now shift our attention to . . .

But what are the reasons for . . .

For a moment let us digress . . .

These steps should lead the reader to understand your thesis in the way you want it understood. The connections between these steps, and thus the connections between paragraphs, should come out of the logic of the thesis and the order of the parts that support it.

The surest way to achieve a flow from one part to the next is to present the parts in the best order possible: time, space, order of importance, order of climax (see Chapter 4). Writing an essay is not like creating a list for the A&P where you write one item under another in any order that occurs to you:

eggs
strawberries
ginger ale
bread

The best connections between ideas are planned for in the writing of sentences. The idea of each sentence propels you to the next sentence, as in the following paragraph by James Dickey, the poet and novelist:

> At any rate, in the Air Force I read a lot of poetry. I was not introduced to it by anybody in my family or any teacher or acquaintance. This has its disadvantages, but it also has one enormous advantage. If you get into poetry in this way, you come to look upon poetry as *your* possession, something that you discovered, that belongs to you in a way it could never have belonged to you if it had been forced on you.

Here, the sentence *This has its disadvantages, but it also has one enormous advantage* sets up an expectation of the next sentence in the heart of the original sentence. The writer need not add an announcement: *The advantage is* . . . Without being told, the reader knows that the sentence *If you get into poetry in this way* . . . explains the advantage. (See Chapter 11 for a discussion of sentences and the ways in which they move your reader forward.)

But connections can be made unmistakably clear when the text itself cannot prepare for the next idea. The writer resorts to emphasizing connections with useful phrases and techniques. *Key words and phrases* that appear at the end of one paragraph can be repeated at the beginning of the next for continuity:

> End of paragraph: . . . Feeling like a prima donna, I closed my eyes and *relaxed.*
>
> Start of next paragraph: That is, I *relaxed* until half of the hair on my head got slurped into the blow dryer's motor! . . .

Pronouns that replace previously stated nouns (see Chapter 15) highlight the connection between paragraphs:

> End of paragraph: . . . *Woodward* would leave his sixth-floor apartment and walk down the back stairs into an alley.
>
> Start of next paragraph: Walking and taking two or more taxis to the garage, *he* could be reasonably sure that no one had followed *him.* . . .
>
> Bob Woodward and Carl Bernstein

Using *synonyms* and *associated words,* rather than repeating exactly the same words, cements the connection between paragraphs:

> End of paragraph: . . . I am grateful to God that, through the influence of the Negro church, the *way of nonviolence* became an integral *part of our struggle.*

> Start of next paragraph: If *this philosophy* had not emerged, by now many streets of the South would, I am convinced, be flowing with blood.

> Martin Luther King, Jr.

To make connections explicit, to state connections plainly, writers have a bank of *set transitional phrases* to draw on. Some of the available phrases are grouped below according to purpose. These words often signal the need to indent for a new paragraph:

Likeness:	likewise, similarly
Difference:	but, however, still, yet, nevertheless, on the other hand, on the contrary, in contrast, at the same time
Addition:	moreover, and, in addition, equally important, next, first, second, third, in the first place, in the second place, again, also, too, besides, furthermore
Example:	for example, for instance, to illustrate
Time:	soon, in the meantime, afterward, later, meanwhile, earlier, simultaneously, finally
Place:	here, there, over there, beyond, nearby, opposite, under, above, to the left, to the right
Purpose:	for this purpose, to this end
End:	in conclusion, to summarize, finally, on the whole
Restatement:	in short, in other words, in brief, to put it differently
Result:	therefore, then, as a result, consequently, accordingly, thus

Because these words provide obvious handles that a floundering reader can hang on to, cautious students are known to overindulge in these terms. Be on guard against using transitional phrases where your text would be clear without them. When you do use transitional phrases, be especially careful not to use them inaccurately where your material doesn't warrant the connection you choose. They are not ready-to-wear links to be used in desperate measures to fasten together reluctant ideas. Every link between sentences and paragraphs must make sense:

> Last year I couldn't hold down a job. *Similarly,* I took a plane to California for a rest.

Similar to what? Because there is no similarity stated, this is an unclear use of *similarly.*

> We both liked jazz and looked all over for a good spot. *Nevertheless,* we found one out in the suburbs, of all places.

Why use *nevertheless,* which suggests an opposition? The connection here is time, not opposition:

> We both liked jazz and looked all over for a good spot. *Finally,* we found one out in the suburbs, of all places.

Link sentences within a paragraph   The same words and phrases that connect one paragraph to the next can be used to connect one sentence to the next within a single paragraph. Remember that sentences that flow into one another naturally without the need for obvious links should be left on their own. Trust that most of your connections will be there naturally as your ideas sweep you forward. But if, as you reread your work, you sense that your reader may be looking for a clearer connection between two sentences, give it to him and get rid of his guesswork.

Keep your paragraphs unified   The writer who writes slowly and painfully is not the only one working under unbearable stress. The writer who writes freely and never stops to refuel is the victim of another curse—the curse of plenty. Wandering from his subject, moving too far afield, offering too many examples that push the reader off the track, he finds all details equally irresistible and has them down on his page before he realizes it. If you have a tendency to long-windedness, proofread your writing for irrelevant sentences and unnecessary details that sabotage paragraph unity and dilute your effect.

Here is a lighthearted—and well-unified—paragraph of definition by Nora Ephron, taken from *Esquire* magazine:

> There have been only a few times in my adult life when I have known for certain that I made a terrible decision in choosing to become a writer—and all of them have taken place at the theatre, at the musical theatre, when someone stopped the show. Anyone in the theatre can give you a nice, precise, obvious definition of what that means: a showstopper, they tell you, literally stops the show, to the point where the audience will not let the actors in the next scene get on with it. But that is not exactly what I am talking about. As far as I am concerned, a showstopper is someone who does something onstage so electrifying, so marvelous, so magical, and, most important, so seemingly within reach, that I want to go out and kill myself for not having stuck with my tap-dancing lessons at the Nick Castle School of Dance on La Cienega Boulevard in Los Angeles.

Here is a rerun of Nora Ephron's paragraph sabotaged by excessive details and irrelevant sentences:

> There have been only a few times in my adult life when I have known for certain that I made a terrible decision in choosing to become a writer—and

all of them have taken place at the theatre, at the musical theatre, when someone stopped the show. *I saw Gwen Verdon do it in* "Can-Can" *and Ella Fitzgerald do it with Count Basie and Barbara Luna stop* "A Chorus Line" *when she sang* "Nothing." Anyone in the theatre can give you a nice, precise, obvious definition of what that means: a showstopper, they tell you, literally, stops the show, to the point where the audience will not let the actors in the next scene get on with it. *At the Kabuki theater in Tokyo, people in the audience shout out for a beloved star to strike a pose and hold it throughout their interminable applause. A Kabuki play usually takes most of the day to be performed.* But that is not exactly what I am talking about. As far as I am concerned, a showstopper is someone who does something onstage so electrifying, so marvelous, so magical, and, most important, so seemingly within reach, that I want to go out and kill myself for not having stuck with my tap-dancing lessons at the Nick Castle School of Dance on La Cienega Boulevard in Los Angeles.

The roll call of examples (Gwen Verdon, Ella Fitzgerald, and so forth) in the second sentence slows down the momentum of the paragraph and takes the reader away from the real point, Nora Ephron's personal and autobiographical definition of showstopping. The second assault on this paragraph's unity is the introduction of Kabuki theater, a subject totally removed from the writer's point and an even worse distraction.

A perfectly good paragraph of student writing has had its unity sabotaged in similar **ways:**

It was my first day of classes, and I began having difficulties as soon as I arrived at my first class. *I had hoped to have Economics first, but instead I had Spanish.* I thought that I had gotten there in plenty of time, but there was no available space in that room. It looked as if the people in the room were staging a sit-in because they were sprawled out all over the floor. *I remember reading a lot about sit-ins during the sixties.* The instructor for the course finally appeared. He called my name for attendance, and I replied from the hall. He smiled and said, "I'm sorry, you will have to come a little early next time." *Now, I have known a lot of great men who were always late.* I don't know what he thought when I turned around and marched out of the building, but I know what I was thinking of.

In truth, this student wrote the paragraph without the three offending sentences:

I had hoped to have Economics first, but instead I had Spanish. (The kind of class has no bearing on the "difficulties" the student experienced.)

I remember reading a lot about sit-ins during the sixties. (An irrelevant recollection that takes the reader on a detour to the sixties.)

Now, I have known great men who were always late. (This comment shifts the attitude of the writer from not being able to cope with the overwhelming difficulties of his first day of classes to a weasling kind of self-righteousness.)

*Sample essay suffering from lack of purpose, lack of unity,
and lack of paragraph development*

A MADMAN

It is incredible that one man could be responsible for the deaths of six million people. The madman, Adolf Hitler, committed this unthinkable, horrifying deed.

Hitler brainwashed close to the entire German population into feeling a sense of Aryan supremacy. A huge Nazi army brutally murdered six million Jewish people in carrying out the wishes of this power-crazed dictator.

My grandmother, now ninety years old, was born in Russia, where many Jewish people were killed. She was fortunate enough to have escaped the clutches of Hitler's brutal army. At about the age of ten, my grandmother traveled with her family on a boat to the United States. I am very grateful that she was able to arrive here safely and start a family.

I can have faith that there will never be another maniacal leader like Hitler who will be able to cause such a disaster as the death of virtually an entire race.

Your comments on this paper might run to triple the length of the essay itself. Confining your criticism to purpose, unity, and paragraph development, you would note that the writer has taken a wild, unfocused stab at the career of Adolf Hitler. The final sentence in the first paragraph (a position, by the way, often used for the thesis) suggests that the writer is aiming at a biographical or a psychological study of the man who could commit this "unthinkable, horrifying" destruction of "virtually an entire race." The second paragraph, undeveloped as it is, announces that Hitler brainwashed the German population yet never develops and explains the idea of brainwashing. Without giving examples or support for these ideas, it is no wonder that the writer herself wanders away. This piece is too short and undeveloped to hold the reader's attention. A surprise comes when the writer introduces her grandmother, who, at age ninety, was ten years old long before 1932 when Hitler rose to power. This example scarcely supports the indictment of Hitler as a madman destroying Jews, because the grandmother left Russia forty years before the prolonged tyranny of Hitler's anti-Semitism and violence. So the third paragraph does nothing to prove the idea that Hitler was a madman: its facts are questionable and its arithmetic careless. The conclusion is sheer magic and flies up from nothing in the paper. On what is the writer's faith based? Where does she explain, in any of these paragraphs, *why* there will never be another Hitler? How does she know?

The truth is that the problems in a paper as unfulfilled as this one cannot be laid to a single fault. Lack of purpose prevents a writer from stating a thesis clearly. And an unclear thesis breeds lack of unity and meager, undeveloped paragraphs because the writer is casting about in many directions hoping to discover a purpose. When a paper has no clear purpose, paragraphs lack their own purposes and cannot contribute to the orderly and unified development of the essay's ideas. Still, even a draft whose thesis and paragraphs are as wobbly as this one's can be reapproached by its writer in search of the nagging point that drove her to write about this general subject. Respect your own urges. The next draft may not look anything like the first, and in fact this student's revision was not a discourse about Hitler at all but a competent, warm-hearted study of her ninety-year-old grandmother's zest for life.

WILLING TO LIVE AT NINETY

My grandmother has many characteristics, but they all add up to one: she has had the ability to stay alive for ninety years.

At the age of ninety, Grandma is still in complete control of her faculties. When I have the time to ride my bicycle over to her small but adequate garden apartment, I often have interesting conversations with her. We have diverged into such subjects as interracial marriage and legalizing abortion, which I am glad she approves of. Sometimes she tells me *bubba meinsers,* Jewish versions of old wives' tales, which always seem to end on a depressing note so that I can learn a moral or lesson. When I was younger, my mother used to tell me not to pay attention to these tales of Grandma's but now I'm old enough to see some truth in them. My grandmother is also quite a Scrabble player. In fact, she is the reigning champion of the family.

She must have had a lot of things to do to have lived so long, very often suffering from much pain in her arthritic legs. Pain and all, Grandma is a talented artist and an excellent cook. She has done beautiful oil paintings of her grandchildren, and more recently she has been painting landscapes. She is another "Grandma Moses." No one cooks as well as Grandma. She often spends hours sitting in the kitchen cooking. She makes not only delicious blintzes and chopped liver but fabulous pizza and chow mein, and no one in the family can roast a Thanksgiving turkey the way she can.

Grandma may be old, but she is still strong-willed and domineering. When she wants her children or grandchildren to do something, they do it whether they like it or not. If she wants us to take her shopping, to the doctor, or to our house for a visit, we do it, and quickly. Grandma, sometimes unfortunately, has quite an influence on her family. Sadly enough, she once prevented one of her sons from marrying a woman with whom he is still in love to this day.

In spite of her age and her frequent pain, Grandma is still a cheerful person. She spends much time sitting on her porch absorbing the sun and talking to her neighbors.

Grandma has said in the past that she was only living so that she could attend the wedding of one of my two sisters or myself. But since it is apparent that none of us has any immediate marriage plans, there must be something else that is keeping her alive. I feel that it is her will to live and "take care" of her family that is keeping her going. It would be very hard to settle on Grandma's outstanding characteristic, so I must say that the sum and final outcome of all her traits is her will to live.

It is reassuring to remember that the second draft might never have been written if it were not for the mistakes of the first draft. Be willing to let your mistakes happen, but know when you are not satisfied. The route to a successful piece of writing is not *think,* then *write,* then *hand it in*. The route is a cycle of acts, any of which you can repeat whenever you need to. Remember that most of your thinking takes place *as* you write. Whether you are freewriting, writing a first draft, or adjusting a detail in a paragraph, you are working back and forth through your ideas, thinking, and writing, and rewriting. The route is a cycle:

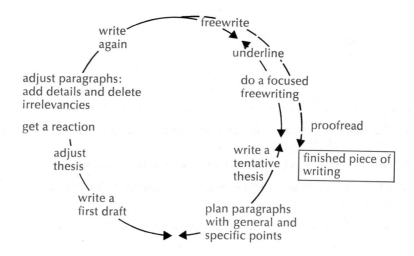

Be patient as your paragraphs become increasingly detailed and purpose-ful. Your essay ends whenever you want it to end. But the cycle of writing habits resumes in your next piece of writing as you freewrite, think, and write the thesis and paragraphs of your next essay.

Exercise 3 Justify the paragraphing in your most recent essay. Why did you indent when you did? Would you change any of your decisions to indent? Why?

Exercise 4 Use the ideas in Column 1 to write two paragraphs comparing high school to college. Sort out the details so that your first paragraph is about high school and your second paragraph about college. Use the words or phrases in Column 2 to connect the ideas within your paragraphs. Provide a link between the two paragraphs.

Column 1	*Column 2*
hated to go to school	no longer
felt stuck in a classroom	once
able to choose my own subjects	for example
wanted to be outside playing	first
teachers treat students as adults	second
despised homework	most important
homework was busy work	now
teaching methods are more	but
interesting	finally
subjects, like psychology, are more	
relevant to my life	
unimportant assignments	
students glued to chairs	
feel freer	
hated new math	
work hard	
achieve high grades	
uninterested and unhappy student	
mature and happy student	

(After an exercise by Kenneth Libo of the City College of New York)

After you have written your paragraphs, look at the order of your details. Explain why you arranged them as you did.

Exercise 5 Write topic sentences for paragraphs that develop the word *student* in the following ways.

1. Define student.
2. Compare a student to a nonstudent (or a poor student to a "grind").
3. Classify types of students.
4. Tell what conditions support a good student.
5. Tell what the special consequences of being a good student are.

Exercise 6   Write a paragraph of the kind indicated for each of the following topic sentences.

1. Dominant impression—general statement and details:
   As soon as she stepped into the room, you knew she had plenty of money to spend.
   Anyone could tell she had just come from the hairdresser's.
   Anyone could see he had just broken up with his girl friend.

2. Cause and effect:
   Several reasons were offered for changing the October camping rules.
   Several things happened after I switched my major from _____ to _____.
   Several changes led Professor _____ to give up teaching.

3. Classification:
   In my Utopia there would be three kinds of work.
   In my Utopia citizens would move from place to place in two ways.
   Marriages in my Utopia would be preceded by several kinds of trial arrangements.

4. Definition:
   Before I go any further, I should offer my definition of "a writer."
   Let me first establish what I mean by "retirement."
   I should say what I have in mind by the term "hard work."

Exercise 7   Develop two different paragraphs for each of the following topic sentences. Do not use the same method of development for both paragraphs. For example, one paragraph may show causes or results and the second a comparison. One may build on details and the second on reasons. One may offer a single illustrative anecdote and the second many smaller details.

1. Sitting in outdoor cafés is an entertaining pastime.

2. Some comedians tell you the truth about yourself.

3. What constitutes "pornography" is always open to disagreement.

4. My favorite spot in the whole world is _____.

5. Children's after-supper games have a distinctive quality.

6. He did not fit the stereotype of someone with a falcon tattooed on his arm.

7. She was certainly not a typical dental hygienist.

Exercise 8 Choose five of the following sentences. Use each sentence as the opening sentence of a paragraph. Write the next four or five sentences to support what you decide to be the primary idea contained in the opening sentence.

1. It was a marriage that was headed for the rocks.
2. I left school because I needed time to think.
3. I went to the woods because I wished to live deliberately.
4. Although I have forgotten most of what I learned about playing the piano, I do remember how to play "Autumn Leaves."
5. Whenever I visit my Aunt Sara, she piles me up with her old costume jewelry.
6. Whenever I see Jim, I think of the good times we used to have at the beach.
7. Ever since I was a child, I've been terrified of escalators.
8. Although my father suffered through wars and revolutions, through the loss of family and friends, he has a zest for life.
9. It was a face that only a mother could love.
10. Joan married Jim because he was faithful.

Exercise 9 Notice how Leonard Michaels, in the following one-paragraph essay entitled "Eating Out," establishes his point of view toward four men dining. Write a thesis statement for this essay.

Four men were at the table next to mine. Their collars were open, their ties loose, and their jackets hung on the wall. One man poured dressing on the salad, another tossed the leaves. Another filled the plates and served. One tore bread, another poured wine, another ladled soup. The table was small and square. The men were cramped, but efficient nonetheless, apparently practiced at eating here, this way, hunched over food, heads striking to suck at spoons, tear at forks, then pulling back into studious, invincible mastication. Their lower faces slid and chopped; they didn't talk once. All their eyes, like birds on a wire, perched on a horizontal line above the action. Swallowing muscles flickered in jaws and necks. Had I touched a shoulder and asked for the time, there would have been snarling, a flash of teeth.

Drafting Effective Sentences

Chapter 11

Part Two is a major section of this book because it gives systematic and
patient attention to the important work of seeing sentences. If you need
to, do not hesitate to return to Part Two to review the skills that enable
you to take a sentence apart and put it back together again: finding verbs,
recognizing subjects, noticing basic sentence patterns, and joining ideas
by means of coordination and subordination.

All along you have been writing whole essays *as* you are learning
about sentences, and this regular exercise has steadily increased your
confidence that grammatical sentences can best deliver the meaning of
your essay to your readers.

Now that you have these sentence skills, you can begin to take *control*
of your sentences, experiencing considerable pleasure as you tame them
into saying precisely what you want. You are ready to shift your emphasis.
Now you can attend not only to writing acceptable sentences without
blunders, but to writing *energetic* sentences that work well together, sentences that have a job to do: they must begin to reward your readers for
their effort and move them unhesitatingly forward into the teeth of your
ideas and into the complex development of your paragraphs. It is up to
your sentences to safeguard the interest of your essay by holding your
readers' attention to each sentence as it arises and by suggesting the promise
in the sentences that follow. This chapter, then, will help you get your
sentences moving. By all means, keep referring to the techniques discussed
in Part Two whenever you have questions, but remember that only *you*
can unlock the energy in your sentences. Reorder the parts, cut out

filler words that contribute nothing — we call this "deadwood" — change words and connectors and keep them as clear and flexible as your ideas require. Your sentences should be plain and vigorous at all times. They must be in the best shape possible to do the fascinating work of showing your readers the clear, sure direction of *your* thinking.

STRAINING FOR A "COLLEGE" STYLE

Many people with powerful things to say are embarrassed to show their writing to others because their sentences are not "elegant" or "complicated" enough. They strain to produce sentences that sound "academic" and "college" level. They say *In the event a young person is prevaricating . . .* instead of *If a child is lying . . .* when they *know* the simple language is clearer. The truth is, the trend in good writing is always toward simplicity and clarity. Even some insurance companies, whose policies have always been impossible to read, have begun to revise the sentences they write so that anyone can read them. Note the difference in the following two sentences taken from Aetna Life and Casualty policies:

> Old policy: Upon the happening of an occurrence reasonably likely to involve the Company hereunder, written notice shall be given as soon as practicable to the Company or any of its authorized agents.

> Readable policy: If there's an accident or incident that may be covered by this policy, notify us in writing as soon as possible. You can give this notice to any of our authorized agents.

It is not always simple to write a sentence that *sounds* simple. Even experienced writers face uncertainties all along the way. The illustrations on the next pages show you the muddled but indispensable rough drafts of our own opening paragraph of the chapter you are now reading. Are you surprised at what an unruly beginning this chapter had? Maybe you imagine that all the sentences of professional writers stream flawlessly onto the page, whole. We hope these exhibits will confirm that, for most writers, writing sentences *means* revising them.

Revision may include changing a single word of a sentence as well as rewriting the entire sentence. Notice our change from *a lot of attention* to *systematic and patient attention.* Any change you make, however trivial it may seem to you at the time, is an attempt to find out as precisely as you can what you are thinking. Any improvement you make in any part of a sentence puts you more and more securely in control of your idea because as you write it out in a sentence, as you force yourself to say it in a sentence, you are always working to refine your idea and make it clear.

Since sentences must be read in order and cannot be read upside down or backward or absorbed all in one glance, the very first sentence of your essay often sets the direction your reader will take. Every sentence that follows is linked into place because its idea in some way springs from the sentence before it and rolls toward the sentence after it and because the language in it refers to words or groups of words that appear in the

Sentences in Paragraphs -- Sentences in Essays

Part II is a large ~~chunk~~ section of this book because it
~~We've~~ gives a lot of attention to seeing sentences.

Seeing sentences in the writing all around you and seeing ~~them~~

in your own writing is the beginning of taking control of

your sentences. The important skills are ~~knowing how to~~ finding

a verb, recognize subjects, objects, indirect objects, noticing

the basic sentence patterns, and make ideas more exact through

modifiers. Although you have been writing whole essays as you are

learning about sentences, a certain mastery in the grammatical sentence

will now ~~allow~~ you to shift your emphasis ~~from.~~ You will be

moving from writing merely acceptable sentences to writing in

sentences which gather momentum and ~~become~~ paragraphs and essays.

Sentences--Sentences in Paragraphs--Sentences in Essays--Sentences

in Letters--Sentences in Memos--Sentences in Motion

Part Two is a ~~large~~ section of this book because it gives

systematic and patient attention to the ~~fundamental~~ work of seeing

sentences. ~~Seeing sentences in the writing all around you and~~

~~seeing sentences in your own writing lead to the~~ pleasure ~~you can~~

~~feel~~ as you take control of your sentences. You may need to review

the skills that ~~Part Two emphasizes~~ :

    findind verbs
    recognizing subjects
    noticing basic sentence patterns
    joining ideas by means of coordination and subordination

~~Although~~ you have ~~already~~ been ~~putting down~~ whole ~~pages of writing (in~~

~~freewriting, in journals, and in essays)~~ as you are learning about

sentences, your confidence in the grammatical sentence ~~has been~~

~~increasing steadily.~~ ~~You can now~~ shift your emphasis.

attending not ~~so much~~ to writing ~~merely~~ acceptable sentences ~~as~~ to

writing ~~interesting~~ sentences that work well together, sentences that

have a job to do: they must ~~gather interest~~ and move ~~your readers~~ forward

into the teeth of your ideas and into the complex development of your

paragraphs and essays. ~~You must now write sentences that uncover what you~~

~~mean and hold tight to your readers as they journey into the center of~~

~~what you have to say.~~ This chapter, then, will help you get your

---

surrounding sentences. Even the rhythms of your sentences are interconnected—suddenly yanking a sentence from the middle of your essay may be like gashing out a line in the middle of a song. Whenever you delete or change a sentence, you should adjust the stream of sentences before and after to close the gap in ideas, language, and rhythm. Adjusting only a single word or moving a phrase from the end of the sentence to the beginning, or from the beginning to the end, can often be enough to restore a seamless flow to your writing.

Writers enjoy options as they compose their sentences, options that you, too, are entitled to enjoy, though the choices may cause you such indecision that you are more likely at first to suffer from them than enjoy them. It would be a lot easier, you think, were there only one way to express an idea, but you will soon find out that without options your sentences would be a lot less colorful and less accurate as well. So you ask yourself questions:

What is the best place in the sentence for this phrase? Where will it create the best link with the sentence before it or the sentence after it?

Should I shift this successful phrase to the opening of the sentence? to the end?

Does this idea belong in a new sentence? Will it overload the sentence?

Should I repeat my verb for emphasis? Or should I use a different verb to add another shade of meaning?

What can I say next? Where will my next sentence come from?

Should I turn to a new idea? Or does the idea in my last sentence need to be expanded or illustrated?

Will there *be* a next sentence?

Much of the discussion about the sources of ideas for your sentences has been included in Chapter 10 on paragraphs. But a quick review will summarize the ideas presented there.

WHERE DO IDEAS FOR SENTENCES COME FROM?

Thesis statement and topic sentences One place you can turn to for ideas is your thesis. By underlining the most important words in your thesis statement, you can write the topic sentences of your paragraphs.

THESIS STATEMENT

Working while you go to college, even when you have no choice about it, can extend your education.

KEY WORDS: working, no choice, extend education

TOPIC SENTENCES:

Paragraph 1: In my family if you want to go to college you have to work.

Paragraph 2: My job as a counterman at Baskin-Robbins gives me the cash I need to be somewhat independent.

Paragraph 3: A major benefit of my job is that it gives me a chance to learn about the public.

Paragraph 4: Because I am under considerable pressure, I try to take time out occasionally.

Topic sentences, in turn, suggest the remaining sentences for each paragraph.

The preceding sentence Paragraphs grow in two ways. Sentences can spring out of the topic sentence, or they can explain, elaborate, or comment on the preceding sentence. The words of every sentence you write are a source of ideas.

Do not ignore the words of the sentence you have just written. If you are stuck for a moment, underline the key words in your last sentence and then write another sentence making one or more of those key words more specific. (See Chapter 9, "Modifying," page 182.)

In the following paragraph, for example, the topic sentence and the sentences that spring directly from the topic sentence are italicized:

> *The disadvantages of living on the ground floor of your dormitory result from its accessibility. Interruptions are everlasting.* "Did you see Amelia?" "Which room is Twitch Lasky in?" "Do you happen to know where we sign up for the room lottery?" and on and on all day and far into the night. *Not only do you hear the noise from your own floor, but the guys upstairs thump around so that the noise comes at you in quadraphonic sound. If you live downstairs, you lose privacy.* The hall is invariably full of people, and passers-through tend to use your bathrooms all the time. *And, finally, if you're interested in aesthetics, forget it.* The view from your downstairs window is probably directly into the sox department of the bookstore.

(See Chapter 4 for the complete essay from which this excerpt is taken.)

The unmarked sentences in the paragraph clarify the others and do not spring directly from the topic sentence:

Interruptions are everlasting.

(Gives examples)	"Did you see Amelia?" "Which room is Twitch Lasky in?" "Do you happen to know where we sign up for the room lottery?" and on and on all day and far into the night.
	If you live downstairs, you *lose privacy.*
(Tells why)	The hall is invariably full of people, and passers-through tend to use your bathrooms all the time.
	And, finally, if you're interested in *aesthetics*, forget it.
(Tells why)	The view from your downstairs window is probably directly into the sox department of the bookstore.

HOW DO YOU MOVE YOUR READER FORWARD?

Write a variety of sentences There's nothing excellent about a long sentence simply because it's long or a short one because it's short. But too many long ones or too many short ones can be monotonous. If you want to intensify the power of your writing, reread what you've written—out loud if you can—with an ear cocked for too much sameness. Sentences that change patterns and lengths will keep your reader awake instead of zzzzzz, lulled by the same old subject–verb–object rhythms that drone on and on.

Exercise 1 Let us suppose that Judy Syfers' essay "Why I Want a Wife" originated in a draft composed entirely of short sentences. It is unlikely that it did, of course, since most people naturally express ideas in longer strings of elements. Nevertheless, consider these short sentences:

I belong to a classification of people. It is known as wives. I am a Wife. And I am a mother. That is not incidental.

A male friend of mine appeared on the scene. It was not too long ago. He had had a recent divorce. He had one child. The child is with his ex-wife. Of course. He is looking for another wife. I was ironing one evening. I thought about him. Something suddenly occurred to me. I would like to have a wife, too. This is why I want a wife.

Revise these sentences. Imagine your reader riding forward on a moving stairway through a display of identical sentences. Think about breaking the monotony of the short subject–verb–object sentences he glides past. Rewrite the sentences by combining some and shifting others so as to rescue the reader from boredom and keep his attention. You may reorder or change any words you feel would slacken the reader's interest. After you rewrite the sentences, compare your version with the published version by the author on pages 83–85.

Look at the variety of sentences in the following example.

> The bankrupt man dances. Perhaps, on other occasions, he sings. Certainly he spends money in restaurants and tips generously. In what sense, then, is he bankrupt?
>
> He has been declared so. Firstly, he declared himself so. He returns from the city agitated and pale, complaining of hours spent with the lawyers. Then he pours himself a drink. How does he pay for the liquor inside the drink, if he is bankrupt?
>
> We are too shy to ask. Bankruptcy is a sacred state, a condition beyond conditions, as theologians might say, and attempts to investigate it are necessarily obscene, like spiritualism. We know only that he has passed into it and lives beyond us, in a condition not ours.
>
> John Updike

There are short subject–verb–object sentences. (*The bankrupt man dances.*) There are sentences with interrupters tucked in the middle. (*Perhaps, on other occasions, he sings.*) There are questions. (*In what sense, then, is he bankrupt?*) There is a long sentence right after a short one. (*We are too shy to ask. Bankruptcy is a sacred state, a condition beyond conditions, as theologians might say, and attempts to investigate it are necessarily obscene, like spiritualism.*)

Notice how much forward energy the next passage gains by questions and answers, by the variety of sentence patterns, by short and long rhythms, and by repetitions and exclamations:

> Why am I so happy? It must be the triumph of the human spirit over genetics and environment. I know the same bad things Howard knows. I have my ups and downs, traumas, ecstasies. Maybe this happiness is only a dirty trick, another of life's big come-ons. I might end up the kind who can't ride on escalators or sit in chairs that don't have arms. Who knows?
>
> But in the meantime I sing as I whip up waffle batter, pour golden juice into golden glasses, while Howard sits in a chair dropping pages of The *Times* like leaves from a deciduous tree.
>
> I sing songs from the Forties, thinking there's nothing in this life like the comfort of your own nostalgia. I sing *Ferry-Boat Serenade*, I sing *Hut-Sut Rallson on the Riller-ah*. The waffles stick to the iron. "Don't sit under the apple tree with anyone else but me," I warn Howard, willing the waffle and coffee smells into the living room where he sits like an inmate in the wintry garden of a small sanitorium.
>
> Hilma Wolitzer

Keep your verbs active Read the following sentences taken from college catalogs (the *Queens College Bulletin* and the *Yale College Programs of Study*):

In the event of any increase in the fees or tuition charges, payments already made to the College will be treated as a partial payment and notification will be given of the additional amount due and the time and method for payment.

Made by whom?

Treated by whom?

Given by whom?

Application Fee: All students are required to pay a non-refundable fee of $10.00 at the time of filing application for either matriculant or non-matriculant status in a master's degree program.

Required by whom?

Transcripts are prepared upon written request and payment of a charge depending upon the number of copies requested at one time. Request forms are available in 11 sss.

Prepared by whom?

Requested by whom?

Members of the military are also accustomed to receiving such orders:

Platoon A has been reassigned to the automotive pool effective immediately.

All enlisted personnel will be issued class B passes for twenty-four hours except platoon A, whose passes have been revoked.

Who can overlook the air of mysterious authority in these statements? An unknown and depersonalized authority shields the college administrators and buffers the military brass from complaints and blame. All this mystery lies in the passive forms of the verbs (*has been reassigned, will be issued, have been revoked*). This is the language of the institution concealing the faces of the real people behind it. It is deliberately lifeless.

If you want the essays you are writing to come alive, you've got to show your face. You've got to invite people with your voice. If you express ideas, you must be ready to accept responsibility for them. You will gain directness and simplicity by eliminating all unnecessary passive constructions. In particular, your voice is steadier when you avoid shifting midway in a sentence from an active verb to a passive one with no clear performer. Look at how these student sentences spring to life when an active verb replaces a passive one and the performer is named:

NO: The willingness of a person to help in his community comes through when urban projects are participated in.

YES: The willingness of a person to help in his community comes through when *he participates* in urban projects.

NO: The child soon learns to put the alphabet together to form words. These words may later be recognized in the book.

YES: The child soon learns to put the alphabet together to form words. Later *he may recognize* these words in the book.

NO: The teen-age years are the most difficult times in a person's life. During this stage of life, many problems must be resolved. New adjustments toward life must be made. More responsibilties are imposed upon teen-agers.

YES: The teen-age years are the most difficult times in a person's life. During this age, *adolescents encounter* many problems that *they must* resolve. *They must make* new adjustments toward life and *accept* more responsibilities.

Use parallel structures   Write sentence elements that have similar impact in similar structures. Match a noun with a noun, a verb with a verb, a phrase with a phrase, a clause with a clause. The balance and rhythm of parallel forms will move your reader right along:

Subject-verb, subject-verb:

times change
traditions survive   *Times Change, Traditions Survive*

Verbal, verbal, verbal:

Mark Fidrych is a loose-limbed, open-mouthed, wide-eyed youth. . . .

William Barry Furlong

loose-limbed
open-mouthed
wide-eyed

Verb, verb, verb:

looks
performs
costs

There is still a watch that looks elegant, performs beautifully, and costs half what you think.

Prepositional phrase, prepositional phrase, prepositional phrase:

BY THE CHIMNEY, UNDER THE TREE, OR IN THE MAILBOX.

by the chimney
under the tree
in the mailbox

in high school
on the job
in life

College credit for knowledge gained in high school, on the job, in life.

Clause, clause:

The more you know about life insurance, the more your agent can help you.

the more you know about life insurance
the more your agent can help you

Here are some student sentences that become more effective when the writers line up the elements in parallel forms. The trick to making the elements parallel is to have the appropriate vocabulary words ready and to be able to use them in the form required by the sentence—adjectives to match other adjectives, adverbs to match other adverbs, and so forth:

NO: Reading is very instructive, entertaining, and it can only benefit the reader.

YES: Reading is an *instructive, entertaining,* and *beneficial* pastime.

Vocabulary: shift from *it can only benefit the reader* to *beneficial pastime*

NO: The kids from the South Side were poor, tough, and wanted to get ahead.

YES: The kids from the South Side were *poor, tough,* and *ambitious*.

Vocabulary: shift from *wanted to get ahead* to *ambitious*

NO: Michael jokes a lot, he is liked by all the kids, and books are among his favorite activities.

YES: Michael is *witty, popular,* and *well read*.

Vocabulary: shift from *jokes a lot* to *witty*, from *he is liked by all the kids* to *popular*, and from *books are among his favorite activities* to *well read*

NO: Laughing loudly and I know she will never stop, my sister watches me do my Yoga.

YES: Laughing *loudly* and *incessantly,* my sister watches me do my Yoga.

Repeat words, phrases, and clauses to move ideas forward

The repetition of words, phrases, or clauses in a sentence is parallel structure carried to its extreme. The reader, gliding forward on the rhythm and words of the repetitions, looks ahead with pleasure to the next unit. Read this paragraph about movies by James Agee:

> Charles Brackett and Billy Wilder have a long and honorable record in bucking tradition, breaking rules, and taking risks, according to their lights, and limits. Nobody thought they could get away with *Double Indemnity,* but they did; nobody thought they could get away with *The Lost Weekend,* but they did; apparently nobody thought they could get away with *Sunset Boulevard,* but they did; and now, one gathers, the industry is proud of them.

Through three examples, Agee impresses us with the daring of Brackett and Wilder; we move on eagerly to read about each exploit as three times Agee repeats "nobody thought they could get away with [it] . . . but they did." The repetition carries us forward.

Emphasize words or phrases by changing their position in the sentence

You can insure your reader's attention by emphasizing the important elements of your sentences.

The usual order of words in English sentences is subject–verb–completer:

> I love chocolate cake.
> I've heard nothing about his wife, but I've heard a lot about Joe.

When you want to emphasize a part of your statement, you may have been doing it in ways that are terribly obvious:

I love chocolate cake!!!!!!!
I've heard nothing about his wife, but I've heard a lot about <u><u>Joe</u></u>.

Good writers avoid a smear of underlinings or a parade of exclamation points. They try to build emphasis into the grammatical construction of their sentences. A change in the usual order of sentence elements will pin the reader's attention to a word in an unexpected location:

Chocolate cake I love.
I've heard nothing about his wife but about Joe I've heard a lot.

Remember that the positions in the sentence that draw the greatest natural emphasis are the beginning and the end. Suppose the positions of words in a sentence had the following price tags: $5, 39¢, $10. With these prices in mind, you wouldn't throw ten dollars away on an unimportant word, as in the following sentences:

       $5   39¢
Unemphatic: I went to the Montreal museum and found some interesting
        $10
      Eskimo sculpture there.

Emphatic (emphasis on *Montreal museum* and *Eskimo sculpture*):
       $5   39¢
      At the Montreal museum I found some interesting Eskimo
      $10
      sculpture.

        $5   39¢
Unemphatic: It makes a person grow if he is responsible for someone
      $10
      or something.

Emphatic (emphasis on *responsible* and *grow*):
       $5   39¢
      Being responsible for someone or something makes a person
     $10
     grow.

        $5
Unemphatic: Feeling inadequate or ugly would not prey on our minds if
       39¢ $10
      we took care of ourselves and taught our children to do so.
      (This sentence starts off well but peters out.)

Emphatic (emphasis on *took care* and *inadequacy or ugliness*):
       $5   39¢
      If we took care of ourselves and taught our children to
        39¢
      care for their bodies, we would not be haunted by feelings
      $10
      of inadequacy or ugliness.

$5   39¢ $10

Unemphatic: You are drenched, I believe.

Emphatic (emphasis on *you* and *drenched*):

$5   39¢ $10

You are, I believe, drenched.

$5   39¢ $10

Unemphatic: I have not always been honest, I am sorry to say.

Emphatic (emphasis on *honest*):

$5   39¢ $10

I have not, I am sorry to say, always been honest.

$5   39¢ $10

Unemphatic: Without a doubt, money is the answer to all my problems.

Emphatic (emphasis on *answer* and *money*):

$5   39¢ $10

The answer to all my problems is, without a doubt, money.

$5

Unemphatic: We found out when we checked our baggage that the plane

39¢ $10

was fifty minutes late, so we browsed among the duty-free shops.

Emphatic (emphasis on *The plane was . . . late* and *duty-free shops*):

$5   39¢

The plane was fifty minutes late, we found out when we

$10

checked our baggage, so we browsed among the duty-free shops.

'This, simply put, is a hatchet job.'

Tucking an unimportant phrase (like *I believe, I am sorry to say, without a doubt, we found out when we checked our baggage*) in between commas as an interrupter in the middle of a sentence has the effect of emphasizing the beginning and the end. The sentence has a starting burst of energy, then stalls, holds its breath, until the energy is released in an important word at the end.

Exercise 2 Rewrite the following sentences so that the least important element is tucked into the middle of the sentence.

Example: I believe you are drenched.
     You are, I believe, drenched.

1. He noted that the landscape was lovely.
2. However, improvements can be made.
3. It is safe to say that everyone is a little weary now.
4. We discovered that the weather was never neutral.
5. Much later in the year we found out that he had won a Nobel Prize.

6. After long months of study, you learn to rely on nobody but yourself.

7. We must remember that throwing something away is really throwing it back into the universe.

8. It occurred to me that the piano needed tuning.

9. They say that once they have their licenses they'll drive me anywhere.

10. We discovered when we got to the airport that it was shut down because of fog.

WHAT SLOWS YOUR SENTENCES DOWN?

Don't use unnecessary words Unnecessary words—deadwood—slow your reader's progress. Be concise. Reduce elaborate constructions by cutting out such filler words. Use strong verbs wherever you can, and eliminate introductory elements like *there is, there are,* and *it is* whenever the meaning will allow:

NO: In our town, there are a great many people who do care and want to help.

YES: Our town has a great many people who care and want to help.

NO: Give me the exact, precise directions that will take me to your house.

YES: Give me precise directions to your house.

NO: My failure on the final examination was due to the fact that I had an aching tooth.

YES: I failed the final examination because I had a toothache.

NO: Volunteers, including those who are candy stripers in hospitals, provide a service in this community.

YES: Volunteers, including hospital candy stripers, serve this community.

NO: They began to fight a war that was costly in spirit and lives.

YES: They began a war costly in spirit and lives.

NO: The teen-ager is no longer a child who is still attached to the "umbilical cord." Adolescence is the time when teen-agers are developing into individuals and when they cut away from "family ties."

YES: The teen-ager is no longer a child attached to the "umbilical cord." During adolescence, teen-agers become individuals and cut family ties.
(Cut from 32 words to 21 words)

NO: Today's modern American citizen should be given a certain amount of responsibility so that he can grow to become an independent and productive member of our contemporary society.

YES: The American government should give citizens enough responsibility to enable them to live independently and contribute to society.
(Cut from 27 words to 18 words)

NO: I don't know why she left her place of employment without completing the assigned work or giving her boss notice.

YES: I don't know why she quit her job so suddenly.
        (Cut from 20 words to 10 words)

Study the next paragraph and compare it with the revised version that follows. Notice the difference in conciseness:

Hockey is a very quick sport. In order to keep it very fast-moving, hockey is the only sport in which substitutions are made while play is actually in progress. Players whiz up and down the rink at speeds of 20 M.P.H. Wearing ice skates, they just weave in and out of the opposition while moving the puck. Their main objective is to score by firing a fast or unexpected shot that goes through the opposing team's goalkeeper and into the goal. It is the goalkeeper's job to dive in front of the goal when shots that frequently go as fast as 100 M.P.H. have to be blocked.

Revision:

Hockey is a very quick sport. To keep it fast-moving, substitutions are made while play is in progress. Players on ice skates whiz up and down the rink at speeds of 20 M.P.H., weaving in and out of the opposition while moving the puck. Their objective is to score by firing a fast or unexpected shot past the opposing team's goalkeeper. Diving in front of the goal, the goalkeeper blocks shots that frequently go as fast as 100 M.P.H.

Eliminate all unnecessary *just*'s, *actually*'s, *very*'s. Combine sentences. Reduce *in order to* to *to*. Eliminate obvious statements.

Good writing results from learning to express your ideas gracefully and fully. Sudden shortcuts, omissions of words crucial to your exact meaning, missing connections between ideas result in sentences that sound like telegrams and wring the pleasure out of reading. For example, here is the paragraph about hockey that is too concisely written. It no longer conveys the sense of speed implicit in the fuller language of the earlier paragraph:

Hockey is a quick sport. Substitutions are made while play is in progress. Players on ice skates going 20 M.P.H. score by firing a shot past the opposition's goalkeeper, who tries to block shots as fast as 100 M.P.H.

For further exercise in conciseness, see Chapter 12 on words. Sometimes only the right word can rescue a sentence that meanders forward with a dreary, roundabout expression known as a *circumlocution:*

NO: We ate what had not been eaten the night before.
YES: We ate *leftovers.*

NO: The student union was a place where we could feel safe.
YES: The student union was our *refuge.*

Exercise 3 The following sentences suffer from wordiness. Rewrite them as simply and as emphatically as possible.

1. In case you lose your way and drive around, call us on the telephone.
2. It was during the winter of 1976 that I learned to ski.
3. In New York, there are many theaters and restaurants.
4. Why weren't you happy with regard to the way your paper turned out?
5. Until the winter of 1976, I had never skied before.
6. There should be greater emphasis on friendliness in hospitals.
7. There is a woman in my French class who sits next to me and is always tense and nervous.
8. I can definitely see a number of improvements that could be made to make registration easier without a doubt.
9. We should never underestimate our opponents and think they are not as fast as we are.
10. Our success was due to the fact that our team had positive hopes and expectations.
11. I will never cease to be optimistic that good things can always come to pass, especially through hard work.
12. Up until the midterm, I had been receiving passable grades on my tests and papers, but nothing spectacular.
13. I was getting ready to go out of my mind due to the fact that I was so frustrated, when I came up with a beginning opening paragraph that chimed like a choir of church bells.
14. I don't think that a teacher should ever accuse a student without first having proof of what he is accusing the student of.
15. There are many times when a person begins to feel he has been treated unjustly.

Exercise 4 The following paragraphs are full of deadwood. Revise each one by eliminating all self-evident ideas, unnecessary repetitions, and vague statements. Write in a single sentence whatever is left of each paragraph.

1. A child in a family at a young age does not have that much responsibility. When he gets older and is not so young any more, the parents give him more responsibility. They give him this responsibility because he has learned what is right and wrong, and they feel he now can judge for himself what to do and which way to go in life.
2. Reading has been an important factor in the development of our nation. The founding fathers of our country were able to do their job because of their ability to read. They were able to look back into books and then

establish our country. With books in the hands of many Americans, the nation will be in good shape for years to come.

3. Laughter is the only real universal language in the world. Everyone can share in laughter, whether it is a small chuckle or a large whoop. Everyone understands laughter.

Don't skip an essential link between two ideas in a sentence

Some sentences put forward one idea and present no problem. Other sentences attempt to deliver two or more ideas in a single container. If you jam two ideas into a sentence without showing the link between them, the continuity of your essay may suffer a break right there in that sentence. Without a link, your readers may slow down and become stalled because they have no way to get across to the next idea. Consider the following sentence:

NO: Children should be taught to think of their bodies as enjoyable and knowable as no one's body can be considered perfect.

A link is missing in this sentence. The writer probably means that children can enjoy their own bodies even if they are not perfect or beautiful, but he has not expressed this connection. He has lined up the two ideas without relating them:

Children should be taught to enjoy their bodies.
No one's body is perfect.

Improved: Even when a child's proportions are not graceful and perfect, he can learn to enjoy his body through exercising, moving his muscles, and fulfilling his own needs independently.

Now consider another sentence:

NO: By reading a lot, you develop your mind and your vocabulary, and these two things are good in any walk of life.

This writer fails to explain the connections between reading, a good vocabulary, and an enhanced life. To make the connections clear, the writer decided to use more than one sentence:

Improved: Reading develops your mind because it trains you to grasp and express ideas through words. This ability to express yourself will improve your relationships with people no matter what you do in your life.

Don't overload a sentence with unconnectable elements

Sometimes you draft a sentence with parts that have no sensible connection. Rather than create a forced connection, break the sentence down into more than one sentence or explain the connection between the parts. See the examples in the preceding section.

Exercise 5 In each of the sentences below, an important connection between two ideas is missing. Ask yourself what the connection between the two ideas is and rewrite the sentence to show the connection fully. Write additional sentences if you need to.

Example: There have been such advances in medicine that general practitioners are hard to find.

Rewritten with connection: Advances in medicine require that many doctors specialize to understand a single field fully. As a result, general practitioners are hard to find.

1. If a person feels loved by his family, he will know how to act in the future.
2. Since the human brain is not like the human eye, Arthur Rubinstein at eighty-six played better than he ever did.
3. In the "Mary Tyler Moore Show," the emphasis was not on a series of funny scenes, and we felt a concern for all the people in the cast.
4. If you are a good typist, you can get an A in anthropology and law.
5. A person who refuses to alter his views cannot be a teacher.

Avoid mixing sentence parts that don't make sense together

A critical task that awaits you every time you reread a first draft of an essay is checking to see that the parts of your sentences make sense together. Consider the following sentence:

NO: Another unique function of reading is the media.

As a reader, you may feel troubled by this sentence. You have a right to expect the words to tell you something, something about reading and the media, but they don't. It is not your fault if you don't understand, for the sentence doesn't make sense. How can a function of reading *be* the media?

Let's backtrack and try to rearrange the idea in our minds. Does the sentence mean:

Newspapers, magazines, pamphlets, periodicals, and other forms of the media depend uniquely on the public's ability to read.

Or does it mean:

We read to keep up with daily changes and opinion that are expressed in the media.

Both sentences are possible. As a writer, try to take apart your idea and say it as precisely as you can. In particular, test your subject's connection to its verb to make sure that together they express your intended idea. Reread your sentence to make sure that you have actually *said* what you think you've said.

Here is another example of a mixed construction:

NO: The word *laughter* can be one of the best things to do these days.

We cannot *do* the word *laughter*. The combination of words doesn't make sense. The writer may mean:

One of the best things to do these days is laugh.
>   or
The word *laughter* suggests one of the best things to do these days.

Laughing is something to *do*. But a *word* cannot be done. It can only suggest or mean something to be done.

Here is a third example:

NO: The make-up of our bodies is one of the most complex pieces of machinery there is.

This writer is saying that the *make-up* of our bodies is a *piece of machinery*. What does the writer mean?

The human body is one of the most complex pieces of machinery there is.
>   or
Our bodies are made up like complex machines.

That is, the human body is a complex machine, or, the body is made up like a machine. But not that the *make-up* is a *machine*.

Avoid is when and is because The word *is* behaves like an equal sign. What comes before *is* equals what comes after *is*. When you write "something is when" or "something is because," you are saying that something *equals* when something else occurs or because something else occurs rather than something equals some*thing* else. A noun should equal another noun. In the same way, clauses beginning with *the reason is* are followed by a noun clause beginning with *that*. Constructions using *is when* and *is because* create sentence difficulties:

NO: A teen-ager is when you are neither an adult nor a child.

YES: A teen-ager is neither an adult nor a child.

YES: A teen-ager is a person who is neither an adult nor a child.

(A teen-ager = a person)

NO: A wedding is when two families have their first showdown.

YES: A wedding is an occasion when two families have their first show-down.

(A wedding = an occasion)

NO: The reason I retired is because I wanted to enjoy my health.

YES: The reason I retired is that I wanted to enjoy my health.

(The reason is that . . .)

Don't disappoint expectations you create

not only . . . but also

both . . . and

either . . . or

neither . . . nor

so . . . that

As soon as one half of any of these constructions appears, the reader expects the other half to follow. When the other half fails to materialize, the reader has a sense of incompleteness, as though he were still listening for the "other shoe" to fall.

NO: He was not only a poor typist and his voice was not clear on the telephone.

YES: He was *not only* a poor typist *but* his voice was not clear on the telephone.

NO: *Scenes from a Marriage* was so unusual and it was the uncut version.

YES: *Scenes from a Marriage* was *so* unusual *that* Public Broadcasting presented the uncut version.

Here is a sequence of sentences with so many traps and false leads that the reader has little chance of moving forward, sentence by sentence:

My sister and brother-in-law's landlord is so mean. Not only does he withhold heat in the wintertime and he won't let their friends park in front of the house. When their friends come by bus, it stops eight long blocks away. My sister and brother-in-law's landlord was humiliated one day by Steve, their friend, and was expressed by a small back yard fire. A new apartment has been found either by their friend Steve, who is not usually too prompt in helping people and has the most friends in real estate.

Sentences like these disappoint our expectations and force us to reread whole sentences or else abandon the text in despair. When half of a paired construction appears, we want to find the other half in the sentence: *So . . . that, not only . . . but also.*

My brother-in-law's landlord is *so* mean *that* . . .
Not only does he withhold heat in the wintertime *but* he also . . .

In paired constructions, ask yourself which words are paired. Two verbs? Two adjectives? Two clauses? Then use *not only . . . but also,* or similar words directly before the words they apply to:

NO: They are *not only planning* to give the Seminoles lunch at the pool *but also dinner* at the club.

YES: They are planning to give the Seminoles *not only lunch* at the pool *but also dinner* at the club.

YES: They are planning to give *not only the Seminoles but also the coaches and administrators* lunch at the pool.

NO: *Either the mugger* demands your money *or your life.*

YES: The mugger demands *either your money or your life.*

NO: You will *either ask* for Ruth *or Helen.*

YES: You will ask for *either Ruth or Helen.*

NO: *Either I'll* buy a denim skirt *or wear* jeans.

YES: I'll *either buy* a denim skirt *or wear* jeans.

WATCH OUT FOR <u>EITHER</u> AND <u>NEITHER</u>

Either goes with *or.*

Neither goes with *nor.*

NO: *Neither* Delta, Eastern, *or* TWA has a morning flight.

YES: *Neither* Delta, Eastern, *nor* TWA has a morning flight.

      Do not use *either* where *neither* is required in a negative sentence.

NO: Joe's name wasn't on the passenger list, and *either* was mine.

YES: Joe's name wasn't on the passenger list, and *neither* was mine.

Don't make illogical comparisons

It is not logical to compare unlike things. Write a comparison fully enough to show the similarity between the things you are comparing:

NO: I like *the pitching on the Astros* better than *the Mets.*
             (*Pitching* is compared with a *team.*)

YES: I like *the pitching on the Astros* better than *the pitching on the Mets.*
             (*Pitching* is compared with *pitching.*)

NO: Floating in the Mediterranean is more serene than the Atlantic.
             (*Floating* is compared with an *ocean.*)

YES: Floating in the Mediterranean is more serene than floating in the Atlantic.
             (*Floating* is compared with *floating.*)

YES: Floating in the Mediterranean is more serene than it is in the Atlantic.

(*Floating* is compared with *floating*.)

NO: Mark's talent in mathematics is as imaginative as Ann in art.
(*Talent* is compared with a *person*.)

YES: Mark's talent in mathematics is as imaginative as Ann's in art.
(*Talent* is compared with *talent*.)

WATCH OUT FOR <u>SO</u> AND <u>SUCH</u>

Do not use *so* or *such* for *very*.

Do not use the superlative for *very*.

NO: Dr. Callahan is *so* strange.

YES: Dr. Callahan is *very* strange.

NO: It was *such* a waste of food.

YES: It was a *very great* waste of food.

NO: Leslie looked *so* beautiful.

YES: Leslie looked *very* beautiful.

NO: Dr. Callahan is the *strangest* person.

YES: Dr. Callahan is a *very strange* person.

Exercise 6 Fill in the blanks in the following sentences with logical constructions.

1. I not only _____ after the guests left but _____ as well.

2. Not only can you _____ but you can _____.

3. We cooked not only _____ but also _____.

4. Ask for either _____ or _____.

5. Either _____ the man or _____ him.

6. This country will either _____ in the next four years or _____.

7. The chairperson explained, simplified, and _____ the new rules.

8. Bernice is educated, employed, and _____.

9. We elected Raymond because he was compassionate, knowledgeable, and _____.

10. Paris is so romantic that _____.

11. I am so hungry that _____.

12. Your feet are so big that _____.
13. They stayed so late that _____.
14. The wound may be too deep to _____.
15. The wound may be so deep that _____.
16. Neither _____ nor _____ can handle the electric chainsaw.

WATCH OUT FOR <u>LIKE</u> AND <u>AS</u>

Use *like* with a *noun*. Use *as* with a *clause*.

He stood there *like* a blind man.

He stood there *as* a blind man does.

Exercise 7 Rewrite the following sentences to correct illogical comparisons. If a sentence is correct, mark it C.

1. Running at the beach is more exhilarating than the yard.
2. I like jazz played on the clarinet better than the flute.
3. Going to school in Vermont is more fun than New York.
4. Annette's hair is shorter than Mark.
5. California's weather is more reliable than Florida's.

Fill in the blanks in the following sentences.

6. We like a picnic at the lake better than _____.
7. The direction of *Guys and Dolls* pleased the audience more than _____.
8. Driving to the Grand Canyon is more expensive than _____.
9. Cruising in a whaler is more exciting than _____.
10. The President speaks before Congress more often than _____.

Avoid writing sentences without internal connectors

Sometimes a sentence may be faulty and hard to understand because one part of the sentence is included directly next to another part without a proper connector written out between the two. It is particularly important to see that a subject makes a logical connection with its verb. (See the discussion of subordination and coordination in Chapter 8.)

NO: There are four more years here will have a great influence on my life.

YES: The next four *years* here *will have* a great influence on my life.

NO: You said you are a Taurus I feel you understand what I am talking about.

YES: *Since* you said you are a Taurus, I feel you understand what I am talking about.

NO: You want to be a policeman, there is good news and bad news.

YES: There is good news and bad news *if* you want to be a policeman.

NO: Dancing all weekend I am a good dancer.

YES: I go dancing all weekend *because* I am a good dancer.

YES: I am a good dancer, *and* I go dancing all weekend.

Don't use more than one negative   One negative word (no, not, nobody, none, no one, nothing) is all that you need. Two negative words will not intensify your meaning. Using more than one negative is considered an error.

NO: I *don't* want *no* help from you.

YES: I *don't* want *any* help from you.

NO: *Nobody* asked *no* questions at all.

YES: *Nobody* asked *any* questions at all.

NO: They were*n't* planning to do *nothing* tonight.

YES: They were*n't* planning to do *anything* tonight.

Avoid using combinations like *don't hardly, won't scarcely, can't barely:*

NO: They *can't hardly* wait for the bell to ring.

YES: They *can hardly* wait for the bell to ring.

NO: They *can't barely* see the lights on the bridge.

YES: They *can barely* see the lights on the bridge.

Exercise 8 Rewrite each of the following news clippings, which suffer from over-loaded sentences. You may need several sentences to include all the elements contained here in a single sentence.

1. WHILE DISTRESSING to Coach Ed Kennedy and Panther fans at the time, Monticello High's opening-season setback on the soccer field may have been just what the doctor ordered as the rejuvenated Blue and White have thrown off their lethargy to win their last three starts and take over the lead in the Orange County League's big school division.

2. Frankly, it's an education for me to write this column. For example, due to letters I've received which are diametrically opposed to each other re the importance of Art; a topic I focused on for two weeks running because of timely associative events — namely: season's end art shows in the vicinity — I've been doing some reflective digging and in the process learned something about art.

3. MONTICELLO — Police Chief Roger Bisland reports that the village is getting along very well so far without a sobering-up station for alcoholics by approaching the problem in different ways.

4. Very often the fluke and flounder are thought to be the same fish. Although in the same class, under the heading of flat fish, and in appearance very much similar, it will be found upon closer examination that there is considerable difference in many details of form and make-up.

5. George E. Bauer called attention to the predicament the firemen were up against last week when the large barn on the Gallagher property was burned. Mr. Bauer said the water pressure was so low on connecting that the service was absolutely useless. It was disgusting, he said, on connecting the fire hose, to find hardly enough water to fill a bucket, and with a big fire raging right under their noses and no means of fighting it except by forming a bucket line from a nearby cistern, which was soon exhausted.

6. In a presentation lasting nearly two hours, attorney John Coffey, with the help of planning, real estate and traffic experts, discussed why his client should be granted a change of zone on 16 acres of land on Jericho Tpke. in Woodbury to allow for construction of a shopping center. They contend such development would not be detrimental to the area.

Choosing Exact Words

Chapter 12

ACCURACY—USE CONCRETE WORDS FOR VAGUE WORDS

There is no arguing with your math teacher who urges, over and over again, that you check every number. "Be accurate," you are told. "There's a big difference between 84 and 48. 1,568.87 is the right answer; 1,563.87 is wrong. 'Around' 1500 is not exact enough. Be precise!"

What inexperienced writers often don't know is that preciseness can be just as crucial to good writing. What the professionals do is take a final close look at their words, especially their verbs and nouns, to make sure that they've chosen the words that convey their meaning most precisely. Suppose you saw the following announcement in the business section of a newsmagazine:

> Something that you wanted to see is on at the same time as something
> else. And tomorrow something is on when you have to go somewhere.
> This is taken care of by a lot of people who own something that can tape
> T.V. shows. This type of thing is not cheap but it works easily. So do what
> you want—and see anything you don't get to see.

You would suspect that the writer had in mind one of the new video-recorder units now on the market, but you wouldn't know much more than that. Words like *something, somewhere, thing,* and *anything* don't make for informative—or exciting—reading. Every time you use a vague word, you sacrifice a chance to interest your reader with concrete, lively information.

Now read this version:

The hilarious installment of "The Odd Couple" that you've always wanted to see is being rerun tonight on Channel 11 at precisely the same time that Channel 5 is featuring the latest episode of "Mary Hartman, Mary Hartman." And tomorrow night "Upstairs, Downstairs" is coming over the tube at 9 P.M.—when you will have to be at a dinner downtown. This sort of problem is easily solved by the 50,000 U.S. owners of Tokyo-based Sony Corp.'s Betamax video-tape record-and-playback system (price: $1,300 list, about $1,000 at discount). The Betamax, which can be attached to any T.V., records on a $16 cartridge one hour's worth of color (or black and white) programming—either off a channel being watched or another channel. So watch what you please, go out when you like—setting the handy timer—and replay at your leisure the shows you loved or you missed.

Time, April 11, 1977

Reading the second passage after the first is like seeing the white line again after driving through fog. The second paragraph leaves you with precise understanding. You know what the machine is. You know what it does, how much it costs, and who can benefit from owning it. Every word in the paragraph is working.

Look at this paragraph:

One of the worst factors about being a teen-ager is the situation of the age itself. You're too old for the kinds of things a child does and too young for the things an adult does. I want to discuss three aspects of the case of being in this bad situation.

Vague words like *factors, situation, kinds of things, aspect, case* choke the personal energy out of your writing. Not only is such writing dull, impersonal, and lifeless, but it is imprecise. You can never be 100 percent sure of what it means. Compare this revised version of the same paragraph:

What is most bewildering about being a teen-ager is the age itself. You're too old to yell and cry for what you want and too young to argue with assurance and experience. Three incidents from my own life show how I was hurt during this period of transition.

The writer made the following substitutions:

Concrete	*Vague*
most bewildering	worst factors
	situation [unnecessary filler] of the age itself
age itself	
yell and cry	kinds of things a child does

argue with assurance and experience things an adult does

incidents from my own life aspects of the case

period of transition bad situation

Substituting concrete and precise words for unnecessarily abstract and vague words puts zest and personality as well as specific meaning into your writing. The reader now has a sense of the human being behind the words, who is describing a perplexing time in his own life. For practice in choosing exact words, go back over the early draft of an essay you've written and replace inexact words with the most accurate words you can find.

Exercise 1 Rewrite the following vague sentences to make them more precise. Change whichever words you have to, and invent any concrete details you need.

Example: Recently, he was in the city doing some work.
From 1976 to 1977, he worked as a claims inspector for an insurance company in Detroit.

1. Because of his sickness, he felt bad.
2. Something in the bathroom makes a funny noise.
3. The athlete had on nice clothes.
4. The lady in the bank looked at someone who had just come in.
5. The people who wrote the book received complaints from a lot of people.
6. It took them a long time to get furniture for their house.
7. The soldier thought about the holiday at home.
8. The appliance went on and off all night.
9. Because of what happened, the people came out of the building not dressed properly.
10. The students were in front of the theater waiting for one of the actors.

You can improve a passage enormously by replacing a good word with the *best* one possible in that context, the one that says exactly what you mean:

Good: The tennis court was *empty*.
(*Empty* means no one was there.)

Exact: The tennis court was *deserted*.
(*Deserted* means no one was there but also suggests that it usually has players who for some reason have left.)

Good: After the interview, I *walked* downtown.
(*Walked* is a neutral word that means to go on foot at a moderate pace.)

Exact: After the interview, I *strode* downtown.
(*Strode* means to go with vigor and confidence. *Strode* suggests a successful or decisive interview.)

Exact: After the interview, I *wandered* downtown.
(*Wandered* means to go aimlessly. *Wandered* suggests that the interview was puzzling to the writer or that the writer was unhurried once the pressure of the interview was off.)

Exact: After the interview, I *sped* downtown.
(*Sped* means to go quickly. *Sped* suggests an appointment was waiting, and the writer had little time to spare.)

(See Chapter 9, "Modifying," for discussion of how to make writing more specific.)

ECONOMY Guard against using unnecessary words. *More* words are not always better than *fewer* words. Learn to use one accurate word instead of two vague ones. Use one word instead of two that mean roughly the same thing:

NO: At thirteen I gave up my toys and began to search for a *replacement and substitution.*

YES: At thirteen I gave up my toys and searched for a *replacement.*

NO: Parents usually won't let you *be alone or by yourself.*

YES: Parents usually won't give you *privacy.*

NO: Pressures from friends can lead to *distressing and disturbing* situations.

YES: Pressures from friends can lead to *disturbing* situations.

Unless a second word *adds* meaning to your sentence, count on one well-chosen word to do the job:

NO: With all the *sad and tragic* events in the world today, we should learn to laugh out loud.

YES: With all the *tragic* events in the world today, we should learn to laugh out loud.
(The word *tragic* implies *sad.*)

NO: The cat *maliciously and deliberately* attacked King.

YES: The cat *maliciously* attacked King.
(The word *maliciously* implies *deliberately.*)

DENOTATION AND CONNOTATION The exact meaning of a word, the definition that you will find in a dictionary, is its *denotation*. We say that the word *weed* denotes an uncultivated plant. But the word *weed* may also have certain associations for you—weeds crowd out desirable flowers, they hurt the tomatoes and peppers you spent long hours cultivating, they run wild and take over your garden. These associations are the word's *connotations*. We say that the word *weed* connotes destruction and uncontrolled growth. We say the word *weed* has *bad* connotations.

The word *wildflower,* on the other hand, also denotes an uncultivated plant, but this word carries with it pleasant overtones. Its "vibes" are good ones, of colorful roadside blossoms and delicate Queen Anne's lace that grow in pale profusion in country fields and meadows. We say the word *wildflower* has *good* connotations.

Think of the word *house.* Its denotation is neutral: a building for human beings to live in. It is an uncharged word. Its connotations are neither bad nor good. The word *residence,* which is also a building for human beings to live in, has connotations of size and elegance. The word *dwelling* is slightly charged because it has poetic connotations or connotations of legality. *Dwelling* is the word lawyers use in contracts and documents to describe a house. The word *hut* means a humble house and connotes crudeness and roughness. *Cottage,* which is also a humble house, connotes instead a cozier place. The *American College Dictionary* tells us that, along with *cabin* and *lodge, cottage* is often used by the "well-to-do" to refer to a second house where they go for recreation: for example, a summer cottage, a ski lodge, a mountain cabin.

Learn to use a reliable dictionary to determine the exact denotations of words. Many dictionaries list synonyms under the definitions. This list will show you the differences among words that mean almost the same thing, and make it easier for you to select the best word for your sentence.

LIVELINESS In math, when you are accurate, you are correct. You solve your problem. In writing, when you are accurate, you are clear and precise. You deliver your message.

But in writing, accuracy has another virtue. It can pull your writing out of a slump. Once accuracy becomes a habit, you will be on a continuing word hunt. You will begin to notice words, not just words that you don't understand but words that you admire yet never seem to use in your own writing. As you read the newspaper or watch TV, you will become more sensitive to the exact meanings of the words you hear. Your own desire to come up with the "right" word will put you in touch with a great variety of words that are fresh, strong, and vivid. One relatively painless but effective way to improve your vocabulary is to hoard words, to save the words you like in a notebook. Make a list of the liveliest words you run into—not just the ones you don't understand—and try to use them in your writing whenever they are appropriate. Lively words make writing come alive. They enable your reader to live through your experience or think through your idea as *you* did. If you actually *sped* somewhere, why say you *walked?* If you mean *deserted,* why settle for *empty?* When you want to suggest a *towering inferno,* why let it go at *tall,* or *big,* or *high?* (Can you imagine the impact of a movie called *The Tall Inferno?*)

Use vigorous verbs Pay particular attention to your verbs. Because the verb is at the crossroad of your sentence's grammar (see Chapter 6, "Finding the Verb and Subject"), it's also at the place where interest takes a turn for better or worse. We have already talked about the dangers of indefinite, all-purpose nouns like *thing, situation,* and *aspect.* Your readers now move to their most critical intersection. This is where *noun meets verb,* and a vigorous verb can turn your sentence from a limp string of ordinary words into magic.

Compare the following sentences with the livelier ones written by Joan Didion:

> Flames were *coming* up behind her.
> Lively: Flames were *shooting* up behind her.

> A window *closed* once in Barbara's room.
> Lively: A window *banged* once in Barbara's room.

> The gas heater *goes* on and off.
> Lively: The gas heater *sputters* on and off.

> College girls *were* at the courthouse all night.
> Lively: College girls *camped* at the courthouse all night.

> I'd *go* seven hundred miles to Brownsville, Texas.
> Lively: I'd *hitchhike* seven hundred miles to Brownsville, Texas.

> Beyond the [old frame houses] *are* the shopping centers.
> Lively: Beyond the [old frame houses] *spread* the shopping centers.

> [It is] so hot that the air *has a shine*, the grass *is* white and the blinds *are* drawn all day.
> Lively: [It is] so hot that the air *shimmers*, the grass *bleaches* white and the blinds *stay* drawn all day.

> [The sailors] *are* on the sidewalk avoiding the Hawaii Armed Forces Patrol and telling one another to get tattooed.
> Lively: [The sailors] *jostle around* on the sidewalk avoiding the Hawaii Armed Forces Patrol and *daring* one another to get tattooed.

The difference between the dull sentences and the lively ones results from the verbs:

Dull	*Lively*
coming	shooting
closed	banged
goes	sputters
were	camped
go	hitchhike
are	spread
has a shine	shimmers
is	bleaches
are	stay
are	jostle around
telling	daring

Examine your own sentences for repeated use of all-purpose verbs like *is, are, were, goes, has, come*. Replace them with striking verbs that put some action into your sentences.

Exercise 2 List as many verbs as you can that make each of the verbs in the list below more specific.

Example: *walk*

wander	run	stroll
amble	race	stumble
stride	saunter	limp
lope	meander	trot

1. look   **5.** love

2. laugh   **6.** tear

3. frighten   **7.** talk

4. hold

Exercise 3 Find a synonym for each of the italicized words in the following paragraphs. Does your synonym work? Is it more or less effective than the original word? What is the essential difference in meaning that makes it more or less effective?

1. Ever since childhood, when I lived within *earshot* of the Boston and Maine, I have *seldom* heard a train go by and not wished I was on it. Those whistles *sing bewitchment:* railways are *irresistible* bazaars, *snaking* along perfectly level no matter what the landscape, *improving* your mood with speed, and never *upsetting* your drink. The train can *reassure* you in *awful* places—a far cry from the *anxious* sweats of *doom* airplanes inspire, or the *nauseating* gas-sickness of the long-distance bus, or the paralysis that *afflicts* the car passenger. If a train is *large* and comfortable you don't even need a *destination;* a corner seat is enough, and you can be one of those travelers who stay in motion, straddling the tracks, and never arrive or feel they ought to—like that *lucky* man who lives on Italian Railways because he is retired and has a free pass. Better to *go* first class than to arrive, or, as the English novelist Michael Frayn once rephrased McLuhan: "the journey is the goal." But I had *chosen* Asia, and when I remembered it was *half a world* away I was only *glad.*

Paul Theroux, *The Great Railway Bazaar*

2. *Apprehensive* that the old woman might be *alarmed* at their being alone, and without any *hope* that his appearance would *reassure* her, he *took hold* of the door and *pulled* it towards him, so that she should not be tempted to lock herself in again. Although she did not pull the door shut again at this, she did not *relinquish* the handle, so that he almost *pulled* her out on the stairs. When he saw that she was standing across the doorway in such a way that he could not pass, he *advanced* straight upon her, and she stood aside *startled*. She seemed to be trying to say something but finding it *impossible,* and she kept her eyes *fixed* on him.

Feodor Dostoevsky, *Crime and Punishment*
(Coulson translation)

3. Many of our *national* problems can be traced directly to our *faulty* eating habits. For example, a third of our population is *obese;* high-protein breakfast alone would largely *correct* this problem. Ninety-eight per cent of Americans have tooth decay caused by eating too much sugar; the *craving* for sweets *disappears* when the blood sugar is kept high. *Lassitude, fatigue, nervousness, irritability,* even *exhaustion* and *foggy* thinking are *widespread* indeed. Prevention or remedy are easy; for the essentially healthy person, fatigue can be changed to *amazing vitality* in a single day. School children are difficult to *handle* and often learn slowly; thus much school-tax money is wasted. *Confused* thinking in political, public, and *private* life is all too common. The greater number of *automobile* accidents occur when the blood sugar is lowest, when thinking is confused and reactions are slow. Our *excessive* use of coffee, cigarettes, and alcohol is related to our level of blood sugar; they stimulate the production of adrenal hormones which cause the blood sugar to be increased, thereby producing the needed *"lift."* *Irritability* resulting from low blood sugar can be a *factor* in divorces. It now appears that polio is contracted only when the blood sugar is particularly low; the summer heat decreases the *appetite* for proteins and increases the *craving* for sugar-filled *iced* drinks and ice cream; exercise, such as swimming, *uses up* the sugar available.

Adelle Davis, *Let's Eat Right to Keep Fit*

METAPHORS AND SIMILES

Metaphors and *similes* are figures of speech. They use words imaginatively instead of literally. The woman pictured on the next page has never really driven her living room behind her. But driving her big American station wagon felt that way to her.

Metaphors and similes show a comparison that exists in the imagination of the writer between two unlike things. Sometimes figures of speech are called *images* because they help us "see." When you use figures of speech in your writing, you help your reader to "see" with sharp, fresh insight.

For suburban driving, Barbara Coats finds that her white BMW "maneuvers beautifully." Driving her previous car, an American wagon, "was like driving my living room behind me."

The following sentences are taken from an essay by Robert Lipsyte about a New York race track and its special subway train.

Simile A simile *expresses* a comparison. Look for the words *as* or *like,* which signal that a simile may be under way:

> The subway car is *as* free of talk *as* the reading room of a library.
> (This sentence explicitly states that the subway car is as quiet as a library.)

> The hot young jockey finishes fourth in the first race, and the praying man collapses on the fence *like* a steer caught on barbed wire.
> (This sentence explicitly states that a spectator falls on the fence like a steer caught on barbed wire.)

> An old, hooded man from Allied Maintenance moves over the asphalt picking up torn tickets with a nail-tipped stick, tapping *like* a blind man among the empty wastebaskets.
> (This sentence explicitly states that the maintenance man picking up tickets with a stick is like a blind man tapping.)

Metaphor A metaphor *suggests* or *implies* a comparison. It does not use the words *like* or *as:*

> The fans troop out to the subway station.
> (The writer suggests that the fans move out in an orderly line like a body of soldiers. Only the verb *troop* implies the comparison.)

> A minute later they are straggling back, chanting the old litany, "I woulda . . . coulda . . . shoulda . . ."
> (The writer suggests that the losers repeat their regrets as they would in a prayer. The words *litany* and *chanting* imply the comparison.)

> There are ebbs and flows throughout the day.
> (The writer suggests the crowd of people at the track comes and goes like an ocean. *Ebbs and flows* implies the comparison.)

Personification Personification compares an inanimate object or nonhuman thing to a person:

> An old shuddering train lumbers in to carry them away.
> (The train is compared to an old person moving clumsily and trembling as if from the cold.)

See Chapter 11 for practice in completing logical comparisons.

Figures of speech let us see more clearly or in a suddenly new way. They suggest what a writer *feels* toward his subject and stir us to respond emotionally. They also delight our imagination with the writer's personal vision and language. For the full effect of these images, read Robert Lipsyte's complete essay from which the above sentences are taken:

SHORT TRIP

The fare to the Aqueduct Race Track is 75 cents on the special subway train from Times Square. This includes a send-off: the narrow escalator down to the platform ends beneath the words Good Luck printed on the grimy-gold arch of a huge wooden horseshoe. The subway car is as free of talk as the reading room of a library, and, in fact, all the travelers are reading: The Morning Telegraph, The Daily News, the latest bulletin from Clocker Lawton. They are very ordinary-looking men and a few women, a bit older than most people these days.

It hardly seems 30 minutes before the train bursts out of the black hole and onto an elevated track that winds above the two-family houses and cemetery fields of Queens. It is nearing mid-day, in the butt-end of another year, and the travelers blink briefly in the flat, hard sunlight. They are standing long before the train skids to a stop. They run down the ramp toward the $2 grandstand entrances, then on to daily-double windows five minutes away from closing.

Before the race of the day, at any track, anywhere, there is a sense of happening, of a corner that might be turned, a door that might open. There is almost a merry ring to the parimutuel machines punching out fresh tickets to everywhere, and the players move out smartly, clapping down the wooden seats of chairs, briskly stepping onto the pebbled concrete areas that bear the remarkable signs, "No Chairs Permitted on Lawn." Seconds after noon, the first race starts. It lasts little more than a minute, just long enough to hold your breath, to scream, or fall to your knees against a metal fence and pray, "Angel, Angel, Angel."

But on this day, Angel Cordero, the hot young jockey, finishes fourth in the first race, and the praying man collapses on the fence like a steer caught on barbed wire. Another man smiles coldly as he tears up tickets, and says: "Dropping down so fast like that, you mean to tell me he couldn't stay in the money? Sure. Haw."

It is suddenly quiet again, and the day is no longer fresh and new, the day is tired and old and familiar. An old, hooded man from Allied

Maintenance moves over the asphalt picking up torn tickets with a nail-tipped stick, tapping like a blind man among the empty wastebaskets. Men watch him to see if he is turning over the tickets looking for a winner thrown away by mistake. He is not.

The race track settles into a predictable rhythm. In the half hour or so between races, men study their charts, straddling green benches or bent over stew and stale coffee in the drab cafeteria or hunkered down beneath the hot-air ceiling vent in a cavernous men's room, the warmest spot at Aqueduct. As the minutes move toward post time, they gather beneath the approximate odds board. They interpret the flickering numbers—smart money moving, perhaps the making of a coup. At the last moment, they bet, then rush out on the stone lawn for the race. A minute later they are straggling back, chanting the old litany, "I woulda . . . coulda . . . shoulda . . ."

There are ebbs and flows throughout the day. People leave, others come, the machines jangle on. There is a great deal of shuffling in the grandstand area, and little loud talk. People move away from strangers. When men speak of horses, they use numbers, not names, and when they talk of jockeys, they frequently curse. It was, they whisper, an "election"; the jockeys decided last night who would win.

The day ends pale and chilly a few minutes before 4 P.M. and the fans troop out to the subway station. There is no special train returning: the city will get you out fast enough, but you can find your own way home.

Horseplayers are smart, and they all wait in the enclosed area near the change booths, ready to bolt through the turnstiles onto the outdoor platform when the train comes, and not a moment sooner. They stamp their feet, muttering, "Woulda . . . coulda . . . shoulda." The losers rail against crooked jocks, gutless horses, callous owners, the ugly track, the greedy state that takes 10 cents of each dollar bet.

Then they bolt through the turnstiles, quick and practiced, tokens in and spin out upon the platform. But there is no train yet, they all followed a fool, and now they curse him for five minutes in the cold until an old shuddering train lumbers in to carry them away.

Exercise 4 List all the figures of speech in the essay "Short Trip" and explain in detail why you think they are successful or unsuccessful. Tell how each figure of speech made you *feel* as you read it.

Mixed metaphor A *mixed metaphor* troubles the reader by blurring two or more images rather than presenting one distinct image. In trying to create a bold comparison, an inexperienced or careless writer may begin a second image before completing the first one. The result is always confusing and often absurd:

The spiritual heart of northern Italy, the great Cathedral of Milan, reaches hundreds of marble fingers to the sky.

(Can a heart have fingers, not to mention hundreds of marble fingers? The image is confusing to imagine.)

She sailed into the room, her mane of hair thrown to the wind.
(Her motion is first likened to that of a sailboat in a breeze, but then the writer confuses the picture by likening her to a fast-moving horse.)

Often, a mixed metaphor is the preposterous product of mixed clichés:

Sly as a fox, he was rotten to the core.

Exercise 5 In the following excerpt from a *New York Times* article about CB radios, list all the figures of speech you can find.

Interference by C.B. Radios Causing a National Earache

By WAYNE KING
Special to The New York Times

ATLANTA, Jan. 22 — Citizens' band radio, that Southern-born phenomenon that has a sizable part of the country saturating the air waves, is now causing a great national earache. Because of an electronic quirk, Rubber Ducky is no longer talking only to receptive listeners like Jelly Belly and Dragon Lady, who talk back on C.B.'s of their own; he is also talking to vast numbers of people who never wanted to listen.

Unsolicited voices are trampling on Beethoven on home stereo systems, interrupting Walter Cronkite on television sets, barging into weddings, funerals and prayer meetings on church public address system or electronic organs and. —even, according to one bizarre account, suddenly blaring out at a woman from the oven of the electric range while she was cooking dinner.

The phenomenon is more than just a curiosity: The Federal Communications Commission received over 100,000 mostly angry complaints about citizens' band intrusion last year, Congress is casting about for a legislative solution, and two large industries, the manufacturers of high fidelity equipment and those who make the C.B. radios, appear to be at odds over who should pay for correcting the intrusions, either by altering the radios or by filtering home entertainment equipment.

Meanwhile, reports from around the country provide a deluge of examples of citizens' band intrusion on equipment never meant to receive it.

Exercise 6 Write a simile to convey each of the following impressions:

Example: What it is like to drive your station wagon.
          Driving my station wagon is *like driving my living room behind me.*

1. What it is like to drive your car.
2. What it is like to take a final exam.
3. What it is like to vote for a candidate you're not 100 percent sure of.
4. What it is like to do some freewriting.
5. What it is like to live in your house (or room or apartment).
6. What it is like to be stopped by a policeman for speeding.

Exercise 7 In the sentences below, change each simile to a metaphor. In each case you will have to change the verb to a more specific word that expresses the essential quality of the italicized simile.

Example: The graduates moved toward the stage *like water.*
The graduates *streamed* toward the stage.

1. Loretta got through her research paper *like a sailboat.*
2. Loretta got through her research paper *like a hurricane.*
3. Loretta got through her research paper *as if she were dancing.*
4. Loretta got through her research paper *as if she were lame.*
5. Loretta got through her research paper *as if she had been enslaved by it.*
6. Loretta got through her research paper *as if she were in a race.*

CLICHÉS

Living is easy

IT'S HIGH TIME *A Helping Hand* **out of**

a warm heart **this**

The Secret of Our Success **a warm welcome** **world**

A golden opportunity **False Starts**

The above phrases are *clichés*—expressions that were once interesting and imaginative but have become dull from overuse. All the zing is out of them. Beginners often reach for clichés to fill gaps in their writing because it is simpler to use a ready-made slogan than to think up a new phrase to capture an idea exactly. The effect is often zero. Your writing becomes tired and juiceless. Generally, avoid clichés and other trite, stereotyped expressions.

Occasionally, clichés (*one in a million*), slogans from advertising (*If you've got it, flaunt it*), famous quotations (*Don't shoot until you see the whites of their eyes*) can stimulate your writing because they can move easily into many different contexts and make sense. When that happens, include them in your first draft and don't worry about them. Keep writing. Then, in a later draft, get rid of all the phrases that have lost their sparkle.

Here is a little reading in clichés. See how many you can find:

Al, who followed in his father's footsteps, was one in a million. Besides, lady luck always smiled on him. One fine day that was as pretty as a picture, soon after he had moved into the little house he called his castle, Al received a phone call. You could have knocked him over with a feather, he was so surprised. The phone call offered a warm welcome from the local radio station W-O-R-N. It said they had a jackpot prize for him that was out of this world. All Al had to do was name the tune now playing on W-O-R-N.

"Stay tuned," they said.

But Al's radio was still packed up. He shrugged his shoulders. "At this point in time," he said without beating around the bush, "my radio's buried six feet under. I guess it's just one of those things."

"The right answer!" cried the voice of W-O-R-N. "You win the W-O-R-N jackpot prize."

"Who me?" said Al. "Well, truth *is* stranger than fiction," muttered Al, but then he secretly knew everyone in his family was smart as a whip.

Exercise 8   Write an essay that is filled with clichés. Use the story about Al for a model.

INFLATED LANGUAGE   Words sometimes suffer from inflation. Words of importance are often worth less than you think.

incredible   PERFECT   Great Wine

Great Get-away weekend   essential

GREAT GOLF & TENNIS   A FABULOUS BARGAIN WEEKEND

indispensable

fantastic

Be on the lookout for inflated words that have lost their value. For *great, unbelievable, incredible, fantastic,* substitute words that describe specifically:

540 airy rooms

540 spacious rooms

540 rooms with a view

540 elegantly furnished rooms

540 modern rooms

Exercise 9 Make each of the following inflated ads more concrete by substituting as many specific words for the word *great* as you can.

1. Great Wine

2. Great Get-Away Weekend

3. Great Golf and Tennis

WORDS REVEAL YOUR ATTITUDE

In all kinds of writing (except perhaps the most objective scientific reports), the words you choose do more than supply facts. Words, like metaphors, often reveal how you feel about your subject. If you think about the clothes you are wearing right now, you see that they do more than cover your nakedness and keep you warm; they tell whether you are formal or informal, outgoing or shy, fashionable or practical, or they suggest something about the circumstances of the occasion. In the same way, words do more than convey your meaning; they may suggest whether you are pleased or angry, critical or admiring, and they may imply that the occasion for writing is a serious one or one that allows you to be mischievous and mocking.

See if you can detect in the next pairs of sentences how the writer's attitude changes from sentence to sentence:

Jerry nagged at me to walk the dog.
Jerry reminded me to walk the dog.

Dad always snarled at the neighborhood kids when they sat on his jalopy.
Dad always chatted with the neighborhood kids when they sat on his trusty Chevy.

Gloria was tall and skinny. As she left, she hung a fur jacket around her shoulders.
Gloria was tall and slender. As she left, she draped a fur jacket around her shoulders.

Marco is short and fat.
Marco has a stocky build.

Jerry thought Marco was a loudmouth.
Jerry thought Marco was outspoken.

Gloria was a biology major and a dull grind.
Gloria was a biology major and a conscientious student.

Marco wore loud synthetic shirts and told stupid jokes.
Marco wore bright, silky shirts and told original jokes.

Grandmother said Dad was a mama's boy all his life.
Grandmother said Dad was a devoted son all his life.

When you ask a friend for a reaction to something you have written, see in what way the words you have used determine that reaction. Are the words loaded for or against your subject, and is your reader for or against your subject as a result? Is that what you intended? Do the words flatter or criticize? Which word is "for" Gloria's looks—*skinny* or *slender?* Which word is "against" Jerry's behavior—*nag* or *remind?*

Against	*For*
snarled	chatted
jalopy	trusty Chevy
skinny	slender
hung	draped
short and fat	stocky
nagged	reminded
loudmouth	outspoken
dull grind	conscientious student
loud	bright
synthetic	silky
stupid	original
mama's boy	devoted son

Exercise 10 Imagine that you are about to leave on a cross-country trip and do the following:

1. Write a classified newspaper advertisement for a traveling companion to split expenses with you. In the ad, emphasize that you are a sophisticated person, that you find great pleasure in good food and drink, and that you are eager to have a good time.
2. Now rewrite the ad to emphasize that you are a responsible person, that you are a competent driver, and that you have modest living habits.
3. In each ad, circle the words that concretely convey your intended personal image.

LEVELS OF USAGE—FORMAL, INFORMAL, SLANG

One of the difficulties in choosing your vocabulary is knowing when it is appropriate to use a certain word. You know intuitively that, while you talk to your best friend one way ("Hey, man!"), you talk to the personnel manager who is interviewing you for a job quite another way ("Yes." "Yes, sir." "Yes, Miss Taylor."). You have a natural sense of audience that screens the words that come out of your mouth. Usually, you can trust your common sense to know what to say when.

In writing, as in talking, certain words are appropriate for certain readers. Professional writers, who are especially concerned about their audiences, always consider their articles before they begin writing. They consider the kind of magazine they are writing for and the type of person who reads that magazine. They write one kind of article about rifles for the *Ladies' Home Journal* and another for the *National Rifleman;* one essay about men's underwear for *Ms.* magazine and another for *Playboy.*

If you are in a writing class, the other men and women in your class are your audience, and you can count on their interest. Readers in a writing class may differ sharply from each other in many respects, such as the morality under which they were brought up, how much money they or their parents make, how old they are, and, above all, what interests they have. But in spite of these differences, their common attempts to write and to expand their understanding of themselves as they write provide a mutual bond. By now, you've probably noticed that the people in your class are willing to read anything you write as long as you make every sentence informational and lively.

But there are levels of language that you can choose for a particular audience or a special occasion. The level we use in this book, and the level you are probably using as you write, is an informal level. American writing—like American living rooms and American restaurants, like the clothes many of us wear to work, to teach, to study, even to attend weddings—tends to be informal rather than formal. You saw in Chapter 11 (page 266) the changes insurance companies have introduced in the language of insurance policies. Some policies are now written on an informal level, and almost anybody can understand them. This is a level that is "safe" for most occasions.

Still, we know that not all language is safe on all occasions. Who hasn't suffered from using an inappropriate expression at one time or another? Older slang terms like "cut it out" and "shake a leg" and newer ones like "off the wall," "out to lunch," "bread" (for money), and "split" (for leave) may mark your academic or business writing as too informal, too much like casual conversation for those important transactions. For personal writing and for a special effect in other writing, of course, slang expressions may sometimes be precisely right.

The next paragraph may arouse your curiosity, but you will have to work to get its meaning. It is written in slang, but a highly specialized kind of slang whose meaning is known only to a special group. Thieves, ballplayers, construction workers, serious musicians, and CB operators all have their own kind of slang (sometimes called *argot*) that only members of the particular group understand. Try reading the following excerpt, which is written in the slang of the jazz musician:

When I think back to those days back in 1940, nothin' but good memories fill my head. Since I was a boulevard cowboy, I always had a glory roll filled with long green and plenty of time on my hands. Some hipsters were really off the cob, but I was one bopper that cooked with gas. There were plenty of fine fryers available because a lot of guys my age weren't able to get around Davy Crockett. All those cats had the issue put on 'em and were on the clip side of the big moist. Yes sir, in those days, the Big Apple, especially the main drag of many tears, was Seventh Heaven.

Dexter Jeffries

Like the slang of groups, the technical language of any special branch of learning often gets so specialized that it becomes hard for outsiders to understand. If you are not a psychologist, a sociologist, or a literary critic, you may have trouble reading the writings of those professionals. This hard-to-read technical language is called *jargon*. Try to avoid jargon by using words simply and in their truest meanings.

Jargon	*Free of jargon*
Twenty patients were *sleep-deprived.*	Twenty patients were *deprived of sleep.*
The children developed *problem-solving strategies.*	The children developed *skill in solving problems.*
A *third-person narrative restricts* the writer to the *consciousness of the protagonist.*	*Telling a story in the third person keeps* the writer *inside the mind of the main character.*
The *word processing center* can help you with your manuscript.	The *typing pool* can help you with your manuscript.

Advertisers often pick up jargon to offer their products in the language of "experts." Here is an example of sociological jargon in an ad for the Datsun 710.

UPWARD MOBILITY FOR THE WHOLE FAMILY...THE LIVELY DATSUN 710.

Jargon	*Free of jargon*
Upward mobility for the whole family . . . the lively Datsun 710.	If you buy a lively Datsun 710, your whole family will *improve its standard of living.*

Formal writing still appears today in some textbooks, dissertations, government bulletins, legal documents, and similar serious or scholarly works. Students often mistakenly strive for the formality of such writing, badly straining their language on the way. We talked briefly about language "strain" in Chapter 11 (page 266). Here is another example of strained writing, a condition you can avoid by writing in words and sentences that feel comfortable and natural to you:

> I seriously regret that I cannot be in attendance at the rehearsal which eventuates today. It is essential that I present myself for the preservation of justice and freedom before a presiding judge in a court of law because I was issued a summons by an officer of the law, the charges against me being one of several instances of a moving violation, in particular, exceeding the limits established by local ordinance.

What the writer should say is this:

> I'm sorry I cannot attend the rehearsal today. I have to appear in court because I got a speeding ticket.

Your choice of words, or *diction,* as word choice is called, ought to strike a balance between the simple, homey word and the pompous word with many syllables. Generally, it is a safe bet to choose a plain, everyday word wherever possible:

NO: After a *double attempt to insert herself* through the *aperture,* she *conceded failure.*

YES: After *two tries* at *climbing in* through the *window,* she *gave up.*

Occasionally, you can strike an interesting contrast by combining a small word (like *hut, mud, wind, twin*) with a word of many syllables:

immovable liar

mad computation

legendary sag

These combinations add surprise and variety to your diction. In addition to collecting words you admire for their liveliness, keep a section of your notebook for words whose meanings you do not know. Write the word, the sentence in which you find it, and the best meaning that you find in your dictionary. Then, when your writing calls for it, you'll be ready to use the new word.

EUPHEMISMS Another kind of strain in your writing may occur when you wish to avoid using "unpleasant" words. Although it is generally the best advice in writing to call even an unpleasant thing by its name, some expressions have become painkillers in our culture, and it is more important to recognize such substitutions for what they are than to expect to eliminate them entirely. Words that sugar-coat "impolite" or "unpleasant" ideas are called *euphemisms.*

For example, we say *men's room* or *powder room* instead of *toilet, mortician* instead of *undertaker.* We say *permanent* flowers instead of *artificial* flowers and *senior citizens* instead of *old people.* School systems refer to students with *poor reading and writing skills as underprepared.* They *excess* teachers instead of *firing* them. Soldiers in Vietnam were *wasted* instead of *killed.* Animals *killed* in laboratories are *sacrificed.* Students receive a *no credit* in a course instead of a *failure.* Appropriateness guides us in deciding when to use euphemisms to make life more bearable. While you may say *My uncle passed on last week,* you would think twice before telling a new widow that *her husband kicked the bucket while on the job that day.* That would be insensitive. But you must understand the real meanings of words like *passed on, wasted, excessed, no credit,* and *underprepared.*

USING YOUR DICTIONARY

Whatever the price of a good college dictionary, it is a bargain, because in a single volume it provides a quick reference guide to an enormous amount of usable information. Kurt Vonnegut, the author of *Slaughterhouse Five* and many other books, confesses that:

> As a child, [I] would never have started going through unabridged
> dictionaries if I hadn't suspected that there were dirty words hidden in
> there, where only grownups were supposed to find them. I always ended
> the searches feeling hot and stuffy inside, and looking at the queer
> illustrations—at the trammel wheel, the arbalest, and the dugong.
>
> *New York Times Book Review,*
> October 30, 1966

A reliable dictionary does more than list words. It spells words, shows you how to pronounce them, and gives you their meanings. It gives their histories, and describes how they are used. Most recommended dictionaries also offer synonyms (words that have almost the same meaning) and antonyms (words that have almost the opposite meaning); they list forms with suffixes added, abbreviations, and foreign terms; and they provide facts of general interest, such as population figures, geographical names, names of famous people, names and locations of colleges, weights and measures, and symbols, as well as pictures of machines and creatures like a *pawl,* a *manatee,* or Vonnegut's *dugong.*

When Americans say "Let's look it up in *the* dictionary" as a way to settle arguments and keep the peace, they are mistakenly implying that every dictionary says the same things and carries the same unarguable authority. That is not true. Dictionaries are different. Each one represents the work of a separate committee of people who study the way words are used in the pages of contemporary writers. They keep rooms full of files noting new meanings for old words, new words, and special words, perhaps from the sciences or the arts, that appear in current newspapers and magazines. Then they write a dictionary based on their research. Usually, they have their own way of organizing entries. Some dictionaries, for example, list the oldest meaning first; others list the most important meaning first. Some dictionaries have separate alphabetically arranged sections at the back for names of people, places, and colleges, while other dictionaries include these proper nouns among the words in the main part of the dictionary itself. Some dictionaries offer comments in the main entry on how a word is to be used. A college dictionary, which is a convenient size for most college students, contains about 100,000 words, whereas a full-sized unabridged dictionary has about 450,000 words. Regardless of their length, all dictionaries, somewhere in the front of the book, explain how they are organized. *Buy a good college dictionary and learn how to make the most of it.*

Here is a list of some good college dictionaries:

The American College Dictionary (New York: Random House)

The American Heritage Dictionary of the English Language (Boston: Houghton Mifflin)

Funk & Wagnalls Standard College Dictionary (New York: Harcourt Brace Jovanovich)

The Random House College Dictionary (New York: Random House)

Webster's New Collegiate Dictionary (Springfield, Mass.: Merriam)

Webster's New World Dictionary of the American Language, college edition (Cleveland: Collins-World)

Get acquainted with your dictionary

1. Browse through the introductory material. Read the sections that explain how the book is organized.

2. Study the table of contents. Turn to each section listed and skim through the main headings.

3. Look at the pronunciation key (usually at the bottom of a page; sometimes on the inside cover). Try to say the sample words aloud. Notice the mark on the vowel as you say it. Then say the vowel sound alone.

   ăct   ă
   āble ā

4. Read one or two entries for common words. Study the definitions. Pick out the one definition *you* think is most important. Notice whether it is listed first.

5. Study any special charts or tables, for example, an etymology key, which tells what other languages words come from; a key to foreign sounds; a list of abbreviations; and so on.

6. Browse through the dictionary, pausing to read whole entries of words here and there. (See the analysis of two typical entries below.)

7. Notice entries that start with a capital letter. These are chiefly names of people and places. Read whole entries to see what biographical and geographical information your dictionary gives you.

Now let's look at two entries from *The American College Dictionary:*

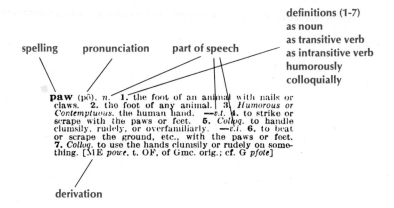

definitions (1-7)
as noun
as transitive verb
as intransitive verb
humorously
colloquially

spelling   pronunciation   part of speech

paw (pô). *n.* 1. the foot of an animal with nails or claws. 2. the foot of any animal. 3. *Humorous or Contemptuous.* the human hand. —*v.t.* 4. to strike or scrape with the paws or feet. 5. *Colloq.* to handle clumsily, rudely, or overfamiliarly. —*v.i.* 6. to beat or scrape the ground, etc., with the paws or feet. 7. *Colloq.* to use the hands clumsily or rudely on something. [ME *powe*, t. OF. of Gmc. orig.; cf. G *pfote*]

derivation

spelling and
syllable divisions   main accent   pronunciation   part of speech   definitions (1-3)

other parts
of speech

peace·ful (pēs′fəl), *adj.* 1. characterized by peace; free from strife or commotion; tranquil: *a peaceful reign.* 2. pertaining to or characteristic of a state of peace: *peaceful uses of atomic energy.* 3. peaceable. —**peace′-ful·ly**, *adv.* —**peace′ful·ness**, *n.*
—**Syn.** 2. PEACEFUL, PLACID, SERENE, TRANQUIL refer to what is characterized by lack of strife or agitation. PEACEFUL today is rarely applied to persons; it refers to situations, scenes and activities free of disturbances, or, occasionally, of warfare: *a peaceful life.* PLACID, SERENE, TRANQUIL are used mainly of persons; when used of things (usually elements of Nature) there is a touch of personification. PLACID suggests an unruffled calm that verges on complacency: *a placid disposition; a placid stream.* SERENE is a somewhat nobler word; when used of persons it suggests dignity, composure, and graciousness (*a serene old age*); when applied to Nature there is a suggestion of mellowness (*the serene landscapes of Autumn*). TRANQUIL implies a command of emotions, often because of strong faith, which keeps one unagitated even in the midst of excitement or danger.

synonyms with
exact distinctions
in meaning

examples of
definitions
in common
phrases

Some common dictionary terms and abbreviations

For a complete list of terms and abbreviations, see the prefatory pages of your dictionary.

parts of speech:		classification of words (noun, pronoun, adjective, adverb, preposition, verbs, conjunction) according to meaning and usage in sentences. A word may be a noun in one sentence and a verb in another, e.g. *paw* as a noun:
n.	noun	
pron.	pronoun	
adj.	adjective	
adv.	adverb	
prep.	preposition	

The dog's paw was injured.
paw as a verb: *The dog pawed the ground under the tree.*

v.t.	transitive verb	action verb always accompanied by a direct object
v.i.	intransitive verb	verb that never is accompanied by a direct object
conj.		conjunction
colloq.	colloquial	refers to use in ordinary or familiar conversation
etymology		study of the history of words to trace origin and change
derivation		origin or source of word
O.E.	Old English	(indicates a word was derived from English as it was spoken before 1100 A.D.)
M.E.	Middle English	(indicates a word was derived from English as it was spoken before 1500 A.D.)
obs.	obsolete	describes a word or a meaning no longer in use

Tips on using your dictionary

Suppose you are looking up the word *peaceful*.

1. Use the guide words at the top of the page. They will save you from hunting for your word up and down the columns of a dozen pages. *Peaceful* is between the guide words *paynim* and *Pearl Harbor*.
2. If you can't find *peaceful,* ask someone else how to spell it. If no one knows, write down several spelling possibilities:

peesful	piecefull
peasful	peesfull
pieceful	peaceful

Try them all.

3. Match the sounds of the word to the pronunciation key. Look for the bold accent. Notice the heavy dot that separates syllables. Say the word.

p ē s′ · fǝl

Note: Most vowels that are in unaccented syllables are pronounced "uh." This is written as a schwa—ǝ.

4. Test the meaning of the word for the one that suits your sentence. In the case of *peaceful*, notice below its definitions the abbreviation *Syn.*, which means *synonyms*. Words that have almost the same meaning as *peaceful* are listed here. Now, in one place, you find a choice of words for your sentence. Will it be *peaceful, placid, serene,* or *tranquil?*

Sentence: I can remember that my father was _____ even when his rug business was on the verge of bankruptcy.

The synonym section indicates that *serene* is used for people and suggests that a person who is serene also keeps his dignity. You choose *serene* to describe your father. And you found it by looking up *peaceful*.

Sentence: I can remember that my father was *serene* even when his rug business was on the verge of bankruptcy.

If you have any further interest in the word *serene*, you may be tempted to look it up next.

Exercise 11 Place the following words in alphabetical order, as they would be listed in a dictionary.

garnish	immense
cardiogram	revivify
revive	sweet potato
Telstar	onion
oozy	sweater
airsick	lonesome
garish	imitate
one-way	cardigan

Exercise 12 Look up the following words in your dictionary and be prepared to pronounce them. Rewrite each word showing the accented syllable and where the word would be divided at the end of a line.

1. Vietnam
2. victual
3. vinaigrette
4. viola
5. vineyard

6. vegetable
7. vodka
8. versatile
9. various
10. vaudeville

Exercise 13 Look up the following pairs of words in your dictionary and state the crucial difference in meaning between the words in each pair.

1. delay/postpone
2. describe/narrate
3. drag/haul
4. trip/pilgrimage
5. empty/deserted

6. leap/vault
7. brief/momentary
8. quick/hastily
9. precious/valuable
10. rigid/strict

Part Four

Choosing Correctly

Chapter 13 / Verbs

As a writer, you must know how to write sentences, each one containing a subject-verb unit. You must also know how verbs work in sentences, and how different forms of the verb express different times and conditions. The choices may baffle you, especially when you confront alternatives like these:

> Jeannette's jeans have shrank.
>
> > or
>
> Jeannette's jeans have shrunk.
>
> Sam lived in California for ten years.
>
> > or
>
> Sam had lived in California for ten years.

You're not facing general questions of *time* in the above sentences because in each situation you're talking about past time. You know that Jeannette's jeans shrank in the past. You know that Sam lived in California in the past. What may confuse you is the exact *forms* you need to express the past. Is it *have shrank* or *have shrunk? Lived* or *had lived?* Is there a difference? To answer these questions, you need to understand exactly how verbs work.

VERB FORMS

Verbs enable you to show differences in time. You can talk about the present, the past, and the future, and you can show activities that continue over a period of time. The verb in a sentence shows a relationship between the time you are speaking (or writing) and the time you are speaking (or writing) about. The "moment of writing" is always the present moment. From this moment, you can comment on the present:

> I am hungry.
> This coffee tastes bitter.
> The soup is too hot.

Or you can refer to the past:

> I was hungry (in the past).
> The coffee tasted bitter (in the past).
> The soup was too hot (in the past).

Or you can refer to the future:

> I'll be hungry (in the future).
> The coffee will taste bitter (in the future).
> The soup will be too hot (in the future).

The following examples show the relationships of time that exist between the writer's moment of writing and the time he is writing about.

The time of writing and the time written about are the writer's present:

> Here I am in Paris, staying at a small hotel on the Left Bank, near the Odéon Theatre. Every morning I sit down to a breakfast of warm milk and hot rolls with the other hotel guests, who are from several countries: Germany, Japan, and Holland. I am practicing my shaky French. I wish I had studied harder in French 101.

The time of writing is the writer's present. The time written about is the writer's past:

> Last year I spent the summer in Europe. I hitchhiked from Rome to Paris and later took the ferry to London. I stayed in hostels and picked up odd jobs when my money ran low. The whole trip cost me less than $700.

The time of writing is the writer's present. The time written about is the writer's future:

> Next week I'll fly to Madrid. I plan to stay in cheap hotels and eat frugally. I'll try the "cheapest restaurant in the world" according to Arthur Frommer, author of the book *Europe on $5.00 a day*. I wonder if I'll still be able to buy a three-course meal for 35¢.

You also can write as if you were *in* the past or the future. You can create an as-if-you-were-there effect by assuming, for example, the voice of Napoleon in a historical novel. Or you might be a reporter at the time of Columbus's birth:

> Today is October 12, 1451. In this quiet city of Genoa, a midwife from the outskirts of town helps to deliver a woman of a child. He is a healthy boy, and his mother calls him Christopher.

As a science fiction writer, you can project your present moment into the future, say, to June 9, 2152. Time after that date would be the future; time before it, the past:

This is my first day on this planet. All around I see the great white beaches sloping into mountain ranges. There is no one else in sight. It is June 9, 2152.

Time before June 9, 2152, would be the past for the writer:

Yesterday I was approaching this planet in my spacecraft. I saw the great white beaches far below. I had a headache from my spacecraft. It was June 8, 2152.

Time after June 9, 2152, would be the future for the writer:

Next week I'll board my craft again. I'll set my sights for Venus, and then I'll head for home. The year is 2152.

When you write, you can view time as you choose. You can move freely from the past to the present to the future. You can choose both the time of writing and the time you are writing about. But you must also choose the verb form that precisely expresses the time you have chosen.

Exercise 1   The following news account of the first moon landing has been re-written in the present for this exercise. Change the verbs back to the past.

Houston, July 20—Man steps out onto the moon tonight for the first time in his two-million-year history. . . . The two men walk easily, talk easily, even run and jump happily so it seems. They pick up rocks, talk at length of what they see, plant an American flag, salute it, talk by radiophone with the President in the White House, and then face the camera and salute Mr. Nixon.

Armstrong shares his first incredible moments on the moon with the whole world, as a television camera on the outside of the wingless Eagle landing craft sends back an amazingly clear picture of his first steps on the moon. . . .

Armstrong seems as if he is swimming along, taking big and easy steps on the airless moon despite the cumbersome white pressure-suit he wears. . . .

Armstrong next takes the television camera out to a spot about 40 feet from the Lem and places it on a small tripod.

Incredibly clear, the picture shows a distant Lem, squatting on the bleak but beautiful lunar surface like some giant mechanical toy. It appears to be perfectly level, not at all tilted on the rough lunar terrain. . . .

Just after 11:30, both men remove a pole, flagstaff, and plastic American flag from one of the Lem's legs. They gently press the flag into the lunar surface.

Adapted from "The Eagle Has Landed:
Two Men Walk on the Moon," by
Thomas O'Toole, in the *Washington Post*.

To express the past, present, and future in your writing, you need to understand the verb choices that are open to you. The following selection shows all the verb forms and many phrases derived from the verb *eat*.

THE MAD EATER

I *eat*, you *eat*, he *eats*, we all *eat*—who can deny it? When I get home, all I can think is "When do I *eat?*" Perhaps I am only happy when I *am eating*. Do I *eat* to live or live *to eat?* "*To eat* or not *to eat*, that is the question." *Eating*, I transcend myself. I become one with what *is eaten*.

My whole life seems like one long meal. As a child I *ate* whatever came my way. I *used to eat* dirt; there were times when I even *ate* little bits of paper or wood. My parents were alarmed. One day my father asked me, "You *didn't eat* that whole cake, did you?"

"Yes I did," I shouted. "I *did eat* the cake!" What did I care? I *ate* and smothered my sorrows.

Often I am seized with fear and dread. I have a recurring dream in which a voice says, "You live only that you *may eat!*" "Yes," I scream, "that I *may eat!* And I *shall eat*, and *go on eating!*" A five-hundred-pound chicken suddenly appears. I wake up in a cold sweat, crying, *"Eat, eat, let us eat!"*

I fall back into a fitful sleep. Suddenly I see the face of a British doctor. He speaks slowly, distinctly: "If I were you, Old Chap, I *should eat* a bit less. I *have eaten* in my time, of course, but a fellow must be careful. I've worked that I *might eat*, but one can go too far."

The words "go too far" sometimes echo in my brain after I *have eaten*. But I realize now that I cannot escape my fate.

Once during a gala supper, I locked myself in the main dining room of the Gourmets' Society. On the door, I left a note:

"Gentlemen: By the time you break down this door. I *will have eaten* everything in sight. Formerly you thought that I *had eaten* only because I liked food. This is not true; *eating* is a mania, an obsession, with me. All that I *may* or *might have eaten*, all that I *have* or *had eaten*, all that now is nothing; because I am the Mad Eater! I live only *TO EAT!*"

Now look at the forms of the verb *eat:*

eat	ate
eats	eaten
eating	

Every verb has a *base:*

eat	love	ring	have
learn	go	cut	do

We *add* to the base or change the spelling of the base to produce the different verb forms:

eat, eats, eating, ate, eaten
learn, learns, learning, learned
love, loves, loving, loved
go, goes, going, went, gone
ring, rings, ringing, rang, rung
cut, cuts, cutting, cut
do, does, doing, did, done

All verbs have an *-s form* and an *-ing form:*

Base	-s Form	-ing Form
eat	eats	eating
learn	learns	learning
love	loves	loving
go	goes	going
ring	rings	ringing
cut	cuts	cutting
have	has	having
do	does	doing

All verbs have *past forms*. Some verbs have *one* past form:

Base	Past	Past participle
learn	learned	(have) learned
love	loved	(have) loved
jump	jumped	(have) jumped
live	lived	(have) lived

Other verbs have *two* past forms:

Base	Past	Past participle
do	did	(have) done
sing	sang	(have) sung
go	went	(have) gone
fly	flew	(have) flown

In the following section, you will see how these forms are used to express different *times* in the English language.

WATCH OUT FOR TENSE AND TIME

When you're thinking about verbs, it is important to distinguish between two often confusing terms: *tense* and *time*. *Time* refers to actual time, generally understood as past, present, and future. *Tense* is a grammatical term that refers to verb forms as they relate to time. Grammarians say that there are two tenses among the parts of the verb: the present tense and the past tense.

PARTS OF THE VERB

base	-s form	-ing form	past
learn	learns	learning	learned

The *present tense* is made up of the base and the *-s* form of the verb:

PRESENT TENSE

I *learn*	we *learn*
you *learn*	you *learn*
he, she, it *learns*	they *learn*

The *past tense* is made up of the *-ed* form of regular verbs and the past form of irregular verbs (see "Regular and Irregular Verbs ").

PAST TENSE

I *learned*	we *learned*
you *learned*	you *learned*
he, she, it *learned*	they *learned*

Other *tenses* are expressed by using the base, the *-ing* form, and the past participle with words called auxiliaries. See "Verbs and Auxiliaries."

USING VERBS TO EXPRESS PRESENT TIME

The following examples illustrate ways in which we express present time.

Remember: the present tense is the base and the *-s* form of the verb.

I *feel*	we *feel*
you *feel*	you *feel*
he, she, it *feels*	they *feel*

1. To express an activity taking place at the present moment for verbs of being, feeling, knowing, and sensing.

> I *feel* tired.
> I *am* hungry.
> The sun *feels* warm.
> The coffee *tastes* bitter.

'I Am a Doctor'

2. To express habitual activities—actions that occur repeatedly.

> I *exercise* every morning.
> Sam *eats* yogurt every day.
> Every other Sunday I *go* to the country auction.
> In the summer we *visit* my great-aunt in Montana.

3. To express facts and universal truths—things that are always true.

> Susan *lives* in Minneapolis.
> The earth *revolves* around the sun.
> Water *freezes* at 32 degrees Fahrenheit.
> She *earns* $15,000 a year.
> Plants *take in* carbon dioxide.

97% of the World's Water Is in Oceans

4. To express continuous activity in the present.

am, is, or *are*
+ *-ing* form

> I *am typing.*
> Harry *is doing* his hard thinking now.
> Rich and Clyde *are waiting* at the corner store.

Our fame is spreading.

5. To capture an immediacy. Newspaper headlines are usually written in the present tense to draw attention to events as *news.*

Mrs. King Beats Miss Evert At Wimbledon by 2-6, 6-2, 6-3

Farm prices drop   *Yanks Win*

Refer to the following time charts for more information about ways to express present time.

WAYS TO STATE PRESENT TIME

Regular verb form	Irregular verb form	Tense	Usage	Examples
I *learn* you *learn* he, she, it *learns* we *learn* you *learn* they *learn*	I *do* you *do* he, she, it *does* we *do* you *do* they *do*	present	Expresses an activity taking place at the present moment for verbs of being, feeling, sensing, and knowing. **Adverbials** focus on present time.	I *love* you. I *hear* the train coming **now.** She *knows* him well. I *believe* in you.
			Expresses a habitual activity that is still practiced. **Adverbials** focus on recurring times.	I *do* the crossword puzzle **every morning.** She *visits* her uncle in California **every summer.** They *play* poker **on Saturday nights.**
			Expresses facts and universal truths.	He *lives* in Chicago. She *earns* $15,000 a year. Water *freezes* at 32 degrees Fahrenheit.
I *am learning* you *are learning* he, she, it *is learning* we *are learning* you *are learning* they *are learning*	I *am doing* you *are doing* he, she, it *is doing* we *are doing* you *are doing* they *are doing*	present progressive	Expresses an activity that is occurring at the present moment. **Adverbials** specify the time.	He *is doing* the crossword puzzle **right now.** I *am eating* dinner. She *is talking* **on the phone.** They *are sleeping* **through the storm.**
			Expresses an activity that is continuing from the *past* through the present and into the future. **Adverbials** specify short or long intervals.	I *am learning* carpentry **this summer.** He *is earning* a good living **this year.** The British *are coming* **now.**
				He *does learn* **quickly.** I *am accustomed to doing* the crossword puzzle **every morning.** The mail *is delivered* **about noon.**

ADDITIONAL WAYS TO STATE PRESENT TIME

1. Use *do* or *does* plus the base for emphasis.
   (do learn, does fly)
2. Use *am accustomed* plus *-ing* form to express habit.
   (am accustomed to doing)
3. Use *am, is,* or *are* plus past participle for passive.
   (is delivered)
   (See "Active and Passive Verbs," p. 341.)

USING VERBS TO EXPRESS FUTURE TIME

1. To express an activity that will take place in the future. The future is often expressed with the word *will* (or *shall*) plus the base. Sometimes the *will* is dropped from the future, and the present form of the verb remains.

Will or
shall + base
(future
tense)

In the morning I will fly to Mexico.
In the morning I   fly to Mexico.

I *will fly* to Miami tomorrow.
I *shall finish* this report by tomorrow.
They *will eat* dinner tonight at nine o'clock.
He *will attend* a Pete Seeger concert tonight.

Will (or shall) be
+ *-ing* form

To express an activity that will be in progress in the future.

I *will be swimming* in the Pacific this time next week.
We *will be studying* for exams next week.

Refer to the following time charts for more information about ways to express future time.

WAYS TO STATE FUTURE TIME

Regular verb form	Irregular verb form	Tense	Usage	Examples
I will learn you will learn he, she, it will learn	I will do you will do he, she, it will do	future	Expresses an event that will happen in the future. **Adverbials** indicate future time. Contractions (I'll, you'll, he'll) are often used.	I will do the crossword puzzle. She'll send you a check **tomorrow.** They'll leave for California **in a few days.**
we will learn you will learn they will learn	we will do you will do they will do			
I will be learning you will be learning he, she, it will be learning	I will be doing you will be doing he, she, it will be doing	future progressive	Expresses an event that will continue over a period of time in the future. **Adverbials** often express the length of time.	I will be staying in California **for the whole summer.** I'll be working on this anthropology paper **during vacation.**
we will be learning you will be learning they will be learning	we will be doing you will be doing they will be doing			

ADDITIONAL WAYS TO STATE FUTURE TIME

1. Use *will have* plus the past participle for an event in the future that occurs before another event in the future.
(will have learned, will have done)

future perfect	Expresses an event in the future that is completed before another time or event in the future.	She *will have finished* dinner by then. He *will have completed* the crossword puzzle by the time she comes home.

2. Use *will have been* plus the *-ing* form for a continuing event in the future that occurs before another event in the future.
(will have been learning, will have been doing)

future perfect progressive	Expresses a continuing event in the future that occurs before another future event begins.	She *will have been sleeping* for several hours by the time he arrives. I *will have been studying* carpentry for a year when he begins college.

3. Use other words combined with the base to express future possibilities, obligations, and so on.

   a. To express determination, use *shall* or *am going to* plus the base.
   (shall learn, shall do, am going to learn, am going to do)

   I *am going to learn* skydiving if it kills me.

   b. To express obligation, use *should, ought to,* or *must* plus the base.
   (should learn, ought to learn, must do)

   I *ought to say* something clever.

   c. To express possibility, use *may* or *might* plus the base.
   (may learn, might do)

   I *may go* away this weekend.

   d. To express ability (in the future), use *can* plus the base.
   (can learn, can do)

   I *can learn* French if I try.

   e. To express an action that will occur in the future, use *about to* plus the base.
   (about to learn, about to do)

   I *am about to leave* for California.

USING VERBS TO EXPRESS PAST TIME

Problems most often arise with past time because in the English language there are several ways to express the past. As you study the following chart, think about each expression of the past in relationship to *time continuing*.

I had lived in California for ten years when I moved to Toronto.

I lived in California.	I have just moved to California.	I have lived in California for several years.

past   present   future

A past action ended before another past action began.

The action has recently been completed.

The action continues from the past into the present.

The action has been completed.

Now we can return to our question about Sam and decide which of the two sentences to use:

Sam lived in California for ten years.

    or

Sam had lived in California for ten years.

The answer depends on the writer's *intention,* on what he wanted to say. The writer has several options depending upon that intention.

The past tense—*lived*—expresses an action that is completed. If Sam formerly lived in California, to emphasize this completed action, you would say:

Sam *lived* in California.

To tell how long Sam lived there or when he lived there, simply add an adverbial:

Sam *lived* in California for ten years.
Sam *lived* in California in 1950.

Clearly, Sam doesn't live there any longer.

The past perfect tense—*had lived*—expresses a past action that ended before another action in the past occurred. Suppose, for example, that Sam lived in California until 1968, when he moved to Toronto. Then you would say:

Sam *had lived* in California for eighteen years when he moved to Toronto.

Notice that *moved* expresses a time *closer to* the present.

Sam had lived . . . before he moved . . .
  distant past   more recent past

WAYS TO STATE PAST TIME

Regular verb form	Irregular verb form	Tense	Usage	Examples
I learned you learned he, she, it learned we learned you learned they learned	I did you did he, she, it did we did you did they did	past tense	Expresses an action completed before the present moment. **Adverbials** specify a moment in time in the past or an extended period of time in the past when the action occurred.	I *learned* my lesson. I *learned* my lesson **a long time ago.** I *learned* my lesson **yesterday.** She *did* the crossword puzzle **a few hours ago.** He *lived* in California **in the 1930s.** I *sold* Fuller brushes **from 1951 to 1955.** They *moved* to Las Vegas **in September.** He *did* the crossword puzzle **every morning.**
I have learned you have learned he, she, it has learned we have learned you have learned they have learned	I have done you have done he, she, it has done we have done you have done they have done	present perfect tense	Expresses an action that began at some time in the past, continues into the present, and may or may not extend into the future. The event may have begun years ago or just a few seconds ago, or the event may have happened recently. **Adverbials** may or may not specify the beginning of the event.	I *have learned* my lesson **time and time again.** She *has done* the crossword puzzle **already.** He *has lived* in California **for many years.** I *have sold* Fuller brushes **since 1951.** They *have* **just** *moved* to Las Vegas.

Regular verb form	Irregular verb form	Tense	Usage	Examples
I *had learned* you *had learned* he, she, it *had learned* we *had learned* you *had learned* they *had learned*	I *had done* you *had done* he, she, it *had done* we *had done* you *had done* they *had done*	past perfect tense	Expresses a past event that occurred before another past event or before another time in the past. **Adverbials** are often subordinate clauses that emphasize the time relationships.	I *had learned* my lesson **by then.** She *had done* the crossword puzzle **before she went to sleep.** I *had just finished* the crossword puzzle **when she arrived.** He *had learned* to swim **by the time he was five.**
I *was learning* you *were learning* he, she, it *was learning* we *were learning* you *were learning* they *were learning*	I *was doing* you *were doing* he, she, it *was doing* we *were doing* you *were doing* they *were doing*	past progressive tense	Expresses a past action that was in progress at the same time that another activity occurred in the past. Expresses an activity that was in progress in the past. The activity could have occurred for a short or extended period of time. **Adverbials** often work as subordinate clauses to specify past time.	She *was doing* the crossword puzzle **when the repair man rang the bell.** They *were sleeping* **while I watched the late movie.** The sun *was shining* **the whole day.** The mechanic *was working* on the car **yesterday.**

Regular verb form	Irregular verb form	Tense	Usage	Examples
I *have been learning* you *have been learning* he, she, it *has been learning* we *have been learning* you *have been learning* they *have been learning*	I *have been doing* you *have been doing* he, she, it *has been doing* we *have been doing* you *have been doing* they *have been doing*	present perfect progressive	Expresses an ongoing action that began at some time in the past, continues into the present, and may extend into the future. **Adverbials** emphasize the duration of time up to the moment of speaking.	I *have been doing* this same crossword puzzle **for days.** I *have been living* in South America **for three years.**
I *had been learning* you *had been learning* he, she, it *had been learning* we *had been learning* you *had been learning* they *had been learning*	I *had been doing* you *had been doing* he, she, it *had been doing* we *had been doing* you *had been doing* they *had been doing*	past perfect progressive	Expresses a past event that continued over a period of time in the past and ended before another past action began or before another past time. **Adverbials** are often subordinate clauses that express time relationships.	I *had been living* in South America **when I met Julio.** I *had been saving* $100 a month **before my job ended.**

Little Maria had been hungry all her life.

Is Maria still hungry? According to this sentence, she no longer is. *Had + been* presents a completed action that occurred in a time in the past before another past time. If the sentence read "Maria *has been* hungry all her life," we would know that she is still hungry, that her hunger has not yet been satisfied.

Refer to the following time charts for more information about ways to express past time.

ADDITIONAL WAYS TO STATE PAST TIME

1. Use *did* plus the past tense for emphasis.
   (did read)

   I *did read* a lot.

2. Use *used to* plus the past tense to express a habit.
   (used to read)

   I *used to read* a lot.

3. Use *could have* plus the past participle to express possibility.
   (could have learned)

   I *could have learned* to swim years ago.

4. Use *might have* plus the past participle to express a condition that existed in the past.
   (might have learned)

   I *might have learned* to swim (had I been given lessons).

5. Use *should have* plus the past participle to express obligation.
   (should have learned)

   I *should have learned* to swim years ago.

6. Use *was* or *was being* plus the past participle to form the passive.
   (was delivered)
   (See "Active and Passive Verbs," page 341.)

   The mail *was delivered.*
   The mail *was being delivered.*

REGULAR AND IRREGULAR VERBS

What about Jeannette's jeans? Have they *shrank* or *shrunk?* The question really is which form of the verb *shrink* do we use with the word *have?* And before we can answer that question, we must consider *regular* and *irregular* verbs. There are thousands of verbs in the language. Most of them are *regular,* which means that they have only one past form, an *-ed* form that is used for the past and for the past principle. *The past participle is the form of the verb that is used with* have, has, *or* had.

Base	*Past*	*Past participle*
learn	learned	(have) learned
jump	jumped	(have) jumped
laugh	laughed	(has) laughed

Regular verbs are generally not troublesome when you join them with a form of *have* because you use the same form with or without *have.*

The cow *jumped* over the moon.
Sally *has jumped* over her last hurdle.

About 150 verbs in the English language are irregular, which means that they do not form the past by adding *-d* or *-ed* to the base. They usually have two past forms, one that is used *alone* and one that is used with a form of *have.*

Base	*Past*	*Past participle*
go	went	(have) gone
sing	sang	(has) sung
shrink	shrank	(have) shrunk

Use the past alone	*Use the past participle with* have, has, *or* had
Sam *went* to the greenhouse.	Sam *has* already *gone* to the greenhouse.
He *sang* to his begonias.	He *has sung* to his begonias, but nothing *has happened* yet.
Jeannette's jeans *shrank.*	I see now that Jeannette's jeans *have shrunk.*

To help you determine which verbs are irregular, we provide three charts at the end of this chapter: Chart I lists the *principal parts*—the base, the past tense, and the past participle—of a few regular verbs so that you can review the forms of the regular verb. Chart II shows the patterns that irregular verbs follow. Some irregular verbs end in *-en*. Others show no change at all (*cut, set, put*). Chart III alphabetically lists the principal parts of the most common irregular verbs in the language. Dictionaries also include these parts. If a verb that you are considering is not included in this chart, consult your dictionary. Since all verbs have an *-s* form and an *-ing* form, these forms are not listed in the charts.

Have Jeannette's jeans shrunk or shrank? To answer the question, we look at the principal parts of the verb *shrink* on page 357. We find that the past form is listed as *shrank*. This is the form to use alone (without *have*).

Jeannette's jeans *shrank*.

My slacks didn't stretch. I "shrank" 79 pounds.

The past participle is listed as *shrunk*. This is the word to use with *have*.

Jeannette's jeans *have shrunk*.

WATCH OUT FOR THE PAST PARTICIPLE

Whenever the verb phrase in a sentence contains two words and one of these words is *have*, *has*, or *had*, you must use the past participle.

have, has, had + past participle

       have spoken
       have become
       has built
       has seen
       had gone
       had given

Use the past form alone without *have*, *has*, or *had*.

       The bell *rang*.
       Harold *went* to the store.
       Bruno *did* his dance.

Use the past participle with *have*, *has*, or *had*.

       The bell *has* just *rung*.
       Harold *has* already *gone* to the store.
       Bruno *has done* his dance.

Exercise 2 Familiarize yourself with the charts on pages 353–357. Find the principal parts of these verbs:

bring	dive	feel
pay	sleep	climb
swim	wish	dream

Exercise 3 Change the verb in each of the following sentences to a single-word past form. Then use the past participle of each verb with *have, has,* or *had*. Check the charts on pages 353–357 or your dictionary for the principal parts of verbs.

Example: # I Hear the People

Single-word past: I *heard* the people.

Past participle with *have, has,* or *had:* I *have heard* the people.

Viking Robot Sets Down Safely on Mars

Yankees Split With Tigers

Pittsburgh takes club to Raiders

Congress overrides job veto

Cubs Sweep Pair With Pirates, 6-1, 2-1

U.S. women swim to new Olympic high

Summer Schools Undergo a Large Cut

Phillies Beat Pirates, 13-7; Schmidt Hits 26th Homer

Exercise 4 Choose either the past form or the past participle of the given verb to fill each empty slot. The past form of the verb stands alone, but the past participle must be combined with *have*, *has*, or *had*. Check the verb charts on pages 353–357.

Example: After the soprano had <u>sung</u>   "America the Beautiful,"
          she   <u>sang</u>   "The Star Spangled Banner." (sing)

1. The telephone has _____ the entire morning; it even _____ during my lunch break. (ring)

2. Jeannette's new jeans, which have _____ three sizes, _____ beyond an acceptable tight fit. (shrink)

3. After Sharon had _____ from one end of the lake to the other, she _____ back again. (swim)

4. As soon as Charles had _____ the mystery, the phone _____ to ring. (begin)

5. He had _____ a long time to get ready for the party; he _____ much too long. (take)

6. Yesterday, when it was 99 degrees, I _____ more water than I should have _____. At the end of the day, I _____ like a balloon. (drink, feel)

7. He had _____ all the way to the store when he realized that he forgot his wallet, so he _____ all the way home again. (run)

8. I _____ to North Beach every day in the summer although years ago I had _____ to South Beach. (go)

9. You've _____ a long way, Baby, but you _____ too late. (come)

10. How could you have _____ this to me? You _____ the same thing last week. (do)

11. You've _____ all the pretzels, and Clyde _____ the potato chips, ice cream, and peanuts. (eat)

12. Henry has _____ till noon the whole week, but this morning he _____ only until 11:30. (sleep)

WATCH OUT FOR THE -ED ENDING

The final -ed is sometimes a problem for writers who are not accustomed to pronouncing the "d" sound for past time. If you are one of these writers, you need to be especially careful in your writing to use -ed for the past:

NO:	YES:
Seymour *ask* to borrow my lighter.	Seymour *asked* to borrow my lighter.
The heiress *beg* me to marry her.	The heiress *begged* me to marry her.
Sharon *learn* her lesson well.	Sharon *learned* her lesson well.

Exercise 5 Fill each empty slot with the appropriate -ed form of the verb. Then read the sentence aloud emphasizing the endings.

Example: I am on a ___restricted___ diet. (restrict)

1. I am _____ to foods that are high in protein and low in calories. (limit)

2. My milk is _____ rather than _____. (skim, homogenize)

3. I'm told all milk is _____. (pasteurize)

4. I avoid old-_____ desserts with _____ cream. (fashion, whip)

5. _____ and _____ potatoes are on my forbidden list. (mash, fry)

6. For lunch I have a _____ green salad. (toss)

7. Since dressings are out, I add lemon juice and _____ fresh or _____ dill. (chop, dry)

8. I sprinkle a teaspoon of _____ onion over _____ tomatoes and cucumbers and a _____ green pepper. (grate, slice, seed)

9. I prepare _____ bass with soy sauce, _____ ginger, and a tablespoon of vinegar. (steam, mince)

10. When I eat meat, it is carefully _____ of fat and then _____. (trim, broil)

11. _____ butter, _____ brownies, _____ vegetables, _____ lasagna, and _____ ravioli are memories. (melt, frost, cream, bake, stuff)

12. I eat leisurely and take bite-_____ pieces. (size)

13. I have _____ thoughts of thirty-eight _____ pounds so far. (satisfy, drop)

14. Only sixty-two _____ more to go! (damn)

VERBS AND AUXILIARIES

Consider again these parts of the verb:

Regular verb	*Irregular verb*
learn	eat
learns	eats
learning	eating
learned	ate
	eaten

Verb forms can stand alone as verbs:

Base: — They *learn* quickly. — We *eat* lunch at McDonald's every day.

-s form — He *learns* even more quickly. — He *eats* like an elephant.

Past form: — We *learned* quickly. — They *ate* all the cheeseburgers.

Or they can combine with auxiliaries. Auxiliaries are words like:

can	is	must
could	are	ought to
has	was	shall
have	were	should
had	may	will
be	might	would
been		

Combined with one or more auxiliaries, the verb in a sentence is not a single word but a verb phrase.

Your worn shocks could be wearing you out.

could be wearing

LIBERATION CAN BE TOUGH ON A WOMAN.

can be

"I would like to create a cologne that will last as long as there are men and women."

would like   *will last*

THE MAN WHO CONTROLS CORPORATIONS OUGHT TO BE ABLE TO CONTROL HIS OWN CAR.

ought to be able to control

We rely on auxiliaries to restrict the meanings of verbs in the following ways. They show:

1. ability: *can, could, be able to*

   I *can* fix this bathroom sink without a plumber.

2. requests or permissions: *may, can, could*

   May I borrow your wrench?
   Could you help me?

3. obligation or necessity: *should, ought to, must, have to, had to, had better*

   I *ought* to call the plumber.
   You *should* have called him before you started.

4. possibility or probability: *may, might, should, ought to, must*

   The sink *might* overflow.
   You *may* have to call the plumber and the fire department before you're through.

5. references or wants: *would, would rather*

   I *would* like my boots.
   I *would rather* forget the whole thing.

6. emphasis: *do, does, did*

   I *did* forget the whole thing.

Be and have   The most important and frequently used auxiliaries are formed from two verbs: *be* and *have*. *Be* is the most irregular verb in the English language because it has eight forms:

Base	*-ing form*	*Present forms*	*Past forms*	*Past participle*
be	being	am, is, are	was, were	been

The verb *have* has four forms:

Base	*-ing form*	*Present forms*	*Past forms*	*Past participle*
have	having	have, has	had	had

These two verbs can be used by themselves:

Irving *has* a health-food store.
He *had* a passion for apricot fruit rolls.
Irv *is* a yogurt addict.
He and his wife, Mabel, *are* vitamin freaks.

Or they can be used as auxiliaries:

Irving *has been* working late hours.
He *is working* too hard.
He *has not taken* a vacation.
Instead, he *has increased* his vitamin dosage.

Using the forms together In writing, the past, present, and future may merge in one sentence. You may say:

After I *have finished* typing this letter, I *will take* a walk to the beach.

This sentence contains a past form—*have finished*—and a future form—*will take*.

Writers need to express time relationships accurately. The present and the future are generally more obvious than the past. In the past, however, you can show one event following or preceding another by using different verb forms and by using different subordinators. The following sentences, for example, express events occurring roughly at the same time in the past:

I *finished* typing the letter. I *walked* to the beach.

You can make the time relationships more precise by making one event happen before the other:

After I *had finished* typing the letter, I *walked* to the beach.
Before I *walked* to the beach, I *had finished* typing the letter.

When you use more than one verb form in a sentence, make certain that the forms express time accurately. Study the charts on pages 353-357.

Exercise 6 Fill each empty slot with a form of the verb that suits the time already established in the sentence. State a reason for your choice. Check the time charts on pages 353-357.

> Example: I forgot that there ___are___ 5,280 feet in a mile. (be)
> Reason: Use the present tense for facts.

1. Sam and Harriet were married fifteen years ago; they _____ for fifteen years. (marry)
2. Janice had just taken an aspirin for her headache when the phone _____. (ring)
3. If you _____ me before, I wouldn't have made such a mistake. (tell)
4. An "R" movie rating recommends that children _____ accompanied by an adult. (be)
5. By the time he arrives, I _____ for several hours. (go)
6. While the child _____ in the surf, the mother was napping on the beach. (play)

7. From 1973 to the present, I _____ in a white house on Locust Avenue. (live)

8. If I had finished this report last night, I _____ this afternoon. (swim)

9. By the time he was four, he _____ to read. (learn)

10. Before I joined Xerox, I _____ for IBM. (work)

11. Tomorrow Jacques _____ to Paris. (return)

12. I didn't realize that Baltimore _____ only forty-five miles from Washington. (be)

13. For the past year, Clyde _____ English to Chinese students in Taiwan. (teach)

14. While he teaches English to the Chinese, he _____ his Chinese. (improve)

Intransitive, transitive, and linking verbs

Chapter 7 presents the three basic sentence patterns (see pages 129–132):

1. Subject-Verb (S-V)
2. Subject-Verb-Object (S-V-O)
3. Subject-Linking Verb-Completer (S-LV-C)

Three kinds of verbs fill the verb slots in the three sentence patterns:

1. S-V   Intransitive Verb

The intransitive verb does not take an object. The subject-verb unit completes the sentence grammatically.

     s   v
Harpo smirked.
     s   v
Chico roared.

2. S-V-O   Transitive Verb

A transitive verb requires an object to complete the sentence grammatically.

     s   v   o
Johnny Bench whacked the ball.
     s   v   o
Johnny Bench slammed a home run.

3. S-Linking Verb-Completer   Linking Verb

A linking verb relates the subject of the sentence to its completer.

     s   LV   c
Namath is a superstar.

```
  S   LV   C
```
He feels terrific.
```
  S   LV      C
```
He looks smashing.

Some verbs can be transitive or intransitive depending upon the way they work in a sentence:

```
                    S      V      O
```
Transitive: Van Cliburn plays the piano.

```
                    S        V  (MODIFIER)
```
Intransitive: Van Cliburn plays eloquently.

ACTIVE AND PASSIVE VERBS

Rangers are beaten by Philadelphia.

A verb is *active* if the subject of the sentence performs the action expressed by the verb. If the subject of the sentence receives the action of the verb, then the verb is *passive*.

```
              S      V      O
```
Active: Philadelphia beats Rangers.
```
              S      V
```
Passive: Rangers are beaten by Philadelphia.

Sentences with active verbs and objects (S-V-O) can be transformed into passives:

```
            S      V       O
```
Active: Bench whacked the ball.

```
            S      V
```
Passive: The ball was whacked by Bench.

When you move from active to passive, the object (*ball*) of the active verb becomes the subject (*ball*) of the passive verb. The subject (*Bench*) of the active verb may become part of a prepositional phrase (*by Bench*) that names the performer of the action. Often the prepositional phrase is dropped.

The ball was whacked by Bench.
The ball was whacked.

Rangers are beaten by Phillies.
Rangers are beaten.

The passive takes the following forms. Use a form of the verb *be* with the *-ed* form of regular verbs (*loved*) or the past participles of irregular verbs (*cut*): (I *was loved*, they *were* cut).

Active	
	Present

Active	Passive

	Present	**Past**
They love me.	I *am loved* (by them)	I *was loved*
They love you.	you *are loved* (by them)	you *were loved*
They love him, etc.	he, she, it *is loved* (by them)	he, she, it *was loved*
They love us.	we *are loved* (by them)	we *were loved*
They love you.	you *are loved* (by them)	you *were loved*
They love them.	they *are loved* (by them)	they *were loved*

	Present progressive	**Past progressive**
	I *am being loved*	I *was being loved*
	you *are being loved*	you *were being loved*
	he, she, it *is being loved*	he, she, it *was being loved*
	we *are being loved*	we *were being loved*
	you *are being loved*	you *were being loved*
	they *are being loved*	they *were being loved*

	Future	**Present perfect**
	I *will be loved*	I *have been loved*
	you *will be loved*	you *have been loved*
	he, she, it *will be loved*	he, she, it *has been loved*
	we *will be loved*	we *have been loved*
	you *will be loved*	you *have been loved*
	they *will be loved*	they *have been loved*

	Future perfect	**Past perfect**
	I *will have been loved*	I *had been loved*
	you *will have been loved*	you *had been loved*
	he, she, it *will have been loved*	he, she, it *had been loved*
	we *will have been loved*	we *had been loved*
	you *will have been loved*	you *had been loved*
	they *will have been loved*	they *had been loved*

Exercise 7 Write ten sentences in the passive; then transform each one into the active.

> Example: Passive: The train was stopped by the brakeman at the railroad crossing.
> Active: The brakeman stopped the train at the railroad crossing.

WATCH OUT FOR THE -ED ENDING IN THE PASSIVE

Remember to write the -ed ending in the passive:

NO:	YES:
The moon was *walk* on by man.	The moon was *walked* on by man.
Lincoln was *assassinate* by John Wilkes Booth.	Lincoln was *assassinated* by John Wilkes Booth.
The report was *complete* on time.	The report was *completed* on time.
The plants have already been *water*.	The plants have already been *watered*.

The best phone system in the world didn't just happen. It was planned a long time ago.

Passive: *was planned*

Exercise 8 Rewrite any passive sentence that you think will work better as an active sentence. Watch out for unnecessary shifts from the active to the passive in the same sentence.

1. While I patiently waited on the phone, the telephone number was checked by the operator.
2. A touchdown was scored by Joe Namath in the last four seconds of the fourth quarter. The score was tied.
3. The kitchen floor was swept clean by the maid.
4. Lincoln was assassinated by John Wilkes Booth.
5. The moon was walked on by man.
6. The report was completed on time.
7. The auto-safety report was considered for adoption by the transportation committee.
8. The assignment to write a 500-word narrative essay was given to the class by the instructor.
9. Gold was first discovered in California in 1848.
10. We packed our camping equipment, shopped for supplies, cleaned the house, and the plants were watered.
11. After the package was opened by Janet, she ran to her husband with the news that a wedding gift had been sent to them by her college roommate.

THE SUBJUNCTIVE

Another form of the verb, used only rarely, is called the *subjunctive*. The subjunctive calls for the use of the verb *be* in unusual ways. It also involves using the base form rather than the *-s* form of the verb for subjects *he, she,* or *it* (see below).

1. Use the subjunctive in the following situations:

a. Wishes or unlikely situations
Use the subjunctive to express wishes or unlikely situations. Rather than say, "If I *was* Robert Redford," use the verb *were* to express an unlikely situation. By using the subjunctive, you tell your reader that you know you aren't and never will be Robert Redford:

I wish I *were* Robert Redford.
If I *were* Robert Redford, I could win friends and influence people.

b. Requirements
Use the subjunctive for *that* clauses that express requirements or recommendations. Rather than say, "The law requires that a working father *supports* his children," use the verb *support* to express the possible force of the requirement.

The law requires that a working father *support* his children.
The court recommended that the child *live* with his grandparents.
I asked that they *be* excused from class.
The court ordered that he *pay* a $50 fine.

2. Form the subjunctive as follows:

a. Use *be* for the present subjunctive of the verb *be*.

The law requires that I *be* in court for jury duty.
The law requires that you *be* . . .
The law requires that he, she, it *be* . . .
The law requires that we *be* . . .

Present subjunctive
The law requires that you *be* . . .
The law requires that they *be* . . .

b. Use the base form for the present subjunctive of other verbs.

Present subjunctive
The law requires that a working father *support* his children.
The law requires that she support her children.
The law requires that he support his children.

c. Use *were* for the past subjunctive when the verb would otherwise be *was.*

Past
subjunctive

If I *were* a millionaire, I would be generous with my money.
If you *were* a millionaire . . .
If he, she, it *were* a millionaire . . .
If we *were* millionaires . . .
If you *were* millionaires . . .
If they *were* millionaires . . .

VERBALS A verbal is a verb form that *does not* function as a verb in a sentence. Verbals function as nouns or modifiers.

Verbal as noun An *-ing* word that functions as a noun in a sentence. When the *-ing* word functions as a noun, it is called a *gerund*.

Reading is one of life's great pleasures.

A gerund can be part of a phrase:

Reading a book is one of life's great pleasures.
He enjoys *swimming in the ocean.*

An *infinitive* (*to* + the base: *to run, to go, to win*) can function as a noun in a sentence:

To err is human; to forgive [is] divine.
Alexander Pope

In each of these sentences, the subject of the verb is the infinitive:

    s   v
To err is human.
    s   v
To forgive is divine.

An infinitive can be part of a phrase:

           s   v
To forgive sinners and spoilers is divine.

Verbal as modifier An *-ing* word (*learning, jumping, willing*) or a past participle (*learned, fallen, burnt, condensed*) can function as a modifier in a sentence. When these words function as modifiers, they are called *participles.*

She is *willing* to risk her life for him.
The judge is a *learned* man.
The *burnt* leaves littered the driveway.

A participle can be part of a phrase:

The novel, *burnt to ashes,* was the remains of her literary career.
She sat at the kitchen table, *revising her final draft.*

For more discussion about verbals as modifiers, see Chapter 9, pages 206–207.

PROBLEMS WITH VERBS

1. He walked down the hall and stops./He walked down the hall and stopped.

If you're writing about one time, you confuse your reader when you switch to another time for no apparent reason. You must choose and stay with a time that *governs* your essay. If you begin an essay about a past event, you can't suddenly switch to the present unless you have a good reason, and if you begin in the present, you must have a reason for switching to the past.

But there are reasons. Perhaps you're *reminiscing:*

I *remember* how I *walked* down that dirt road to school every day.

The remembering is occurring now in the writer's mind, but the walking occurred in the past.

Perhaps you're *stating a fact:*

I *forgot* that Chicago *is* near Gary, Indiana.

The forgetting has occurred in the past, but the fact that Chicago *is* near Gary, Indiana, remains true now.

In the following paragraph, the writer switches from one time to another so that you are uncertain when the action occurred.

NO:

First the man *walks* to the window. Then he *moved* over to the counter. His hands *shake.* He *took* a cup of coffee and *sips* it slowly. He *sat* down to watch the news. He *keeps* looking to the window. The phone *rang.*

In the next paragraph, the writer chooses a time (the past) and stays with it so that it *governs* his writing:

YES:

First the man *walked* to the window. Then he *moved* over to the counter. His hands *shook.* He *took* a cup of coffee and *sipped* it slowly. He *sat* down to watch the news. He *kept* looking to the window. The phone *rang.*

Exercise 9 Study the way movie critic Liz Smith stays with the present tense in her review of the movie *The Hot Rock:*

Cool Caper on a Hot Rock

Movie screen, movie screen, on the wall—who is fairest of them all? Robert Redford, that's who, and here's Mr. Gorgeous in **The Hot Rock,** playing a cool, calm, good-looking thief. Minutes out of prison, Redford gets talked into a new heist by his inept but endearing brother-in-law, George Segal. The pair conspire to steal a giant diamond from the Brooklyn Museum, and hire two amateur grand larsonists in the kooky personalities of Ron Leibman and Paul Sand to help out. This is a "caper" movie as played by fools: lovely, handsome, entertaining, agreeable crazies whose brilliant bumbling turns a caper into *four* capers. (I mean, how many times can the same diamond be stolen?) William Goldman's screenplay has more twists than a Chinese road map, and the movie is slick, like most of director Peter Yates's work. (He did *Bullitt* and *Murphy's War.*) New York is the setting, and never has the city looked so honestly beautiful. Star Redford is at his best when most natural. A sneeze is left uncut, and his attempt to rub something doggy off his shoe endears him to you. He does an awful lot of just walking around, but he's so pretty I didn't mind.

Now write a summary of a movie you have seen. Keep to the present tense throughout your summary.

WATCH OUT FOR PLOT SUMMARIES

When summarizing the plot of a movie, a short story, or a novel, the present tense is usually used as in the following summary:

One of my favorite movies *is Bye, Bye, Birdie.* The movie *is* a musical comedy about a rock singer who *comes* to a small town to give a concert. The movie *shows* how he *becomes* involved in the lives of the townspeople, When a teen-ager *is* chosen to appear with him on television in a pinning ceremony, her boyfriend *flies* into a jealous rage.

Treat the events of a movie or story as facts that are always true.

Fact: Water *freezes* at 32 degrees Fahrenheit.

Movie fact: In *Gone With the Wind,* Scarlett O'Hara *is* a Southern belle with an eighteen-inch waist. She *falls* in love with Ashley Wilkes but *marries* Rhett Butler.

---

2. Yesterday I return the book./Yesterday I returned the book.

Some writers do not include the *-ed* ending on the verb because they're not accustomed to pronouncing or hearing the *-ed*. If you are one of these writers, be especially careful to use the *-ed* ending for the past of regular verbs:

NO: Yesterday I *return* the book to the library.
NO: Last week I *climb* up to the roof.

YES: Yesterday I *returned* the book to the library.
YES: Last week I *climbed* up to the roof.

When there are several verbs in the past in a sentence, use the *-ed* ending of regular verbs (or the past form of irregular verbs) for each verb in the sentence:

NO: He *walked* down the corridor, *stop* at Apartment 3C, *hesitate* a moment, and then *tap* on the door.

YES: He *walked* down the corridor, *stopped* at Apartment 3C, *hesitated* a moment, and then *tapped* on the door.

3. I use to go./I used to go.   I am suppose to go./I am supposed to go.

Give special attention to past forms of *use* and *suppose:*

NO: I *use* to go.
YES: I *used* to go.

NO: I'm *suppose* to come.
YES: I'm *supposed* to come.

4. He has came./He has come.

Combine *have, has,* or *had* with the past participle of irregular verbs (*have come, have run*). Do not combine *have, has,* or *had* with the *past form* of irregular verbs (not *has came, has ran*). The problem occurs only with irregular verbs because the past and past participle of regular verbs are identical:

She *smiled* at me.   She *had smiled* at me a long time ago.

They *laughed*.   They *have* often *laughed*.

Use the past participle of irregular verbs with *have, has,* or *had:*

NO:	YES:
I should *have went*.	I should *have gone*.
They *had did* it.	They *had done* it.
The water *hasn't froze* yet.	The water *hasn't frozen* yet.
I should *have took* him along.	I should *have taken him along*.

The following verbs are often used incorrectly with *have, has,* or *had.* Learn to recognize them as problem verbs:

	NO:	YES:
break	have broke	have broken
choose	has chose	has chosen
do	had did	had done
draw	have drew	have drawn
drive	has drove	has driven
eat	had ate	had eaten
begin	have began	have begun
come	have came	have come
sing	had sang	had sung

5. *I done my homework./I did my homework.*

Do not use the past participle of an irregular verb (*done*) for a past form (*did*). The past participle cannot be used without an auxiliary:

NO:	YES:	YES:
I *gone* to the movies.	I *went* to the movies.	I *have gone* to the movies.
They *done* it.	They *did* it.	They *have done* it.
We *seen* it.	We *saw* it.	We *have seen* it.

Remember, there's no problem with regular verbs, for the past and the past participle are identical:

YES:	YES:
I *learned* an unforgettable lesson.	I *have learned* an unforgettable lesson.
She *walked* home.	She *has walked* home.
They *loved* each other.	They *had loved* each other.

6. *The lilies growed./The lilies grewed./The lilies grew.*

If the verb is irregular, don't tack on an *-ed* ending as if it were a regular past (*growed*) or as if the irregular past form required *-ed* (*grewed*). Use the past forms of irregular verbs listed on pages 355-357:

NO:	YES:
The lilies *growed* along the freeway. The lilies *grewed* along the freeway.	The lilies *grew* along the freeway.
Jeannette's jeans *shranked* three inches. Jeannette's jeans *shrinked* three inches.	Jeannette's jeans *shrank* three inches.

7. *She swimming./She is swimming.*

The *-ing* form alone cannot be used as the verb in a sentence. It must be combined with a time word (is, are, were, etc.) See Chapter 6, pages 116-117.

NO:	YES:
Samantha *swimming* in the lake.	Samantha *is swimming* in the lake.
She *wearing* a scanty bikini.	She *was wearing* a scanty bikini.

8. *I planned writing./I planned to write.*

Certain verbs must be followed by certain verbals. Familiarize yourself with the following lists:

a. These verbs are followed by an infinitive (*to dance, to think, to wish*):

ask	She'll *ask* him *to dance.*
beg	He *begged* her *to marry* him.
care	She doesn't *care to tango.*
decide	She could *decide to sit* this one out.
expect	He *expected* her *to say* that.
forget	She *forgot to apologize.*
hope	He's *hoping to win* her hand.
learn	She's *learning to control* herself.
plan	He *plans to captivate* her.
promise	She *promised to consider* him.
want	He *wants to kiss* her.
wish	She *wished to leave.*

b. These verbs are followed by an *-ing* word (*dancing, thinking, wishing*):

admit	He *admitted dancing* with Janet.
appreciate	I *appreciate* your *coming.*
avoid	They *avoided paying* their bills.
consider	We *considered leaving.*
deny	He *denied seeing* her.
enjoy	She *enjoys swimming.*
escape	He *escaped going* bowling tonight.
finish	She's *finished considering* him.
imagine	He *imagined kissing* her.
keep	She *kept* him *waiting* all night.
mind	Would you *mind eating* out?
miss	He *missed seeing* her.

9. *sit/set   lie/lay   rise/raise*

Three troublesome verb pairs have much in common. Three of the verbs are transitive; that is, they take objects. These verbs are *set, lay,* and *raise.* Three of the verbs are intransitive; that is, they do not take objects. These verbs are *sit, rise,* and *lie.* The difficulty lies in remembering the principal parts of each verb and in knowing the particular verb's meaning.

set/sit

set (takes an object)

Present	*set*
Past	*set*
Past Participle	*have set*

Meaning:
Set means to put something in a place—to *set* the suitcase down, to *set* the problem aside.

s   v   o
I *set* the book on its shelf.

Yesterday I *set* the book on its shelf.

I *have set* the book on its shelf.

Note: All three forms of *set* are the same: *set, set, set.*

sit (never takes an object)

Present	*sit*
Past	*sat*
Past Participle	*have sat*

Meaning:
Sit means to rest—to *sit* in a chair, to *sit* on a bench.

s   v
The book *sits* on the shelf.

Yesterday the book *sat* on the shelf.

The book *has sat* on that shelf for years.

lay/lie

lay (takes an object)

Present	*lay*
Past	*laid*
Past Participle	*have laid*

Meaning:
Lay means to place or put something down.

s   v   o
I *lay* the pencil down

Yesterday I *laid* the pencil on the desk.

I *have laid* the pencil down.

lie (never takes an object)

Present	*lie*
Past	*lay*
Past Participle	*have lain*

Meaning:
Lie means to rest in a reclining position.

s   v
I usually *lie* down after dinner.

Yesterday I *lay* in bed all day.

I *have* often *lain* down after dinner.

Notice where the confusion is: The past of *lie* (recline) is *lay,* which is also the present of *lay* (put).

Present: I usually *lay* (put) my glasses on that table, and now they aren't there.

Past: Yesterday I *lay* (reclined) in bed all day.

raise/rise *raise* (takes an object)

Present	*raise*
Past	*raised*
Past Participle	*have risen*

Meaning:
Raise means to lift something up, or to increase something in size or intensity—to *raise* a voice, to *raise* prices.

  S V O
She *raises* the window blind at dawn.

She *raised* the window blind at dawn.

She *has* often *raised* the window blind at dawn.

rise (never takes an object)

Present	*rise*
Past	*rose*
Past Participle	*have risen*

Meaning:
Rise means to stand up after lying or sitting down, or to go up—the price of eggs *rose* this week.

  S V
The sun *rises* early in the summer.

Yesterday the sun *rose* at 4:46 A.M.

The sun *has risen* before 5:00 A.M. this week.

Exercise 10 Choose the correct verb form of *rise/raise, sit/set,* or *lie/lay* to fill the empty slots.

Although I had _____ the alarm for six o'clock this morning, I couldn't _____ my weary body when the alarm rang. The sun had already _____, but I needed to _____ in bed awhile. I remembered the *Time* magazine that I had _____ next to the bed last night and began to read it. The national news section noted that the price of eggs and dairy products had _____ again. Farmers in the West had _____ the price of wheat so that bread prices would surely _____ in the fall. The news was certainly not promising.

After awhile, I _____ up in bed, _____ the magazine aside, and _____ the window shade behind me. The day was glorious. I wished that I could _____ in bed the whole morning, but I knew I should _____ out the dog's breakfast and begin the day.

10. *would of/would have   could of/could have   should of/should have   gonna/going to*

Although it is natural to slur sounds of words as we talk, do not drop endings of words or merge words in writing. A common writing error is to use *of* instead of *have*. Another is to write *gonna* for *going to*.

NO:
I could *of* danced all night.
I should *of* bought that dress.
He's *gonna* be President.

YES:
I could *have* danced all night.
I should *have* bought that dress.
He's *going to* be President.

11. *if I would have/if I had*

Do not use *would have* in an *if* clause.

NO:
If I *would have* studied Chapter 3, I would have passed the exam.

YES:
If I *had* studied Chapter 3, I would have passed the exam.

CHART I: PRINCIPAL PARTS OF REGULAR VERBS

Base	*Past tense* (*used alone*)	*Past participle* (*used with* have, has, *or* had)
ask	asked	asked
beg	begged	begged
learn	learned	learned
love	loved	loved
rush	rushed	rushed

CHART II: PATTERNS OF VERB CHANGES IN IRREGULAR VERBS

Base	*Past tense* (*used alone*)	*Past participle* (*used with* have, has, *or* had)
a. cry	cried	cried
pay	paid	paid
say	said	said

Verbs like these in IIa show a spelling change before adding *d*.

b. break	broke	broken
choose	chose	chosen
drive	drove	driven
draw	drew	drawn
take	took	taken

Verbs like these in IIb show a past participle ending in *n* or *en*.

c. begin	began	begun
ring	rang	rung
swim	swam	swum

Verbs like these in IIc show a vowel (*a, e, i, o, u*) change within the base.

d. cut	cut	cut
hit	hit	hit
hurt	hurt	hurt
put	put	put
set	set	set

Verbs like these in IId show no change in the past or past participle.

e. bring	brought	brought
catch	caught	caught
fight	fought	fought
keep	kept	kept
stand	stood	stood
teach	taught	taught

Verbs like these in IIe show the same past and past participle.

f. become	became	become
come	came	come
run	ran	run

The three verbs in IIf show the same base and past participle.

g. awake	awaked, awoke	awaked, awoke, awaken
forget	forgot	forgotten, forgot

Verbs like these in IIg have more than one past or past participle. Each is acceptable.

CHART III: PRINCIPAL PARTS OF IRREGULAR VERBS

Base	*Past tense*	*Past participle*
awake	awaked, awoke	awaked, awoke, awoken
be	was, were	been
beat	beat	beaten, beat
become	became	become
begin	began	begun
bend	bent	bent
bite	bit	bit, bitten
bleed	bled	bled
blow	blew	blown
break	broke	broken
bring	brought	brought
build	built	built
burst	burst	burst
buy	bought	bought
catch	caught	caught
choose	chose	chosen
come	came	come
cost	cost	cost
cut	cut	cut
deal	dealt	dealt
dig	dug	dug
dive	dived, dove	dived
do	did	done
draw	drew	drawn
dream	dreamed, dreamt	dreamed, dreamt
drink	drank	drunk
drive	drove	driven
eat	ate	eaten
fall	fell	fallen
feed	fed	fed
feel	felt	felt
fight	fought	fought
find	found	found
fit	fitted, fit	fitted, fit
fly	flew	flown

Base	*Past tense*	*Past participle*
forget	forgot	forgotten, forgot
freeze	froze	frozen
get	got	gotten, got
give	gave	given
go	went	gone
grow	grew	grown
hang (an object)	hung	hung
hang (a person)	hanged	hanged
hear	heard	heard
hide	hid	hidden, hid
hit	hit	hit
hold	held	held
hurt	hurt	hurt
keep	kept	kept
kneel	knelt, kneeled	knelt, kneeled
knit	knit, knitted	knit, knitted
know	knew	known
lay (put)	laid	laid
lead	led	led
lean	leaned, leant	leaned, leant
leave	left	left
lend	lent	lent
let (allow)	let	let
lie (recline)	lay	lain
light	lighted, lit	lighted, lit
lose	lost	lost
make	made	made
mean	meant	meant
meet	met	met
pay	paid	paid
prove	proved	proved, proven
put	put	put
quit	quit, quitted	quit, quitted
read	read	read
rid	rid, ridded	rid, ridded
ride	rode	ridden
ring	rang	rung
run	ran	run
say	said	said

Base	Past tense	Past participle
see	saw	seen
sell	sold	sold
send	sent	sent
set	set	set
shake	shook	shaken
shine	shone, shined	shone, shined (trans.)
shoot	shot	shot
show	showed	showed, shown
shrink	shrank	shrunk
shut	shut	shut
sing	sang, sung	sung
sink	sank	sunk
sit	sat	sat
sleep	slept	slept
slide	slid	slid, slidden
speak	spoke	spoken
speed	sped, speeded	sped, speeded
spend	spent	spent
spin	spun	spun
spring	sprang, sprung	sprung
stand	stood	stood
steal	stole	stolen
stick	stuck	stuck
sting	stung	stung
strike	struck	struck, stricken
swear	swore	sworn
swim	swam	swum
swing	swung	swung
take	took	taken
teach	taught	taught
tear	tore	torn
tell	told	told
think	thought	thought
throw	threw	thrown
wake	waked, woke	waked, woke, woken
wear	wore	worn
win	won	won
wring	wrung	wrung
write	wrote	written

Chapter 14 / Subject-Verb Agreement

PERSON AND NUMBER Look at the following sentences about the President of the United States, noticing how each pronoun refers to the subject differently:

> *I* am the President.
> *You* are the President.
> *He* is the President.

When the subject of a sentence is *speaking about himself*, he uses the singular pronoun *I*, or he uses the plural pronoun *we* if he is part of a group:

> *I* am the President.
> *We* are supporters of the President.
> *We* must win.

When the subject of a sentence *is being spoken to*, the pronoun *you* is used:

> *You* are the President.
> *You* are supporters of the President.
> *You* must win.

When the subject of a sentence is *being spoken about*, we use the pronouns *he, she, it*, or *they;* or we can use any word or group of words that can be reduced to these pronouns:

> *Jimmy Carter* is the President.
>   or
> *He* is the President.

> *Rosalynn Carter* is the President's wife.
>   or
> *She* is the President's wife.

358

The Steelers must win.

or

They must win.

The subject, as you have seen, can *speak about himself, be spoken to,* or *be spoken about.* We call each of these three ways of referring to a subject *person.* The idea of *person* may have nothing to do with people. All nouns (or noun substitutes) can be changed to *he, she, it,* or *they. It* is called a third-*person* pronoun although it never refers to a human being.

Another quality of the subject is *number,* which means that a subject may be *singular* (one) or *plural* (more than one). We can talk about the *person* and *number* of every subject. Let's look closely at these qualities.

First person   In the first person, the subject speaks about himself. Whenever the pronouns *I* (singular) or *we* (plural) appear in the subject slot, the pronoun is in the first person.

Second person   In the second person, the subject is being spoken to. Whenever the pronoun *you* appears in the subject slot, the pronoun is in the second person. Note that the second-person pronoun has the same form for both singular and plural.

You are the one I adore. (singular)

You are the men and women of tomorrow. (plural)

Third person   In the third person, the subject is being spoken about. Whenever the pronouns *he, she, it* (singular), or *they* (plural) appear in the subject slot, the pronoun is in the third person. Whenever a subject can be reduced to one of these pronouns, the subject is in the third person. *Every subject,* in fact, that does not contain the pronouns, *I, we,* or *you,* will be in the third person.

He's Swinging in the Rain

She was young

They call us old-hat.

Giants Win Two Ball Games

or *They* win.

The Carters Make a Date For Lunch

or *They* make a date for lunch.

San Francisco Has Some of the Best

or *It* has some of the best.

As you see in the following list, every subject in every sentence in the English language can be described by *person* (first, second, or third) and by *number*—singular (one) or plural (more than one).

	Singular	*Plural*
First person	I	we
Second person	you	you
	he	they
	she	
	it	
Third person	dog	dogs
	boy	boys
	tree	trees
	one	many

AGREEMENT BETWEEN SUBJECT AND VERB

Whenever you hook up a subject in the *third-person singular* with a verb in the *present tense,* you run into one of the peculiarities of the English language. No other subject presents a problem; no other tense presents a problem.

Let's look now at the verb forms in the present tense:

	Singular	*Plural*
First person	I *walk*	we *walk*
Second person	you *walk*	you *walk*
Third person	he *walks*	they *walk*
	she *walks*	John and Susan *walk*
	it *walks*	
	John *walks*	
	Susan *walks*	

You see that the present tense of a verb is made up of the base (*walk*) and the *-s* form (*walks*). A *third-person singular subject always takes the -s form of the verb in the present tense.* This matching of the subject and verb is called *agreement.*

Watch what happens to the verb in the present tense when you change a third-person singular subject to a third-person plural subject:

Third-person singular

A cat love*s* Purina.

A cat☐ love⑤ Purina.

Third-person plural

Cats love Purina.

Cat⑤ love☐ Purina.

Purina knows what cats love most

It is a peculiarity of English that when the verb in a sentence has an *-s* ending, there is usually no *-s* on the subject (cat☐ loves☐). But when the *-s* (for plural) occurs on the subject, no *-s* occurs on the verb (cats☐ love☐). For the one exception to this rule, see "Agreement Problems," p. 363.

There are no problems in agreement between subject and verb in the past or the future tense because all forms of the verb are the same for all three persons, singular and plural:

Past

I *walked*	we *walked*
you *walked*	you *walked*
he, she, it *walked*	they *walked*

Future

I *will walk*	we *will walk*
you *will walk*	you *will walk*
he, she, it *will walk*	they *will walk*

WATCH OUT FOR <u>BE</u> AND <u>HAVE</u>

Remember the parts of the verbs *be* and *have:*

BE		HAVE	
PRESENT		PRESENT	
I *am*	we *are*	I *have*	we *have*
you *are*	you *are*	you *have*	you *have*
he, she, it	they	he, she, it	they
John *is*	*are*	John *has*	*have*
the dog	the dogs	the dog	the dogs

PAST	
I *was*	we *were*
you *were*	you *were*
he, she, it *was*	they *were*

Remember how *be* and *have* combine with other verbs.
The *dog is growling* at his Gainesburger.
The *dogs are growling* at their Gainesburgers.
That *dog has been growling* all morning.
Those *dogs have been growling* all morning.

WATCH OUT FOR -S ENDINGS

Some words end in *-s:*

LAS VEGAS

SWISS This *Actress* **fuss**

gas Tennis

Plural nouns end in *-s:*

SINGULAR	PLURAL
athlete	Athletes
problem	Problems
lifestyle	*Lifestyles*
ceremony	Ceremonies

Singular nouns form possessives with an *'s:*

Scott

SCOTT'S LAST VOYAGE

emperor

The Emperor's New Clothes

All verbs have an *-s* form:

BASE	*-S* FORM
get	**gets** Says
say	does
do	
keep	**keeps** **opens**
open	

AGREEMENT PROBLEMS

Using the -s form Although you may be able to recognize when your subject is singular (*Vincent, cat, actress*), you may not distinguish between a verb form with *-s* at the end and a verb form without *-s* at the end. You may, in fact, be using the same base form (with *-s*) for all your subjects, whether they are singular or plural:

YES: They *walk* to the bus every night.
NO: Vincent *walk* to the bus every night.
YES: Vincent *walks* to the bus every night.

YES: They *love* to go shopping with their wives.
NO: Vincent *love* to go shopping with his wife.
YES: Vincent *loves* to go shopping with his wife.

Occasionally, speakers of dialects overcorrect and use the *-s* verb form for every subject:

NO: I *loves* mint chocolate chip.
NO: They *loves* cherry vanilla.

Learn to distinguish the *-s* ending of plural nouns and the *-s* form of verbs. Read the following sentences aloud, pronouncing each *-s* you come upon. Notice how the *-s* box for the verb is filled when the subject is singular. (A cat□ loves☒.) Notice how the *-s* box of the subject is filled when the subject is plural. (Cats☒ love□.)

pain* interferes...

pain□   interferes☒

Ali Rests in Ring; Joe Just Rests

Ali□ Rests☒

Three authors discuss work informally

Southern Farmers Debate

farmers☒ debate□

authors☒ discuss□

Nouns do not need to end in *-s* to be plural. When a plural noun does not end in *-s*, neither box is filled.

Singular noun	*Plural noun*
man	men

The Almond People Invite You To Nibble Your Way Through The Week

2 policemen deliver baby

almond people□   invite□   policemen□   deliver□

Exercise 1 For each subject in the left column, write a sentence using a verb in the right column. Every verb should be in the present tense and end in -s. See page 435 to form -s endings on *screech, buzz,* and other words ending in *s, z, x, ch,* and *sh*.

the IRS	to be
Joni Mitchell	to have
the queen	to sing
an owl	to want
"Happy Days"	to buy
Barbra Streisand	to sound
Bill Cosby	to buzz
Hubert Humphrey	to seduce
my stereo	to screech
	to collect
	to suggest

Exercise 2 Write the following headline in the past tense, the present tense, and the future tense. In which time does the headline appear here?

Your college degree cost over $15,000

Exercise 3 Rewrite the following passage from Judy Syfers' "Why I Want a Wife," changing *I* to *she*. Make any other changes necessary because of the shift from *I* to *she*.

> Example: She wants a wife who will take care of her
> physical needs. (continue)

I want a wife who will take care of *my* physical needs. I want a wife who will keep my house clean. A wife who will pick up after me. I want a wife who will keep my clothes clean, ironed, mended, replaced when need be, and who will see to it that my personal things are kept in their proper place so that I can find what I need the minute I need it. I want a wife who cooks the meals, a wife who is a *good* cook. I want a wife who will plan the menus, do the necessary grocery shopping, prepare the meals, serve them pleasantly, and then do the cleaning up while I do my studying. I want a wife who will care for me when I am sick and sympathize with my pain and loss of time from school. I want a wife to go along when our family takes a vacation so that someone can continue to care for me and my children when I need a rest and change of scene.

Recognizing the subject To make certain that your subject and verb agree, you must be able to isolate the subject-verb unit. If you have trouble deciding what the subject of a sentence is, look again at the advice in Chapter 6, "Finding the Verb and Subject," page 104. Once you've found the verb in the sentence, ask a *who* or *what* question to find the subject.

What is the subject in the following sentence? *Water? Costs?*

Higher Water Costs Raise Rents

The verb is	*raise*
Who or what	raise?
Higher water costs	*raise*

Now reduce the subject to a pronoun (*he, she, it,* or *they*) that fits the subject slot:

What	*raise?*
They	raise

The word that is the subject of the verb is *costs,* not *water.*

When you're not certain if your subject is third-person singular or plural, reduce the subject to the third-person pronoun, *he, she, it,* or *they.* Practice these steps:

Groucho is snickering.
He   is snickering.

Groucho, Harpo, Zeppo, and *Chico* roar.
They   roar.

The *comedians* roar.
They   roar.

Lucille Ball is a brilliant comedian.
She   is a brilliant comedian.

Slapstick *comedy* is hilarious.
It   is hilarious.

Problems in determining whether a subject is singular or plural arise with *abstract nouns,* that is, nouns that describe ideas or qualities. Abstract nouns are usually singular:

life	improvement	beauty
liberty	necessity	nature
freedom	kindness	solitude
happiness	loveliness	peace

Necessity is the mother of invention.

Liberty creates patriots.

Experience is the best teacher.

No matter how long and involved the subject is, you can determine whether it is singular or plural by reducing it to a third-person pronoun:

An extreme nationalism that drains a country's energy is destructive
          It   is destructive

Life, liberty, and the pursuit of happiness are privileges we expect.
      They   are privileges we expect.

Winning the election in November is his first goal.
     It   is his first goal.

Exercise 4 No matter how long and involved the subject of a sentence is, you can reduce the subject to one of these personal pronouns:

	Singular	*Plural*
First person	I	we
Second person	you	you
Third person	he	they

Reduce the following subjects by determining their person and number and then substituting an appropriate pronoun.

	Person and number	*Pronoun*
Example: Charles Smith and his sister Mary	third-person plural	they

1. one man and his dogs
2. one man
3. his dogs
4. Charles Smith, his sister Mary, and I
5. Charles Smith and his sister Mary
6. his sister Mary
7. I
8. the pursuit of happiness
9. the man in the purple suit and I
10. the man in the purple suit
11. freedom
12. international companies
13. gross national product
14. electric bills
15. the task force

Exercise 5 Reduce the subjects in the following sentences.

Example: Musicians' talks hit another snag.   talks ☒ hit ☐
they ☐ hit ☐

Losing 37 pounds doesn't sound like much, but look at the difference it made in me.

Indiana Triumphs Over Mich. State

Those quaint New England inns do exist

Fedders heat pump air conditioner cuts winter fuel bills

Solving other agreement problems Errors in subject-verb agreement often occur when writers lose sight of their subject because other words separate the subject and verb:

s
The *man* in the navy blue suit talking to those salesmen
v
is my English professor.

Problems also arise when writers are uncertain whether words like *each, either, none, everyone* are singular or plural, or when they are unsure whether such expressions as *along with, as well as,* and *in addition to* make a singular subject plural. Should they write:

Each of the committees *is* meeting this week.
        or
Each of the committees *are* meeting this week.

Marie as well as her class *is* going to the museum.
        or
Marie as well as her class *are* going to the museum.

The following section demonstrates some of the trickiest agreement problems. Study these pages carefully now, and then return to them whenever you have specific questions about subject-verb agreement in your own writing.

Words that come between Words that come between the subject and verb may be misleading. Often
the subject and verb you'll have to untangle the subject to find the head noun.

> The woman in the yellow bikini serving the sandwiches to the girls in dungarees is my grandmother.

> s   v
> woman ——————————————————————————— is

What may confuse you is that the phrase *girls in dungarees* comes closer to the verb than the subject does. Don't let it fool you. You're not saying *the girls in dungarees are my grandmother.* You're saying *the woman is my grandmother.*

> The *price* of eggs *is* high.
> The *price*_____*is* high.

Don't let the plural form *of eggs* mislead you. What is high is the *price*, and *price* is singular. The phrase *of eggs* that comes between the subject and verb should not influence the number of the verb.

> NO: The *price* of eggs *are* high.
> YES: The *price* of eggs *is* high.
>   s-v: *price is*

> NO: The *dog* who wants quality biscuits *love* Purina.
> YES: The *dog* who wants quality biscuits *loves* Purina.
>   s-v: *dog loves*

JAMBALAYA
THIS SAVORY CREOLE CONCOCTION FROM THE LOUISIANA BAYOUS CALLS FOR CHICKEN, HAM, RICE, ONION AND THE MEAT OF THE TOMATO.

The verb is	*calls for*
Who or What	calls for?
This savory Creole concoction from the Louisiana Bayous	*calls for*
What	calls for?

Reduce the subject to a personal pronoun
(*he, she, it,* or *they*) that fits the subject slot: *it*   *calls for*
The word that is the subject of the verb is *concoction.*

> *concoction calls for*

Do not let the modifiers that come before or after the one word that is your simple subject distract you. Put parentheses around the modifiers so that you can see the one word that is the subject of your verb:

> (This savory Creole)   s   (from the Louisiana Bayous)   v
> . . .   concoction   *calls for*

See Chapter 9, "Modifiers," pages 182–224.

Exercise 6 Here is one long sentence from the *New York Times* with an error in it. Identify the subject and verb, explain the error, and correct the sentence.

> Until now, with rare exceptions, the nation's tenured professors, whose jobs are virtually guaranteed for life, has escaped wholesale dismissals as institutions of higher education adjusted to the economic realities of standstill budgets and dwindling enrollments.

Compound subjects When two or more subjects are joined by *and*, the verb is usually plural:

> Max's chipped front *tooth and* his *dimple attract* the girls.
> > s-v: *tooth and dimple attract*
>
> *Breakfast and lunch are served* at Max's pool.
> > s-v: *breakfast and lunch are served*

When two subjects joined by *and* constitute a single unit, consider the subject singular:

> Peanut butter and jelly is my favorite sandwich.
> Johnson & Johnson sells Band Aids to the world.

When two subjects joined by *and* refer to a single item, consider the subject singular.

> A wife and mother is an overworked member of the labor force.
> (Wife and mother refers to one person who is both.)

Alternative subjects When two or more subjects are joined by *or* or *nor,* use the form of the verb that agrees with the *subject nearest the verb:*

> Either Lillian or her *parents are* walking the dog.
> Either Lillian's parents or her *brother is* walking the dog.

Occasions will arise when strict adherence to this rule will produce awkward phrasings:

> Neither the Dean nor I am happy with the sleeping arrangements.
> Neither I nor the Dean is happy with the sleeping arrangements.

It is often neatest to change the construction altogether:

> I am not happy with the sleeping arrangements, and neither is the Dean.

as well as/together with/in addition to When a subject is followed by a phrase beginning with *as well as, together with,* or *in addition to,* decide whether your *intent* in the entire phrase is singular or plural.

> My *mother*, as well as my father, *has* a key to the office.
> A cop together with Gideon and Kevin are getting out of a patrol car.

each, either,   *Each* is singular and is usually understood to mean "each one":
    neither

> *Each has* his own stopwatch and is ready to begin.

When *each* is followed by *of them* (an intervening phrase), the subject remains singular:

> NO: *Each* of them *have* their own stopwatches and are ready to begin.
> YES: *Each* of them *has* his own stopwatch and is ready to begin.

When *each* immediately follows a plural subject (*the contestants each, they each*) the subject is plural, as it would be if *each* were omitted:

> The *contestants* each *have* their own stopwatches and are ready to begin.

Either and *neither* are both singular:

> NO: *Either* Sharon or Lauren *walk* the dog in the morning.
> YES: *Either* Sharon or Lauren *walks* the dog in the morning.

> NO: *Neither* of them *like* to swim.
> YES: *Neither* of them *likes* to swim.

<u>anybody</u>, <u>anyone</u>, <u>anything</u>/<u>somebody</u>, <u>someone</u>, <u>something</u>
<u>nobody</u>, <u>no one</u>, <u>nothing</u>/<u>everybody</u>, <u>everyone</u>, <u>everything</u>

Since these words are always singular, verb problems rarely arise when they are used as subjects:

> *Everybody swims* in Lake Winnipesaukee.
> *Something is* wrong with Robert.

None, any, all, more, most, and *some* can be either singular or plural, depending on the meaning of the sentence:

> Plural: *Some* of the storks *are* standing on two legs.
> Singular: *Some* of the sand *is* in my shoe.

> Plural: *Most* of the lifeguards *were* striking.
> Singular: *Most* of the bathhouse *was* under a foot of water.

> Plural: *None* of us *know* what cholesterol does to our bodies.
> Singular: *None* of our Irish setters *is* expected to win in the state dog show.

(See Chapter 15, pp. 387–388, for a fuller discussion of these pronouns.)

kind of/*type of*   Any expert in grammar will say that the following sentence is correct:

> The type of eyeglasses you want is rimless.

But this construction is jarring. *Eyeglasses,* which has a plural meaning, actually dominates the true singular subject *type. Type* becomes a throwaway subject and yields to *eyeglasses* in the contest for control of the verb:

> The type of eyeglasses you want are rimless.
> The kind of shoes now in style hurt my feet.

In the next sentence there is no contest because *lens* and *type* are both singular nouns.

The type of lens you want is plastic.

Collective nouns Though a collective noun names a group, it usually refers to that group as a single unit and functions in the sentence as a singular subject. Notice the *-s* form of the verb in the following ads:

SITUATIONS WANTED

Live-in European couple seeks position, handyman, caretaker, auto mechanic, references. 628-2656 after 5 pm.

Couple with 2 children wants live-in, part time caretakers job in exchange for rent. References. 212-CY 8-6259.

Mature couple desires room & bath or small apartment. Away on weekends. 759-0622.

---

seek*s*   wants   desire*s*

s-v: *couple seeks*   *couple wants*   *couple desires*

When you focus on the individual members of the group and not on the group as a unit, the subject is plural and requires a plural verb:

WANTED TO RENT

Young married couple, lawyer & school teacher with baby, seek apartment for the summer. Willing to work in turn for rent. Call bet. 9 & 5, 364-2700 ext. 295.

---

s-v: *couple seek*

Other collective nouns are *jury, orchestra, family, audience, crowd, committee, United States, flock, band, team, faculty,* and so forth.

Singular: Beverly's family is in the car waiting for her.

Singular or plural: Beverly's family is scattered all over Canada.
                     Beverly's family are scattered all over Canada.

Plural: Beverly's family—her parents, her brother Otto, and her sister Amelia—are scattered all over Canada.

Quantities as subject A noun of quantity is singular when the quantity is considered as a single unit:

Ten miles is too long to hike in July.
Six dollars is a fair price for that haircut.

But when a noun of quantity refers to the individual items, the subject is plural:

Two-thirds of the nation *are* ill-housed, ill-fed, and ill-clothed.
Three quarts of orange juice *are* barely enough for Steve's breakfast.

the number of/ a number of The number of is always singular, but a *number of* is plural:

The number of travel books about Kenya *is* increasing.

A number of officials in Nairobi *have* expressed concern about relations with Uganda.

A lot . . . are/
A lot . . . is *A lot* is plural if the upcoming noun in the *of* phrase is plural and singular if the noun in the *of* phrase is singular:

A lot of Coke *bottles were* strewn along the highway to Jericho.
A lot of *Coke is* drunk in East Africa.

one of those who The verb agrees with the plural noun (*poets, lawyers, artists*), and not with *one:*

Aileen is one of those *poets* who *study* art.
Isabel is one of the *lawyers* who *are going* to Washington.
Phyllis is one of the *artists* who *like* poetry.

Reversed word order/ **there is** / **there are** / **it is**

A preceding noun should never influence a verb whose true subject follows it in the sentence:

In the early morning fog *come* the *sounds* of fishing boats off Deer Isle.

s-v: *sounds come*

Seated behind her as she spoke were her husband and children.

s-v: *her husband and children were*

There is/there are reverses the usual word order: the verb is first and the subject second. Usually, the number of the delayed subject controls the verb:

There *were Joe and Bob barbecuing* the chickens in their backyard.

s-v: *Joe and Bob were barbecuing*

There *is* no *explanation* for food preferences.

s-v: *explanation is*

There are still some things Americans know how to do best.

s-v: things are

The word *it* always takes the *-s* form of the verb:

It *was* the O'Connells at the door.
It'*s* the books I ordered.

Nouns ending Nouns ending in *-ics* that represent a single field of study are considered
in -ics singular:

Mathematics *is* a mystery to Harry.
American politics *has* been Janet's lifelong passion.
Dean Flint's campus politics *are* scandalous.

(In the third sentence, Dean Flint's *politics* are not a field of study but are all his maneuvers and strategies to gain power and therefore are considered plural.)

Subject, not the completer, controls the verb

Even when the completer of a linking verb differs in number from the subject, the subject controls the verb:

The *disturbance* outside the window *was* three men beating on garbage can lids.

s-v: *disturbance was*

Titles   The title of a book, song, play, and the like, even when it is plural in form, is thought of as a single work and requires the *-s* form of the verb.

Ideas and Beliefs of the Victorians is not exactly bedside reading.
Wuthering Heights is about an uncouth fellow named Heathcliff.

Exercise 7   Write your own sentences using each of the following words as subject. The verbs in the sentences should be in the present tense. Include a phrase or clause between the subject and verb so that your sentence looks like this:

subject _____ verb
Example: confusion
        The *confusion* of registering for classes gets me down.

United Nations Organization
my education and my background
the original intent
power brokers
the most exposed part
the glamour and glitter
the noise and the confusion

Exercise 8   Supply a verb in present time in the following sentences.

Example: The Bijou or the Valencia _____ *Gone With the Wind* this week.

The Bijou or the Valencia *is showing Gone With the Wind* this week.

1. Clark and Lois _____ each other.
2. Either a cold rain or some snow _____ every afternoon.
3. Some of the musicians _____ to sight read.
4. Most of the Planetarium _____ undergoing a paint job.
5. None of the telephone operators _____ clearly.
6. Some of the mathematics _____ easy to understand.
7. Lucy, together with William, _____ to play Little League ball.
8. Some of the fastest traveling galaxies _____ no longer visible.
9. Nobody _____ the trouble I've seen.
10. Ten minutes in that ice cold swimming pool _____ to cardiac arrest.
11. The number of businesses in our neighborhood _____ steadily increasing.
12. A number of supermarkets in our neighborhood _____ open all night.
13. Well, if it _____n't the Waterhouse boys, all dressed to kill and coming up the walk!

Chapter 15 / Pronouns

PRONOUNS

There are some words you would hesitate to use at the beginning of a conversation if you want your listener to understand your meaning:

"Hello, Alice. Do you remember *him? He's* at Annapolis now."

Or:

"Hi, Jake. *It's* not giving me any more trouble. *It's* been fixed."

What are these speakers talking about? Except for *I* (which always refers to the person speaking) and *you* (which always refers to the person spoken to), the italicized pronouns (*him, he, it*) make little sense. As you can see, when no noun has previously been named, pronouns only hint at meaning. By contrast, you can easily understand the following two statements:

"Hello, Alice. Do you remember *Paul? He's* at Annapolis now."

And:

"Hi, *Jake. Whatever was wrong with my car* isn't giving me any more trouble. *It's* been fixed."

An *antecedent* is the word or words that provide the meaning. An antecedent is a noun (*Paul*) or a phrase or clause functioning as a noun (*whatever was wrong with my car*) that goes before the pronoun and gives it meaning.

Similarly, in your writing, every pronoun must have a clear antecedent if your reader is to understand your meaning:

My friend Tony gave a *party* last weekend. *It* lasted until four in the morning.

Twenty-five *people* attended, and *they* all had a terrific time.

In a paragraph, you can work a thread of continuity from one sentence to another by using pronouns in place of a previously stated noun. On the one hand, pronouns make your reader work harder. By using *she, him, it,* or *them* to refer to a noun that appeared in an earlier sentence, you are demanding your reader's continuing interest because you are depending on your reader to carry your idea forward without your saying it again. But on the other hand, because pronouns are briefer and seem less repetitious than nouns and noun phrases, pronouns speed your ideas along and allow your reader to read more efficiently. The following paragraphs from *The Peter Principle* depend on pronouns for unity:

> Mr. N. Beeker had been a competent student, and became a popular science teacher. *His* lessons and lab periods were inspiring. *His* students were cooperative and kept the laboratory in order. Mr. Beeker was not good at paper work, but this weakness was offset, in the judgment of *his* superiors, by *his* success as a teacher.
>
> Beeker was promoted to head of the science department where *he* now had to order all science supplies and keep extensive records. His incompetence is evident! For three years running *he* has ordered new Bunsen burners, but no tubing for connecting *them*. As the old tubing deteriorates, fewer and fewer burners are operable, although new *ones* accumulate on the shelves.
>
> Beeker is not being considered for further promotion. *His* ultimate position is *one* for which *he* is incompetent.
>
> Dr. Laurence J. Peter and Raymond Hull

PRONOUNS IN SENTENCES

In a sentence, pronouns can fill the subject slot:

S   V
You   're

You're more than a face in the crowd.

Pronouns can be direct objects of verbs:

Our guests
love us
for our view.

S   V   D OBJ
Our guests   *love*   *us*

Pronouns can be objects of prepositions: **Come sail with us!**

with   *us*

Pronouns also show possession: **Stride Rite fits your baby for each stage of foot development.**

your baby

KINDS OF PRONOUNS

I, you, he, she, it, we, and they These words are called personal pronouns, not because they refer to people (for example, *it* never refers to a person), but because they refer to the concept of the three persons in grammar (see Chapter 14 on agreement):

First person: I am the President.
(Subject is the speaker—*I, we.*)

Second person: You are the President.
(Subject is spoken to—*you.*)

Third person: He is the President.
(Subject is spoken about—*he, she, it, they.*)

Nouns usually show plural by adding *-s* (*pencil/pencils, waiter/waiters, book/books*). They always add an apostrophe or *'s* to show possession (the pencil's eraser, the waiters' jackets, the book's cover). Unlike nouns, most pronouns change their forms completely to show plural (*I/we, he/they*). They change to show a subjective form (*I, he, she*), an objective form (*me, him, her*), and a possessive form that never has an apostrophe (*my, his, hers*).

PERSONAL PRONOUNS

SINGULAR

	Subjective pronoun	*Objective pronoun*	*Possessive pronoun*	*Possessive modifier*
First person	I	me	mine	my
Second person	you	you	yours	your
Third person	he	him	his	his
	she	her	hers	her
	it	it	its	its

PLURAL

First person	we	us	ours	our
Second person	you	you	yours	your
Third person	they	them	theirs	their

Note: *You* is the one personal pronoun that does not change form to show plural. The plural of *you* is *you*. *Youse* and *you all* are not used in standard English.

Nouns and Here is a listing that shows how personal pronouns can take the place
personal pronouns of nouns in sentences. Notice that a pronoun (*he*) frequently replaces more
than a noun. It replaces a noun plus its modifiers (*the tall waiter*)

Subjective:	*The tall waiter* spilled the ketchup.
	He spilled the ketchup.
Objective:	The tall waiter spilled *the ketchup.*
Direct object of verb	The tall waiter spilled *it.*
	The boss fired *the tall waiter.*
	The boss fired *him.*
Indirect object of verb	The boss gave *the waiter* severance pay.
	The boss gave *him* severance pay.
Object of preposition	The waiter smiled at *the cashier.*
	The waiter smiled at *her.*
Subject of infinitive	The boss asked *the tall waiter* to leave immediately.
	The boss asked *him* to leave immediately.
Possessive:	The *tall waiter's* red jacket hung in the kitchen.
	His red jacket hung in the kitchen.
	The friendly cashier's smile faded.
	Her smile faded.

Pronoun problems Problems with personal pronouns arise when writers are not certain which
form to use.

1. *Alice and I / Alice and me*

When the pronoun is part of a compound, writers have trouble
deciding whether to use *I* or *me.* Choose the form of the pronoun you
would use if the pronoun were alone.

Subject: Alice and *me* / Alice and *I* love Professor Greenberg.

Alice and _____ love Professor Greenberg.

(drop *Alice*) I love Professor Greenberg.

(No one would say *Me love Professor Greenberg.*)

YES: Alice and *I* love Professor Greenberg.

Subject: *Her* and the TV repairman / *She* and the TV repairman argued about Eric
Sevareid.

_____ and the TV repairman argued about Eric Sevareid.

(drop *the TV repairman*) *She* argued about Eric Sevareid.

(No one would say *Her argued about Eric Sevareid.*)

YES: *She* and the TV repairman argued about Eric Sevareid.

Direct object: Professor Greenberg admires Alice and *me*/Alice and *I*.

Professor Greenberg admires Alice and _____.

(drop *Alice*) Professor Greenberg admires *me*.

(No one would say *Professor Greenberg admires I*.)

YES: Professor Greenberg admires Alice and *me*.

Indirect object: Professor Greenberg gave Alice and *I*/Alice and *me* two tickets to *Room Service*.

Professor Greenberg gave Alice and _____ two tickets to *Room Service*.

(drop *Alice*) Professor Greenberg gave _____ two tickets to *Room Service*.

Professor Greenberg gave *me* two tickets to *Room Service*.

(No one would say Professor Greenberg gave *I* two tickets to *Room Service*.)

YES: Professor Greenberg gave Alice and *me* two tickets to *Room Service*.

Object of preposition: At the end of the semester, Professor Greenberg took home a bottle of wine from Alice and *I*/Alice and *me*.

At the end of the semester, Professor Greenberg took home a bottle of wine from Alice and _____.

(drop *Alice*) At the end of the semester, Professor Greenberg took home a bottle of wine from _____.

At the end of the semester, Professor Greenberg took home a bottle of wine from *me*.

(No one would say *from I*.)

YES: At the end of the semester, Professor Greenberg took home a bottle of wine from Alice and *me*.

As objects of the preposition *between,* both pronouns should be in the objective form: *you* and *me*. Never write *between you and I*.

NO: Between you and *I*, I think Eric Sevareid would like to be President.
YES: Between you and *me*, I think Eric Sevareid would like to be President.

2. *My mother, she thinks/my mother thinks*

Do not add an unnecessary subject to a sentence in the form of a reinforcing pronoun.

NO: My mother, *she* thinks she's a psychiatrist.
YES: My mother thinks she's a psychiatrist.

3. *We Democrats/us Democrats*

When the pronoun is followed by an appositive, choose the form of the pronoun you would use if the pronoun were alone.

Subject: Every four years *we* Democrats/*us* Democrats heal our wounds.

(drop *Democrats*) Every four years____we____heal our wounds.

YES: Every four years *we* Democrats heal our wounds.

Object: of we Democrats/of us Democrats

In accepting the Democratic nomination for Vice-President, July 15, 1976, Walter Mondale's use of *we Democrats* after the preposition *of* appears to have been an attempt at correctness and elegance. But when a pronoun is the object of a preposition, the correct form is the objective—*us Democrats*.

NO:

> **Delegates and friends:**
> I am proud to accept your nomination as your candidate for Vice President of the United States.
> I thank you for this confidence and I thank you for your confidence, and I pledge to you tonight and I pledge to all Americans that I will do everything in my power to elect Jimmy Carter the next President of the United States.
> Tonight Jimmy Carter is the embodiment of the hope and the dream not only of we Democrats but of all Americans.

YES: . . . the hope and dream not only of *us* Democrats but of all Americans.

4. *It's me/it's I*

It's me is now an accepted form in standard English. Although a linking verb is usually followed by a subjective form, *it's me* is commonly used in informal, and even in formal, speech and writing. To the question *Who is it?* a reply of *It is I* would sound super-correct and unnatural.

It is him (*her, them*) is commonly used in informal speech and writing, though less often in careful writing. Since language is always in the process of changing, it will be interesting to watch these forms as they make further inroads. Meanwhile, you decide or ask your teacher which form to use. In college writing, your teacher may prefer that you write *It is he*, even if you have been saying *it is him* all your life.

Spoken English: *I could swear it was her.*
Careful writing: *I could swear it was she.*

5. *Let him and me/let he and I*

Test which form sounds more comfortable by dropping one of the words after *let*.

Let *him and me/ he and I* do the dishes.

Let ___ do the dishes. Let ___ do the dishes.
Let *him* do the dishes. Let *me* do the dishes.

YES: Let *him and me* do the dishes.

<u>Who</u>, <u>whose</u>, <u>whom</u>, <u>which</u>, and <u>that</u>

These are relative pronouns:

Subjective	*Objective*	*Possessive*
who	whom	whose
that	that	
which	which	

Relative pronouns are used to combine sentences:

Jill is the girl. Jill went up the hill.
Jill is the girl ___ went up the hill.

Combined sentence:

Jill is the girl who went up the hill.

In the combined sentence, the subject-verb unit of the independent clause is *Jill is*, and the subject-verb unit of the dependent clause is *who went*.

Here is another example of combining sentences with a relative pronoun:

We have the air conditioner. It drips.
We have the air conditioner ___ drips.

Combined sentence:

We have the air conditioner *that* drips.

We have is the subject-verb unit of the independent clause, and *that drips* is the subject-verb unit of the dependent clause.

Pronoun problems **1.** *Who/whom*

Choose *who* or *whom* according to its function in the dependent clause.

NO: Jill is the girl *whom* I think went up the hill.
YES: Jill is the girl *who* I think went up the hill.

Who is subject of *went* and not object of *I think.*
I think is an explanatory remark inserted in the sentence.
(S-V OF DEPENDENT CLAUSE: *who went*)

NO: All night Mark worried about *whom* would win the free-style.
YES: All night Mark worried about *who* would win the free-style.
(S-V OF DEPENDENT CLAUSE: *who would win*)

Who is subject of *would win* and not object of preposition *about.* The entire clause *who would win the free-style* is the object of the preposition *about.*

2. *Whoever/whomever*

Choose *whoever* or *whomever* according to its function in the dependent clause.

NO: The Sanitation Department will accept *whomever* volunteers.
YES: The Sanitation Department will accept *whoever* volunteers.
(S-V OF DEPENDENT CLAUSE: *whoever volunteers*)

Whoever is subject of *volunteers* and not object of *accept.* The entire clause *whoever volunteers* is object of *accept.*

WATCH OUT FOR LOOK-ALIKES

Who, which, that serve other functions in other sentences. In the question *Who are you?* who is not a relative pronoun but a question pronoun. In *I want that record* and *I don't care which scarf you wear,* that and which are not pronouns but are paired with nouns (*that record, which scarf*) as modifiers.

Who? Whose? Whom? Which? What?

These pronouns introduce sentences that ask questions:

Who are you?
Whose hat are you wearing?
To *whom* is the letter addressed?
What was his name?
Which of these do you like best?

WATCH OUT FOR <u>WHAT</u> AND <u>WHICH</u>

What is a general inquiry. *Which* asks what one or ones of a limited number or group.

> *What* would you like to eat?
> *Which* dessert would you prefer, the pie or the mousse?

Question pronouns also introduce indirect questions:

> I want to know *who* is in the kitchen.
> I wonder *whose* raincoat you are wearing.
> He asked to *whom* the letter was addressed.
> We never asked *what* his name was.
> We want to know *which* of these detergents you like best.

Pronoun problems **1.** *Who* is it for?/*Whom* is it for?

Popular usage has been moving toward the elimination of *whom,* especially when it comes first in a question. Although *whom* used to be required in all positions as object of a verb (*Whom* did you see?) and as object of a preposition (*Whom* is it for?), constructions such as the following, in which *the question word comes first,* are now accepted in standard spoken English and in most forms of written English:

> *Who* is it for?
> *Who* did you see?
> *Who* are you looking for?
> *Who* did you give it to?

Nonetheless, in very careful writing (and this may include writing done for your college assignments), the outlook on these constructions is still undergoing change, leaving some readers unsatisfied unless *whom* appears as the object:

> *Whom* is it for?
> *Whom* did you see?
> *Whom* are you looking for?
> *Whom* did you give it to?

If you are not sure which form to use in your writing, decide for yourself or consult your teacher.

2. For *who?*/For *whom?*

When the question word is not the first word of the question, standard usage has not yet given up *whom* after a preposition (*To whom* is he married?) and at the end of a question (He saw *whom?*).

> For *whom* was the party given?
> You listened to *whom?*
> He saw *whom?*
> With *whom* did you go? (Though we commonly hear *Who with?*)
> To *whom* is he married?

Myself, yourself, himself, herself, itself, ourselves, yourselves, and themselves

These pronouns are used when the subject and object of a sentence (or of a preposition) are identical:

> We surgeons pride *ourselves* on our steely nerves.
>   (we surgeons = ourselves)
> He absented *himself* from the final autopsy.
>   (he = himself)
>   (I = myself)

'I Did It For Myself'

Pronoun problems **1.** *Himself/hisself*

Never use *hisself, theirself,* or *theirselves.* These forms are not acceptable in standard English.

> NO: He looked at *hisself* in the operating-room mirror.
> YES: He looked at *himself* in the operating-room mirror.

> NO: They congratulated *theirselves* on the tonsillectomy.
> YES: They congratulated *themselves* on the tonsillectomy.

The same pronouns are also used for emphasis.

> He *himself* cleaned the house.
> The owners *themselves* couldn't locate the door.

2. *Louise and I/Louise and myself/Louise and me*

Myself is often mistakenly used instead of *I* or *me* as a polite or "super-correct" subject or object of a sentence. Do not substitute *myself* for *I* or *me* in an effort to sound grand or polite.

> NO: Louise and *me* won first prize.
> NO: Louise and *myself* won first prize.
> YES: Louise and *I* won first prize.

Although *Louise and myself won* is sometimes heard, *myself* is not fully accepted when it is used as a subject. As the second or later member of a compound object, however, *myself* is accepted in current usage.

> NO: David congratulated Louise and *I*.
> YES: David congratulated Louise and *me*.
> YES: David congratulated Louise and *myself*.

3. *Than myself/than I   as myself/as I*
Standard usage now accepts *myself* after *as* or *than:*

> NO: No one understood the will as clearly as *me*.
> YES: No one understood the will as clearly as *I*.
> YES: No one understood the will as clearly as *myself*.

This, that, these, and those   *This, that, these,* and *those* point out or show what they refer to. When the same forms are paired with nouns, they function as modifiers.

Modifiers	*Pronouns*
These surfboards are huge.	*These* are huge.
This ring sparkles.	*This* sparkles.

Pronoun problems   **1.** *Them workmen/those workmen*

Do not use *them* with a noun. *Them* is always a pronoun and stands alone. Use *these* or *those* before a noun.

> NO: *Them* workmen will never get finished.
> YES: *Those* workmen will never get finished.

> NO: He's been watching *them* workmen all day.
> YES: He's been watching *those* workmen all day.

2. *This taxi/this here taxi   that lady/that there lady*

Do not use *this here* or *that there. This* and *that* point things out without assistance.

> NO: *This here* taxi is waiting for *that there* lady.
> YES: *This* taxi is waiting for *that* lady.

3. *This kind/these kind*

Though modifiers in English do not generally change their form to show plural (*yellow* rose, *yellow* roses), demonstrative modifiers do change form (*this* rose/*these* roses, *that* rose/*those* roses).

We often hear the usage *these kind of shoes/those type of earrings* because the emphasis in the mind of the speaker is on the plurals, *shoes* and *earrings,* rather than on the singular word *kind* or *type.* Although you are sure to hear these constructions frequently in speech, they are not yet fully accepted in careful writing. The "safe" constructions match singular *this* with singular *type* (*this type of shoes*) or plural *these* with plural *types* (*these types of shoes*).

Each other, one another, each other's, one another's

There are two reciprocal pronouns—*each other* and *one another*. They are used to show an exchange of action:

The cast congratulated *each other* on their performance.
The cast congratulated *one another* on their performance.

Jane and Lisa wore *each other's* clothes.
Jane and Lisa wore *one another's* clothes.

Pronoun problem **1.** *Each other's/each others'   one another's/one anothers'*

Even though these phrases refer to two or more individuals, they are always spelled in the singular.

NO: The students read *each others'* essays.
YES: The students read *each other's* essays.

NO: The sisters rode *one anothers'* bicycles.
YES: The sisters rode *one another's* bicycles.

Indefinite Pronouns An indefinite pronoun does not refer to a specific person or thing. There are many indefinite pronouns:

each	none	one another	everybody
either	several	another	everyone
neither	all	anybody	everything
both	any	anyone	nobody
some	most	anything	no one
few	each	somebody	nothing
many	each one	someone	
much	one	something	

All of these words can function alone in a sentence as if they were nouns. (See page 390 for agreement problems and page 396 for a discussion of pronoun reference.) When indefinite pronouns are paired with nouns, they function as modifiers:

Modifiers	*Pronouns*
Many electric typewriters were broken.	*Many* were broken. *Many* (of the electric typewriters) were broken.
Several applicants were successful.	*Several* were successful. *Several* (of the applicants) were successful.
Some wines go well with fish.	*Some* go well with fish. *Some* (of the wines) go well with fish.

Note: *Some* can be singular or plural, depending on its antecedent.

Pronoun problems _Someone/his, someone/their, everybody/his, everybody/their, no one/he, no one/ they_

Use a singular pronoun when the intent of the antecedent is singular. An indefinite pronoun is usually considered to be singular and is referred to by singular pronouns.

NO: _Someone_ left _their_ raincoat on the chair.
YES: _Someone_ left _his_ or _her_ raincoat on the chair.
(One person left one raincoat.)

NO: _Everybody_ drove _their_ own car to the field.
YES: _Everybody_ drove _his_ own car to the field.
(Each person got into his own car and drove it to the field.)

NO: _No one_ is actually coerced into doing what _they_ don't want.
YES: _No one_ is actually coerced into doing what _he_ doesn't want.
(Focus should remain on individual's freedom.)

NO: If somebody did something wrong, Ms. Black really let _them_ have it.
YES: If somebody did something wrong, Ms. Black really let _her_ have it.
(for group of women)

Some/their, everyone/they

Use a plural pronoun when the intent of the antecedent is plural.

YES: _Some_ of the guests left _their_ raincoats in the hall.
(Many people left many raincoats.)
YES: _Everyone_ was in the library, but _they_ all left to get pizza.
(Although _everyone_ looks singular (one) and always uses a singular verb (_was_), this sentence would be illogical if carried out in the singular: _Everyone was in the library, but he left to get pizza._)

Rewrite in plural If you are uncertain about whether to use a singular or a plural pronoun (or if you waver between the two), rewrite the sentence so that the antecedent is unmistakably plural. Then use the pronouns _they_ and _them_.

NO: If somebody did something wrong, Ms. Black really let _them_ have it.
YES: If her _students_ did something wrong, Ms. Black really let _them_ have it.

Exercise 1 Fill each empty slot in the following sentences with the appropriate form of the pronoun.

> Example: Let _____ and me give you the details. (he/him)
>
> Let *him* and me give you the details.

1. Antonio is a tailor _____ I think sews meticulously. (who/whom)

2. They hurried to her house to break the news _____. (themselves/theirselves)

3. Gordon and _____ jogged to the meeting of "Citizens on the Run." (I/myself/me)

4. The commissioner lectured Gordon and _____ about industrial carelessness. (I/myself/me)

5. Benjamin Franklin and _____ adored Paris. (I/me)

6. Between you and _____, Edward would have made a dandy king. (I/me)

7. Humphrey invited Ida and _____ to tea. (I/myself/me)

8. Watch out for _____ bumps in the road. (those/them)

9. "Who is it?" "It's _____." (me/I)

10. Let Ben and _____ meet her at the Optimistic Cafe. (I/me)

Exercise 2 Fill each empty slot in the following sentences with an appropriate form of the pronoun.

> Example: Miss Irene gave Grandma and _____ identical haircuts. (I/me/myself)
>
> YES: Miss Irene gave Grandma and *me* identical haircuts.
> YES: Miss Irene gave Grandma and *myself* identical haircuts.

1. Rosemary and Leonard ate _____ lunches. (each others'/each other's)

2. No one worked harder than _____. (I/me/myself)

3. I know _____ you are. (who/whom)

4. _____ hat did Bella wear, the straw or the felt? (what/which)

5. The only hope for _____ students is to have Dean Flint speak to the president. (we/us)

6. The burglar and _____ stared at each other through the dining room curtains. (I/me)

7. The Air and Space Museum is the first place in Washington that you and _____ should visit. (I/me)

8. The waiter at The Iron Gate poured honey wine for Bridget and _____. (I/me)

9. To _____ is the mailgram addressed? (who/whom)

10. World War I fliers used to dress _____ in fur-lined leather hats and coats. (themselves/theirselves)

PRONOUN AGREEMENT   The following paragraph from *The Peter Principle* demonstrates how a writer moves a subject forward in a piece of writing:

> Mr. N. Beeker was promoted to head of the science department where *he* now had to order all science supplies and keep extensive records. *His* incompetence is evident! For three years running *he* has ordered new Bunsen burners, but no tubing for connecting *them*.
>
> Dr. Laurence J. Peter and Raymond Hull

Beeker continues in the paragraph in the form of *he* and *his*. *Bunsen burners* continues in the form of *them*.

As you develop a subject, you don't have to keep repeating the same word over and over again. You can use a pronoun to refer to it. Pronouns keep the reader on the trail of a noun because they offer built-in clues about the noun they refer to. The form of a pronoun helps the reader remember the unrepeated noun.

He and *his,* for example, refer us back to *Mr. N. Beeker. He* and *his* remind us that *Beeker* is third person, masculine in gender, and singular in number. *Them* is always third person and plural. *Them* clearly refers to the plural noun *Bunsen burners*. This built-in linking principle—of gender, number, and person—is known as agreement between a pronoun and its antecedent.

Lack of agreement can create serious problems in writing, because whenever the gender, number, and person of the pronoun do not correspond to the gender, number, and person of the antecedent, the reader is suddenly thrown off the trail of the original noun. Although pronouns help you link ideas, they succeed only if you use them consistently. Don't frustrate your reader with chains of pronouns that mysteriously lose their antecedents.

See the confusion that can result when pronouns do not agree with the nouns they refer to:

> When <u>a person</u> reads about *an earthquake* in another country, *it* hardly affects <u>them</u>. Of course <u>they</u> feel bad and upset that people were killed. But because *they* happen in such distant places, and because *they* don't affect *their* own lives, <u>a person</u> wouldn't be too traumatized by *it*. If *an earthquake* killed <u>their</u> relatives in California <u>they</u> would be much more emotionally upset by *them*.

Notice how these chains of reference break down because plural pronouns are used to refer to a singular noun:

<u>a person</u>: <u>them</u>, <u>they</u>, <u>their</u>
an earthquake : they, them, as well as *it*

Here are other sentences in which the pronouns do not agree with their nouns.

NO: When a *student* starts a writing course, *they* may want to keep a journal.

YES: When a *student* starts a writing course, *he* may want to keep a journal.

YES: When *students* start a writing course, *they* may want to keep a journal.

Pronoun and antecedent agree:

student—he
students—they

NO: If *anybody* goes to the admitting office of the hospital, *you* have to fill out *your* Blue Cross forms first.

YES: If *you* go to the admitting office of the hospital, *you* have to fill out *your* Blue Cross forms first.

YES: *Anybody* who goes to the admitting office of the hospital has to fill out *his* Blue Cross forms first.

YES: *People* who go to the admitting office of the hospital have to fill out *their* Blue Cross forms first.

Pronoun and antecedent agree:

Anybody—his
People—their

As a writer, you can move your ideas forward smoothly and efficiently by using pronouns. Be sure that your pronouns agree with the nouns they refer to, especially in number.
Plural:

People—they—them—their
Students—they—them—their

Singular:

A person—he or she—him or her—his or her
A student—he or she—him or her—his or her
Anybody—he or she—him or her—his or her

<u>One . . . his/
one . . . their</u> Never use *their* with *one. One* is always singular. Use *one's* or *his* or *her* or else rewrite the sentence.

NO: When a girl's father appears, *one* experiences danger signals going off inside *their head.*

> YES: When a girl's father appears, *one* experiences danger signals going off inside *one's* head.

> YES: When a girl's father appears, danger signals go off inside a guy's head.

France and Belgium . . . their/France or Belgium . . . its

Two nouns joined by *and* require a plural pronoun.

> YES: France and Belgium fly *their* flags at the border.

Two singular nouns joined by *or* require a singular pronoun. The intent is alternative, that is, one or the other but not both.

> YES: France or Belgium has repainted *its* flagpole at the border.

If one of two nouns joined by *or* is singular and the other is plural, the pronoun usually agrees with the closer noun:

> Either the company doctor or the accountants are scheduled to receive *their* bonus today.

> Either the accountants or the company doctor is scheduled to receive *her* bonus today.

The band is unpacking/the band are unpacking

Collective nouns having a singular intent are referred to by a singular pronoun. Collective nouns having a plural intent are referred to by a plural pronoun.

> The band is unpacking *its* instruments and is keeping an eye on the conductor.

> (The band is a musical unit that is preparing to play as a unit.)

> The band are unpacking *their* instruments and are chatting with each other.

> (The emphasis is on the individual members of the band, who are separately taking instruments out of cases and talking.)

CHOOSING A PRONOUN TO PRESIDE *Point of view* is a term writers use to describe the angle of vision they take in their writing. They may use the personal *I* or *we,* or address their audience by using *you,* or speak about their subject by using *he, she, it,* or *they.* Choosing a point of view and a personal pronoun to establish that point of view tangles up the best writers at one time or another, though how many false starts are to be found in the rough drafts of America's famous writers we may never know, since most of them edit their sentences carefully before their writing goes to press. There are two main problems in determining which pronoun will preside over a piece of writing.

The first problem is the careless shift from one subject to another within a sentence or from one sentence to the next. It is usually the unlucky beginner whose sentences show up with their pronouns wobbling. They may begin a paragraph with *Most people believe,* shift to *Some of you may doubt* in the second sentence, and further along shift to *One can never be certain unless he.* See how the following paragraph, which has obviously snarled up its writer, ends by confusing the reader.

> When *a person* reads about an earthquake in another country, it hardly affects *you.* Of course, *I* feel bad and upset that people are killed. But because earthquakes happen in such distant places and because they don't affect *your* own life, *people* aren't too traumatized by them. If an earthquake killed *my* relatives in California, *you* would be much more emotionally upset by it.

The solution is to rewrite the paragraph using a consistent presiding pronoun, or point of view. (See below for alternative ways to rewrite the paragraph.)

Now the second problem arises: which pronoun should you choose—*I, you, we, he, one, they*—and what will help you decide?

Much contemporary writing seems to present the subjective point of view of the writer—journalism, books, film scripts, magazine articles, and particularly the essay, which depends for its character not on the event, but on the writer's view of the event. (For example, a car accident might be the subject of a news report, but the speculations and personal experience of one of the victims of the accident would constitute the makings of an essay.) Such writing makes habitual use of the personal pronouns *I, you, we.* In fact, until you become a more experienced writer, you would do well to refrain from using *one* as the pronoun to preside over your writing, since *one* tends to be impersonal and difficult to maneuver as you write. (Certainly, there may be occasional impasses where *one* or *one's* will be the word to break down the block and allow you to proceed.) You can establish your personality at the outset by the choice of an appropriately relaxed, personal, and informal pronoun. *I,* of course, is the indispensable pronoun in essay writing. Except in technical writing and in an objective narrative or report, the first-person pronoun is always appropriate. It says you are ready to come forward as the bearer of the news here printed, as the individual who has experienced these events and is willing to be known by name. *We* is also useful, a pronoun that many writing teachers especially recommend as a compromise between the personal, sometimes confessional, *I* and the distanced third-person *he* or *she.*

Can you describe the changes in the effect of the following paragraphs as the presiding pronoun changes:

> 1. When *I* read about an earthquake in another country, it hardly affects *me.* Of course, *I* feel bad and upset that people are killed. But because earthquakes happen in such distant places and because they don't affect *my* own life, *I* am not too traumatized by them. If an earthquake killed *my* relatives in California, *I* would be much more emotionally upset by it.

2. When *we* read about an earthquake in another country, it hardly affects *us*. Of course, *we* feel bad and upset that people are killed. But because earthquakes happen in such distant places and because they don't affect *our* own lives, *we* are not too traumatized by them. If an earthquake killed *our* relatives in California, *we* would be much more emotionally upset by it.

3. When *one* reads about an earthquake in another country, it hardly affects *one*. Of course, *one* feels bad and upset that people are killed. But because earthquakes happen in such distant places and because they don't affect *one's* own life, *one* is not too traumatized by them. If an earthquake killed *one's* relatives in California, *one* would be much more emotionally upset by it.

4. When *a person* reads about an earthquake in another country, it hardly affects *him* (or *her*). Of course, *he* feels bad and upset that people are killed. But because earthquakes happen in such distant places and because they don't affect *his* own life, *he* is not too traumatized by them. If an earthquake killed *his* relatives in California, *he* would be much more emotionally upset by it.

5. When *people* read about an earthquake in another country, it hardly affects *them*. Of course, *they* feel bad and upset that other people are killed. But because earthquakes happen in such distant places and because they don't affect *their* own lives, *they* are not too traumatized by them. If an earthquake killed *their* own relatives in California, *they* would be much more emotionally upset by it.

6. When *you* read about an earthquake in another country, it hardly affects *you*. Of course, *you* feel bad and upset that other people are killed. But because earthquakes happen in such distant places and because they don't affect *your* own life, *you* are not too traumatized by them. If the earthquake killed *your* own relatives in California, *you* would be much more emotionally upset by it.

Above all, you have to think of consistency in choosing presiding pronouns. Avoid shifting pronouns without a good reason. Study the sample paragraphs closely. Read them aloud. Paragraphs 1, 2, and 5 are comfortable and contain entirely respectable forms for use in your essays. Paragraphs 3 and 4, on the other hand, may strike your ear as rather strained, and paragraph 4 raises the issue of sexist language, which is discussed below. Paragraphs 2 and 6 actively and directly involve the audience. All of these options are available to you. As you perceive their different possibilities, you will begin to involve your readers by choosing the appropriate pronouns.

SEXIST LANGUAGE Most writers today are sensitive to the use of sexist language, and few would wish to contribute further to the problem by referring to women in some "second-class" way or by burying women in all-male language. Until recently, people never gave much thought to sentences like these:

> A student will enroll in *his* appropriate English course according to *his* placement test score.

> It is the passenger's responsibility to keep *his* ticket visible at all times.

Today, writers pay more attention to the implications of such sentences. To help you avoid sexist language in your own writing as often as possible, we offer these guidelines:

1. Convert from singular to plural whenever your meaning will not be altered by the change in number:

> *Students* will enroll in *their* appropriate English *courses* according to *their* placement test scores.

TIPS FOR WRITERS

Avoid sexist terms:

> *Authoress, poetess, woman doctor* are terms that suggest there is a difference between a real author, a real poet, and a real doctor and a female author, a female poet, and a female doctor. Call an author an author. Similarly, call a Jew a Jew (not a Jewess). Avoid using *lady* as the corresponding term for *man*. The opposite of *man* is *woman*.

> Some new designations, like *chairperson,* are catching on. Others, like *policeperson,* seem to resist.

> Remember that a woman who is a psychiatrist would rather be known as a psychiatrist than as a "lady psychiatrist."

Be alert to new proposals and combinations:

> *A student will enroll in their appropriate course* still sounds like a mistake to many ears.

> *S/he* has not yet caught on.

At best, these designations are likely to continue changing and arousing debate.

As you think about language, consider your own attitudes, but consider also those of your readers. Until improved strategies arise, our suggestions may help you to offend as few readers as possible and keep your writing free of cumbersome usages.

> It is the *passengers'* responsibility to keep *their* tickets visible at all times.

2. Use *he or she* sparingly. You may want to use the whole phrase to show that you are fair, but if used excessively *he or she* becomes cumbersome and tedious to read:

A student will enroll in *his or her* appropriate English course according to *his or her* placement test score.

It is the passenger's responsibility to keep *his or her* ticket visible at all times.

3. Omit all unnecessary pronouns:

Placement test scores determine which English courses students enroll in. Tickets must be kept visible at all times.

4. Use *she* and *her* when the persons referred to are female.

Everybody in the girls' locker room grabbed *her* sneakers and ran out on the field.

5. Use *he* and *him* when the reference continues over a long passage and none of the above alternatives satisfies you. Although this practice may offend some people, we suggest it in the interest of emphasizing vigorous language, even at the occasional expense of advancing a worthwhile cause.

REFERENCE
OF PRONOUNS A pronoun should unmistakably refer to a noun (or a group of words functioning as a noun) stated in the same sentence or in a preceding sentence. Your reader should be able to identify, immediately and with no confusion, the exact antecedent of a pronoun. If there is any chance that your reader will be unsure of the antecedent, replace the doubtful pronoun with an explicitly stated noun or rewrite the sentence.

1. Explicit reference to a noun creates no problems:

What were the first languages ever spoken? How did *they* sound and how were *they* structured?
(*They* clearly refers to *first languages*.)

2. Implied reference to a noun that is not stated in the sentence requires that you rewrite to include the noun:

Confusing: If you are exempted from English 1, *it* won't give you three credits.
(What won't give you three credits? English 1 or exemption from English 1? Add an explicit noun.)

Rewritten: An *exemption* from English 1 won't give you three credits.

3. You must also rewrite if the reference is to a noun in the possessive case:

Confusing: After Rhoda's analysis of my handwriting, she respected me more as an artist.

Rewritten: After Rhoda analyzed my handwriting, she respected me more as an artist.

4. Replace a vague pronoun with an exact noun:

Confusing: In my old high school, *they* broadcast *Wizard of Oz* records between classes.
   (Who is *they?*)

Rewritten: In my old high school, the media center broadcasts *Wizard of Oz* records between classes.

5. Get rid of unnecessary pronouns:

Wordy: In this comment, *it* says I tend to want to be too wordy.

Rewritten: This comment says I tend to be wordy.

6. If a pronoun can easily refer to more than one noun, rewrite the sentence to eliminate ambiguity:

Ambiguous: The priest sat next to an old man and read *his* book.

Copout: The priest sat next to an old man and read his (the priest's) book.

Rewritten: The priest sat next to an old man and read a book.

7. The pronouns *this, that, such,* and *which* can stand for an entire preceding statement as well as a single, explicit noun:

She wouldn't spend her two-week vacation behind a fishing pole. *That* was the problem, and David knew it.
   (The problem was that she wouldn't spend two weeks fishing.)

But don't rely on *this, that, such,* and *which* to link poorly stated ideas and cover incomplete or illogical references:

Confusing: Esther would not admit turning left which later became an issue in court.
   (What became an issue? Esther's not admitting a left turn or the left turn itself?)

Rewritten: Esther would not admit turning left, and a left turn later became an issue in court.

8. To avoid confusion, do not use the pronoun *it* near an *it* used as a structure word. Rewrite to eliminate the structure word.

Confusing: Although your gardenia plant produced flowers last year, *it's* good that *it* has been repotted.

Rewritten: Although your gardenia plant produced flowers last year, repotting *it* was a good idea.

Exercise 3 Rewrite each of the following sentences entirely in the plural. At the conclusion of the exercise, write a sentence explaining why it is preferable to use the plural rather than the singular in these sentences.

Example: Everyone should do as well as they can on the road test.

Rewritten: Candidates for a driver's license should do as well as they can on the road test.

1. If a voter is not properly registered, they may not vote.
2. When a student reads a poem, they often give their own interpretations.
3. Every passenger on this bus has their eyes on the masked gunman with the jar of mayonnaise.
4. Each of them use heavy makeup on their eyes and barbarous language in their conversation.
5. If one tilts one's head to the far left, they can see Orion slipping into view.
6. Johnson and Johnson never cut their knee.
7. The committee worked on its report all weekend, but they still weren't finished by Monday.
8. Everybody in the encounter group stares at their partners for a half hour without touching.
9. Whenever a collection agent calls my Dad, they threaten to notify his employer.
10. Everybody waited onstage to do their dance for Mr. Champion.

Exercise 4 Rewrite the following sentences to establish clear reference between pronouns and their antecedents. If a sentence is clear, mark it C. If a sentence is not clear, improve it.

1. For instance, there are many children living in slum and poor areas with great potentials, but they are not enhanced because they feel they can't get ahead.
2. We've been conditioned to want, to need, to be greedy. We're never satisfied. All this must be changed.
3. I was bombarded with warnings about registration. My friends told me they close down everything by the time freshmen register.
4. Since the French class already had thirty students registered for it, I had to get an overtally slip to enroll but two other girls wanted them at the same time.
5. Everyone calls me crazy and that may be true.
6. As people began to think about death, it became ritualized.
7. The governor will allow more water into the rivers which the city says will threaten its water supply.

8. The cottage was situated on a hill which had a splendid view from every window.

9. Walking the dog in the wet grass which I never like is a nuisance in the early mornings.

10. I put the frozen strawberries in the sink because it was leaking.

Exercise 5   Correct any pronoun errors that you find in the following sentences.

1. A college student should be able to buy their lunches at reduced rates.

2. A parent has their eye on you at all times.

3. They brought they tape recorders to the zoo.

4. A person going into business has to decide what kind of business he or she wants to spend their life in.

5. People on airplanes can have the kind of food he or she likes best.

6. Most of us know that if we want to cook nourishing meals you need fresh food.

7. Many people take a holiday to rest yourself.

8. Everyone who parks their car at school is usually late for class.

9. Students can't expect to have a career waiting if you are afraid to speak out and say what's on your mind.

10. Employees have to get to work early if you want a parking place.

Exercise 6   Rewrite the following short paragraphs of sabotaged student writing, using a consistent presiding pronoun, or point of view, in each:

1. We are all born into this world as equals, but for various reasons, not all people are treated as equals. This inequality begins when you reach the age of five, for that is when you will enter elementary school. In school, the child is no longer "Mommy's little darling." You now have to prove yourself to the other children and also to your teacher. If one seems different from the other students, they are treated differently, and these differences could be anything: pants, shoes, speech, religion, and so forth. It really doesn't matter. Right from the start, you think that as long as you are different, there is something wrong with you.

2. I know that I will not feel successful if I am not married by the age of twenty-four. Even though with the Women's Lib movement it is now acceptable for you to be thirty years old and unmarried, a person's views can't change. I truly believe that we are all products of our parents' values. And since one's parents have always assumed that they would be married by that age, I have assumed that notion also.

3. Last Wednesday Allen Ginsberg appeared in Academic 170, and I went to see him perform. I must state at the outset that my feelings about this event were totally ambiguous even to myself. Even if a person

knows what to expect of him before going to the reading, you still haven't reached a verdict when you get there, and I can honestly confess that Ginsberg's performance left an indelible impression on me.

There are a couple of reasons to explain this phenomenon. The first reason is that the main objective of an artist is to express your innermost feelings. Secondly, the way in which one does this and how well they do it equals the sum of his success. Allen Ginsberg not only presented his innermost self but went way beyond it. From one's personal experience, you would contend that he was successful in communicating with a person on a one-to-one basis rather than on the group level. As I looked about, you could readily notice that he had also successfully put everyone else in a trance.

Exercise 7 Rewrite the following student writing so that each pronoun has a clearly identifiable antecedent with which it agrees. Choose a point of view and keep it consistently. Let one pronoun preside.

When it comes to making a conscious effort to help keep a public place clean, most people just don't make the effort. I'm a maintenance man for a department store. If you did make the effort to help keep the public place where I work clean, we probably wouldn't have a job.

The area that you have to spend the most time cleaning is the employees' lunchroom. They go there during breaks, lunch, and dinner. The maintenance department supplies the waste containers for garbage and the ashtrays for cigarette butts. When they finish their food, they will generally either throw their papers on the floor or leave it on the table. One will on occasion throw their papers in the garbage. An employee who smokes will either flick their ashes on the floor or on their table. Everybody's butts I usually find on the floor and in half-filled soda cups. The cigarettes may be found anywhere other than in the ashtray because you steal the ashtrays or you fill it with gum. Sometimes an employee will remark, "Aren't these people pigs? They don't even clean up after themselves," as they proceed to walk away from their littered table.

Punctuation and Capitalization

Chapter 16

PURPOSES OF PUNCTUATION

punctuationasweknowittodayisonlyafewhundredyearsoldmanuscripts
ofthe1400sdidn'thavespacebetweenwordssentencesorparagraphsoneword
ranintoanotherandonesentenceranintoanotherandoneparagraphraninto
another

Did you have trouble reading this? It says: *"Punctuation, as we know it today, is only a few hundred years old. Manuscripts of the 1400s didn't have space between words, sentences, or paragraphs. One word ran into another, and one sentence ran into another, and one paragraph ran into another."* No comma, period, capital letter, or paragraph indentation guided readers through a piece of writing. Without punctuation, they had to guess their way through uncharted ground each time they read anything. Many inexperienced writers today don't allow punctuation to work for them. They might as well be back in the 1400s. They're never certain where a comma belongs; they signal wrong turns and full stops where only a pause is needed. Some writers are helpless in the face of a semicolon or quotation marks and simply never use them. Other writers, to play it safe, over-punctuate and hope for the best:

Would you believe? that, I, alone (and nobody else!) learned to sail, that sunfish, out into the bay? I, also, learned to waterski; on "one" ski!

Punctuation like this can be as bothersome as no punctuation at all. It forces the reader to stop and start and start again to understand the message.

With punctuation, you offer your reader the hesitations, pauses, whispers, and shouts that are common to speech. More important, you show the relationship between ideas and emphasize those ideas that are important. A period at the end of a sentence tells your reader to come to a full stop and *separate* that idea from the next. A semicolon between clauses, on the other hand, tells your reader to *make* connections between your ideas. The same sentence can often be punctuated in several ways, allowing for varied emphases and effects. As a writer, you must punctuate each sentence in the way that best expresses your intent. Keep in mind that your primary goal is *clarity:* your reader should be able to understand your intent without stumbling over excess punctuation marks or passing over pauses that need to be signaled by additional punctuation. The smooth, uncluttered sentence containing just the necessary punctuation is what you're after, because overpunctuation can handicap your reader as much as no punctuation.

The key to effective punctuation is an understanding of the sentence and its elements as well as coordination, subordination, and modification. (See Chapters 6–9.) This chapter, built on your understanding of the whole sentence, is divided into three parts:

1. How to end the sentence
2. How to join sentences
3. How to punctuate within the sentence

This chapter presents the currently accepted rules of punctuation and also discusses the options. We encourage you to use punctuation to support your meaning—to join related ideas with a semicolon; to introduce a list with a colon; to show a break in thought with a dash. As you experiment with your writing, you will discover how to call attention to your meaning through effective punctuation.

HOW TO END A SENTENCE

Period Use a period to end a *statement.*

A smile doesn't cost much.

YOU JUST INHERITED $400,000.

Question mark Use a question mark to end a direct *question*.

What is Organic Food?

ARE YOU READY FOR ADULT MUSIC?

Exclamation point Use an exclamation point to end an *emphatic or strongly worded statement*.

Call the police! These hands are a crime!

Use the exclamation point sparingly. You lose emphasis rather than gain it when you overuse exclamation points:

I will not join you for dinner at the Pizza Barn! I hate pizza! I must eat something else, or I'll turn into a cheese-covered pie crust! I've had it!

Your reader says, "Ho-hum. There she goes ranting and raving again," and the exclamation points mean little.

You can turn many statements into questions or exclamations by using a question mark or an exclamation point.

Seeing is believing.   (statement)
Seeing is believing?   (question)

Seeing is believing!

(exclamation)

Occasionally, you will use a sentence fragment to emphasize a point. Punctuate the fragment as a complete sentence.

Yes.
Of course!
Really?
Oh no!
Why?

WATCH OUT FOR INDIRECT QUESTIONS

End an indirect question with a period. End a direct question with a question mark.

Do not confuse an indirect question with a direct question.

> DIRECT QUESTION: She asked, *"Are you hungry?"*
> INDIRECT QUESTION: She asked whether I was hungry.

Learn the differences between a direct question and an indirect question. An indirect question is a statement, not a question, because it includes the idea, but not the exact words, of a question. Since an indirect question is a statement, it ends with a period.

	Direct Question	Indirect Question
VERB CHANGES	*Are* you hungry?	She asked whether I *was* hungry.
	Will you *join* us?	She asked if I *would join* them.
PRONOUN CHANGES	Are *you* hungry?	She asked whether *I* was hungry.
	Will *you* join *us*?	She asked if *I* would join *them*.
SUBJECT-VERB ORDER	V S Are you hungry?	S V She asked whether I was hungry.
	V S V Will you join us?	S V She asked if I would join them.

If and *whether* are clues that the sentence is an indirect question **and does not end with a question mark.**

Exercise 1 Rewrite the following direct questions as indirect questions. Provide a speaker for each indirect question.

> Example: Are you hungry?
> Mary Ann asked if I was hungry. (Mary Ann is the speaker.)

1. Do you want to eat lunch now?
2. Do you want to try Burger King or stay with McDonald's?
3. Does Henry like Burger King?
4. Should I go with you or stay with Henry?
5. How are their onion rings?
6. Will you ask for extra pickles?
7. Do you have enough money?
8. Does Mary Ann eat a Big Mac every day?
9. Does she order French fries and a Coke?
10. How does she stay so thin?

There are two ways to join whole sentences when you want to give them equal emphasis.

1. Join sentences with a comma plus a coordinator:

, and

, but

, or

, nor

, for

, yet

, so

_____ , and _____

He hit a home run in the bottom of the ninth, and the crowd went wild.

**Their engines
may be in the same place,
but their prices aren't.**

2. Join sentences with a semicolon:

_____ ; _____

He hit a home run in the bottom of the ninth; the crowd went wild.

Knicks Defeat Kings; Haywood Stands Out

Words like *however, therefore,* and *meanwhile* may begin a second clause (_____; however, _____). Compare the following sentences:

Kingman hit a home run, and the crowd went wild.
When Kingman hit a home run, the crowd went wild.
Kingman hit a home run; meanwhile, the crowd went wild.

Meanwhile, unlike *and* or *when,* can be shifted, with some change in emphasis, to another part of the clause:

Meanwhile, the crowd went wild.
The crowd, *meanwhile,* went wild.
The crowd went wild, *meanwhile.*

When a word like *meanwhile* introduces a second clause, use a semicolon before it and a comma after it:

Kingman hit a home run; _____, the crowd went wild.
Kingman hit a home run; *meanwhile,* the crowd went wild.

The following is a special group of words like *however, therefore,* and *meanwhile.* Become familiar with the words in the list, and remember that

TIPS FOR WRITERS

The semicolon doesn't slow your reader down as the period does. The period separates; the semicolon joins, adding a forceful connection between two sentences.

> She was in an exuberant mood; her laughter was childlike, bright, brittle.
>
> Joyce Carol Oates

Notice in the following sentence how three sentences are joined:

_____; _____; _____.

> We in education must remind ourselves that this generation of critics is a product of our system. We taught them to question the status quo; we encouraged their hope and aspiration for all; we trained them to seek reform through the democratic process.
>
> Sydney Marland

when the word begins a second clause, a semicolon goes before it and a comma after it.

accordingly	however	on the other hand
also	indeed	otherwise
as a result	in fact	similarly
at the same time	likewise	still
besides	meanwhile	that is
consequently	moreover	then
for example	nevertheless	therefore
furthermore	nonetheless	thus
hence		

Run-on sentences   A run-on sentence occurs when two or more sentences are incorrectly joined. There are two types of run-ons. When no punctuation mark joins the sentences, the run-on is called a *fused sentence:*

Kingman hit a home run in the bottom of the ninth the crowd went wild.

When only a comma is used as a connector, the run-on is called a *comma splice:*

Kingman hit a home run in the bottom of the ninth, the crowd went wild.

There are several ways to eliminate run-on sentences:

1. Use a period:

Kingman hit a home run in the bottom of the ninth. The crowd went wild.

WATCH OUT FOR COMMAS

1. Use commas to join very short, related sentences:

> Drivers shout, dogs bark, the race is on.

Do not use a comma to join longer coordinated sentences. When in doubt about when to use a comma, you're always safe to use the options for joining sentences on page 405.

2. Do not separate compound parts of a sentence. Do not use a comma to separate the elements of a compound verb:

> NO: They often visited the lighthouse, and watched the fishing boats return to the pier.
>
> SV: they visited and watched
>
> Compound verb: visited and watched
>
> YES: They often visited the lighthouse and watched the fishing boats return to the pier.

Do not use a comma to separate the elements of a compound subject:

> NO: Sam, and Harriet visited their children in California.
>
> SV: Sam and Harriet visited
>
> Compound subject: Sam and Harriet
>
> YES: Sam and Harriet visited their children in California.

3. When two clauses are joined by a coordinator (*and*, *but*, or *nor*), do not use a comma *after* the coordinator:

> NO: I've worked hard this year, and, I need a vacation.
>
> YES: I've worked hard this year, and I need a vacation.
>
> NO: I usually vacation in Mexico, but, I'll go to Buenos Aires this year.
>
> YES: I usually vacation in Mexico, but I'll go to Buenos Aires this year.

---

2. Use a semicolon:

> Kingman hit a home run in the bottom of the ninth; the crowd went wild.

3. Use a comma plus a coordinator.

> Kingman hit a home run in the bottom of the ninth, and the crowd went wild.

4. Use a semicolon plus a word like "meanwhile":

> Kingman hit a home run in the bottom of the ninth; meanwhile, the crowd went wild.

5. Subordinate one clause to another:

> When Kingman hit a home run in the bottom of the ninth, the crowd went wild.

> The crowd went wild when Kingman hit a home run in the bottom of the ninth.

See Chapter 8 for a discussion of coordination and subordination of sentences.

Exercise 2   Write four pairs of sentences and connect each pair with a semicolon. Begin the second sentence in each pair with one of the following openers. Watch the punctuation.

Example: I could never hit a softball very well; however, I still try.

however

on the other hand

in fact

at the same time

meanwhile

therefore

for example

Exercise 3   The following sentences, taken from a student's paper called "How Lucky Can't You Be," are representative of problems that occur when sentences are joined. Supply the necessary punctuation for each sentence.

1. I had already taken four out of five finals but the most difficult was yet to come.
2. Two weeks later the date for the final was arranged and I spent hours and hours studying for the exam.
3. I didn't mind so much that the final had been canceled or that I had to travel to the college to find out but I regretted the extra weeks I had spent studying.
4. Everything seemed to be going wrong but I knew that my luck had to change eventually.
5. I began to win rather steadily so naturally they switched dealers.
6. I was betting five dollars a shot and had three chances to win twenty when I was up fifteen but it never came and I lost my original ten.
7. I picked numbers seven five and three and five seven and three came in.
8. I always believed in Lady Luck but after these experiences I decided to study astrology.

TIPS FOR WRITERS —THE COLON AND THE DASH

1. The colon (:) can draw sentences together when the clauses that follow the colon define or explain the first clause. Consider the following example:

> Life in America has indeed become easier for most people: the car is more efficient than the horse; death in childbirth has sharply fallen; certain diseases have totally disappeared; and even a kind word can be said occasionally for a computer.
>
> Lillian Hellman

(The four independent clauses that follow the colon explain *how* life in America has become easier.)

2. The dash (—) can also link parts of sentences. Since the material that follows the dash often sounds like an afterthought, use the dash only when you want this special effect. Observe how Peter Elbow uses the dash:

> If you are serious about wanting to improve your writing, the most useful thing you can do is to keep a freewriting diary. Just ten minutes a day. Not a complete account of your day; just a brief mind sample for each day. You don't have to think hard or prepare or be in the mood: without stopping, just write whatever words come out— whether or not you are thinking or in the mood.
>
> Peter Elbow

(Elbow's words, *whether or not you are thinking or in the mood,* sound as if they have been tacked on to the end of the sentence.)

HOW TO PUNCTUATE WITHIN A SENTENCE

Sentence openers   When a word, phrase, or dependent clause precedes the main clause of a sentence, a comma is often used to separate the introductory material from the main clause.

Sentence: He was an honest man.

Introductory word: *Yes,* he was an honest man.
Introductory phrase: *Of course,* he was an honest man.
  Throughout his life, he was an honest man.

Introductory clause: *When you come to think of it,* he was an honest man.

  Although he was unhappy most of his life, he was an honest man.

WATCH OUT FOR SEPARATION OF SENTENCE ELEMENTS

Do not separate the subject from its verb. What looks like introductory material may actually be the whole subject:

NO: The orange-feathered hat with a bullet through the rim, belonged to Jesse James.

YES: The orange-feathered hat with a bullet through the rim belonged to Jesse James.

Subject and verb: *the orange-feathered hat with a bullet through the rim belonged*

Do not separate a verb from its completer:

NO: He believed, that men should be equal to women except in the kitchen.

YES: He believed that men should be equal to women except in the kitchen.

Verb and completer: *believed that men should be equal to women except in the kitchen*

Modern usage is moving away from the comma after introductory material as long as the introductory words are brief and there is no chance the sentence will be misunderstood if the comma is omitted:

In 1492 Columbus sailed the ocean blue.
On Elm Street there is a monument to Columbus.

Sometimes, however, a comma is needed to avoid confusion, even when the sentence opener is brief:

Confusing: Inside everything smelled of burnt wood and smoke.

Clear: *Inside,* everything smelled of burnt wood and smoke.

Note how essential a comma is in the following sentence:

Before the car had stopped rolling over the officers were out with their hands on their guns.

Without a comma, it sounds as if the car is *rolling over* the officers. The reader must go back to the beginning of the sentence to understand the meaning. A comma following the introductory clause clears up the confusion:

Before the car had stopped rolling over, the officers were out with their hands on their guns.

Use commas *before* and *after* introductory material that begins a second independent clause.

YES: I usually vacation in Mexico, but, of course, Eddie goes to Hawaii.

Do not let one end of the phrase or clause dangle:

NO: _____, but of course, _____.
NO: _____, but, of course _____.
YES: _____, but, of course, _____.

An alternate way to punctuate this sentence would be to use a semicolon to separate the two clauses:

YES: I usually vacation in Mexico; but, of course, Eddie goes to Hawaii.

TIPS FOR WRITERS

Words, phrases, and dependent clauses that follow the main clause of a sentence generally do not require a comma. We pause after a sentence opener, but we sail through the whole sentence when the same material *follows* the main clause. Read these sentences aloud to sense the difference:

Inside, the cabin was warm.	The cabin was warm inside.
On old Madison Avenue, there is a house of wonders.	There is a house of wonders on old Madison Avenue.
If he hadn't lost his wallet, he would have joined us.	He would have joined us if he hadn't lost his wallet.

Exercise 4 Write four pairs of sentences, and connect each pair with a comma and a coordinator. Begin the second sentence in each pair with the following introductory material. Watch the punctuation.

Example: I am flying to San Francisco on Tuesday, *and, when I arrive,* I will phone you from the airport.

but during the summer
or for that matter
and in the heat of the argument
nor after the exam

Items in a series Words, phrases, and clauses in a series are usually separated by commas:

Wheaties *suits you, courts you, and keeps you hopping.*

He'll use it, enjoy it, and love you for it.

Think of this formula:

a, b, and (or) c

Although it is not wrong to drop the comma before the *and* or *or* in a series, it is a good idea to include it; otherwise, you run the risk of running the last two items in a series together. When there are pairs involved, omitting the final comma leads to confusion:

CONFUSING: The concert featured *Simon and Garfunkel, Elton John, Carly Simon and James Taylor and Pete Seeger.*
(It sounds as if Carly Simon and James Taylor and Pete Seeger are a group.)

CLEAR: The concert featured *Simon and Garfunkel, Elton John, Carly Simon and James Taylor, and Pete Seeger.*
(Pete Seeger is separated from Simon and Taylor.)

Items in a series joined by *and* or *or* do not require commas:

I am taking biology and chemistry and physics next semester.

When the items in a series themselves contain commas, it may be difficult to tell where one item ends and the next begins. To avoid confusion use semicolons instead of commas to separate the items:

And there were the comings and goings of the other occupants of the house—Morris Fink, muttering malevolently to himself as he swept the front porch; Yetta Zimmerman herself, clumping down from her quarters on the third floor to give the place her morning onceover; the whalelike Moishe Muskablit, departing in a ponderous rush for his yeshiva, improbably whistling "The Donkey Serenade" in harmonious bell-like notes.

William Styron

Notice how the dash sets off the series. Two options are available for introducing a long series in a sentence: the colon and the dash. A colon is two periods : (one on top of the other). A dash, on the typewriter, is two hyphens - - with no space between them or the words before or after the words they separate.

A dash may introduce a series when you do not want the formality of the colon:

There are three sides to every question—*the pro side, the con side, and the inside.*

The colon is most often used to introduce a series. Note how the series is set off from the rest of the sentence.

When words like *is, are, like, such as, in,* and *on* introduce a series, they should not be followed by a comma or colon:

NO: The boys in the band are: *John, Jerry, Henry, and Clyde.*
YES: The boys in the band are *John, Jerry, Henry, and Clyde.*

NO: We have traveled in, *Europe, Africa, and Asia.*
YES: We have traveled in *Europe, Africa, and Asia.*

There are three sides to every question: the pro side, the con side and the inside.

Adjectives in a series Use a comma between adjectives that independently modify the same noun:

There Is a Rugged, Wild, Exotic, Sprawling, Colorful, and Magnificent America

All the adjectives in the above series describe the noun, *America*.

There is a *rugged* America.
There is a *wild* America.
There is an *exotic* America.
There is a *sprawling* America.
There is a *colorful* America.
There is a *magnificent* America.

These adjectives are interchangeable and can be separated by the word *and:*

There is a rugged *and* wild *and* exotic *and* sprawling *and* colorful *and* magnificent America.

Some adjectives, however, fit together to form a phrase and are not separated by a comma:

We had a *fine old* time.

Here the phrase *fine old time* means the same thing as a *good time*. If you separated the two adjectives (*fine* and *old*), you would be saying that you had a fine time and an old time, which doesn't make sense.

Do not separate adverbs from the adjectives that they modify:

NO: They played a *wildly, competitive* game of poker.
YES: They played a *wildly competitive* game of poker.

NO: We saw a *very, funny* movie at the Bijou last night.
YES: We saw a *very funny* movie at the Bijou last night.

Exercise 5 Punctuate the following passage, which contains items in a series. Distinguish between those adjectives in a series that need to be separated by commas and those that belong together and require no commas.

This summer American families will be holding reunions in the Bronx in Georgia in El Paso and in the Caribbean islands. Toddlers eating hot dogs will be introduced to great-aunts in wheelchairs great-uncles will be cooing to grand-nephews in baby carriages and middle-aged cousins meeting for the first time will be curiously looking each other over for family resemblances. Ever since the publication of Alex Haley's book *Roots* and the television series about it families are calling together their dispersed members in an effort to promote personal worth record family history and —especially among black families—emphasize racial pride. Prizes are offered to the ones who come the furthest bring the largest delegation have the most sets of twins wear the funniest T-shirts or draw the most detailed genealogy charts. High school gymnasiums backyard patios apartment living rooms and wide-open national parks are some of the scenes for gathering in the clan depending on the size and financial ability of the attending members.

Parenthetical expressions A parenthetical expression is a word, phrase, or clause that interrupts the flow of a sentence to make an additional point. When a parenthetical expression falls within a sentence, it must be sealed off at both ends by *a pair of commas, a pair of dashes,* or *a pair of parentheses:*

SENTENCE: The local school has been at the heart of the community.

Add a parenthetical expression with:

COMMAS: The local school has been, *and usually still is,* at the heart of the community.

PARENTHESES: The local school has been (*and usually still is*) at the heart of the community.

DASHES: The local school has been—*and usually is*—at the heart of the community.

Margaret Mead

Remember to seal off the parenthetical expression at *both* ends when it falls within the sentence. Do not let one end hang loose:

NO: The local school has been, *and usually still is* at the heart of the community.

NO: The local school has been *and usually still is,* at the heart of the community.

Use commas to set off parenthetical expressions that interrupt the sentence only slightly:

He was, *after all,* an honorable man.
They were all, *I would say,* honorable men.

Use dashes when you want to emphasize parenthetical material:

Even the secret of the universe's own structure—*the atom*—served our nation's goals, which were mankind's and the world's goals.

Lillian Hellman

The talk of brassieres or no brassieres, who washes the dinner pots, whether you are a sex object—*whatever the hell that is*—has very little meaning unless the woman who slams the door can buy herself dinner and get out of a winter wind.

Lillian Hellman

Use parentheses when you want to separate parenthetical material from the mainstream of the sentence. Parentheses ( ) come in pairs; never use one without the other.

Parentheses clarify:

Seymour spent twenty years (from 1947 to 1967) in Sausalito.

Parentheses enclose comments (a question or a statement of disbelief, for example) that interrupt the main idea of the sentence:

I often wonder (*don't you?*) if he needs all that underwear.

Sam finally proposed to Harriet (*imagine that!*) after they had lived together for eleven years.

Parentheses enclose explanatory material:

Mayor Beame sampled the world's largest ice cream sundae (*seventy-two hundred and fifty pounds of vanilla, chocolate, and strawberry Sealtest*).

The Mayor also drank a toast poured from a salmanazar, the world's largest champagne bottle (*it holds three hundred and twelve ounces, and there are only a hundred and eighty salmanazars in existence; this one was flown to New York in an Air France first-class seat*), and with a sword, cut into the sixteen-foot-long cake. . . .

The New Yorker

No punctuation marks are used *before* parentheses, but commas and end punctuation can *follow* parentheses if necessary:

After Sam and Harriet were married (*April 24, 1965*), they moved to San Francisco and opened a coffeehouse.

When the parenthetical material is set off as a separate sentence, use the necessary end punctuation within the parentheses:

The Mayor also drank a toast from a salmanazar, the world's largest champagne bottle. (*It holds three hundred and twelve ounces.*)

The matter of choosing how to set off a parenthetical expression is up to you, the writer. Practice setting off material in the same sentence to discover which pairs work most effectively.

Modifiers   Use commas to seal off modifiers that follow the word or words they describe when the modifiers are *not essential* to the meaning of the sentence:

The police chief, *with ease,* recommended the promotion.
The police chief   recommended the promotion.

My brother, *who usually spends his Sundays reading the newspaper,* offered to help me paint the house.
My brother   offered to help me paint the house.

Study the way the commas work to seal off the modifiers in the following sentences:

Grandmother Skinner, *whose sugar cookies never turned out the same twice and whose jars of fruits and vegetables exploded,* used to pinch her son's nose to give it a distinguished look. Grandfather Skinner, *a sometime housepainter,* lacked ambition; the parts of his unsuccessful stove polisher filled the hayloft. Grandmother Burrhus, *who plied the young with apple pie and maple sugar,* was a worrier. Grandfather Burrhus, *who worked for the railroad,* apparently gave her cause to worry.

Elizabeth Hall

Do not use commas to set off modifiers that are essential to the meaning of the sentence:

Hot dogs steamed in beer have a gourmet flavor.

(Only hot dogs *steamed in beer* have that flavor.)

This bakery specializes in cakes decorated the way you want them.

(The bakery's specialty is cakes *decorated the way you want them.*)

What should you feed a dog who's in love with hamburger?

(You're not feeding *any* dog; you're feeding a dog who's in love with hamburger. So you would not put a comma after "dog.") See Chapter 9, page 182, for a fuller discussion of punctuation of modifiers.

Appositives Use commas to set off most appositives from the nouns they describe:

> Monty Python, *King of the Goons,* is a nutty guy.
> James, *my only brother,* flew in from Brazil yesterday.
> Lawrence Roberts, *a well-known podiatrist,* died.

For an explanation of appositives, see Chapter 9, page 217.

Exercise 6 Write five sentences in which you use modifying clauses that are essential to the meaning of the sentences.

Example:

THE MAN WHO CONTROLS CORPORATIONS OUGHT TO BE ABLE TO CONTROL HIS OWN CAR.

> The man is not *any* man; he's the one *who controls corporations.*
> No commas are needed in the sentence.

Now write five sentences in which you use modifying clauses that are *not* essential to the meaning of the sentences.

Example:

> John F. Kennedy, who died in 1963, sparked the imagination of the nation's youth.

Here the modifying clause *who died in 1963* is not essential to the meaning of the sentence: *Kennedy sparked the imagination of the nation's youth.*

Nouns of direct address Use commas to seal off the name of a person or persons directly spoken to:

> All right, *gang,* let's go.
> Okay, *Joe,* you're on your way.
> *Sharon,* will you brush your hair?
> Please sit up straight in that chair, *Lauren.*

Nice going, Shorty.

Direct address: *Shorty*

Failure to set off nouns of direct address results in confusion:

> NO: Will you please eat Sharon.
> YES: Will you please eat, *Sharon.*
>
> NO: Joe Margaret is already here.
> YES: *Joe,* Margaret is already here.

Dates, locations, and addresses   Use commas to seal off dates, addresses, and locations when they provide additional information in a sentence.

Dates and locations   Ross was born on *January 13, 1939,* in *New York, New York.*

(1939 identifies the year in which the specific January 13 occurred.)

Ross was born in *New York, New York.*

(The second New York identifies the state of New York.)
You can also write:

Ross was born on *13 January 1939* in *New York.*
Ross was born in *January 1939* in *New York.*

When the day of the month comes before the month or when the day of the month is not given, commas may be omitted.

Addresses   304 Elm Street, Pittsburgh, Pennsylvania 15213

Linear: 504 Weaver Street, New York, New York 10024
Block: 304 Elm Street
        Pittsburgh, Pennsylvania 15213

(Note: There is no comma between the state and the zip code.)

Quotations   Quotation marks are always used in pairs to set off the exact words of a speaker or writer, such as these statements by Benjamin Franklin.

"There never was a good war or a bad peace."

"God helps those that help themselves."

Use a comma or a colon after the introductory remarks that introduce a quotation:

Benjamin Franklin said, "There never was a good war or a bad peace."

But he is probably best known for these words: "Early to bed and early to rise, / Makes a man healthy, wealthy, and wise."

(Note: The slash / shows where one line of verse ends and another begins.) Notice that the colon separates the quotation from the statement and draws attention to it. The comma allows the quotation to be integrated into the sentence. (See Chapter 19 on the research paper for further information about quoting sources.)

Using quotation marks with other marks of punctuation is often tricky. Follow these guidelines:

1. Place introductory commas or colons before the opening quotation marks:

Franklin said, "There never was a good war or a bad peace."
Franklin said: "There never was a good war or a bad peace."

2. Place periods and commas inside the closing quotation marks:

Franklin said, "There never was a good war or a bad peace."

Franklin said, "There never was a good war or a bad peace," and he also said, "Little strokes fell great oaks."

3. Place semicolons outside the closing quotation marks:

Franklin said, "There never was a good war or a bad peace"; he also said, "Little strokes fell great oaks."

4. Place question marks and exclamation points inside the closing quotation marks when they are part of the quotation:

Juliet called out, "O Romeo, Romeo! wherefore art thou Romeo?"
"O Romeo, Romeo!" Juliet cried, "wherefore art thou Romeo?"

5. Place question marks and exclamation points outside the quotation marks when they apply to the whole sentence and are not part of the quotation:

Did Shakespeare say, "Uneasy lies the head that wears a crown"?

6. Do not use two punctuation marks at the end of a sentence. When the quotation ends with a question mark or exclamation point, the period that would ordinarily end your own sentence is omitted:

NO: Juliet called out, "O Romeo, Romeo! wherefore art thou Romeo?".

YES: Juliet called out, "O Romeo, Romeo! wherefore art thou Romeo?"

7. Set off with commas any statements that identify the speaker:

"There never was a good war," said Franklin, "or a bad peace."

Note where the commas are placed:

"_____," said Franklin, "_____."

8. Use single quotation marks to set off a quotation within a quotation:

An admirer of Eleanor Roosevelt said, "We came to know by heart her maxims: 'You can do it,' 'People matter,' 'Try, try again,' 'We must remember those less fortunate than ourselves.' "

Remarkable American Women

There are two sets of quotations here:

An admirer said, "We came to know by heart her maxims."

Eleanor Roosevelt said, "You can do it," "People matter," "Try, try again," "We must remember those less fortunate than ourselves."

WATCH OUT FOR INDIRECT QUOTATIONS

Use quotation marks around the exact words of a speaker:

Samantha said, "I'm tired of Tony's pizza."

Do not use quotation marks around an indirect quotation, which *rephrases* the speaker's words:

Samantha said *that she was* tired of Tony's pizza.

The word *that* signals an indirect quotation:

Researchers say *that* TV ads can hurt children.

Frequently, however, the word *that* is omitted:

Researchers say TV ads can hurt children

This is an indirect quotation because there are no quotation marks. If it were a direct quotation (the exact words of a speaker), the sentence would read:

Researchers say, "TV ads can hurt children."

Note how the commas all fall within the quotation marks and how the period, which is the end punctuation of the whole sentence, is enclosed within the single *and* double quotation marks.

Dialogue Use quotation marks to set off dialogue, which is conversation between two or more people. Notice that a new paragraph begins each time the speaker changes. Note also that commas and periods set off tag statements that identify the speaker.

"How long will you be gone?" she asked faintly.

"Two weeks," he replied with a wide smile. He went on business trips to Boston like a sailor going on shore leave after months of deprivation on the high seas.

"Business?"

"Mostly. I don't know if I told you—we're thinking of moving to Boston." Scandalized, Ginny looked at him quickly. "How could you? This is our *home*."

"Not mine it isn't. I've always hated this town. You know that. I intended to stay here just a year, as part of my training for a job in Boston. But then I met your mother, who couldn't bear the thought of leaving Hullsport. Though God only knows why."

"But how could you just forfeit thirty-five years of memories?" Ginny wailed, knowing the incredible difficulty she experienced in letting go of anything out of her past, however objectionable.

"Easily. Very easily," he said with a laugh.

Lisa Alther

Brackets   Use brackets to insert your own words into a quotation:

You may draw in a bracket or use the slant key on the typewriter /   / and then add the edges by hand [   ].

"He [Toscanini] used to sing along with the orchestra when he conducted."

Use brackets to provide a correction:

"The play ran for sixty-four [sixty-five] weeks on Broadway."

(The number sixty-four, according to the writer, is an error, which he corrects in the brackets.)

To point out that a misspelling or wrong grammatical form was part of an original text, enclose the Latin word *sic,* which means "thus," in brackets:

"His was an unneccesary [*sic*] crime."

Use brackets for parentheses within parentheses:

(After all the talk [and there was a great amount of talk], she did what she wanted, anyway.)

Ellipses   Use an ellipsis mark, which is three spaced dots, to show that words have been omitted from a quotation:

Joan said, "I haven't seen her since . . . last summer. How is she?"

If words have been omitted immediately following the end of a quoted sentence, the ellipses follow the period of the sentence for a total of four dots:

Ellipses   . . .

Period + ellipses   . . . .

Joan said, "I haven't seen her since she had her appendix out last summer. . . ."

If the material omitted from a quotation contains a period, use ellipses with a period:

Joan said, "I haven't seen her. . . . How is she?"

When quoting from a longer passage, use the ellipsis mark to show that you have used only part of the quote:

One of the functions of a society is to make its inhabitants feel safe, and

Americans devote more of their collective resources to security than to any other need. Yet Americans do not feel safe, despite (or because of) shotguns in the closet and nuclear bombers patrolling overhead.

Philip Slater

"One of the functions of a society is to make its inhabitants feel safe. . . ."

or

"One of the functions of a society is to make its inhabitants feel safe . . . yet Americans do not feel safe. . . ."

Exercise 7 Provide the necessary quotation marks and other marks of punctuation in the following dialogue.

Ralph turned over and sat up in bed.

What are you doing Meg mumbled.

Just getting up for awhile I can't sleep Ralph answered.

Where are you going she asked.

I need some air I'll just walk around the block.

What time is it asked Meg as she turned on the light.

Two o'clock.

That late. If you take a walk you'll just wake up more she argued.

Just a few minutes Ralph yawned.

Wait I'll go with you.

But you're tired Ralph rubbed his eyes.

I'll go with you. We can walk down to Sam's and get some ice cream.

But it's two 'clock he said.

Suddenly I'm not tired Meg answered throwing off the covers.

I think I'm sleepy said Ralph lying back down.

Terrific said Meg now what am I supposed to do I'm wide awake.

Other uses of quotation marks

Titles Use quotation marks for the titles of works found inside published volumes:

Chapter:	"Punctuation and Capitalization"
Article:	"It's Never Too Late to Start Living Longer"

Use quotation marks for the titles of short stories, poems, and songs:

Short story:	"Uncle Wiggily in Connecticut"
Poem:	"Ode on a Grecian Urn" "Kubla Khan"
Song:	"Battle Hymn of the Republic" "The Star-Spangled Banner"

Television program: "Happy Days"

Radio program: "The Gene Klaven Show"

Irony Use quotation marks for irony (when you mean the opposite of what you say).

Irony: You certainly are a "big help."

Italics Use italics (which in printed type are slanted letters) for the titles of books, newspapers, magazines, plays, movies, long poems, ships, trains, airplanes, foreign words, or words used as words. Italics can also be used for emphasis. In written or typed papers, words to be italicized are underlined.

Books:	*The Catcher in the Rye* *The Borzoi College Reader*
Newspapers:	*New York Times* or New York *Times* (either is acceptable)
Magazines:	*Playboy* *Time*
Plays:	*Hamlet* *The Night of the Iguana*
Movies:	*Gone With the Wind*
Long poems:	*Paradise Lost*
Ships:	*Titanic* *Queen Elizabeth II*
Trains:	*Super Chief*
Airplanes:	*Spirit of St. Louis*
Foreign words and phrases:	**It's *amore* at first sip.**
Words used as words:	The word *and* is a powerful coordinator. *Because* often introduces a dependent clause.
Emphasis:	**"Some mornings I <u>hate</u> my skin."**

Exercise 8 Supply the necessary quotation marks and italics in the following passage, which is a brief biography of Elvis Presley, the rock singer, who died in 1977.

Elvis Aron Presley began his rock and roll career touring rural areas of Tennessee under the name The Hillbilly Cat. He had a clever manager, a non-military Colonel Thomas A. Parker, who promoted him locally and then catapulted him onto the national scene. In 1956, Presley's first great hit, Heartbreak Hotel, was released by RCA. Exploding on the musical consciousness of America's youth, this ballad has been described by the New York Times as a blood-stirring dirge about love and loneliness. It pounded on every jukebox and radio station across America, selling finally two million copies. In the same year, Heartbreak Hotel was swiftly followed by other songs, Don't Be Cruel, Hound Dog, Blue Suede Shoes, and Love Me Tender. In 1957 Presley began his film career in a movie also entitled Love Me Tender, which, although blasted by the critics, grossed brilliantly at the box-office.

But Presley was not a lucky kid who happened to have a style that caught on. In the years before RCA he worked tirelessly in now historic recording sessions at Sun Records Studios in Memphis, blending into his style and technique white country music and black blues rhythms. Although his career declined after the Beatles came on the scene, most people's earliest recollections of Elvis Presley will remain those of his first wildly mobbed concerts, and of the gyrating, satin-shirted Elvis the Pelvis who seized the imagination of America's young people in the late 1950's.

PUTTING PUNCTUATION TO WORK

Putting punctuation to work means using punctuation marks to draw attention to your meaning. You make decisions about separating or joining ideas; about emphasizing or deemphasizing material; about clarifying, which is what you're always after. Study the ways the punctuation marks—commas, dashes, and colons—are used in the following biographical sketch of Eleanor Roosevelt from a *Life* magazine Special Report, *Remarkable American Women.*

It wasn't what Eleanor Roosevelt said nor even what she did that people remember best about her. It was what she was—a woman of unfailing grace and generosity of spirit, a survivor who outlasted the pain and controversy of her life, and a tireless partisan of the best in herself and in all the rest of us. "She not only believed in but lived all the difficult, optimistic bluestocking virtues," wrote one admirer after

Dash introduces series.
Commas separate parts of the series.

Quotation marks set off exact words of the admirer.
Comma separates adjectives in a series.

her death in 1962. "We came to know by heart her maxims: 'You can do it,' 'People matter,' 'Try, try again,' 'We must remember those less fortunate than ourselves.' " Shy and awkward as a girl, an orphan at nine, she overcame a painful childhood and gradually emerged as a personality as forceful and vivid as her husband. She brought a new dimension to the role of First Lady: going everywhere in Depression America, inspecting coal mines, visiting ghettos, defending the rights of minorities at a time when it was rash for any public figure to speak up for blacks. Her syndicated column, "My Day," and her radio program brought her presence into every American home. She represented the U.S. at the United Nations, traveled the world incessantly and at home extended herself to meet as many people as she could squeeze into her schedule. "She was as indigenous to America as palms to a Florida coastline," a journalist wrote. In many ways she acted as our conscience, and as such was resented as well as cherished. But she earned the ultimate tribute: our lives were better because they were touched by hers.

Comma sets off words that identify speaker.
Colon introduces quotations.
Single quotation marks set off quotation(s) within a quotation.
Comma sets off introductory modifier. (shy and awkward).
Comma sets off a second introductory modifier (an orphan at nine).

Colon introduces series of examples that explain how Eleanor brought a new dimension to the role.

Quotes around title of newspaper column.
Commas set off name of column, which is an appositive identifying the column.
Comma separates series of verbs: *represented, traveled,* and *extended.*

Colon introduces sentence that defines the "ultimate tribute."

Exercise 9 The following sentences, which have been adapted for this exercise from the story "The Little Pub" by Patricia Zelver, begin with capital letters and end with periods. Supply any additional punctuation you think necessary in these sentences.

1. Only a few lights were visible from the picture window where Mrs. Jessup stood having her Happy Hour her first or was it her second vodka martini in her hand.

2. Transfer was in the air this time a very important one the Chairman of the Board was about to retire and Mr. Jessup was in line for this position.

3. She mixed herself another cocktail at the wet bar then she went into the kitchen and opened the oven and looked at the frozen Stouffer cheese soufflé she had put in before her first drink.

4. He had such a nice easy manner with the ladies and everyone else too for that matter.

5. One vodka martini on the rocks for my little Sugar Big Bill would sing out as he mixed the drink himself.

6. Big Bill would undoubtedly present her with a drink on the house perhaps he would even toast her and Mr. Jessup's future.

7. In the meantime it was pleasant to think about the Little Pub.

8. She finished her drink and went into the kitchen and took out the soufflé and put it on the dining room table in its foil container.

9. It was limp and sticky but she managed to get most of it down.

10. She lay in bed watching the middle of an old movie sipping the drink and thinking how surprised and grateful Mr. Jessup would be that she had accomplished so much in his absence.

Exercise 10   The following student writing has been overpunctuated for this exercise. What punctuation can you remove and why?

In these times of industry, and computer technology, have we lost our pride, in tradition? Christmas time, for example, is supposed to be a time of giving, and sharing. But, big business, has distorted Christmas. How can you get into the Christmas spirit, if thousands of people are shopping; and all they want to do, is beat you, to the cashier's counter? Anyone, who has tried to shop during the three days' before Christmas, knows that it can turn you, into a nervous wreck.

Thanksgiving has also, been distorted. It is supposed to be a time, of thanks. For all, our successes, whether big or small; we should be thankful. It should be a day, when we do remember, how fortunate we are. But, do you know what we do? These days, you'll find most Americans glued to the television, watching the Kansas City Chiefs, and the New England Patriots in a football game!

CAPITALIZATION   Capitalize the following:

1. The first word of every sentence and every sentence within a sentence:

   Seeing is believing.
   He said, "Seeing is believing."

2. Names of persons, their titles, and their title abbreviations:

	Do not capitalize
Henrietta Smith	woman
Father Wilhelm	father
Saint Augustine	saint
Queen Elizabeth II or the Queen	queen
President Carter or the President	president

(Use capitals when a specific king, president, or the like, is referred to or addressed. Use capitals when a title is used as a name. *You may leave the convent any time, Sister. The King has arrived.*)

John Williams, M.D.	doctor
Susan Wilson, Ph.D.	
Margaret Roberts, D.D.S.	dentist
Mr. and Mrs. Berger	
Mother (when used as a name)	my mother
Father (when used as a name)	my father

(Example: *It isn't often that Father visits. It isn't often that John visits.* But: *It isn't often that my father visits.*)

3. Names of specific places and locations:

	Do not capitalize
Willow Street	street
Locust Avenue	avenue
Westchester County	county
Pennsylvania	state
Switzerland	country
Monongahela River	river
Lake Minnewaska	lake
Empire State Building	building
World Trade Center	center
University of Texas	university
Hunter College	college

4. Specific languages:

English
French

5. Course titles:

Developmental Psychology	psychology
Sociology 101	sociology

6. Religions:

> Catholic
> Protestant
> Jewish

7. Specific groups, organizations, institutions, and businesses:

> Federal Trade Commission
> Supreme Court
> Alcoholics Anonymous
> Xerox Corporation

8. Months, days, and holidays:

January, September, etc.	Seasons are not usually capitalized:
Monday, Wednesday, etc.	spring
Thanksgiving	summer
Memorial Day	fall
Lincoln's Birthday	winter

9. Titles of works. Capitalize the first and last words in titles and all other words except short words like *a, an, the, and, of,* and *in.*

> "I've Been Working on the Railroad"
> *Death of a Salesman*

10. Names of events or periods in history:

> Revolutionary War
> The Age of Reason

11. Adjectives derived from names:

> Shakespearean
> English
> Lincolnesque

Exercise 11 Supply all the necessary punctuation and capitalization in the following passage, which describes some of the dangers of excessive drinking.

drowning in drink

drinking may help drown your sorrows but excessive drinking before going swimming may literally drown you. according to dr. park elliott dietz and susan p. baker of johns hopkins medical institutions alcohol may be involved in as many as half of the 6500 accidental drownings which occur each year in the united states.

dietz and baker based their conclusion on a study of victims who drowned in maryland in 1972 and in baltimore from 1968 to 1972. of the adults who died in baltimore 47 percent had positive blood-alcohol tests. swimming and drinking just don't mix.

Spelling

Chapter 17

PRACTICAL SUGGESTIONS

If you're a writer who has a spelling problem, you may feel as if you have taffy stuck to your fingers. Just as taffy moves from finger to finger, so spelling errors appear to move from word to word. Whatever you do to get rid of it, you're stuck with your problem. And that's not all. Because, unfortunately, if you have trouble spelling, you may also have trouble writing a paper. Rather than encourage yourself to write through a first draft, you stumble over every word because you're worried about spelling. Worse still, you restrict yourself to "safe" words—words you're certain you can spell—often giving up the word you're really after and opting for a weak substitute. *Nice* won't make it if you're after *scrupulous. Awful* is a cop-out if you really want *obnoxious.*

Being a shaky speller doesn't mean you're a poor writer. Many effective writers have had spelling problems. Winston Churchill and Franklin Roosevelt, for example, had trouble spelling, and Herman Melville and F. Scott Fitzgerald were such poor spellers that they relied on their editors to correct their misspellings.

Since you don't have an editor handy, learn to become your own editor. Don't let your difficulty in spelling keep you from writing; spelling is one technicality you can confront in the final stages of your writing. This chapter presents some practical suggestions for handling spelling problems.

1. *Write immediately.* Keep on writing during a freewriting exercise, a journal entry, or first draft of an essay without pausing to worry about spelling. You can check your spelling when you're revising and proof-reading.

2. *Use your first-choice word.* Your uncertainty about spelling shouldn't prevent you from using the word of your choice. Use the word, and spell it the way it sounds. Underline each word you're unsure of so that you won't forget to check the correct spelling when you're revising or proofreading.

3. *Find out how to spell a word.* If you know the beginning letters of a word, you'll probably be able to find the word in your college dictionary. But the dictionary won't help if you look for *psychology* under the *s*'s. Don't give up. Ask someone—friend, relative, or instructor—for help. Your instructor will respect your initiative and supply you with the beginning *psy* for *psychology*. Above all, don't be afraid to ask.

4. *Keep a record of your misspellings.* Once you find out how to spell a word, record it in a notebook or file box. Keep a list of unusual word beginnings. Learn that the sound *n* can be *pn* as in *pneumonia; gn* as in *gnaw, gnarl,* and *gnome;* and *kn* as in *knew, knight,* and *knob.* Remember that *ps* equals the *s* sound in *psychic, psychosis, psychologist,* and *psychiatrist.* Remember that *ch* equals the *sh* sound in *Chicago, chivalry,* and *chateau.*

5. *Write legibly.* Handwriting can disguise a spelling problem. You may think you're hiding your problem from your readers by blurring letters, hoping they will gloss right over the misspellings. The fact is, you're hiding your problem from *yourself* as long as you avoid it.

6. *Listen to the pronunciation of words.* Pronunciation may be at the heart of your spelling problem. We tend to spell words as we speak them or hear them spoken by others. Often, letters that are not pronounced when a word is spoken are also omitted when the word is written down. You might ignore the *g* in *recognize,* for example, because you pronounce it *reconize.* The same is true of added letters. If you pronounce *height* with an *h* on the end, you might spell the word *heighth* when you use it in your writing.

   When you hear a word but are uncertain of its spelling, record it. Write it down as it sounds, and then ask someone how to spell it. Pronounce the word to *yourself* the way it is spelled as a memory trick. Pronounce the *s* and *w* in *sword* even though the *w* is silent. Pronounce the *d* in *Wednesday* to help you remember that it's there.

   Try mentally to break a word into syllables. Say the word to yourself, separating and emphasizing each syllable. Say SEP-A-RATE, EM-PHA-SIZ-ING. Check in a dictionary.

7. *Read everything:* signs, advertisements, coupons, labels, ticket stubs, as well as newspapers, magazines, and books. When you see a spelling that puzzles you, write it down.

Many misspellings result from unfamiliarity with the written language. You've undoubtedly been surprised by seeing a word or phrase printed for the first time when you had it written differently in your mind. One woman, for example, thought that the phrase "grain of salt" was written "grand assault." Although she understood how to use the phrase, she occasionally wondered why it was a military term and concluded that it had something to do with a great battle. When she saw the written words "grain of salt," she realized that what she had seen in her mind didn't correspond with the written words at all. A man who thought the phrase "up and at 'em" was written "Up and Adam" wondered what Adam had to do with the idea—until he saw the phrase in writing. And in an English class, when students were asked to describe their rooms, several who had never seen the written phrase "chest of drawers" wrote "chester drawers" or "chesto drawers."

On the other hand, you may know perfectly well how to pronounce a word but may mispronounce it when you see it in writing. When you use the word *colonel* in conversation, you may pronounce it *kernel,* but when you see the word in print, pronounce it *col-o-nel.* Since you never matched the written and spoken words, you are likely to go on spelling the word as you say it. The more you familiarize yourself with the written language, the better you'll be able to make that match.

Exercise 1 The following words are taken from the *Wall Street Journal* advertisement below. Break each word into syllables. Study the syllables. Close your eyes and try to see the syllables. Write the words several times.

introductory	minimum
journal	maximum
publication	enclosed
subscribe	possessions
advantage	offer
subscription	choose

8. *Exercise your spelling power.* Play word games. Try your hand at cross-word puzzles, where an omitted or extra letter will strike you out. Try word-search puzzles (like the one below), where you must find words by reading forward, backward, up, down, and diagonally.

Exercise 2 Try the Word Search puzzle below.

(WORD SEARCH 5)

the copy room

The copy room of a newspaper is where the words for the newspaper originate. Here is where reporters pound out their stories on clattering typewriters; where copy boys speed the stories to editors who finalize them for publication; where the telephone never stops ringing!

Word List

Advertising	Cub (*reporter*)	Photo
Article	Daily	Pica (*type size*)
By-line	Deadline	Press
Caption	Editor	Print
Cartoon	Headline	Prose
Circulation	Issue	Report
Classified (*ads*)	Lead (*article*)	Scoop
Column	Lino (*machine*)	Sports
Coverage (*news*)	News	Type
	Page	Weekly

```
P N O O T R A C W E E K L Y
I G P Z O B E O A C G F T D
C A O T O H P N E N I L Y B
A O I Z L N A I I E E Y P G
D D L E X B C S I L G L E F
E D A U H X I S M H D I N H
I D E C M T R U P L M A B E
F Q I R R N C E O R E D E A
I S W E N L U K O L E A O D
S J V P K C L Y C J X S C L
S D Q O G X A I S U P P S I
A I R R P T T P S T D O R N
L S C T U R I U T N V R F E
C U E G A P O I E I H T W K
B V T L H H N S J R O S G L
E G A R E V O C E P O N I L
```

Exercise 3 Try the word power puzzle below.

INTERCHANGE

From the above word, make as many words of four letters or more as possible. Use only one form of a word, "rate" or "rates," but not both. Slang, proper names, and foreign words are not allowed.

9. *Devise ways to remember tricky words.* Remember how to spell a word by your own associations. Remember words within words: record the *dance* in atten*dance*, the *par* in se*par*ate, the *ear* in h*ear* and h*ear*d (the words that have to do with listening). Remember words that rhyme with each other; *loose* rhymes with *goose*, and *tough* rhymes with *rough* but not *cough*.

Draw a picture on paper or in your mind, if you will, to remember the *dance* in atten*dance*, the *ear* in h*ear*. Devise whatever associations will work for you.

10. *Find a way to diagnose your spelling problem.* It may be that you misspell only a few words; it may be that your big problem is using *ie* instead of *ei;* it may be that you're not certain when to drop a final *e* or double a consonant before adding an ending. Make lists of the words you misspell and see if there are any patterns. Perhaps there is a writing or reading workshop in your college where a tutor will help you diagnose your spelling problem.

Your spelling problem may actually be a reading problem. You may not have learned to read phonetically, that is, to recognize the letters that stand for certain sounds. You may transpose or reverse letters. If you keep track of your spelling errors, you may find that you're making the same kinds of letter-reversal errors in many words. You may need to work with letters made from sandpaper, tracing the letters over and over again with your fingertips until you begin to *sense* the formation of letters in particular words. Above all, find out all you can about your problem. Reading problems inhibit not just your spelling; they obviously inhibit your reading as well, so you have two problems instead of one. If there is no one around who can help you diagnose your problem, gather your own data and try to determine the root of your problem yourself.

When you know what your problem is, check your papers—word by word, page by page—to spot your misspellings. The work may be tedious at the beginning, but as you proceed you'll be able to spot the spelling errors more quickly and master your problem.

11. *Proofread every paper.* Read all of your papers aloud. If you type, you're bound to miss a letter or two. Even the strongest spellers make mistakes. Your reading aloud will move you through the paper more slowly than your silent reading, and you will be more likely to catch misspellings. Your voice will also pick up the pauses and hesitations and stops that you may want to punctuate differently. (See Chapter 5, page 99.)

12. *Don't give up.* A spelling problem, especially a serious one, demands work and time if it is to be overcome. Changing spelling habits doesn't happen easily or quickly, but if you confront your problem seriously, you will see results. Don't give up.

SPELLING RULES The following pages present spelling rules that will guide you through some of the most troublesome spots in the English language. Before studying the rules, however, you need a brief spelling vocabulary.

1. A *vowel* is a letter that represents one of these sounds: *a, e, i, o,* or *u.* (The letter *y* often represents a vowel sound; for example, lazy, easy.)

2. A *consonant* is a letter that represents a sound other than the vowels (*a, e, i, o, u*).

Example: *k, m, s, p, t*

3. A *syllable* is a letter or a group of letters that represents a unit of sound with one vowel sound. *Every* syllable must have one vowel sound.

> Example: *Great* is a one-syllable word because the *ea* sounds like one vowel, *a*.

See your dictionary for a full explanation of syllabification.

4. A *root* is the main part of a word to which a prefix or a suffix may be added.

PREFIX ROOT   SUFFIX
Example: dis   appear   ance   =   DISAPPEARANCE

5. A *prefix* is a group of letters that come before a root.

PREFIX   ROOT
Example: un + wise = unwise

6. A *suffix* is a letter or a group of letters that comes after the root.

ROOT   SUFFIX
Example: wise   +   ly   =   wisely

Spelling problems often arise when you add prefixes or suffixes. Some words, *disappearance,* for example, include both a prefix and a suffix:

PREFIX	ROOT	SUFFIX
dis	appear	ance

Adding prefixes Add a prefix to the *whole* root word:

Words like <u>unnecessary</u>

Prefix	+	Root word	=	Word
un	+	necessary	=	unnecessary
co	+	operate	=	cooperate
mis	+	spell	=	misspell
grand	+	daughter	=	granddaughter
dis	+	appear	=	disappear
im	+	mature	=	immature
il	+	legal	=	illegal

Words like <u>roommate</u> Retain all the letters of both words when a word is made up of two words:

room	+	mate	=	roommate
with	+	hold	=	withhold
over	+	rate	=	overrate

Adding suffixes   Most spelling problems occur when you add a suffix to the root. You need to know whether to change a *y* to *i* or whether to drop a final *e;* you need to know whether to add *-s* or *-es*. The following is a list of common suffixes:

-s	-ly
-es	-ous
-er	-able
-ed	-ness
-ing	-ment
-y	-ic
-al	-est

Adding -s̱ or -es̱   Most nouns take an *-s* for a plural. Most verbs take an *-s* for the *-s* form
Words like girls   of the verb:

Nouns

Singular	*Plural*
girl	girls
window	windows
writer	writers
pen	pens

Verbs

Base	*-s form*
seem	seems
feel	feels
hunt	hunts
laugh	laughs

Words like buzzes   When a word ends in *s, z, x, ch,* or *sh,* add the suffix *-es:*

bo*x*	boxes
bu*zz*	buzzes
cru*sh*	crushes
di*sh*	dishes
fo*x*	foxes
hi*ss*	hisses
ki*ss*	kisses
spee*ch*	speeches
waltz	waltzes
wat*ch*	watches
witne*ss*	witnesses

Words ending in y   For words ending in *y*, change the *y* to *i* and add *es* when the *y* is preceded
Words like <u>stories</u>   by a consonant:

story   stories

consonant   *y*   change *y* to *i*   add *es*

al*ly*	allies
ar*my*	armies
ba*by*	babies
bo*dy*	bodies
ci*ty*	cities
cry	cries
dai*ry*	dairies
dia*ry*	diaries
f*ly*	flies
libra*ry*	libraries
mar*ry*	marries
penal*ty*	penalties
sto*ry*	stories
stu*dy*	studies
trop*hy*	trophies

Words like <u>beautiful</u>   Follow the same pattern when adding other suffixes:

beau*ty*	beautiful
cry	cried
de*ny*	denial
ea*sy*	easier
emp*ty*	emptiness
grati*fy*	gratification
la*zy*	laziness
noi*sy*	noisily
love*ly*	loveliest
pret*ty*	prettiest
rep*ly*	replied

Words like crying   Do not drop the *y* when adding *-ing* to a word ending in *y:*

cry	crying
deny	denying
gratify	gratifying
reply	replying
try	trying

Words like monkeys   Add an *-s* to a word that ends in *y* preceded by a vowel:

monkey → monkeys

vowel   *y*   add   *s*

all*ey*	alle*ys*
attorn*ey*	attorne*ys*
b*oy*	bo*ys*
d*ay*	da*ys*
k*ey*	ke*ys*
p*ay*	pa*ys*
s*ay*	sa*ys*
turk*ey*	turke*ys*

Words ending in o
Words like pianos   Add an *-s* to most words ending in *o:*

piano	pianos
memo	memos
radio	radios
Eskimo	Eskimos
yo-yo	yo-yos

Words like echoes   Add an *-es* to these common exceptions:

do	does
echo	echoes
go	goes
hero	heroes
potato	potatoes
tomato	tomatoes
veto	vetoes

Some words take either spelling:

buffalo	buffalos/buffaloes
motto	mottos/mottoes
zero	zeros/zeroes
volcano	volcanos/volcanoes
lasso	lassos/lassoes

Proper names
Words like _Smiths_

Add an *-s* to proper names to make them plural:

McCoy	McCoys
Smith	the Smiths
Ford	the Fords
Archie Bunker	Archie Bunkers
Sally	Sallys (more than one)

Words like _Joneses_

When a proper name ends in *s, z, x, ch,* and *sh,* add *-es* to make it plural. In these names, the plural ending becomes an extra syllable you have to pronounce:

Jones	Joneses
Williams	Williamses
Spitz	Spitzes
Sax	Saxes
Rich	Riches
Kirsh	Kirshes

WATCH OUT FOR APOSTROPHES AND PROPER NOUNS

Do not add an apostrophe to a proper noun to make it plural.

>   NO: The *Smith's* bought a house down the block from us.

>   YES: The *Smiths* bought a house down the block from us.

Use the apostrophe for possession.

>   YES: The Smiths' house is near ours.

See the discussion of apostrophes on pages 455-460.

Exercise 4   Add *-s* or *-es* to each of the following words. Follow the rule on page 436 for changing *y* to *i*.

1. cry	**3.** class	**5.** box
2. rush	**4.** dish	**6.** blush

7. monkey	15. write	23. memo
8. alley	16. lady	24. Hess
9. ally	17. buy	25. hero
10. girl	18. library	
11. witness	19. finish	
12. Schwartz	20. miss	
13. story	21. piano	
14. kiss	22. Betsy	

Exercise 5 Combine each of the following words with the suffix that follows it to form a new word.

1. reply ed _____	9. hasty ly _____
2. cry er _____	10. dainty ness _____
3. beauty ful _____	11. dry ing _____
4. beauty fy _____	12. pity ful _____
5. deny al _____	13. early er _____
6. easy er _____	14. shy ly _____
7. lovely er _____	15. icy er _____
8. gay ty _____	16. noisy ly _____

Words ending in e When a word ends in *e* preceded by a consonant, drop the *e* before adding
Words like <u>writing</u> a *y* or a suffix beginning with a vowel:

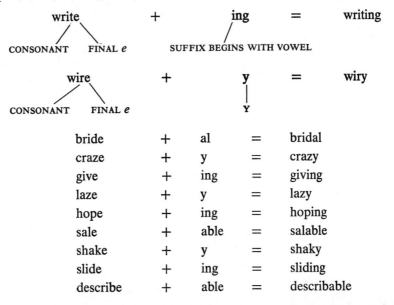

bride	+	al	=	bridal
craze	+	y	=	crazy
give	+	ing	=	giving
laze	+	y	=	lazy
hope	+	ing	=	hoping
sale	+	able	=	salable
shake	+	y	=	shaky
slide	+	ing	=	sliding
describe	+	able	=	describable

desire	+	ous	=	desirous
encourage	+	ing	=	encouraging
ridicule	+	ous	=	ridiculous

Words like <u>encouragement</u>

Keep the *e* when adding a suffix beginning with a consonant:

encourag*e*	+	*ment*	=	encouragement
entir*e*	+	*ly*	=	entirely
hop*e*	+	*ful*	=	hopeful
lat*e*	+	*ness*	=	lateness
lif*e*	+	*less*	=	lifeless
retir*e*	+	*ment*	=	retirement
sincer*e*	+	*ly*	=	sincerely

There are some exceptions to this rule:

true	+	*ly*	=	truly
awe	+	*ful*	=	awful
argue	+	*ment*	=	argument
judge	+	*ment*	=	judgment

Words like **When a word ends in *ce* or *ge*, keep the final *e* when adding a suffix begin-
<u>outrageous</u> ning with *a* or *o*:**

noti*ce*	+	*able*	=	noticeable
coura*ge*	+	*ous*	=	courageous
servi*ce*	+	*able*	=	serviceable
outra*ge*	+	*ous*	=	outrageous
chan*ge*	+	*able*	=	changeable

One-syllable words ending in a consonant

Words like <u>cutting</u> **When a one-syllable word ends in a consonant preceded by a single vowel,
double the consonant when adding a suffix beginning with a vowel:**

cut	—	one-syllable word
cu*t*	—	ends in a consonant
c*u*t	—	preceded by a single vowel
*i*ng	—	suffix begins with a vowel
cu*t*ting	—	double the consonant and add the suffix

beg	+	g	+	ing	=	begging
beg	+	g	+	ar	=	beggar
beg	+	g	+	ed	=	begged
can	+	n	+	ed	=	canned
can	+	n	+	ing	=	canning
dip	+	p	+	ing	=	dipping
dip	+	p	+	ed	=	dipped
flip	+	p	+	ed	=	flipped
plan	+	n	+	ed	=	planned
rob	+	b	+	er	=	robber
run	+	n	+	ing	=	running
snap	+	p	+	ed	=	snapped
sit	+	t	+	ing	=	sitting
swim	+	m	+	er	=	swimmer
win	+	n	+	ing	=	winning

These words have alternate spellings. Both forms are correct:

bus	bused	bussed
bus	busing	bussing
focus	focused	focussed
focus	focusing	focussing

Words like cheered When all of the above conditions do not exist, do not double the consonant:

cheer	+	ed	=	cheered
great	+	er	=	greater
heat	+	ed	=	heated
knock	+	ing	=	knocking
paint	+	ing	=	painting
rock	+	er	=	rocker
sail	+	ing	=	sailing

Multisyllable words with the accent on the last syllable

Words like controlled When a word of more than one syllable with the accent on the last syllable ends in a single consonant, double the consonant when adding a suffix beginning with a vowel.

begín	+	n	+	ing	=	begínning
admít	+	t	+	ed	=	admítted
contról	+	l	+	able	=	contróllable

compél	+	l	+	ing	=	compélling
occúr	+	r	+	ence	=	occúrrence
permít	+	t	+	ed	=	permítted
omít	+	t	+	ing	=	omítting
prefér	+	r	+	ed	=	preférred

Words like
preference   Note these exceptions: when the accent shifts from the last syllable of the word to the first syllable of the word formed by adding a suffix, do not double the consonant:

prefér	+	ence	=	préference
prefér	+	able	=	préferable
refér	+	ence	=	réference
confér	+	ence	=	cónference
infér	+	ence	=	ínference

When the accent is on a syllable other than the last, do not double the consonant:

ópen	+	ed	=	ópened
díffer	+	ence	=	dífference
trável	+	ing	=	tráveling
glímmer	+	ed	=	glímmered
lísten	+	ing	=	lístening

These words have alternate spellings. Both forms are correct:

benefit	benefited	benefitted
kidnap	kidnaped	kidnapped
counsel	counseled	counselled

Troublesome combinations—ie or ei?

Words like believe
and receive   The general rule (although there are a few exceptions) for spelling words in which the letters *i* and *e* appear side by side is as follows:

Use *i* before *e* (believe, friend)
Except after *c* (receive)
Or when sounded like *a*
As in *neighbor* and *weigh.*

i before e	*except after* c	*when sounded like* ā
achieve	receive	neighbor
believe	receipt	weigh
brief	ceiling	vein
chief	conceit	eight
field	conceive	reign
fiend	deceit	freight
fierce	perceive	chow mein
friend		reindeer
frontier		
grieve		
mischief		
niece		
piece		
pier		
quotient		
relief		
retrieve		
review		
soldier		
shield		
thief		
wield		
yield		

Watch out for exceptions to the rule: *cien* exceptions:

proficient	efficient
sufficient	omniscient
conscience	deficient
ancient	conscientious

Other exceptions:

codeine	height	forfeit
counterfeit	leisure	seize
caffeine	neither	science
financier	either	weird
protein		

Exercise 6 Fill in the empty slot in each of the following words with *ie* or *ei*. Remember the general rule for spelling these words.

1 n__ce

2 rec__ve

3 w__ght

4 p__ce

5 c__ling

6 n__ghborhood

7 v__n

8 r__ndeer

9 h__ght

10 f__rce

11 sc__nce

12 impat__nt

13 sh__ld

14 chow m__n

15 ch__f

16 w__gh

17 conc__t

18 bel__ve

19 quot__nt

20 conc__ve

Troublesome combinations— -ceed, -cede, and -sede

Words like proceed, precede, and supersede

Only one word in the English language ends in *-sede;* three end in *-ceed;* all others end in *-cede:*

-sede	-ceed	-cede
supersede	exceed	accede
	proceed	concede
	succeed	intercede
		precede
		recede
		secede

Exercise 7 Combine each word with the suffix following it to form a new word.

1 argue   ment   _____

2 cut   ing   _____

3 great   er   _____

4 begin   ing   _____

5 meet   ing   _____

6 omit   ed   _____

7 chat   ing   _____

8 fat   est   _____

9 open   ed   _____

10 control ed   _____

11 transfer ed   _____

12 notice   able   _____

13 beg   ar   _____

14 ridicule ous   _____

15 win   ing   _____

16 arrive   al   _____

17 cheer   ed   _____

18 slide   ing   _____

19 write	ing	_____	22 retire	ment	_____
20 sale	able	_____	23 wrap	er	_____
21 advantage	ous	_____	24 sincere	ly	_____

SPELLING DEMONS The following commonly used words are often misspelled. Each word has a devilish trouble spot, shown underlined, that usually causes the difficulty. The rules on pages 433–444 will help you with some of the words, but others, which defy any rule, must be memorized. If any word gives you trouble, say it aloud, break it into syllables, practice writing it by itself and in sentences, and think of a device for remembering it.

Example: Remember: *eve* is in d*eve*lopment
dance is in atten*dance*

absence
academic, academically
accessible
accommodate
accomplish
accurate
achievement
acquaintance
acquire
across
actual, actually
adequately
admission
admittance
adolescence, adolescent
advertise, advertisement
advice
advise
affect
aggravate
aggression, aggressive
alleviate
analysis, analyze
answer
apparatus
appropriate
approximate
argument
arouse
article
athlete, athletic
attendance, attendant

attitude
available
balloon
beautiful
beginner, beginning
behavior
breath, breathe
Britain
business
calendar
capitalism
career
ceiling
cemetery
certainly
characteristic
chief
choice
choose, chose
Christianity
commercial
commission
committee
compatible
competition, competitive, competitor
concede
conceivable, conceive
concentrate
connotation
conscience, conscientious
consequently
continuously

controlled, controlling
convenience, convenient
correlate
council
counselor
courtesy
criticism, criticize
curriculum
decision
defendant
definitely
dependent
despair, desperate
dilemma
disappoint
disciple
discipline
dissatisfied
doesn't
during
easily
efficient
eighth
embarrass, embarrassed, embarrassing
emphasize
enough
enthusiasm
entirely
entrance
environment
equivalent
especially
exaggerate
except
existence
experience
experiment
explanation
extremely
familiar
fascinate
February
finally
foreign
forty
fulfill
fundamentally
gaiety
generally
genius

government
governor
grammar, grammatically
guarantee
guidance
height
hindrance
hoping
hypocrisy, hypocrite
ideally
immediate, immediately
incidentally
independence
influence, influential
intellectual
interest, interesting
interpretation
interrupt
irrelevant
irresistible
January
knowledge
laboratory
leisure, leisurely
length
license
likelihood
loneliness
loose
lose
magnificence, magnificent
maintenance
maneuver
medieval
Mediterranean
mischief
misspell, misspelled, misspelling
mysterious
necessary
nickel
niece
ninety
occasion
occur, occurred, occurrence, occurring
omission
opinion
opportunity
original
parallel
particular

pastime
peculiar
perceive
persistent
phenomenon
philosophy
phony
physical
prefer, preference, preferred
prejudice
presence
prevalent
privilege
procedure
pronunciation
psychology
quiet
realize
really
recommend
refer, referred, referring
relieve
reminisce
rhyme
rhythm
schedule
secretary

seize
separate
several
similar
simultaneous
sincerely
sociology
sophomore
straight
strength
subtle, subtly
succeed, success
sufficient
surprise
theory
tomorrow
tragedy
truly
Tuesday
undoubtedly
unnecessary
unusually
vacuum
vengeance
Wednesday
weird
yield

HOMONYMS

Words are often misspelled because they are homonyms; that is, they sound alike but are spelled differently. The following is a list of commonly confused homonyms.

aloud—out loud
allowed—permitted

altar—a place for worship
alter—to change

ate—past tense of *eat*
eight—the number

bare—naked
bear—to carry; a wild beast

brake—a stopping device on a vehicle
break—to split, mash, or divide into parts

by—a preposition
buy—to purchase
bye—as in *good-bye*

cite—to summon; to quote
site—place; position
sight—the power of seeing; a view

core—an innermost part; a center
corps—an organized company, as of soldiers

course—a direction or route taken; a path; a series of classes
coarse—rough, not fine

desert—a dry region with little water
dessert—a final course to a meal

fare—money paid for a trip; food
fair—beautiful; equitable; a market

guessed—estimated at random
guest—one who is entertained

hair—as of the head
hare—an animal

heel—the hind part of the foot
heal—to cure; to grow sound
he'll—contraction of *he will*

here—in this place
hear—to perceive with the ear

isle—a small island
aisle—passage in an auditorium
I'll—contraction of *I will*

it's—the contraction of *it is*
its—the possessive of *it*

led—past tense and past participle of *lead*
lead—a metal

lone—solitary; alone
loan—a temporary grant

male—opposite of female
mail—letters and other postal matter

meet—to assemble
meat—food; flesh

miner—a worker in mines
minor—one under age

new—not old
knew—past tense of *know*

night—opposite of day
knight—a title of honor

our—a pronoun
hour—sixty minutes

pain—physical or mental suffering
pane—a piece of glass (in a window)

pair—two; a couple
pare—to slice thinly
pear—a kind of fruit

passed—gone through; went by
past—having taken place in a time before the present

peace—a state of harmony
piece—a part of a whole

peel—skin; outside
peal—sound of bells

plane—a perfectly flat or level surface
plain—level, flat country

principal—invested funds; chief, head of a school
principle—a fundamental rule or law

quiet—free of noise or disturbance
quite—completely; wholly; entirely

red—a color
read—past tense of *read*

right—just; correct
rite—a ceremony
write—to trace letters or characters

road—a path; a way
rode—past tense of *ride*
rowed—past tense of *row*

root—as of a plant; origin
route—direction; road

sail—to navigate
sale—act of selling

scene—a sight; part of a play
seen—observed

soul—the spirit
sole—only; bottom of the foot; a fish

sow—to scatter seed
sew—to fasten, as with a needle
so—in this manner

sum—the amount of anything; to add up
some—more or less of a quantity

tale—a story
tail—hindmost part of an animal

their—possessive of *they*
there—in that place
they're—the contraction of *they are*

two—a pair; the number 2
too—also; excess, as too much
to—a preposition or part of an infinitive

your—possessive of *you* (a pronoun)
you're—contraction of *you are* (a subject and a verb)

wait—to expect; to stay
weight—heaviness; importance

weather—the general condition of the atmosphere
whether—if it be the case or fact that

whose—a possessive pronoun or an interrogative person
who's—the contraction of *who is*

wood—a forest; timber
would—verb form

Adapted with permission from "Homonyms,"
The Lincoln Library of Essential Information,
edited by W. J. Redding. Chicago:
The Frontier Press Co., 1976.

Fourteen tricky words

Devise a way to remember the trickiest homonyms.

1. **It's**—the contraction of *it is*.

   It's (*it is*) raining cats and dogs.

2. **Its**—the possessive of *it*. Remember that the possessive *its*, like the possessive *his*, has no apostrophe.

   The cat is chasing *its* tail. (the tail of *it*)

3. **Here**—in this place.

   My great-aunt is *here* for a visit.

4. **Hear**—to perceive with the ear. Remember *ear* is in *hear*.

   Did you *hear* what I said?

5. **There**—in that place. Remember that *here, there,* and *where* all refer to places. *Here* is in all three words.

   Here is the entrance to the cave.
   There are too many cats in this house.
   Where is my pogo stick?

6. **Their**—the possessive of *they*. Remember in *their* is the word *heir*, which means one who will inherit another's possessions. An *heir* will take *possession*.

   They inherited *their* house from a relative.

7. **They're**—the contraction of *they are*.

   They're (*they are*) coming at last.

8. **To**—a preposition or part of an infinitive.

   He went *to* market *to* buy a fat hen.

9. **Too**—an adverb that means in addition to; also; in excess. *Remember* if *very* or *also* will substitute, use *too*.

   He is *too* old to act that way.
   I want to buy a fat hen, *too*.

10. Two—the number 2.

You act like a *two*-year-old child.

11. Whose—a possessive pronoun or an interrogative pronoun.

Whose handkerchief is this?
A man, *whose* name is Ivan, stopped by to make an appointment.

12. Who's—the contraction of *who is*.

Who's (*who is*) going to the theater with me?
Who's (*who is*) driving you home?

13. Your—the possessive of *you*.

Your room is a mess.

14. You're—the contraction of *you are*.

You're (*you are*) the one.

Exercise 8 Write the correct homonym in each empty slot in the following sentences:

1. I couldn't _____ to find out the _____ of the fish I caught. (weight, wait)

2. He didn't realize at the time that the girl was _____ in school, but he _____ that he had never met her. (knew, new)

3. After he looked through the _____ in the doughnut, he ate the _____ thing. (whole, hole)

4. I wouldn't _____ those jeans to a party _____ everyone will be dressed formally. (where, wear)

5. She's only a fair-_____ friend, _____ you like it or not. (weather, whether)

6. Everyone finished eating by _____ except Joe, who _____ until he was stuffed. (eight, ate)

7. I will gladly give you a _____ of my cake if you will go outside and leave me in _____. (peace, piece)

8. I'll _____ his neck if he _____s the doorbell one more time. (ring, wring)

9. Please _____ about the difference between _____ and wrong. (right, write)

10. _____ the door before you take off your _____. (close, clothes)

11. Reading _____ is not _____ in the library. (allowed, aloud)

12. When the _____ returned, she _____ dinner. (made, maid)

13. He _____ the ball _____ the arms of the defender. (threw, through)

14. The man who _____ the bandits carried a _____ pipe. (lead, led)

15. I _____ the book with the _____ cover. (read, red)

16. If you could, _____ you chop this _____? (wood, would)

17. I will tell you the _____ of the dog who couldn't wag his _____. (tail, tale)

18. If the _____ man is a _____, why isn't he called a mailmale? (mail, male)

19. _____ over _____ with _____ hands in _____ pockets. (their, they're, there)

20. _____ a shame that the cat lost _____ tail. (it's, its)

21. _____ cooks are _____ many _____ be in the kitchen at the same time. (to, too, two)

22. _____ overdue library book is this, and _____ going to return it? (who's, whose)

23. _____ making a fool of yourself in _____ Holloween costume. (your, you're)

24. _____ is the best place to _____ the concert. (hear, here)

USES OF THE HYPHEN   Hyphens have several important uses. Leaving out hyphens from some words can be considered simple misspellings; but leaving out hyphens from other words can confuse the meaning of your sentences. Hyphens are most often used to draw two or more words together to act as a single word (*eighty-two, high-school* teacher), to separate some prefixes from the words to which they are attached (*non-European*), and to break a word at the end of a line when there isn't room for the whole word (*imposs-ible.*) Here are the uses of the hyphen in greater detail:

1. Use hyphens to form certain compound words:

do-gooder   has-been
do-it-yourself   mother-in-law
forget-me-not   tenth-grader
great-grandfather   stick-in-the-mud

There are some compounds that were once hyphenated but are now one word:

housekeeper   dropout
roommate

Check your dictionary for the accepted way to write other compounds.

2. Use hyphens between two or more words acting together as a single adjective before a noun:

> They lived a *hand-to-mouth* existence during the Depression.
> Walter Johnson is a *well-known* lawyer in town.
> This was a *never-to-be-forgotten* day.

When two or more words acting as a single adjective follow the noun they modify, do not hyphenate them:

> During the Depression, their existence was *hand to mouth*.
> Walter Johnson is *well known* in town.
> The day will *never be* forgotten.

Do not use hyphens between two words when the first word in a pair is an adverb ending in *ly:*

> a poorly written paper
> a barely concealed smile

Some adjectives are always hyphenated whether they precede or follow the noun they modify:

even-tempered   shirt-sighted
high-pressure   simple-minded

Check your dictionary for hyphenated adjectives.

3. Hyphenate compound numbers from twenty-one to ninety-nine:

eighty-two
sixty-three

But:

one hundred and one
four hundred and three

Hyphenate fractions:

one-half cup of sugar
three-quarters empty

Note: Do not hyphenate fractions used as nouns.

one half of a tank of gas
three quarters of the auditorium

Hyphenate decades written in words:

eighteen-nineties
nineteen-twenties

4. Use a hyphen when prefixes are joined with *proper* nouns or *proper* adjectives:

all-	all-American
anti-	anti-American
mid-	mid-Atlantic
pan-	pan-American
post-	Post-Victorian
pro-	pro-Chinese
trans-	trans-Siberian
un-	un-American

When a modifier has two contrasting prefixes, the first one stands by itself with a hyphen.

Pro- and anti-American forces clashed.

Check your dictionary for the hyphenation of prefixes joined with common nouns.

5. Hyphenate words with an *ex-* prefix where *ex* means "former":

ex-husband
ex-president

Hyphenate words with a *self-* prefix (but not words in which the root is *self*):

PREFIX	ROOT
self-respect	selfish
self-made	selfless
self-satisfaction	

6. Hyphenate words that may be mistaken for other words:

They had a *run-in* about letting boys *run in* the girls' race.

The thieves wanted the upholsterer to *re-cover* the stolen pink sofa in green so that the owner could not identify it and *recover* his property.

Do not break up a syllable:

NO: He dropped out of school because he needed to help his family.
YES: He dropped out of school because he needed to help his family.

Do not divide contractions:

NO: He hits well but he can-
't run.
YES: He hits well but he
can't run.

Do not divide numbers written in figures:

NO: The population of the city was 367,-
463 in 1977.
YES: The population of the city was
367,463 in 1977.

Do not leave one letter hanging at the end of a line:

NO: He wanted to be a-
lone.
YES: He wanted to be alone.

7. When you must divide a word at the end of a line because you've run
out of room, hyphenate the word between syllables:

Although the council had considered the proposal, they, nonetheless, turned it down.

Do not break up one-syllable words:

NO: After all was said and done, he did what he wanted.
YES: After all was said and done,
he did what he wanted.

Check your dictionary for the proper syllabification of words.

USES OF THE APOSTROPHE

Incorrect use of the apostrophe is the single most consistent spelling
problem in the work of many writers. If you leave out apostrophes or if
you put them in where they don't belong, you may need to give your writing
a special proofreading in which you examine your work super-closely just
for these errors. Taking the time to add omitted apostrophes and remove
unnecessary ones will help you avoid a major spelling problem and make
your writing easier to read and more publicly acceptable. Chiefly, use
apostrophes to show possession or to show that a letter (or number) has

been left out. Never use *'s* to show the plural of a noun or to show the *-s* form of a verb. Here are some pointers on where (and where not) to put apostrophes:

1. Use the apostrophe plus *s* to form the possessive of nouns not ending in *s:*

NOUN	POSSESSIVE
Rachel	Rachel's boots (boots belonging to Rachel)
children	children's toys (toys of the children)
men	men's room (room for men)

2. Use the apostrophe alone to form the possessive of nouns ending in *s:*

NOUN	POSSESSIVE
boys	boys' team (team of the boys)
Louis	Louis' hat (hat belonging to Louis)
ladies	ladies' room (room for ladies)
friends	friends' house (house of the friends—meaning more than one friend)

Note the difference:

friend's house (the house of *one* friend)
friends' house (the house of *two or more* friends)

You can always determine if the noun is singular or plural by converting the possessive to a prepositional phrase with *of* or *for:*

the dog's tail (the tail of the dog—singular)
the dogs' tails (the tails of the dogs—plural)
ladies' room (room for ladies—plural)
children's hour (hour for children—plural)
Louis' hat (the hat of Louis—singular)
the Smiths' house (the house of the Smiths—plural)
two cents' worth (the worth of two cents—plural)

When a singular noun ends in *s*, form the possessive by adding either the apostrophe alone or *'s*. If adding *'s* would cause difficulty in pronunciation, add the apostrophe alone.

Moses' followers (*Moses's* would be difficult to pronounce.)
Charles's hats (*Charles'* would also be acceptable.)

3. Hyphenated words take the apostrophe after the last part of the word to form the possessive:

a mother-in-law's delight
a do-it-yourselfer's dream

4. To show joint ownership by a pair or group of individuals, add *'s* to the last word only:

Mary and Tom's house (the house belonging to both Mary and Tom)

To show individual ownership, add *'s* to each word in the pair or series:

Mary's and Tom's shoes (the shoes belonging to Mary and the shoes belonging to Tom)

5. Use a possessive form before an *-ing* word:

I was impressed by Mary's learning to drive at fourteen.

(This says *learning to drive at fourteen* was what impressed me.)

I was impressed by Mary learning to drive at fourteen.

(This says Mary herself impressed me because of her accomplishment in learning to drive so young.)

6. Sometimes you need a double possessive (an *of* plus a possessive form) to make your meaning clear:

A song of Sally (Is it a song *about* Sally or is it Sally's song?)

A song of Sally's (Here the meaning is clear; it's Sally's song.)

7. Do not use the apostrophe for the possessive pronouns:

PRONOUNS	POSSESSIVE PRONOUNS
he	his
she	hers
it	its
us	ours
you	yours
they	theirs

8. Use the apostrophe to mark omissions in shortened forms. The apostrophe takes the place of the missing letter or letters:

are not	=	aren't	(missing *o*)
she will	=	she'll	(missing *wi*)
cannot	=	can't	(missing *no*)
could not	=	couldn't	(missing *o*)
do not	=	don't	(missing *o*)
he will	=	he'll	(missing *wi*)
it is	=	it's	(missing *i*)
is not	=	isn't	(missing *o*)
must not	=	mustn't	(missing *o*)
she will	=	she'll	(missing *wi*)
should not	=	shouldn't	(missing *o*)

they are	=	they're	(missing *a*)
they will	=	they'll	(missing *wi*)
you are	=	you're	(missing *a*)
we have	=	we've	(missing *ha*)
would not	=	wouldn't	(missing *o*)

9. Use the apostrophe to indicate omitted numerals:

| 1979 | '79 |
| class of 1981 | '81 |

WATCH OUT FOR OMITTED APOSTROPHES AND UNNECESSARY APOSTROPHES

1. If you're a writer who fails to use the apostrophe, then you need to retrain yourself to *think* about using it and understand why you should use it. The apostrophe is a shortcut in possessives and contractions.
Instead of saying "the book belonging to Bill" or "the book that belongs to Bill," you say "Bill's book."

A trick to using the apostrophe correctly in possessives is to determine whether the word is singular or plural *before* you make it possessive.

The word is	*boy*
The hats belonging to one *boy*	*boy* + 's hats = the (one) *boy's* hats
The word is	*boys*
The hats belonging to many *boys*	*boys* + ' = the (many) *boys'* hats

2. You may be a writer who puts the apostrophe in the wrong place. When you combine two words into one, you shorten their pronunciation by leaving out a letter. The apostrophe shows where a letter has been left out.

NO:	YES:
could'nt	couldn't

There is nothing missing between *could* and *not*. The missing letter is the *o* in *not*. The *o* is replaced by the apostrophe—*couldn't*. Similar contractions containing *not* are formed in the same way:

NO:	YES:
do'nt	don't
would'nt	wouldn't
is'nt	isn't

10. Use the apostrophe to indicate the omission of one or more letters in a word:

sock it to them	sock it to 'em
rock and roll	rock 'n' roll
alligator	'gator
madam	ma'am

Doesn't is a difficult word to spell. Be sure to spell it correctly:

NO:	YES:
dosen't	doesn't

3. You may be a writer who uses the apostrophe where none belongs. Most unnecessary apostrophes are added in an attempt to show the plural. Remember that all English nouns show their plural without apostrophes:

bed	beds
glass	glasses
Carter	Carters, the Carters
	(not: the Carter's)
Kennedy	Kennedys, the Kennedys
	(not: the Kennedy's)

Remember, too, that all verbs show the -s form without apostrophes:

does
cuts
listens

Note these exceptions:

Show the plurals of letters, words used as words, and abbreviations by adding *'s.*

This time, call the *Z's* before the *A's.*
I told that scoundrel, "No *if's, and's,* or *but's."*
They all have *Ph.D.'s.*

11. Use *'s* to form the plurals of letters, numbers, words referred to as words, and abbreviations:

p and q	p's and q's
1 and 2	1's and 2's
1920	1920's
and and *but*	*and's* and *but's*
GI	GI's

If there is no danger of confusion, an *s* alone may be added:

1920	1920s
GI	GIs

Exercise 9 The following sentences are taken from a student paper on golf. This student had difficulty deciding when to use apostrophes, especially in *its* and *it's*. Correct his errors by either adding or omitting apostrophes wherever necessary.

1. If people would take the time to learn about golf, they would appreciate its fusion of mental and physical challenge.
2. Its a great game enjoyed by young and old in increasing numbers.
3. It's a game everyone can learn easily and quickly.
4. It is'nt an easy task hitting that little ball 500 yards, over hills, around trees, across creeks, past sandtraps, and into a hole a few inches' wide.
5. Golf is truly a thinking mans' game.
6. Golfs' appeal is universal.
7. Its easy to understand why it's so popular.
8. Its over 500 years old.
9. This fact alone should attest to the games' timelessness and the dedication of its players.

Exercise 10 Rewrite each of the following phrases so that the noun or pronoun is in the possessive form.

Example: the trees of the neighborhood
          the neighborhood's trees

1. the army of France
2. the voice of Mary
3. the name of someone else
4. the work for Harry

5. the theme of the novel
6. the heat of the day
7. the house of them
8. the room for ladies
9. the toys of the children
10. the book of Charles
11. the hat of my mother-in-law
12. the nerve of him

Exercise 11 Form a contraction in each of the following sentences.

Example: We are lost.
We're lost.

1. It is mine.
2. Do not come late.
3. He will find us.
4. You are being foolish.
5. Give them hell!
6. In 1941 the war began.

Exercise 12 Substitute a possessive pronoun (his, her, its, their, someone's, any-one's) in each of the following phrases.

Example: my sister's husband; <u>her</u> husband

1. a woman's hat _____ hat
2. the pen of the boy _____ pen
3. a family's car _____ car
4. the mane of a lion _____ mane
5. a bicycle belonging to an unknown person _____ bicycle

Exercise 13 Find and correct any misspellings in the following passage from an article about jury selection:

The perspective jury is led out into a small jury room to wait until the judge acomplishes some busness with the attornies. I am the only woman in the room. Three men begin a conversation begining with "She" as if I were not present. They conclude that my chances of bein selected for the jury are zero. "Your a goner," they finally admit to me. My shoulder aches from the wait of lugging around my shoulder bag and two novles all day. One man attemts to cheer me. "Hell dismiss you and you can go home for the day and cook diner. We'll probly be here 'till they get a jury. He looks like a deturmined son of a bitch." I decide I like his forthriteness about the judge. We all have sanctuary in hear. I all ready have a sense of belonging, even though the concensus is that I am washed up. A car-rental execetive offers me a life-saver. "Listen," he says. "That defence laywer is not going to pick a smart lady chemist to sit on a drug pusher's case. Your threw."

Part
Five

Being
Practical

Chapter 18 / Writing the Research Essay

Students in a freshman writing class were asked to write down the first words that popped into their minds when they heard the words *research paper*. Their responses included these:

library

stack of books

card catalog

confusion

boring

time consuming

last minute

typing

microfilm

Reader's Guide

why?

Like some of these students, you may think of the research paper as joyless, boring, uninspiring, and meaningless. With its stacks and cards and numbers, books and magazines and microfilm, the library may seem mazelike as you wander from room to room, trying to appear as if you know what you are doing. As you write your paper, you may feel overwhelmed by the amount of expert information around you and be tempted to bury your own good ideas and judgments by simply recording what the "experts" say. That is why research papers are often dull, lifeless reports and not essays at all.

But the research papers that you write for your English class and for other classes as well will be essays—essays in which all the writing skills you have practiced come into play. In your writing, you are always making connections—between words, between sentences, between paragraphs—so that all the parts of the essay work together to produce a unified piece of writing. The research essay asks you to make connections in a larger, more complex way by relating your own thinking and writing skills to the ideas and information provided by other writers. This chapter highlights the research paper as another essay by attempting to answer the questions students most often ask and by providing the information and techniques you will need to write this paper.

WHY A RESEARCH PAPER? No writer knows everything. Beginners or professionals, all writers must eventually go outside their own experiences to find information. You aren't expected to be an expert—in women's fashions of the 1920s, in the life cycle of a snail, in the economic development of China, or in a zillion other specialized subjects—but you are expected to be able to find information when you need it. You've *already* done research in writing personal essays; you've called on your memory and your personal relationships and experiences. Now you must find out how to call on the research of other writers, on the information that they make available to you in their writings, which are based on *their* research—their memories, their personal relationships and experiences, their observations and insights, their scientific experiments and library research.

The research paper in your English class is not simply an academic exercise. It has the same goals and involves the same procedures as the research you will undertake on your own, on the job or in upper-class courses, when you need to find information on a particular subject. If you need to find out all you can about teen-age acoholism because you know of someone who needs help; if an employer asks you to find out what you can about the baby boom of the 1950s; if you need to find out about the effects of marijuana on the body, you'll have to know how to find the information. You'll need people to talk to and books and articles to read. And you'll have to know what to do with the information you find to get the most out of it.

As a researcher, you learn by finding sources, reading critically, and evaluating and summarizing what you've read. You put all your research together into a paper that you, as a writer, *control*. You credit your sources by providing footnotes and a bibliography. You follow the same procedure as that of professional writers who prepare their manuscripts for publication.

WHAT IS A RESEARCH PAPER? Students who wrote research papers before college often report that they were not encouraged to include their own ideas and judgments. Their high-school research papers were simply *reports* of their findings on a subject. One student (whose college research essay appears in the next chapter) described these high-school reports like this:

> I did the usual high school "research paper." The research paper that I refer to is the type where you run to the encyclopedia, copy half of the words, maybe change a few by means of a thesaurus, scribble your name at the top, and hand it in.

In your college English class, the research paper that you write is, first of all, an essay. All essays require research. Your personal essays rely on personal research into your observations and memory. Although you may check a book or magazine article to get started on a personal essay, your chief research tool is *you.* (See Chapter 2, pages 15–31, for suggestions on getting started.) Now, in the research paper, you turn to information provided by *others. Re-search,* in fact, means to *search* through the same books and magazines and newspapers that others have explored. Your research invites you to see through your own eyes what has gone before and to offer your own ideas about the information that you find.

Because many students feel powerless when confronted with vast amounts of information, they forget the essay part of the research paper. They wind up doing a "patchwork" paper, where they present the ideas of one writer and then another and another. The patches are loosely stitched together, producing a collection of patches but not a quilt. Think of the research paper as a research *essay,* which you, as the writer, must design and write.

WHEN TO BEGIN   One pitfall for many students who are assigned research papers is time; they wait until the assignment is just about due and then dash to the library to find that the books they need for their paper have already been checked out. Time must be on your side when you write a research paper because it is going to take you time to find a subject, settle on a thesis, do the research, take notes, write the paper, rewrite it, produce accurate footnotes and bibliography, and, finally, revise. The research essay, because it involves a more intricate balancing of parts than any other kind of essay you have written, needs time for careful revision, for a studied look *after* you have completed what you think is a close-to-final draft. Ideally, you should let this draft sit for a week and then go back to it and revise—checking each sentence and each paragraph for clarity and organization.

HOW TO BEGIN   Chances are your instructor will provide you with a general subject for your paper—women, politics, the media, education, drugs—and you'll have to narrow the subject to a workable, limited topic. Don't mistake the subject for a topic. In their eagerness to begin, students often adopt a broad subject such as "women" as their topic and forget all they know about narrowing a subject. If you haven't been provided with a general subject, then you'll need to find one and go through the same narrowing process.

You can begin narrowing your subject by talking to an expert, by finding an instructor on campus who will talk with you about his or her field—about urban politics or mass media or Chinese communes—so that you can begin to think about the range of your subject. You can begin by talking to a reference librarian—by asking where to find materials on housing problems or women in politics or government agencies. Every library provides information on how to use the library, and many provide excellent pamphlets on using the library to do research. Find out.

You may begin by freewriting to find a topic that has *research potential*. The freewriting you've done for personal essays reveals your personal feelings and experiences. Now you can use the same writing at the beginning of a research project to tap your own ideas and *questions* about a general subject. Suppose that you have been assigned a broad subject, "the media." You have vast experience with the media: you've attended movies; watched television; read books, magazines, and newspapers. Where do your experiences take you in your writing? Your focused freewriting may lead you to an interesting idea that has research potential.

Consider the following sample of a student's freewriting on the media:

> Media, newspapers, magazines, newspapers. Ben Franklin—didn't he do something with early newspapers? Philadelphia. Didn't he work with his brother in Boston? Dogood papers, newspapers. How did Americans get their information in colonial America? What was the first American newspaper? When and where did it begin? Who started it? What was its circulation? How long did it last? When did it fold? Why? How many newspapers are there today? What is the largest selling newspaper in America today? If it's the Enquirer, why? What do we want in our newspapers? Violence—to read about murder and killings? Why? Why is there so much violence in newspapers—in news in general—on television? All you have to do is turn on the evening news or flip the channel at night to see bombardments of violence. Violence.

The student began with Benjamin Franklin and early American newspapers and ended with a specific question about a newer medium—television—and violence. Along the way, he asked numbers of questions, some of which call for factual answers: *What was the first American newspaper? Who started it? How long did it last?* Although these questions lead to facts, they can also lead to dead ends unless the student asks more provocative questions. He can find out that Benjamin Harris started the first American newspaper in colonial Boston in 1690. The paper, called *Publick Occurrences Both Forreign and Domestick,* was suppressed by the governor four days later. These are facts, but from them, the student can ask powerful questions that may lead to a topic that has research potential: *Why did the governor of Massachusetts suppress Harris's paper?* With this question in mind, he may be on the way to a study of freedom of the press. Or he may follow another lead from his freewriting, researching the subject of violence on television (as he actually did in his research paper, which appears in Chapter 19).

The student next must turn his spontaneous questioning into a *working question* for his research: *Why were early American newspapers suppressed?* or *What are the effects of television violence on our society?* He can now go to the library armed with a purpose because he has narrowed a broad subject into a manageable, researchable topic. Along the way, he has discovered a *working question,* which may be discarded or which may, in fact, be turned into the thesis of his paper. Now the research begins. The student will have to read and read hard and extensively; he will have to think hard and rethink, write and rewrite.

HOW TO RESEARCH —THE HUNT

Finding sources for the information you will need is like participating in a hunt. The trail leads to one clue and then to another and finally to the sources you will use in your paper. Another clue may lead to a dead end. In all the research papers you write, the moves are similar: you check through the card catalog, encyclopedias, and periodical indexes.

Check the card catalog

The card catalog can be the first step in your research. The card catalog is an alphabetical index to the printed materials within a library. Find out how the card catalog in your library works. Does it catalog books by the Library of Congress System or the Dewey Decimal System? The following tips for researchers show you how to use the cards.

What's in the cards?

Author card

```
001.5
S      Schramm, Wilbur Lang, 1907--
```

Title card

```
001.5
S      Men, messages, and media;  a look
       at human communications
```

Subject card

```
001.5
S      MASS MEDIA

       Schramm, Wilbur Lang, 1907--

          Men, messages, and media;  a look at
       human communication
       New York, Harper & Row, 1973.
          341 p. illus.  21cm.
          Includes bibliographical reference.

       1. Communication  2. Mass Media  3. Title
```

The card catalog lists every nonfiction book in the library by *author's name,* by *title,* and by one or more *subject headings.* The sample cards reveal the following information:

1. Call number indicates where the book can be found in the library.
2. Subject heading.
3. Author's name and date of birth. The 1907— (without a second year) indicates that he is living.
4. Title of book, place of publication, publisher's name, and year of publication.
5. Format of book: "341 p." indicates the number of pages; "illus." indicates that the book contains illustrations; "21 cm." indicates the size of the book in centimeters.
6. Additional information about the book: this is a cataloger's note indicating that this book includes a bibliography.
7. Lists the subject headings under which the book is cataloged.

Clues:

The cataloger's note "Includes bibliographical references" is an important clue, telling you that this book offers a listing of other related books that may be useful to you in your research.

The subject heading "communication" at the bottom of the card offers an additional clue, telling you that the book is cataloged under another heading. Go to the subject heading *Communication* to see what other sources you can find. As you begin your project, you need to follow clues that take you from one possibility to another. If you are looking at cards for a broad subject, for example, you may be tempted to look under only *one* subject heading. That may lead you nowhere. The subject heading *Media* in one library turns up a few cards on *Media and Education,* but at the bottom of the cards under the subject headings, there are other clues—additional reference cards:

See MASS MEDIA
See MASS COMMUNICATION
See TELECOMMUNICATION

Following the clue *See Mass Media,* you find over 200 cards under such headings as:

MASS MEDIA—BIBLIOGRAPHY
MASS MEDIA—CENSORSHIP
MASS MEDIA—POLITICAL ASPECTS
MASS MEDIA—PSYCHOLOGICAL ASPECTS
MASS MEDIA—SOCIAL ASPECTS
MASS MEDIA—UNITED STATES

Following the clue *See Telecommunication,* you find over 100 cards under these headings:

TELEVISION ADVERTISING
TELEVISION AND CHILDREN
TELEVISION BROADCASTING
TELEVISION BROADCASTING—BIBLIOGRAPHY
TELEVISION BROADCASTING—SOCIAL ASPECTS
TELEVISION BROADCASTING—UNITED STATES
TELEVISION IN ADVERTISING
TELEVISION IN EDUCATION
TELEVISION IN POLITICS
TELEVISION INDUSTRY—UNITED STATES
TELEVISION—LAW AND LEGISLATION
TELEVISION—PROGRAMS
TELEVISION—STAGE SETTING

Check the call numbers for library locations As you work through the card catalog, notice the call numbers under which books are listed. Because libraries categorize books by subject, you can find the *general locations* where most of the books on your subject are shelved. In continuing your search for books on the media, you see that many books are stored under:

> P   92

and

> 001.5

This information takes you to the stacks.

Check the stacks Many libraries store their books in open stacks, where the books are accessible. In open stacks, once you know where most of the books on your subject are shelved, go directly to those stacks to browse. A book that you can hold in your hands will turn up more possibilities (or fewer possibilities) than a card in the catalog can indicate. So take the time to look through the shelves.

If your library has closed stacks, you cannot go directly to the books. From the card catalog, decide on the titles of books that look promising. You request these books by giving an attendant a slip of paper on which you have written the author, title, and call number of each book. After a short wait, the book is sent to the desk, where you collect it.

Find an overview Find a book that provides an overview of your subject. The overview enables you to see the range of a subject and its research possibilities. You will be able to do some general reading.

How do you find such a book? Again, there are clues for you to follow, contained in the book itself:

1. Consider the title of the book.
2. Read the table of contents.
3. Look at the date of publication.
4. Find out if there is a bibliography within the book.

As you look through the titles of books on the media, for example, you may turn up these titles:

American Journalism
The Press and America
A History of Book Publishing
The Book in America
The Presidents and the Press
The Correspondent's War
A Tower in Babel: A History of Broadcasting in the United States to 1933
Media in America
Newspapers in Colonial Times

If you know that you want to research American journalism, two books, *American Journalism* and *The Press and America,* may offer you the overview you need. If you want to study book publishing, *A History of Book Publishing* and *The Book in America* will be possible sources. The next two, *Presidents and the Press* and *The Correspondent's War,* will not provide overviews because their titles indicate more specific studies. *A Tower in Babel: A History of Broadcasting in the United States to 1933* concerns broadcasting. If you're interested in television, you'll know at once that this book will not be helpful because its study ends in 1933. If your topic is radio, however, then *A Tower in Babel* may be a valuable source. *Newspapers in Colonial Times* offers a specific study, but *Media in America* sounds general enough to offer the overview you need. You pull *Media in America* from the shelf, glance through the table of contents, and see that the book begins with colonial America:

PART ONE: The Media and the Idea of Freedom
1. How the Media Began
2. The Development of Freedom
3. The Revolution and the Media

The last section of the book is called "The Media in the Twentieth Century" and includes chapters on both radio and television.

You note the date of publication is 1974. This means that the book's study of the media includes seventy-four years of the twentieth century. Another book on the media in America published in 1947 will cover only forty-seven years of this century. It will not include recent developments.

In the last pages of *Media in America,* you find a section called "For Further Reading." Here is another clue; the author is leading you to other books and articles. Some of them may be possible sources. You conclude that *Media in America* is the place to start.

Check an
encyclopedia

The following encyclopedias offer general information on most subjects:

Chambers's Encyclopaedia
Collier's Encyclopedia
Encyclopedia Americana
Encyclopaedia Britannica
New Columbia Encyclopedia

The *Encyclopaedia Britannica* is one of the best general encyclopedias. The newest edition (1974) is divided into three parts: the *Propaedia* (one volume), the *Micropaedia* (ten volumes), and the *Macropaedia* (nineteen volumes). The Macropaedia offers expansive, in-depth articles on many topics. At the end of each entry is a bibliography that you can scan.

As you read through the encyclopedia, use *note cards* to jot down notes and questions. You can read for general information, but some of the information may lead you to a research topic.

In taking notes, you record what strikes you as interesting or important. The facts may later fit into your paper as evidence or support. The information may lead you to research possibilities. As you read, you weigh the possibilities, think about the evidence, and ask questions. See pages 475–476 on note taking.

Check a
periodical index

Books are not the only sources you bring to your research paper. In fact, if you are researching a contemporary topic or a recent event, you may not find information published in books. Libraries also store periodicals (magazines, journals, and newspapers). Leafing through the 4,000 or so periodicals that many libraries store is an impossibility, but you can use a guide to periodicals that categorizes articles by subject.

The most useful guide to periodicals is the *Reader's Guide to Periodical Literature,* which is published monthly and is an index to about 160 magazines. Printed below is a sample from the *Reader's Guide:*

ADVERTISING
See also
Soft drink industry—Advertising
Awards, prizes, etc.
Saturday evening post television commercial awards. il Sat Eve Post 248:40-1 S '76
Economic aspects
Advertising is having some kind of year! C. J. Loomis. il Fortune 94:136-9+ Ag '76
Freedom must advertise; address. July 1, 1976. T. C. Dillon. Vital Speeches 42:678-82 S 1 '76
Effectiveness research
See Advertising research
Psychological aspects
Mass advertising; the message, not the measure. L. Bogart. bibl f il Harvard Bus R 54:107-16 S '76
Want ads
See Advertising, Classified
→ ADVERTISING, Classified
How to read the newspaper want ads. Ladies Home J 93:40+ Ag '76
Anecdotes, facetiae, satire, etc.
Classified information; jobs for celebrities. R. Kent. il Harp Baz 109:114-15 Ag '76

Subject: Classified advertisements
Title of article: "How to Read the Newspaper Want ads."
Title of magazine: *Ladies' Home Journal*
Volume: 93
Page numbers: 40+
Date: August 1976

Another widely used index is the *New York Times Index,* which catalogs articles printed in the *New York Times* from its first issue, September 18, 1851, to the present date. Recent issues of both magazines and newspapers are usually available on the shelves or on microfilm in the library. Ask the librarian for guidance in locating the periodicals you need. See the list of indexes on page 475.

Until you actually examine the periodicals, especially old magazines and newspapers, you will be unaware of the riches stored within them. You will find, very often, the same social concerns in a magazine from the 1920s that you find today: politicians seeking votes, police fighting crime, Presidents visiting abroad and toasting foreign dignitaries. Pick up an old magazine—leaf through it; look through the articles and advertisements.

Exercise 1 Find the *New York Times* of the day of your birth. Record the important news of the day—local, national, and international. What was the weather on the day you were born? What programs were on television? on radio? What was the lead editorial? Describe the concerns of the letters to the editor. Describe the advertisements.

Exercise 2 Find your local newspaper of the day of your birth. What were the headlines of the day? If there is a "help" columnist like Ann Landers, what were the problems and solutions offered in these columns? Compare the concerns of that day with the concerns you find in a recent newspaper.

Exercise 3 Find an encyclopedia article on your research topic. Check the bibliography entries at the end. Track down one of the sources that looks promising. Describe the source in some detail.

Exercise 4 Find a book that provides an overview of your topic. Check to see if there is a bibliography at the end of the book. Determine whether any of the listed books or periodicals will be of help to you.

Exercise 5 Find five articles on your topic through the *Reader's Guide to Periodical Literature.* Determine the value of each as a source. Tell why each is or is not valuable to *your* research.

General and special reference materials The following list supplies you with information about general and special reference materials: encyclopedias, dictionaries, indexes, and other useful sources.

General encyclopedias *Chambers's Encyclopaedia,* 15 vols.
Collier's Encyclopedia, 24 vols.

Columbia Encyclopedia, 1 vol.
Encyclopaedia Britannica; Micropaedia, 10 vols.; Macropaedia, 19 vols.; Propaedia, 1 vol.
Encyclopedia Americana, 30 vols.

Special Check with the reference librarian to see which specialized encyclopedias
encyclopedias your library stores. The following is a brief list of special encyclopedias:

Paul Edwards, ed., *The Encyclopedia of Philosophy* (1973)
Encyclopedia of Banking and Finance (1973)
Encyclopedia of Educational Research (1969)
Encyclopedia of World Art (1959–1968)
H. J. Eysenck et al., eds., *Encyclopedia of Psychology* (1972)
Peter Gray, ed., *The Encyclopedia of the Biological Sciences* (1970)
William L. Langer, ed., *An Encyclopedia of World History* (1972)
Larousse World Mythology (1968)
Richard B. Morris and Henry S. Commager, eds., *Encyclopedia of American History* (1970)
The New Oxford History of Music (1954)
David L. Sills, ed., *International Encyclopedia of the Social Sciences* (1968)
Robert E. Spiller et al., eds., *Literary History of the United States* (1974)
UNESCO, *World Survey of Education* (1955–date)
Van Nostrand's Scientific Encyclopedia (1968)
Robert C. Zaehner, ed., *The Concise Encyclopedia of Living Faiths* (1959)

Almanacs, *Facts on File* (1940–date)
yearbooks, *Information Please Almanac* (1947–date)
and atlases *The New York Times Encyclopedic Almanac* (1970–date)
The World Almanac and Book of Facts (1868–date)
Year Book of World Affairs (1947–date)
Encyclopaedia Britannica World Atlas (1959)
National Geographic Atlas of the World (1970)
The Times Atlas of the World (1968)

Dictionaries See Chapter 12, pages 308–312.

Biography *Biographical Index* (1947–date)
Chambers's Biographical Dictionary (1969)
Current Biography: Who's News and Why (1940–date)
Dictionary of American Biography (1928–1958)
International Who's Who (1935–date)
Webster's Biographical Dictionary (1971)
Who's Who (1849–date)
Who's Who in America (1899–date)

Quotations John Bartlett and E. M. Beck, eds., *Familiar Quotations* (1968)
Bergen Evans, ed., *Dictionary of Quotations* (1968)
The Oxford Dictionary of Quotations (1953)
Burton E. Stevenson, ed., *The Home Book of Quotations, Classical and Modern* (1967)

Indexes Valuable indexes, in addition to the *Reader's Guide to Periodical Litera-ture* and the *New York Times Index,* include the following:

> *Agricultural Index*
> *Applied Science and Technology Index*
> *Art Index*
> *Biography Index*
> *Business Periodical Index*
> *Education Index*
> *Social Sciences and Humanities Index*
> *United States Government Publications* (monthly catalog)

Special guides The following guides will lead you to the title of a book when you have only the author's name or to the author's name when you have only the title. Because these guides are published annually, you can use them to look for recent books on certain topics or to find out if a book is still in print:

> *Books in Print*
> *Cumulative Book Index*
> *Paperbound Books in Print*
> *Subject Guide to Books in Print*

READING HARD AND TAKING NOTES You must now apply the skills you bring with you as a writer to *reading* the writing of others. As you read, you will be observing and evaluating the support writers provide for their arguments, the development of their theses, their approaches and attitudes toward their subjects.

To determine the value of a book, consider the title, table of contents, and date of publication—the same things you considered when you were looking for an overview (see pages 470–471). You can also skim the preface or introduction to discover whether the book will be useful for your research.

Everything you read provides you with information, but now you must think critically as you read. If you are after facts, you should not be satisfied with articles in popular newspapers, nor should you accept a writer's opinion as fact. You must read hard to find the substantive information you need to support your own thesis. First read headings and topic sentences of paragraphs to get an outline of the author's ideas. Then read for details and facts.

Taking notes does two jobs: it is a way to keep track of what you read, and it is a way to record your own questions and judgments as they occur to you while you are reading. The more accurate your notes, the easier the job of writing your paper will be. In fact, many researchers know that once their note taking is complete, the job of writing the paper itself will go quickly.

Many researchers use 3″ x 5″ index cards to record each note they take and each bibliographical source they consider. Although experienced researchers may use other means to keep track of their notes, it is a good idea to use index cards for your first papers. The note cards provide an easy way for you to organize your material because they can be arranged and, if necessary, rearranged in any order you choose.

Take your note cards with you on the first trip to the library because the first step in your research is to begin a *working bibliography*.

How to keep a working bibliography

Keep track of each source you consider, either on a separate note card or on a list. So that you won't have to relocate the source the night before the paper is due, include all bibliographical information. For a book, include the call number, the author's name, title, edition number (if there is one), place of publication, publisher, and date of publication. For an article, include the author's name, title of article, title of periodical, volume number, date, and page numbers. It is a good idea to assign a number to each source.

Bibliography Card:

> ⑨
>
> Gerbner, George, and Larry Gross,
> "The Scary World of TV's Heavy
> Viewer," *Psychology Today*, 9
> (April 1976) 41-45.

If you keep a running list of each source you consider, include bibliographical information for each book and magazine or newspaper article that sounds promising. As you check each source on the list, cross off those that will not be helpful for your paper. Keep those that will provide you with useful information.

The student whose paper is reprinted in the next chapter used the following working bibliography to guide him through his research. Notice that he numbered each source.

Working Bibliography

1. Arlen, Michael J. "Cold, Bright Charms of Immortality." *New Yorker*, 50 (Jan. 27, 1975), pp. 73-78.

2. Beier, Ernst G. (interview) "Hidden TV Messages Create Social Discontent." *Intellect*, 104 (Feb. 1976), p. 350

3. Bowles, Jerry. "How We Got This Way: TV-Styled America." *Vogue*, 166 (Feb. 1976), p. 169.

4. Bromberg, W. and George, G. "Can TV Crime Shows Prevent Violence." *Today's Health*, 47 (May 1969), p. 88+.

no good 5. ~~Cater, Douglass., and Others. Television as a Social Force: New Approaches to TV Criticism. N.Y.: Praeger Publishers, 1975.~~

6. Chin, Tony. "The Violent World of the TV Viewer." *Sci. Digest*, 77 (Mar. 1975), pp. 80-83.

7. Cripps, Edward J. "Violence and Children's TV." *America*, 135 (Sept. 11, 1976), pp. 116-118.

no 8. ~~"Ending Mayhem." Time, 107 (June 7, 1976), p. 63.~~

9. Gerbner, George. and Gross, Larry. "The Scary World of TV's Heavy Viewer." *Psych. Today*, 9 (Apr. 1976) pp. 41-45+.

10. Harris, George J. "More Blood on the Tube." *Psych. Today*, 9 (Apr. 1976), p. 4.

11. Niemeyer, Gerhart. "Sex and Violence." *Nat. Rev.* 27 (Aug. 1, 1975), p. 834.

How to take notes as you read *Write out essentials in details;* don't rely on your memory. You might think you will remember what you meant by:

> Authors provide important research findings on effects of violence on heavy TV watchers.

But by the time you sit down to read fifty note cards, you will probably have forgotten what the findings were. See the sample note cards on the next page.

1. *Devise an identity heading for each note.* As you read, you find information that belongs together. If you are researching the effects of television, you may study the effects on children, on teen-agers, and on adults. Some information may strike you as useful for the beginning of the paper, other information may seem slated for the end. Based on your tentative plan for your paper, write a heading for each card. (*Effects on Children, Good Material for Beginning,* and so forth). You may change your mind as you shuffle the cards once your research is complete, but you will have a start toward classifying the material.

2. *Assign each note card a bibliographical number.* You don't need to copy all bibliographical information (author's name, title, publisher, date, and so forth) for each note card. Instead, assign each bibliographical source a number (No. 9—Gerbner and Gross). As you write your note, use the code number and page number:

9   Gerbner and Goss, p. 41.

Or simply use the author(s) name(s) and page number:

Gerbner and Gross, p. 41.

MANY CRITICS WORRY about violence on television, most out of fear that it stimulates viewers to violent or aggressive acts. Our research, however, indicates that the consequences of experiencing TV's symbolic world of violence may be much more far-reaching.

We feel that television dramatically demonstrates the power of authority in our society, and the risks involved in breaking society's rules. Violence-filled programs show who gets away with what, and against whom. It teaches the role of victim, and the acceptance of violence as a social reality we must learn to live with—or flee from.

We have found that people who watch a lot of TV see the real world as more dangerous and frightening than those who watch very little. Heavy viewers are less trustful of their fellow citizens, and more fearful of the real world.

Since most TV "action-adventure" dramas occur in urban settings, the fear they inspire may contribute to the current flight of the middle class from our cities. The fear may also bring increasing demands for police protection, and election of law-and-order politicians.

Those who doubt TV's influence might consider the impact of the automobile on American society. When the automobile burst upon the dusty highways about the turn of the century, most Americans saw it as a horseless carriage, not as a prime mover of a new way of life. Similarly, those of us who grew up before television tend to think of it as just another medium in a series of 20th-century mass-communications systems, such as movies and radio. But television is not just another medium.

3. *Write one note per card.* Keep track of each piece of information you find on a separate note card. By reserving a note card for each bit of information, you'll be able to shuffle through your cards, placing together those facts and ideas that seem to belong together.

4. *Summarize, paraphrase, or quote.* You do not always need to copy complete passages on your note cards. Study the guidelines for the summary, paraphrase, and quote in the following sample cards. (From the article "The Scary World of TV's Heavy Viewer," by George Gerbner and Larry Gross.)

Summary   When you *summarize,* you write *in your own words* the most outstanding points in a passage, a chapter, or an article. A summary is much shorter than the original. It highlights important information or ideas. After you have read the material, it is wise to turn away from it before recording your observations. Write down what you can remember, and then return to the original to make certain you have not missed an important point. Also make certain you have not accidentally taken *actual phrases* from the original.

> *Effects on TV addicts*
>
> Gerbner and Gross, p. 41.
>
> Gerbner and Gross discuss most important effects of TV violence. Their research shows that heavy TV watchers fear world and distrust others.

Paraphrase In a *paraphrase*, you record an author's ideas *in your own words*. A paraphrase is usually longer than a summary because you record important points and any *specifics* you think useful.

> *Effects on TV addicts*
>
> 9, 41.
>
> Gerbner and Gross say that effects of violence in television are more powerful than we think. Violence, especially for the heavy viewer ("the TV addict") shapes the way he relates to the world. He sees himself as a victim in a powerful society. He accepts violence as the real state in which he lives. TV addicts fear the world they actually live in and distrust others

Quotation A *quotation* records the exact words of an author. Use quotations when you think the author's words are particularly memorable or convincing. Remember to put quotation marks around the exact words of the author, and be sure that you copy capitalization, spelling, and punctuation exactly.

> *Effects on TV addicts*
>
> 9, 41.
>
> Gerbner and Gross say, "We have found that people who watch a lot of TV see the world as more dangerous and frightening than those who watch little. Heavy viewers are less trustful of their fellow citizens, and more fearful of the real world."

Your comments You can also record your own ideas, comments, questions, and judgments on note cards. Too often you forget ideas because you do not record them. Keep track of your own thoughts on note cards.

> Me: Question about Gerbner and Gross study:
>
> If these are the effects on adults who watch TV, what about effects on kids? Serious question. What do we know? Find out.

WATCH OUT FOR PLAGIARISM

Plagiarism literally means *kidnapping*—stealing another's ideas and passing them off as your own. Some students plagiarize *deliberately*. They know what they are doing, and they risk failing a course or being expelled from school if they are caught.

Other students plagiarize *accidentally*. When they write their papers, they do not credit other writers for the ideas they have borrowed because when they take notes, they stay too close to the original and do not paraphrase. Notice in the passage below how close the phrasing is to the original:

ORIGINAL

Many critics worry about violence on television, most out of fear that it stimulates viewers to violent or aggressive acts. Our research, however, indicates that the consequences of experiencing TV's symbolic world of violence may be much more far-reaching.

PLAGIARISM

Critics worry about television violence because they fear it stimulates viewers to violent or aggressive action. Gerbner and Gross find that the consequences of experiencing TV's symbolic violent world may be much more serious.

PARAPHRASE AND QUOTE

Gerbner and Gross say that TV violence has an even more powerful effect than encouraging crime. They say critics recognize only the obvious symptoms, "that it stimulates viewers to violent or aggressive acts."

The following guidelines will help you *avoid* plagiarism:

1. Take accurate notes. Distinguish in your notes between your own ideas and the ideas of other writers.

2. Place quotation marks around *all* material that is not yours and credit the source.

3. Credit any idea that is not yours even if it is paraphrased or summarized and does not appear in quotation marks.

DESIGNING THE PAPER By the end of your research, you will have a stack of note cards, a working thesis, a working bibliography—and most of the work behind you. Now you will need to design the whole essay, as you have done with other essays. You'll need to examine your thesis and specific points of support to determine how to arrange the essay: cause and effect, comparison or contrast, a generalization with specifics? You'll need to think about the beginning, the supporting paragraphs, and the ending (see Chapter 4, "Reach for the Whole Essay: Three More Arrangements.")

As you shuffle and reshuffle your notes, you plan the essay by writing an outline. It may be an informal outline like the following:

> Introduction—Statistics on effects of TV violence on TV addicts
> Effects—Attitudes of TV addicts toward others
> Effects—Ways TV addicts see the world
> Effects—On society as a whole
> Conclusion—Too much TV dangerous

Or you may write a more detailed outline like the one on page 491 of the next chapter.

The final design of the paper is up to you as you weave the research you have done into a paper that is *yours*.

Use your own words The rule of thumb is to write your research paper in your own words unless you want to capture the exact words of another writer for a special purpose. The following examples show how students have woven their research into their own sentences:

> *I Love Lucy* is an international success. The show has been seen in a total of seventy-seven countries.[1] In 1954, in its third season, it was on Monday nights from nine o'clock to nine-thirty. A large department store in Chicago had to change its evening shopping hours from Monday to Thursday because few customers showed up on Monday night, which was "Lucy" night. The telephone company reported that fewer calls than usual were made during that half-hour period.[2]

The student reports on her research in her own words; she footnotes the material because the information is *not* general knowledge; it is taken from materials that she has researched. (See page 484 on footnoting.)

> Simpson's on-the-field record is outstanding. His NFL records include the most rushing yards gained in one season (2,003), the most rushing yards gained in a single game (250), and the most touchdowns scored in a season (23).[6]

Notice how the student controls the material by his own remark: "Simpson's on-the-field record is outstanding." He footnotes the statistics because Simpson's record is not general knowledge.

> In 1974, Amin was busy writing a helpful book to aid his agents on how to spot a spy. Among the pointers Amin included are these: a spy often speaks with a foreign accent; he may be spotted in the day or night but never in the afternoon (that is when he sleeps); he has a lot of money, a good wife, and, of course, a black dog. Sometimes a spy may even be bald.[4] If Amin is right and these really are dead giveaways, then I must assume that half the men in America are spies.

Notice how the student culls from Amin's pointers. He doesn't list all the advice, but he *selects* the material to fit his own purpose—which is to question Amin's improbable advice about spies. He says, "Among the pointers . . ." "If Amin's right . . . then I must assume . . ."

Quote for a purpose Use the exact words of a speaker or writer for a specific purpose:

1. To capture the exact wording because it is memorable or striking
2. To relate the words of a famous quotation to your original ideas
3. To lend authority to your ideas by presenting the exact words of a recognized authority on your subject

When you do use quotations, follow these guidelines: When you want to include only part of a quotation, use ellipses to indicate where material has been left out (see page 421). When you want to emphasize the name of the author as well as the quotation, give the name in your text (As *Benjamin Franklin* said, "Little strokes fell great oaks."). When you want to use a brief quotation in your own sentence but you do not want to emphasize the author's name, cite his name in the footnote. When you use a long quotation, introduce the words with your own remarks (*as one researcher comments; as Benjamin Franklin said*). Read and study the following samples taken from student papers:

> Carter's diligence and his "ability to fine-tune his campaign to the mood and temper of the people"[4] were not surpassed.

Here the student uses the quotation because he wants to capture the precise phrasing, but he does not want to include the author of the words in his sentence. He fits the quotation into his *own* sentence, and then he tells in the footnote who the author is.

> Promising to return Ugandan politics to a democratic control, Amin was jubilantly welcomed as a "legitimate leader . . . a symbol of peace, unity, and social justice."[7]

Notice how the student tailors the quotation to suit his purpose. Again, he does not include the author of the words (except in the footnote) because his emphasis is on the expression.

> Off the court, Nastase is described as a charming, witty, and even shy individual. Then why the "Nasty" routine? When asked about his unique style, Nastase said, "The madder I get, the more hungry I am to win. I think I play better then."[5]

The paper is about tennis player Ilie Nastase's "nasty" behavior. Rather than speculate on Nastase's purposes, the student lets Nastase speak for himself. Notice how the words of the speaker are introduced: "When asked about his unique style, Nastase said . . ."

> In her essay "Reunion," Nora Ephron describes the disillusionment she felt when she attended her tenth college reunion:
>
>> I can pretend that I have come back to Wellesley only because I want to write about it, but I am really here because I still care, I still care about this Mickey Mouse institution; I am foolish enough to think that someday it will do something important for women. That I care at all, that I am here at all, makes me one of them. . . . This college is about as meaningful to the educational process in America as a perfume factory is to the national economy. And all of us care, which makes us all idiots for wasting a minute thinking about the place.[12]

Notice how the student introduces the long quotation with her own words. She quotes at length because she wants to capture Ephron's phrasing and feeling. Note how she sets off the long quotation by indenting and single spacing it. She does not use quotation marks because indenting and single spacing serve the same purpose: they signal that the words are those of another writer.

Follow these guidelines for using long quotations:

1. Consider why you are using a long quotation: Do you want to capture the style and flavor of a whole passage? Can you just as well restate the information yourself?
2. Introduce the long quotation with your own words.
3. Use a colon or a comma to set off the long quotation.
4. Set off a long quotation of over fifty words by indenting five spaces on both sides and single spacing.
5. Use long quotations sparingly (only one or two to a five-page paper).

For additional pointers on punctuation of quotations, see Chapter 16, pages 418–422.

FOOTNOTES

What to footnote Footnotes serve two purposes: they give credit where it is due, and they permit your reader to find your original sources. Generally, *everything* that you have researched should be footnoted. Footnote every quotation, every paraphrase, every summary. Footnote all information that is not common knowledge. You know, for example, that O. J. Simpson is a fast running back, but your research takes you to his record. The facts of his record, which are not general information, should be footnoted. When in doubt about what to footnote and what not to footnote, it's better to footnote.

How to footnote Footnotes look complicated, but they need not be. Determine what your source actually is. If it's a book, is it written by one author or by several authors? Is it an edited book (often a collection of essays that has been compiled by one or more editors)? Is the book a revised edition (if the book was first published in 1921 and revised in 1959, it is important for your reader to know which edition you are using; page numbers in one will not correspond to page numbers in another edition)? If you are using an encyclopedia, which one? What volume? What year was the encyclopedia published?

All book footnotes have common features. They include the following:

1. Name of the author or authors (first name first)
2. Title of the book (underlined in your footnote)
3. Edition number (if other than the first)
4. City where the book was published
5. Name of the publisher
6. Date of publication
7. Page number(s)

Footnoting books One author:

[1] Eric Barnouw, *Tube of Plenty: The Evolution of American Television* (New York: Oxford University Press, 1975), p. 265.

Two authors:

[2] Carl Bernstein and Bob Woodward, *All the President's Men.* (New York: Simon and Schuster, 1974), p. 43.

An edition other than the first:

[3] L. Joseph Stone and Joseph Church, *Childhood and Adolescence: A Psychology of the Growing Person,* 4th ed. (New York: Random House, 1978), p. 17.

An edited book:

> [4] Michele H. Garskof, ed., *Roles Women Play: Readings Toward Women's Liberation* (Belmont, Calif.: Wadsworth Publishing Company, 1971), p. 116.

An essay in an edited book:

> [5] Marlene Dixon, "Why Women's Liberation," in *Roles Women Play: Readings Toward Women's Liberation,* ed. Michele H. Garskof (Belmont, Calif.: Wadsworth Publishing Company, 1971), p. 165.

An encyclopedia:

> [6] "The Art of Television," *Encyclopaedia Britannica,* 1974, Macropaedia.
> [7] "Television," *Collier's Encyclopedia,* 1965.

(Because the encyclopedia is printed in alphabetical order, a volume number is unnecessary.)

Footnotes are numbered *consecutively* throughout your paper. They are placed at the bottom (or *foot*) of the page. Leave a triple space for the first footnote; double space between footnotes. Notice that the first line of each footnote is indented. See Chapter 19 for the layout of footnotes in a research paper. (You may be permitted to use endnotes—a page of footnotes at the end of your paper. Check with your instructor on college policy.)

Once you footnote a source, you do not need to repeat the entire entry. Use the last name of the author and the page number:

> [8] Margaret Mead, *Blackberry Winter: My Earlier Years* (New York: Morrow, 1972), p. 73.
> [9] Studs Terkel, *Working* (New York: Random House, 1972), p. 63.
> [10] Mead, p. 104.
> [11] Terkel, p. 307.

Or use *ibid.* if you immediately repeat the same source. *Ibid.* is the Latin word for "in the same place." When used in a footnote, it means that footnote 4 is *exactly* the same as footnote 3. If the source is the same but the page number is different, you use *ibid.* plus the new page number:

> [8] Eric Barnouw, *Tube of Plenty: The Evolution of American Television* (New York: Oxford University Press, 1975), p. 265.
> [9] Ibid.
> [10] Ibid., pp. 268–269.
> [11] Douglass Cater, *Television as a Social Force: New Approaches to TV Criticism* (New York: Praeger Publishers, 1975), p. 96.
> [12] Ibid., p. 100.
> [13] Barnouw, p. 271.
> [14] Ibid., p. 270.

Footnotes tell a great deal about your paper because they show whether you have integrated your sources. The footnote scheme that follows shows that the student has used one source, then exclusively another, and then exclusively another (Bradley, Ibid., Ibid., Smith, Ibid., Ibid., and so on). The student has probably not integrated the sources and is in danger of producing a patchwork paper:

[15] Bradley, p. 17.
[16] Ibid.
[17] Ibid.
[18] Smith, p. 43.
[19] Ibid.
[20] Ibid.
[21] Jones, p. 76.
[22] Ibid.
[23] Ibid., p. 78.
[24] Church, p. 11.
[25] Ibid., p. 12.
[26] Ibid.

Footnoting articles A footnote for an article published in a periodical includes the following information:

1. Name of author (first name first)
2. Title of the article (in quotation marks)
3. Title of the magazine, journal, or newspaper (underlined)
4. Volume number (238)
5. Date of publication
6. Page number(s)

The following is a typical footnote for an article from a popular magazine. Notice the differences between it and footnote 9 for an article from a book.

[8] Robert L. Heilbroner, "Middle-Class Myths, Middle-Class Realities," *Atlantic*, 238 (October 1976), 37.
[9] Daniel Goleman, "Hypnosis Comes of Age," *Psychology Today*, July 1977, p. 54.

(Note that when no volume number appears, parentheses around the date should be omitted and *p.* or *pp.* before the page numbers should be included.)

An unsigned article:

[10] "Jimmy Carter: Not Just Peanuts," *Time*, March 8, 1976, p. 15.

(Note that the title of the article appears first when the article is unsigned.)

An article from a newspaper:

[11] Graham Hovey, "Human Rights Group Supports President," *New York Times*, March 6, 1977, p. 5, col. 1.

(An unsigned newspaper article, like an unsigned magazine article, would include the name of the article first.)

If you are writing in a discipline like psychology or biology, your instructor will ask you to follow a footnote form specific to that discipline. If you need footnotes for materials that have not been included here, your school's English Department probably provides a manual of style that describes the particular ways papers and research papers are to be written.

THE BIBLIOGRAPHY   The bibliography is a list of the sources that you have consulted for your paper. Notice that there are slight differences between a footnote entry and a bibliography entry:

indented   comma   parentheses

Footnote form   ³ Margaret Mead, *Blackberry Winter: My Earlier Years.* (New York: Morrow, 1972), p. 73.

page reference

last name first   period   period

Bibliography form   Mead, Margaret. *Blackberry Winter: My Earlier Years.* New York: Morrow, 1972.

indented

Sample bibliography entries

Books   One author:

Terkel, Studs. *Working.* New York: Random House, 1972.

Two authors:

Bernstein, Carl and Bob Woodward. *All the President's Men.* New York: Simon and Schuster, 1974.

An edition other than first:

Stone, Joseph L., and Joseph Church. *Childhood and Adolescence: A Psychology of the Growing Person.* 4th ed. New York: Random House, 1978.

An edited book:

> Garsof, Michele H., ed. *Roles Women Play: Readings Toward Women's Liberation.* Belmont, Calif.: Wadsworth Publishing Company, 1971.

An encyclopedia:

> "The Art of Television." *Encyclopaedia Britannica,* 1974, Macropaedia.

(If an encyclopedia article is signed, include the author's name first.)

Articles A signed article from a popular magazine:

> Heilbroner, Robert L. "Middle-Class Myths, Middle-Class Realities." *Atlantic,* 238 (October 1976), 37–42.

(Include all page numbers of the article.)

An unsigned article from a popular magazine:

> "Jimmy Carter: Not Just Peanuts." *Time,* March 8, 1976, pp. 15–20.

An article from a newspaper:

> Hovey, Graham. "Human Rights Group Supports President." *New York Times,* March 6, 1977, p. 5, col. 1.

(If a newspaper article is unsigned, include the title of the article first.) See the sample bibliography in Chapter 19, page 503.

Student Research Essay

The following sample research essay was written by a student in a freshman writing course. Howard's personal experience, his own opinions, and his research findings merge in his essay on television violence. He begins with a personal anecdote (*On a recent television show that I watched . . .*) and leads to his thesis (*. . . it seems to me that violence on television is a negative force in our society, affecting us in ways we cannot immediately see.*) Howard then weaves his research in among his own ideas to support his developing argument. He ends with a recommendation for change: *we should protest the amount of violence on television.*

Howard's paper fulfilled the assignment for a 1,200-word research essay. The paper relies on limited research because his instructor encouraged the members of the class to emphasize their own ideas rather than the ideas of others. Howard incorporates his research as support for his own ideas. Since most students in the class had not written this kind of paper before, the instructor took them through the research cycle: the class as a group visited the library, the card catalog room, the reference room, the stacks, and the microfilm area. All students wrote a working question, a working bibliography, and notes that summarized and paraphrased their research findings. They all practiced integrating their research into their texts, and they had the opportunity to read their first drafts to other members of the class.

By the end of this paper, Howard had not simply seamed together the ideas of several writers; instead, he had designed and written an essay of his own, weaving his research in and out of the text to lend support to his own thinking.

489

Television Violence: How Does It Affect Us?

Howard _____

English I

March 1, 1978

Television Violence:

How Does It Affect Us?

THESIS: Violence on television is a negative

force in our society, affecting us in

ways we cannot immediately see.

I.   Overwhelming amounts of violence are shown on television.

    A.   6:00 news

    B.   Rising crime rate

    C.   No proof of effect of TV violence on crime rate

II.   Effect: We close our eyes to violence.

    A.   Society immunized

    B.   Death an unreality

III.   Effect: We take the law into our own hands.

    A.   Violence a way to change things we do not like

    B.   Everyone vulnerable to violence

IV.   Effect: Heavy viewers have a distorted view of reality.

    A.   World more dangerous and frightening

    B.   Develop victim mentality

Although your instructor may not require an outline for most of the papers you write, he may ask that you keep track of your ideas for the research paper in outline form because they are likely to be more complex.

   V.   Effect: We assume TV reflects life.

        A.   Marcus Welby example

        B.   Amount of time spent watching

        C.   Los Angeles survey

        D.   No reflection of reality

  VI.   The Opposition: We should use violence to fight crime.

        A.   De-emphasize crime and chase

        B.   Identify with reason for character's loss of control

 VII.   Violence of TV has no positive effect on American Society

        A.   Failure of family viewing hour

        B.   Need for action

3

On a recent television show that I watched, one of
the characters had been severely beaten, had his
head smashed in by a hammer, and had been thrown into a
river with cement blocks tied to his feet. The program was not one of the well-known violent gangster
shows. It was the six o'clock news. From the evening news to children's cartoons, our nation's television programs show overwhelming amounts of violence.
Many researchers have tried to find a cause-effect
relationship between the violence on TV shows and
the rise in crime, examples of which we see in the
news. The nation's crime rate is rising, but in
spite of much research and the enormous amount of
statistical data that have been gathered, such a
cause-effect relationship has not been established.
Even though the results are not clear, it seems to me
that violence on television is a negative force in our
society, affecting us in ways we cannot immediately
see.

The essay begins
with a personal
experience to catch
the reader's
attention.

Thesis statement.

4

One far-reaching effect of TV violence is that

we do not see the brutality and suffering in front

of us because we have become immune to it. Violence

is an everyday event, and death is only a statistic.

We are being conditioned to ignore the reality of death.[1]

On the news, deaths are commonly reported as a result

of catastrophe or violence: twenty thousand die of

starvation in Bangladesh; forty-seven people die in a

train derailment in Chicago; a housewife and her seven

children are murdered in their suburban home. "These

real deaths," says Michael Arlen, "are treated as if

they have no meaning--except as the statistical by-

product of some disaster."[2] We tune out. Death be-

comes just another facet of the day's events--along

with the day's accumulated rainfall and the football

scores.

---

[1]Michael J. Arlen, "Cold, Bright Charms of Immortality," New Yorker, 50 (January 27, 1975), 76.

[2]Ibid.

Footnote for a magazine article.

Ibid. means that footnote 2 is exactly the same as footnote 1.

5

Television violence also encourages us to take the law into our owns hands, to arm ourselves in case we are attacked. Although the villains of gangster and police shows are eventually caught and punished, the hidden message that comes through is that violence supplies a means by which we can change something we don't like. If a person has been offended or "stepped on," a weapon can give him the opportunity to "even the score." A gun can make us feel secure. By arming ourselves against violence, we accept it as a given. We see ourselves, it seems, as "vulnerable in the face of violence."[3]

Communications experts such as Professors George Gerbner and Larry Gross of the Annenberg School of Communications at the University of Pennsylvania have done many studies concerning the effects of heavy television viewing on both adults and children. They

---

[3]Ernest G. Beier (interview), "Hidden TV Messages Create Social Discontent," Intellect, 104 (February 1976), 350.

offer interesting findings about the effects of television violence on avid TV viewers, the TV "addicts,"
as they call them. According to Gerbner and Gross,
television distorts the viewers' perspective of the
real world. TV addicts develop a "victim mentality"
and become more apprehensive about social dangers
than actual conditions warrant. Gerbner and Gross
found that "people who watch a lot of TV see the
real world as more dangerous and frightening than
those who watch very little."[4]

In another study, when the viewers were asked
to respond to the following question, "In any given
week [a. one in 100; b. ten in 100] Americans will
be involved in some kind of violence, most regular
television watchers chose b. The answer is a."[5]

---

[4]George Gerbner and Larry Gross, "The Scary World
of TV's Heavy Viewer," Psychology Today, 9 (April 1976),
41.

[5]Tony Chiu, "The Violent World of the TV Viewer,"
Science Digest, 77 (March 1975), 80.

7

A surprising number of viewers assume that the
stereotyped personalities portrayed on television match
those of the real world. Gerbner and Gross report that
250,000 letters requesting medical advice were sent by
viewers to Dr. Marcus Welby during the first five years
"Marcus Welby, M.D." was on TV.[6]   One can argue that
if TV influences adults so heavily, it must also do a
thorough job on children.

It is relevant to note that "the average American
high school graduate has spent 3,000 more hours watching
television than sitting in classrooms."[7]   If this figure is accurate, then one can hardly begin to comprehend
the number of violent acts the average teen-ager has
witnessed on his television screen.

---

[6]Gerbner and Gross, p. 44

[7]Edward J. Cripps, "Violence and Children's TV,"
America, 135 (September 11, 1976), 116.

Because Gerbner
and Gross have
been cited fully in
footnote 5, the
second and subse-
quent times they
are mentioned, the
shortened footnote
form is used.

8

A Los Angeles survey of nighttime television

during one week in 1960 reports that television

viewers would have seen:

Long quotation
is introduced by
writer's own words.

> 144 murders (scenes of mass murder not
> tabulated), 143 attempted murders, 52
> justifiable killings, 14 cases of
> drugging, 12 jailbreaks, 36 robberies,
> 6 thefts, 13 kidnappings (1 of a small
> boy), 6 burglaries, 7 cases of torture,
> 6 extortion cases, 5 blackmail, 11 planned
> murders, 4 attempted lynchings, 1 massacre
> scene with hundreds killed, 1 mass murder
> of homesteaders, 1 planned mass murder
> by arson, 3 scenes of shooting between
> gangland posses, many killed, 1 other
> mass gun battle, 1 program with over 50
> women kidnapped, this one including an
> hour of violence, kidnapping, murder,
> brutal fighting. These figures do not
> include the innumerable threats to
> kill, the sluggings or the many times
> when characters in the crime programs
> manhandled the victims, the forced
> confessions, and the dynamiting to
> illegally destroy.[8]

Is this the way life is in our society? There are those

who say that TV, with all its violence, is actually a

Footnote for a
book.

[8]Erik Barnouw, Tube of Plenty: The Evolution of
American Television (New York: Oxford University Press,
1975), p. 265.

reflection of American life. But this is not the case.
According to Edward Cripps, "Life on television has
fewer old and sick people, fewer people with family
responsibilities, fewer women, more men in their
middle years, more law enforcers and more violence
than American society has."[9]

Not all people think as I do that TV violence is
unwholesome and acts as a destructive social force.
Walter Bromberg and Gerald George, for example, are
convinced that TV crime programs can become an invaluable asset to the nation's war on crime. To
realize the full anti-crime potential of these shows,
they claim that it would be necessary to de-emphasize
the "crime, chase, and capture, and enlarge instead
on the 'why' of the violent act."[10] In Bromberg and
George's view, television programs would show ordinary

---

[9]Cripps, p. 117.

[10]Walter Bromberg and Gerald George, "Can TV Crime
Shows Prevent Violence," Today's Health, 47 (May, 1969),
88.

people who are not conscious of their own capacity
to act in a violent manner. A character would lose
control when "some deeply hidden, sensitive spot is
touched." Viewers who are predisposed to react violently would be able to identify with the character
in the story.
This would alert the viewer to his own tensions
and anxieties, which, when ignited, could result
in destructive actions.[11]

Expert opinion indicates that constant ex-
posure to televised violence does not provide a
wholesome atmosphere for our society. Yet no
legislative or voluntary regulation to reduce
the amount of violence has been imposed on the
networks. The "family viewing hour," which
supposedly prohibits violence on the air from
8:00 to 9:00 P.M., seemed to be a step in the
right direction. Yet shortly after it was

---

[11]Ibid.

established in 1975, the networks knew that
it was not accomplishing anything. They discovered that most children who watched television from 8:00 to 9:00 continued watching
programs until 10:00 or 11:00.

The debate over television violence and
its effects on society--particularly the
crime rate--will undoubtedly continue for years,
but I think the evidence is already convincing
enough for all Americans to be concerned about
the amount of violence on TV. As I flip through
the dial from night to night, I can choose among
programs on murder, rape, arson, bribery, and
extortion. It seems to me that it is time for a
change in our options. Why can't television
offer a more realistic view of our society?
Why can't it be a better source of information?
Why can't it offer the family more balanced
viewing? Television, I am afraid, will remain
as it is because viewers keep watching these

12

programs. When concerned citizens care enough

to ask for change, only then will change take

place. We must all voice our protests, or else

we will become a nation of gun-carriers who are

afraid to leave our houses. Without our voices

of protest, there is little hope for change.

13

For bibliography
form, see pages
487–488. Note that
not all of these
sources have been
used in Howard's
paper. You may
include works that
you have consulted
but not used in
the paper itself, or
you may include
works that may be
of interest to
your reader.

BIBLIOGRAPHY

Arlen, Michael J. "Cold Bright Charms of Immortality."
    New Yorker, 50 (January 27, 1975), 73-78.

Barnouw, Erik. Tube of Plenty: The Evolution of American
    Television. New York: Oxford University Press, 1975.

Beier, Ernst G. (interview). "Hidden TV Messages Create
    Social Discontent." Intellect, 104 (February 1976),
    350.

Bowles, Jerry. "How We Got This Way: TV-Styled America."
    Vogue, 166 (February 1976), 169.

Bromberg, Walter, and Gerald George. "Can TV Crime Shows
    Prevent Violence." Today's Health, 47 (May 1969), 88.

Cater, Douglass. Television as a Social Force: New
    Approaches to TV Criticism. New York: Praeger
    Publishers, 1975.

Chiu, Tony. "The Violent World of the TV Viewer."
    Science Digest, 77 (March 1975), 80-83.

Cripps, Edward J. "Violence and Children's TV." America,
    135 (September 11, 1976), 116-118.

"Ending Mayhem." Time, 107 (June 7, 1976), 63.

14

Gerbner, George, and Larry Gross. "The Scary World of TV's Heavy Viewer." Psychology Today, 9 (April 1976), 41-45.

Harris, George T. "More Blood on The Tube." Psychology Today, 9 (April 1976), 4.

Niemeyer, Gerhart. "Sex and Violence." National Review, 27 (August 1, 1975) 834.

Chapter 20 / Writing Précis, Exams, and Résumés

In the final chapter of this book we offer you practical suggestions that may make life a bit easier for you—in and out of college. We have found in our teaching and workshop experiences that most college students have never confronted the challenge of writing the précis. Many students have difficulty taking essay exams, and practically everyone has questions about business writing, especially the job résumé and letter of application.

WRITING A PRÉCIS Students in an introductory writing class were asked to write a 100-word condensation of a 3,500-word essay. Impossible? No, but difficult and exacting.

A précis is a condensation *in your own words* of a short work: an article, an essay, or perhaps a chapter in a book. The technique of précis writing requires that you read closely and write precisely. Writing a précis is excellent practice for taking notes (especially for the research paper—see Chapter 18) and for developing reading and writing skills.

Here are the guidelines for précis writing:

1. Highlight the most important ideas and omit the specifics. Record the bare bones of the article, leaving out all subordinate ideas and modifiers. (See the discussion of generalizations and specifics in Chapter 3 and modification in Chapter 9.)

2. Observe accurately. Report exactly what you read *in the order in which it is presented*. Do not inject your own opinion.

3. Make every word count. Eliminate all unnecessary words from your writing. Keep to the bare essentials.

4. Observe the word limit given by your instructor.

A sample précis, plus the article it condenses, follows:

In the first sentence, the précis writer states that he is condensing an essay on Vincent van Gogh written by Mark Roskill.

Précis

Essayist Mark Roskill claims that the popular images of Vincent van Gogh--that he was simpleminded and insane--are misconceptions. Van Gogh was well-read, well-informed, expressive, and in command of his art up until the end of his life.

Although relatively unknown in his lifetime van Gogh greatly influenced the artistic world that was to follow. His admirers overreacted by reading into his later paintings his personal suffering and by not recognizing the flaws in his early paintings.

Roskill calls for a realistic view of van Gogh that recognizes the imperfections of his early works and appreciates his personal approach to color and technique (and not the artist's personal feelings) in his final great works. Roskill believes that when van Gogh died at age thirty-seven, he was just reaching "the height of his powers."

Summary of paragraphs 1–5

Summary of paragraphs 6–7

Summary of paragraph 8

Writer puts into quotes Roskill's exact words.

VAN GOGH

BY MARK ROSKILL

The idea that van Gogh was both simpleminded and crazy still survives, but only, today, at the level of popular myth. If nothing else did, van Gogh's correspondence with his brother Theo and artist-friends—now published in English as the *Complete Letters*—would be bound to show the careful reader the misconception in both cases.

The picture of simplemindedness is contradicted in the first place by the sheer wealth and extent of van Gogh's reading; by his extraordinary articulateness in expressing his ideas; and by the very calculated way in which he constantly kept his brother informed of his plans and practical progress, and thereby assured himself of the financial support on which he was completely dependent. But what lies behind the misconception here is, perhaps, rather the idea of van Gogh's artistic isolation.

Because of the premium placed in modern times—beginning actually in van Gogh's day—on individuality and personal, revolutionary innovation, any modern artist must to a large extent work by himself and develop on his own. And van Gogh, after his two years (1886–88) in the metropolitan cen-ter of Paris, which he found too oppressive to bear, did spend the rest of his life off the artistic map, so to say: first at Arles in the south of France, then at nearby St.-Rémy, and finally at Auvers outside Paris. His dreams of an artistic community in the south equally came to nothing, after the sad debacle of Gauguin's stay with him at the end of 1888. Throughout this time, however, through the friends he had made in Paris, his correspondence and reading and his brother's activities as a dealer, van Gogh remained very well informed and aware of all that was going on in

Paris and around. And his art of those years belongs correspondingly in the main artistic and intellectual currents of the time. All of the major developments, such as symbolism in particular, have their echoes or analogues in van Gogh's achievement.

As for the question of madness, the repeated attacks to which van Gogh was subject from the end of 1888 on, and which eventually drove him to his death, should by no means lead one to suppose that there is any real, direct similarity between his work and the art of the insane. There have been various medical and psychiatric hypotheses as to the nature of those attacks, but none of them is really satisfactory, and the problem remains unsolved. Naturally there is, in a general sense, a relationship between those attacks—the feelings and pressures out of which they came—and the character of van Gogh's art; one sees this particularly in the choice, from the beginning, of themes and motifs that were intensely charged with an inner and personal significance, and in what van Gogh said or revealed about such subjects in his letters. But what is certain is that van Gogh's late works—with one or two exceptions, notably the famous *Crows Over a Wheatfield*— were not done during the periods of attack, but rather in between, when he was completely in charge of himself, or during the weeks of recovery. And the evidence of the works themselves points correspondingly to van Gogh's complete control over what he was doing. The deep, accelerated perspectives of the Arles landscapes, which seem to tie down and hold together a stretch of nature that would otherwise warp or topple down towards the spectator, and the exaggerated, swirling rhythms of such St.-Rémy paintings as the *Starry Night* and the *Olive Trees*—these are elements that van Gogh adopted with complete self-awareness and a lucid deliberateness. He "knew what he wanted"; and the art was, in fact, itself a means of control.

Though van Gogh sold only one or two paintings during his lifetime, he did attract attention even before his death—as the exhibition situation opened up inside and outside France—from the fellow artists and critics most closely involved. His "rediscovery," however, came in the early years of this century with the expressionist generation of painters—the Fauves in France and the Brücke in Germany. For them what mattered was the way that van Gogh had shown of doing things, rather than what he had actually done: the distortions and the expression of inner, subjective feeling which his example sanctioned. He became in this way, like Nietzsche in literature, a figurehead for a whole movement.

The results in time were twofold: first, the detachment of van Gogh's last three years in France (1888–90) as his "great period" and the tendency to read into each painting the drama and psychic urgency of the artist's feelings at the time (though van Gogh made it clear that he wanted his works to speak in themselves, without any such background); and secondly, an amplification of the importance of the works from the early years in Holland (1880–85)—the clumsiness of figure drawing in these works and the concern which they show with the harsh dignity of peasant life being seen as positive virtues.

Today, perhaps, a more sober view is in order. The years in Holland were essentially a period of apprenticeship—to the old masters whom van Gogh revered, particularly Rembrandt and Millet, and to the nineteenth-century Dutch line of landscape painting also. Symbolism, when van Gogh introduced it at this time, tends to be overcontrived or literary; but by the *Potato Eaters* (1885) he was working towards a more subtle and indirect kind of suggestiveness, based on his affiliation to the romanticism of the earlier nineteenth century. In Paris, from the impressionists and post-impressionists, he discovered color and a freer technique and was able to find his way through and beyond impressionism (of the 1870's) by transmuting everything that he successively picked up into personal terms of handling and approach to subject matter. But at Arles he was still learning—as he saw himself. The moving directness of his portraits, the "flaming" vision of the landscape of Provence—images so familiar now that one cannot any too easily make a proper evaluation of them—are still accompanied by unresolved qualities of structure and presentation. And the same holds true for the St.-Rémy works, some of which have in addition, or in compensation, a somewhat forced simplism. It was only, perhaps, at Auvers in the last months of his life that van Gogh fully succeeded in reconciling the crispness and flattening that he adopted from the Japanese print and the quality of allusive suggestion—and then in works that are not the best known, such as the figures against backgrounds of wheat and grasses. It is something of a cliché today to say of an artist who died young (van Gogh was thirty-seven) that he was just reaching the height of his powers and achievement at the time of his death; but in van Gogh's case this would appear to be true.

Exercise 1 Write a hundred-word précis of the following essay on Mark Twain.

MARK TWAIN

BY JUSTIN KAPLAN

Two currents flow through the life of Mark Twain. One flowed away from Hannibal, Missouri; the other, back to Hannibal again. Out of the opposition of these currents, out of the turbulent dark waters, came one of the great styles and dazzling personalities of our literature, one of its few undisputed masterpieces, and half a dozen of its major books.

Samuel Clemens's first fifty years swell the legend of the self-made man. At twelve he ended his formal schooling in Hannibal, where he had been brought at the age of four, and began work as a printer. At seventeen he left home for good, set out on his travels, and was in turn an itinerant typesetter, a river pilot, and for an unforgettable two weeks, a Confederate irregular. As a miner he never struck it rich in the Nevada Territory, but it was there, during the Civil War, that as a journalist he created the name and identity of Mark Twain, whose vocation was "to excite the *laughter* of God's creatures."

His first travel book, *The Innocents Abroad* (1869), made him famous, he prospered as a humorist on the lecture circuit and he became part owner of a newspaper in Buffalo. His marriage to Olivia Langdon, heiress to an Elmira coal combination, completed the decisive stage of his transition from the golden age of his Hannibal boyhood to what he would soon call the Gilded Age. The river rat and sagebrush bohemian became a gentleman and householder, the Western journalist a man of letters and property. During the three decades after his marriage his fame became international. He was the people's author, having reached a mass audience through the subscription book market, but he was also the idol and intimate of the rich, renowned, and titled. He was as much at home in London, Paris, Vienna, or Berlin as he was in his unmistakable, eye-catching mansion in Hartford, which dwarfed the cabin he had been born in to the size of a bird cage. He was capitalist, promoter, entrepreneur, and he invested both his psyche and his fortune in visionary enterprises, including the mechanical typesetter and the publishing house which eventually bankrupted him. In 1885, with the successful publication by his own firm of both *Huckleberry Finn* and the *Personal Memoirs* of his hero, General Ulysses S. Grant, Mark Twain reached the heights of a multiplex career as writer and businessman. All in all, it would seem that he had come as far as any man could possibly come from the drowsing white town of Hannibal.

But the central drama of Samuel Clemens's mature literary life was his discovery of his boyhood in Hannibal as the usable past. He began to make this discovery in his early and middle thirties as he explored the literary and psychological options of the comic identity, Mark Twain. Instead of severing his imagination from Hannibal, his triumphs in the East only reunited them. The first Sunday after his marriage he rained reminiscences of his boyhood day and night, and for the rest of his life, however involved he was with the insistent materialities of houses and machines, business ventures and publishing contracts, his imagination continued to dwell "down there" in Hannibal, with Tom and Huck. His image of Hannibal, as he evolved as a writer, became supple and comprehensive. Instead of purging the idyll of its frontier violence, of the pains of adolescence and the horrors of slavery, Mark Twain reshaped his idyll so that it embraced them. The river towns of *The Gilded Age* (1873) as well as *Pudd'nhead Wilson* (1894) mirror the possibilities of the human condition; and Huck and Tom, in Mark Twain's late notes for continuing their story, reflect some of his own sense of aging and desolation. Comparably, Mark Twain's style became a wonder of suppleness, moving freely from Huck's vernacular poetry to flights of savage invective and satire, at times laconic or eloquent, fierce or caressing, analytic or hyperbolic, always employing a complex rhetoric of comic invention, and, at its best, something incomparably and distinctively native.

Mark Twain's laughter had always been close to his sorrow, but when the opulent structure of his life gave way during the 1890's under a series of terrible blows—his business failures and bankruptcy, the sudden death of his favorite daughter, his fear that he was finished as a writer—he fell into a pronounced mood of despair and misanthropy which was to be as dramatic a manifestation of his late years as his white suits, his strolls on Fifth Avenue, his brilliance as a banquet speaker, his autobiographical dictations. At times he believed that his rags-to-riches, obscurity-to-fame story, which reminded some of his friends of *The Arabian Nights,* was a meaningless story of failure. During his darkest period he turned inward in the hope of solving what had become an intolerable sense of divisiveness and multiplicity, a sense suggested by the fact that Samuel Clemens often felt oppressed by his "conscience" and also shackled to humor by the fame of Mark Twain. But to the end he remained an enigma and a prodigy: "Everyone is a moon and has a dark side which he never shows to anybody," not even to himself.

All his life had been spent in divided and distinguished worlds. Frontier Hannibal had nurtured him, he was its celebrant and chronicler, and eventually he became the living symbol of America's vanished frontiers. Even so, his friend William Dean Howells said, he was "the most desouthernized southerner I ever knew." He came to be associated with the motorcar and steam yacht in place of the stagecoach and riverboat, and he sometimes wore a silk hat. But the subject matter of his fiction went farther and farther back into the past, and as a fiction writer he became an expatriate from his own times, just as in his person he became an expatriate from his own country (between 1878 and 1900 he spent about eleven years abroad) and complained of his "everlasting exile."

The representative of a broad spectrum of paradox, as writer, critic, and moralist. Mark Twain stood outside American society of his times and observed it with a bitter eye, but as a businessman he embraced its business values. Thus he flayed the shams and venalities of the Gilded Age, but he also lived deeply and hungrily in the age, and although he believed money corrupted absolutely, he was determined to be rich, not merely to get along. He identified himself with the masses and elevated the vernacular to literature, yet he sometimes courted the approval of high official culture, was often confused in his goals, and spent his inspiration in such genteel performances as *The Prince and the Pauper* and *Joan of Arc*. He was an exhibitionist who jealously guarded his privacies and sensitivities, an aristocrat who was a passionate foe of social injustice, and a grass-roots radical who, for all his denunciation of the "damned human race," is known the world over as a democrat and general friend of mankind.

TAKING AN ESSAY EXAM

Don't stay up the night before.

Stay up the night before.

Don't cram.

Review.

Take a cold shower.

Take a hot bath.

Go to the movies.

Read a good book.

Eat a good breakfast.

Eat nothing.

How-to-study manuals prescribe numerous and often conflicting suggestions about preparing for an essay examination. If you study all of this advice, you may feel that you'd be better off eating a bowl of chicken soup than reading another one of these manuals.

When it comes down to it, individuals respond *individually* to taking essay exams. Ask any group of students, and you'll get numbers of differing responses. Common ingredients do go into preparing for and writing an exam, but it is up to you, in the end, to rely on your own experience.

In this section of "Practical Helps," we'll consider three steps in exam taking:

1. Preparing for the exam
2. The night before
3. The exam itself

Preparing for the exam Studying for an exam begins with *reading* your text and your notes. How you attack the chapters, how you establish the points that the author is trying to get across, how you write your notes—all these acts are part of an overall strategy for organizing your thinking.

Time Give yourself time to study. Opening a 300-page history text for the first time the night before the exam is asking for disaster. Pace yourself. Keep up with the assignments, portion off material to read and study, take notes from your text and from lectures, write outlines, and study as you go along.

Facts and ideas You need facts *and* ideas. Facts alone are not enough. Many students who memorize dates, names, and places do not piece them together to see or understand ideas. In your reading, search for the general and abstract ideas that hold the facts together (in the same way that your thesis holds the details of your essay). Individual details about the War of 1812 may fascinate you, but you need to know what those details mean. Study the facts in relation to causes and effects, comparisons and contrasts, descriptions and definitions. Try to understand.

Your goal as an exam taker is to know the meaning of the facts you learn so that you can present the broad picture of an historical event, a philosophical position, a cultural theory. Facts are an important part of this picture, for general statements alone will not convince your instructor that you know the material. Pay attention to dates, names, places, and the like, and use them as support for your generalizations.

Mnemonics Mnemonics are ways of remembering information that you think is important. Say, for example, that you want to remember four effects of Columbus's discovery of the New World:

1. Discovering a northwest passage to the East
2. Finding gold, silver, and gems
3. Conquering new lands
4. Converting natives to Christianity

You pick a letter from each of the four effects:

E = East
G = gold
L = lands
N = natives

Then you put the letters together to form a word:

GLEN

Memorize the word; associate it with the four effects of Columbus's discovery. When you confront a relevant exam question, call upon the word, peel off the layers, and get to the information you need.

Dress rehearsal Write practice essay questions. The purpose of writing practice exams is not to try to psych out your instructor (although you may come up with a practice question that is the same one on the exam). Rather, the purpose of practice exams is to stimulate your thinking about an issue and to practice writing these thoughts in an essay.

In studying the War of 1812, you learn not only the facts but the meaning of the facts. You ask yourself questions like these:

Why did the war occur?
Discuss the origins.
Discuss the causes.
Discuss the results (short term, long term).
Describe the most important battles.

And you answer them. During this rehearsal, time is less important than the content of your answers. With your goal a complete, well-organized essay, you can work from an outline and use your text and lecture notes to look up answers. Think about the design of the essay: begin with your most interesting point, support it with facts, and conclude.

The night before

Review Ideally, you should spend the night before the exam reviewing your summaries, outlines, notes, and mnemonics. Many students find it helpful to work with other students, asking each other questions and drilling each other on the ideas and facts to be covered on the exam.

Try not to cram If you establish solid study skills, you won't need to cram (learn new material right before the exam). Cramming generally *interferes* with what you already know. By trying to squeeze in new material, you force out the information that you already know.

Try to relax You sometimes hear people say they work best under pressure, but that may not be the case for you. Pressure can cause anxiety, and anxiety can bring with it fatigue because you've stayed up the whole night worrying. By exam time, you're a wreck, washed out, bleary-eyed, unable to *recall* what you know.

Find your own way to relax if working under pressure doesn't agree with you. Meditation, a TV mystery, a long walk, a banana split—try whatever relaxes you. Don't let anxiety take you over.

The exam   The following tale is a typical one. A student who did poorly on a history examination realized afterward that she had not followed directions. She had been asked to write on *two out of three* questions. She answered *all* three. She had been asked to *compare* the French and American revolutions, but she devoted 90 percent of her answer to the French Revolution and remarked only briefly about the American. She discussed the *causes* of the American Revolution when she had been asked to describe the *effects*. Although the student had studied hard, she fell apart on the exam because she did not pay attention to the instructions.

Read the
instructions   Essay exams usually contain several questions, with a specific amount of time suggested for each. Many exams also indicate the number of points assigned to each question:

Question 1	30 minutes, 30 points
Question 2	30 minutes, 30 points
Question 3	45 minutes, 40 points

By reading the instructions, you know that you have a total of 105 minutes to answer all three questions. Because the last question carries more weight, more time is allotted for it. Without reading the instructions, you might take your time with the first question, thereby forcing yourself to hurriedly answer the most weighted question at the end.

Read all the essay
questions   Take in all key words and directives (see "Tips for Exam Takers" on page 514). If you are given a choice of questions to answer (three out of four, for example), make the decision *tentatively*. You can change your mind later on if you begin to feel more confident about another question.

Brainstorm on
paper   Begin thinking by *writing*. If there is one bit of advice most successful exam takers suggest, it is this: they do not begin writing a response to an exam essay until they have brainstormed—begun their thinking—*on paper*. Here is how brainstorming generally works. On a piece of scrap paper (the last page of the exam booklet, perhaps), you write down as fast as you can all the words that come to mind—words related to *one* of the exam questions. As soon as you feel certain about answering this question, begin to jot down a whole outline. (You don't need to answer the questions in the order in which they are presented.)

It's a common experience to read a question, know the answer, but for the moment feel blocked, unable to recall specific concepts and facts. Don't be alarmed. Go on to a question you *can* answer. Although you can't recall at first reading the information you need for the other questions, your careful reading of them has started a process whereby key words and phrases will come to mind *while* you are working on your first or second essay. When these thoughts occur, don't treat them as intrusions upon the question you are answering. Take a moment and *write them down* immediately on the area of the scrap paper set aside for the question or questions they relate to. *You are, in fact, working on more than one question at the same time.* The key to this process is *thinking* by *writing*. If you sit, staring into space, allowing thoughts to enter and exit, you will not have *concrete evidence* of your thinking. Get that thinking down on paper. Give yourself time to *frame an answer in one sentence*. The first sentence of your essay should respond directly to the question:

Question: Discuss the causes of the fall of the Roman Empire.
Answer: (I believe) There were four distinct causes of the fall of the Roman Empire. (What will follow will be a discussion of the four causes.)

Write   Once you have framed a one-sentence response and have written an outline (from your associative list), you begin to write. As the clock ticks on, you keep writing, referring to your list whenever you need to. You have listed four causes in answer to the question above:

1. _____
2. _____
3. _____
4. _____

In your essay, you explain the first cause, then the second, and so on. Rather than feel panicky as you work through the exam not knowing what to say next, your outline structures your response and your time. What you are writing is a mini-essay that contains your thesis, paragraphs of support, and a conclusion. Your outline allows you to move easily from one part of the essay to another.

If you have time remaining, proofread your responses. Even though you have tried to plan your time carefully, you may run out of time before you've answered a question. If this happens, sketch out a response in outline form. If you write nothing, the instructor has to assume that you know nothing about the topic. But an outline of the essay, as detailed as possible, can go a long way to impress your instructor that you did know a great deal about the question but ran out of time. You may at least receive partial credit for your attempt.

On the following pages you will find sample exam questions with analyses of their key words and directives. Study these questions. Practice answering any that you can. Set up questions of your own by using these samples as models.

TIPS FOR EXAM TAKERS

Pay attention to all *directives* (words that tell you exactly what to do) and *key words* (words that set down specifics and limits). Familiarize yourself with exam language:

DIRECTIVES	KEY WORDS
analyze	after
choose	before
comment	briefly
compare	fully
contrast	only
define	numbers:
describe	250 words
discuss	two out of three
evaluate	all three
explain	three out of five
give an example	
list	
illustrate (give examples)	
outline	
select	
show	
state	
trace	

Consider how these words are used in the sample questions on this page and the next. Notice that some questions are more interesting and inviting than others. Unfortunately, you frequently must answer questions that have no appeal at all.

1. In an *essay* of *250 words,* discuss the following statement made by Enid Haupt, editor of *Seventeen* magazine:

"I've never met anyone who wanted to be a teenager again."

The directive *discuss* often appears in essay exams. As it is used here, *discuss* invites you to *agree* or *disagree* and to support your point of view with specifics. This question asks you to write an *essay* whose thesis statement might be:

Enid Haupt is right when she says, "I've never met anyone who wanted to be a teenager again."

2. *Discuss* the *effects* of sleep deprivation on humans.

In this question, *discuss* means to explain what you can about the effects of sleep deprivation. Agreement or disagreement does not enter into your discussion. A thesis statement for your essay might be:

Sleep deprivation has three major effects on humans.

3. *Compare* and *contrast* the sociological *theories* of Herbert Spencer *and* Karl Marx.

> This question asks you to show likenesses (*compare*) and differences (*contrast*) between the two men's thinking on sociology. A thesis statement for your essay might be:

Although both Herbert Spencer and Karl Marx were responding to similar problems in nineteenth-century European society, their solutions to these problems were quite different.

> In one sentence, you will have mentioned similarities (they were both responding to problems) and differences (their solutions were dissimilar).

4. *Describe* living conditions in Russia *before* the Bolshevik Revolution.

> *Describe* asks you to tell how it was. When a question is as broad as this one, it is useful to limit your response to certain groups and then contrast or classify the conditions among these groups. A thesis statement for your essay might be:

Living conditions in Russia before the Bolshevik Revolution were vastly different for the aristocrats, the common people, and the peasants.

> Note the importance of the word *before*. A quick reading may have omitted the word, resulting in a description of Russia *during* or *after* the Bolshevik Revolution.

5. *Trace* and *discuss* the most *important discoveries* of the *nineteenth* century that *influenced* Einstein's theory of relativity.

> The most important directive in this complex question is *trace,* which asks you to tell about events in their chronological sequence: this happened and then this and then this. Selection of detail is critical in a question like this one; you will not throw in every detail you remember but will select the ones that were influential to Einstein. A thesis statement for your essay might be:

Einstein's theory of relativity can be traced to three specific experiments carried out in the late nineteenth century.

WRITING BUSINESS LETTERS Occasions will arise when you need to communicate with the business world: to request information, register a complaint, place an order, apply for a job. All business letters follow the format of the following sample letter:

(1)

637 Front Street
Frederick, Pennsylvania 16339
March 17, 1978

(2) Mr. Gene Rollins
Customer Service
General Electric Company
405 Summit Street
Uniontown, Pennsylvania 15345

(3) Dear Mr. Rollins:

The General Electric refrigerator I recently bought arrived
with two serious defects. First, the freezer compartment
does not function properly. I have tried to adjust the
freezer dial, but the thermostat is stuck on low. As a
result, nothing freezes. Second, the refrigerator buzzes all
the time, creating an annoyance.

(4) I called your office yesterday and was told by your
secretary, Mrs. Smith, that I must register a written
complaint that includes these details: The refrigerator is
Model No. CU-13546. I bought the appliance at Mern's
Department Store in Frederick on March 1, 1978. According to
the guarantee, I am entitled to free service for one year.

I would appreciate your sending a serviceman to my address
as quickly as possible. Please phone my home to set up an
appointment (412-776-3818).

(5) Yours truly,

Martin Pearl

(6) Martin Pearl

The addressed envelope appears below:

Martin Pearl   STAMP
637 Front Street
Frederick, Pennsylvania 16339

Mr. Gene Rollins
Customer Service
General Electric
405 Summit Street
Uniontown, Pennsylvania 15233

1. The *heading* includes the writer's full address (no abbreviations) and the date. If you are using stationery with a printed address, add the date in the right margin.

2. The *inside address* includes the name of the person to whom you are writing, the company, and the address. If you know the person's title or position, include it also:

> James McNulty, M.D.
> or
> Helen M. Witherspoon
> Director of Admissions

3. The *greeting* includes the name and personal title of the person to whom you are writing. Note that the greeting is always followed by a colon:

> Dear Professor Langley:
> or
> Dear Mrs. Smith:

When you are not writing to a specific person, you may use one of these greetings:

> Dear Sir:
> Dear Madam:
> Gentlemen:
> Ladies:
> Dear Sir or Madam:
> To Whom It May Concern:

Modern usage is beginning to accept *To Whom It May Concern* because it eliminates the risk of offending women by addressing them as men and vice versa.

4. The *body* of the letter includes the specific information you wish to convey. Paragraphs are usually short and separated by two spaces. Paragraphs may or may not be indented, depending on your preference.

5. The *complimentary close* includes words like:

> Yours truly,
> Sincerely,
> Sincerely yours,
> Cordially,

Note that only the first word of the complimentary close is capitalized.

6. The *signature* includes your name written in longhand (without a title). Your name in type appears underneath.

> Gertrude Miller
> Gertrude Miller, Ph.D.
>
> William Rogers
> William Rogers
> President, Faculty Senate

A married woman uses her own first name in her correspondence, not her husband's. A woman may show the title she prefers to be addressed by if she wishes:

(Mrs.) Sally Johnson
(Miss) Sally Johnson
(Ms.) Sally Johnson

Follow these guidelines when writing business letters:

1. Get to the point right away. If you are writing to complain about a broken freezer compartment, do not waste time talking about how badly you needed a new refrigerator.
2. Use plain English. You do not have to use six-syllable words or hide behind convoluted constructions to state your point. If you write:

   On the 12th of March, the undersigned confronted difficulties with a major appliance,

   your reader will have difficulty unraveling your words. You shouldn't, on the other hand, resort to slang or obscenities, no matter how angry you are. You can say what you must in plain English. (See Chapter 12, "Choosing Exact Words.")
3. Include all essential information. If the freezer doesn't work *and* the refrigerator makes a buzzing sound, state both problems. Include any other information you think pertinent: model number, date of purchase, guarantees, and the like.
4. Mention that you have enclosed something—a check, money order, copy of a receipt, résumé, and the like. Your reader will know to look for whatever has been enclosed.

Exercise 2 Write a business letter to a utility company (telephone, gas, water) registering a complaint about an unreasonable bill—for example, long-distance phone calls you know you didn't make.

WRITING A RÉSUMÉ AND A LETTER OF APPLICATION

An advertisement placed in a local paper calling for an experienced summer camp counselor elicited this response on a small piece of blue paper:

```
Dear Sir:
     I saw you ad in the local paper and believe
that I am qualified for your camp job. Please
call me at 452-6178.
                              Yours truly,
```

The prospective employer did not respond.

Writing a résumé and a letter of application are two of the most important writing tasks you will undertake. Here is where your writing counts, for getting to first base with that prospective employer depends on the effectiveness of your application letter and résumé.

The résumé   A résumé is a summary of your life that covers four major areas: *personal information, educational background, work experience,* and *references.* It is the accepted way to present yourself on paper when you apply for a job or to graduate school. Because prospective employers and organizations rely on résumés for initial judgments, writing a strong résumé is like passing the first test on your way to landing a job.

Résumés are usually brief—one or two pages. The following sample is a typical résumé of a recent college graduate:

```
Jerome Winters
113 West End Avenue
Douglaston, New York 11356

Home telephone: (212) 123-4567

PERSONAL INFORMATION

Birth date: September 26, 1956
Marital status: single
Health: excellent

EDUCATIONAL BACKGROUND

B.A. Queens College of the City University of New York, Flushing,
     New York, 1978 (Accumulated grade point average: 3.4 on 4.0 scale)

     Major: Psychology

Special abilities: Fluent in Spanish

High School Diploma: Bronx High School of Science, Bronx, New York, 1974.
```

Begin with most recent experience first

```
WORK EXPERIENCE

     1977-1978: Tutor, Math Workshop, Queens College, Flushing, New York

     1977-1978: Volunteer research assistant, Columbia Hospital, New York, New York

     1976-1978: Counselor, Crisis Hot Line, Queens College, Flushing, New York

     1976 (Christmas): Salesclerk, Macy's department store, Flushing, New York

     1975,1974 (summers): Counselor, Camp Sunshine, Wellfleet, Massachusettts
```

Obtain permission of your referents before listing their names on your résumé.

```
REFERENCES

     Professor Joan Clark          Dr. Ross Tauber            Professor Robert Smith, Director
     Department of Psychology      Department of Psychiatry   Math Workshop
     Queens College                Columbia Hospital          Queens College
     Flushing, New York 11367      New York, New York 10025   Flushing, New York 11367
```

Tailoring your résumé Although many people use the same résumé for each application, others tailor their résumés to fit the specific requirements of each job. You can highlight certain information on the résumé itself. For example, under *work experience,* you can specify your responsibilities or duties:

WORK EXPERIENCE
1977–1978: Tutor: Math Workshop, Queens College, Flushing, New York
 Tutored business math students individually and in groups
1977–1978: Volunteer research assistant, Columbia Hospital, New York, New York
 Interviewed parents and children in studies on hyperactive children; gained experience in analyzing data
1975, 1974 (summers): Counselor, Camp Sunshine, Wellfleet, Massachusetts
 Counselor for emotionally disturbed children

Letter of application Many applicants use the letter of application to highlight their résumé. Although the résumé is in itself a summary, most applicants go one step further by *summarizing* the summary in a cover letter. The cover letter should emphasize the sections of the résumé that will fit the applicant's qualifications to the job or graduate school requirements.

The letter of application follows the business letter format (see page 516) and should include the following:

1. State exactly what position you are applying for and how you heard of the opening (from a friend, a professor, a newspaper advertisement, an agency).
2. State your qualifications for the job.
3. Show how your experience meets the requirements of the job.
4. Mention your enclosed résumé.
5. Indicate the best way to get in touch with you and offer to meet for an interview.
6. Make certain your tone is sincere and courteous.

The following two letters show how you can use your experience in different ways depending on the position you are applying for. The candidate (whose résumé appears on page 520) wrote two letters of application: first, for a job as a research assistant in a psychology lab; second, for admission to a graduate school of social work.

In the first letter, the applicant highlights his work as a volunteer research assistant, his advanced psychology courses, and his mathematical skills. In the second letter, he focuses on his work with people. He stresses his work as a volunteer at Crisis Hot Line at Columbia Hospital, where he learned interviewing techniques and behaviorist approaches. His math skills, in this case, may be less important than his ability to share what he knows with others.

113 West End Avenue
Douglaston, New York 11356
June 30, 1978

Box 786
New York Times
New York, New York 10036

To Whom It May Concern:

Please consider my application for the position of
psychology assistant as advertised in the New York Times,
June 27, 1978. I believe that my background fits the
qualification you require of a college graduate with
research experience. I am enclosing my résumé.

Since June 1977 I have worked as a volunteer research
assistant with Dr. Ross Tauber of Columbia Hospital, New
York, New York. I have assisted him in interviewing parents
and children for his studies on hyperactive children. I have
gained valuable experience participating in every step of
these studies and aiding in the analysis of the data.

I used my experience at Columbia Hospital for a senior paper
on disturbed children. My courses in advanced statistics and
experimental psychology have also given me a firm grasp of
research design. In addition, I have sharpened my
mathematical skills by tutoring undergraduates in the Queens
College Math Workshop.

I would very much appreciate the opportunity for an
interview. You can write to me at my home address or call
me at (212) 123-4567 any weekday after 3:30 P.M.

Sincerely yours,

Jerome Winters

Jerome Winters

113 West End Avenue
Douglaston, New York 11356
June 30, 1978

Dr. James Simpson, Director of Admissions
Bryant School of Social Work
114 Carter Avenue
White Plains, New York 10607

Dear Dr. Simpson:

Please consider my application for graduate study in social
work at the Bryant School of Social Work. I understand that
a social-work student must display an interest in working
with people and have some experience in the field. I believe
my qualifications meet both of these requirements.

My experience as a volunteer in two social agencies has
given me valuable experience working with both children and
adults. As a counselor at Crisis Hot Line, a twenty-four-
hour telephone help center, I learned to respond quickly and
specifically to people in need. During the past year, I
worked as a volunteer research assistant with Dr. Ross
Tauber at Columbia Hospital, where I learned interviewing
techniques and behavorist approaches to use with hyperactive
children.

In addition, for two summers I worked as a group counselor
at a camp for handicapped children. My experience tutoring
undergraduates in the Math Workshop at Queens College
allowed me to understand a one-to-one teaching situation.

The satisfaction I have received from all these experiences
has proved to me that I am interested in working with and
helping other people.

As requested, I have enclosed my résumé and a completed
application form. I have arranged for a transcript of my
grades to be sent to your office. I would very much
appreciate the opportunity for an interview. You can write
to me at my home address or call me at (212) 123-4567 any
weekday after 3:30.

Yours truly,

Jerome Winters

Jerome Winters

TIPS FOR JOB HUNTERS

Think about what prospective employers (or admissions officers) look for when they read résumés and letters of application. First, they look for credentials: college degree, related experience, and the like. Second, they examine the information you have included and the way you have presented it. Third, they look for *what is missing*.

If there are gaps in your résumé, prospective employers naturally wonder why. Unless they are highly impressed by what you have included, you may not have the chance to explain why you omitted items. For people who have been working for many years, a gap of a year or more that is not explained may arouse suspicion: Were you fired from a job? Are you lazy? It is a good idea to account for all your time. Similarly, don't omit needed personal information. Some people, for example, object to stating their birth date, on principle. Keep in mind that when you omit information that employers require, you risk not getting fair consideration.

As you write the letter of application, remember that your words reflect you. A letter discourteously written or a letter filled with typographical errors probably won't get you very far.

A successful résumé and letter of application allow you to move to the next step in the job-seeking processs—the interview. It may take a little time to write a good résumé and letter of application, but it's a good investment.

Exercise 3 Write a résumé for yourself that includes four parts: personal history, education, work experience, and references. Write two letters of application that use the information on the résumé in different ways.

Index